Consuming Culture in the Long Nineteenth Century

Consuming Culture in the Long Nineteenth Century

Narratives of Consumption, 1700-1900

Edited by Tamara S. Wagner and Narin Hassan

LEXINGTON BOOKS

A division of
ROWMAN & LITTLEFIELD PUBLISHERS, INC.
Lanham • Boulder • New York • Toronto • Plymouth, UK

Published by Lexington Books
A division of Rowman & Littlefield Publishers, Inc.
A wholly owned subsidiary of The Rowman & Littlefield Publishing Group, Inc.
4501 Forbes Boulevard, Suite 200, Lanham, Maryland 20706
http://www.lexingtonbooks.com

Estover Road, Plymouth PL6 7PY, United Kingdom

British Library Cataloguing in Publication Information Available

The hardback edition of this book was previously cataloged by the Library of Congress as
follows:

Consuming culture in the long nineteenth century : narratives of consumption, 1700–
1900 / edited by Tamara S. Wagner and Narin Hassan.
    p. cm.
 Includes bibliographical references and index.
 1. Food habits—History—18th century. 2. Food habits—History—19th century. 3.
Food habits in literature. I. Wagner, Tamara S., 1976– II. Hassan, Narin, 1969–
 GT2850.C63 2007
 394.1'209'033—dc22   2006038093

ISBN: 978-0-7391-1207-6 (cloth : alk. paper)
ISBN: 978-0-7391-4510-4 (pbk. : alk. paper)

♾™ The paper used in this publication meets the minimum requirements of American
National Standard for Information Sciences—Permanence of Paper for Printed Library
Materials, ANSI/NISO Z39.48–1992.

Printed in the United States of America

Contents

Preface

Having made her home inside a novel, the first person narrator of *The Well of Lost Plots* (2003), one of the recent installments of Jasper Fforde's satirical series, remarks the "relative absence of breakfast [as] the first and most notable difference to [her] daily timetable."[1] Fforde's series significantly starts with an experimental take on sequels to "classic" eighteenth- and nineteenth-century novels, *The Eyre Affair*, published in 2001.[2] Literary detectives are shown to project themselves into the books they investigate, and life to go on beyond the published pages of canonical works. Thus, a heroine of one of Jane Austen's novels smokes cigarettes and relies on readers to supply her with the products of different ages. Anachronistic consumption of food and drink is almost standard. So what is it about the absence of breakfast? The symbolic significance of meals is, after all, otherwise sustained, discussed, even self-consciously evoked, as are so many other aspects the reader and critic of fiction might take for granted (or perhaps analyze in accordance with likewise satirically presented critical paradigms) in Fforde's parodic play with postmodern self-reflexivity. As the narrator points out, "[i]nside books, dinners are often written about and therefore feature frequently, as do lunches and afternoon tea; probably because they offer more opportunities to further the story."[3] *Consuming Culture in the Long Nineteenth Century: Narratives of Consumption, 1700-1900*, it is important to note for the conceptualization of the study's focus and subsequent shaping, originated in a discussion of this assumed absence of breakfast in traditional, or "classic," literature as in speculations on divergent forms of representation in popular culture. What were the different cultural as well as social functions of meals, how were they represented and why, and how have the ways in which food figures in literary, philosophical, and of course also culinary works, in instructions of household management and fairs as well as in fiction, at once established parameters for the didactic or symbolic use of food and shaped our understanding of the literature and culture of the time? Most importantly, how do these cultural narratives of consumption—and most poignantly perhaps, the ways in which they intersect and overlap—differently illuminate canonical and non-canonical cultural productions of the "long nineteenth century?"

Breakfast, for its very marginality, has proven a particularly fruitful point of entry into a truly intra- as well as interdisciplinary inquiry into the representations of food. When it *is* visible or even discussed in fiction, is the symbolic potential of breakfast as the first meal of the day, served at so many different hours of the morning (as a notoriously flexible and extendable time of day in itself), *per definition* different from that of other meals? What can this tell us about the functions of consumption in fiction more generally? How did cultural discourses of "the long nineteenth century" affect representations of consumption, and not only of breakfasts? The initial discussion of these and related questions on the 18C-List Server in the spring of 2003 was initiated by Jim Chevallier, whose essay on the cultural and social history of breakfast in eighteenth-century Europe now forms an important contribution to this collection. The discussion branched out very quickly indeed, testifying to the remarkable cultural pervasiveness and permeability of the changing narratives of consumption generated during the turbulent centuries that saw the formation of Enlightenment and post-Enlightenment modernity and, at the same time, to significant shifts in the focus of eighteenth- and nineteenth-century studies. The discussion was then continued at a panel one of the present editors, Tamara S. Wagner, organized for the annual conference of the *British Society for Eighteenth-Century Studies*, held at the University of Oxford in January 2004. It was there that the idea to write a book on consumption first arose. An internet discussion list, an international conference, the primarily virtual exchange between the present book's editors, and a guest talk on Dickens's representation of commodity culture by one of the contributors, Andy Williams of Cardiff University, in Singapore in August 2005, have thus shaped what had been from the beginning an interdisciplinary and comparative project.

In order to explore the class-stratified, gender-dependent, and increasingly globalized, habits and problems of consumption, *Consuming Culture in the Long Nineteenth Century*, in fact, seeks to bring together an excitingly diverse range of perspectives, including musicology, philosophy, history and art history, cultural and postcolonial studies as well as the study of literature in English, French, and German. It aims to reconstruct, make problematic, and dissect the social functions, cultural meaning, and changing representations of consumption in the eighteenth and nineteenth centuries. The ways in which food and drink, caffeine and other drugs, consumable exotica, or luxury products in general, have reflected and contributed to the formation of post-Enlightenment modernity is central to this study. What was the role of eating, drinking, and shopping in the growing preoccupation with consumption and leisure in the eighteenth and nineteenth centuries? How did the search for luxury goods redirect discourses of Empire, medicine, or Puritanism? How did food taboos and exoticism figure within their cultural fictions, and how were they represented or harnessed in the politics, literature, and arts of the time? Were debates on the pleasures of the table and the social roles of eating—and shopping—problems specific to the development of modernity, and if so, what was the extent of their influence on the rising consumer culture as we have come to know it? How were vegetarianism, blood lust, the economics of meat production, or the cultural stereotyping of the potato, for example, redeployed and redefined in fiction? In what ways can we understand better the literature, music, or philosophy, and their cultural representation at the time by exploring one of the perhaps seemingly most mundane aspects of popular culture: patterns of consumption?

As these leading questions are addressed from different perspectives and in comparative approaches, this study is structured in three parts. Each section takes up a specific aspect of the cultural myths, or fictions, of consumption. Part I: Making Food Fictions focuses on the making, the preparation and delivery, of food as well as on the construction of the fictions about these variously—culturally, socially, literally—inflected "re-presentation." Part II: Victorian Spectacles of Consumption concentrates on the display of the very processes of consumption as well as of consumables in a markedly different vein, as the sheer spectacle of consuming is shown to be central to its representation. From world fairs to the celebration of nationality through domesticity (and *vice versa*) in the Victorian Christmas dinner, ideas of the spectacular harness representative food as well as the representation of food in ideologically more and more powerful ways. Part III: Blood, Blockage, and Regurgitation: The Consumer's Modernity, by contrast, aims to move away from the preparation, display, and processes of various incorporation of the consumable (beyond the edible). Instead, the essays collected in this section start with a cultural inquiry into the history of breakfast and its embodiments and then move to the question of embodiment and the changing body as end-consumer and end-product of consumption itself. Regurgitation perhaps follows naturally, once preparation and mastication have been absorbed by interconnected cultural fictions. Yet it is also particularly an issue of modernity's definitional consumer culture with all its attendant excesses. From the powerful metaphorical uses of digestion in Kant's writing and Handel's embodiment of excessive output to insatiability in the Baudelairian aesthetic, the consumer's modernity is shown to be premised on an overproduction and consumption of excess. The modern consumer, the study concludes, is like Bram Stoker's *Dracula*, culture's vampire in more senses than one.

Given this emphasis on excess and the study's origins in an awareness of lack (the seeming absence of breakfast in eighteenth- and nineteenth-century fiction), it is peculiarly apt and further forms a pointed entry into the discussion of consumption to start with the representation of bad cooking. In "Badly-Boiled Potatoes and Other Crises," Sumangala Bhattacharya investigates the creation of a fiction of bad cookery as it emerged in the nineteenth century in a number of essays, polemics, cookbooks, and literature. A language of decline of English cooking displayed an anxiety that the culture of modernity—the culture of mass-produced abundance—had replaced one kind of deprivation with another. As ideas of nutrition replaced those of nourishment, a new kind of hunger was engendered. In Charles Dickens's *David Copperfield* (1850), Bhattacharya shows, middle-class anxieties about industrial culture and modernity are transmuted into these fictions of bad English cookery, cultural myths that have been perpetuated in multiple distortions that have unfortunately detracted from the discourse's original focus and significance.

So if the first essay underscores a new kind of hunger of modernity—a modern hunger that ultimately culminated in the vampiric excesses explored by Jared Green in the final contribution—the next two analyses admirably work as a pair. In "Vegetable Fictions in the Kingdom of Roast Beef: Representing the Vegetarian in Victorian Literature," James Gregory examines the cultural meaning of vegetarianism through its representation in fiction. Britain as the birthplace of the modern Western vegetarian movement has fascinatingly brought forth a treatment of dietetic nonconformity that goes far beyond the presence of food reformers or faddists. While the representation of a new vegetarian "type" exemplifies fiction's place in defining cultural norms, it also reveals the Victorian fascination with "eccentricity" and "otherness." The vegetarian-teetotal character, often depicted as combining dietary "ism" with other "progressive" enthusiasms, is shown to play a satirical role, either in condemning present social ills, or in caricaturing the social purity crusades or advanced reform movements of the period. Dietetic difference, in fact, often indicates more serious transgressions, stressing connections between the materiality of food and the spiritual/ moral world. In sharp contrast, Ron Broglio's contribution, "'The Best Machine for Converting

Herbage into Money': Romantic Cattle Culture," analyses landscape painting to show how cattle is co-opted for nationalism and advanced the association of Britain with beef. Agriculture technologies intersected with economic demands and artistic interests in reshaping the material body of cattle and their cultural signification as Britain demanded more and better meat. The juxtaposition of these two essays underscores a central ambiguity in Britain's ever diverse redefinition of its cultural and culinary legacies and the fictions that began to be circulated about it. If beef became an embodiment of British-ness, it was done consciously and deliberately, and side by side with the birth of the Western vegetarian movement. The British vegetarian may have been fictionalized as eccentric, but then eccentricity was a proudly acknowledged definitional characteristic beyond, but more and more emphatically through, patterns of consumption.

The final two essays of the first section similarly work together. Helen Day's "Möbial Consumption: Stability, Flux and Interpermeability in 'Mrs Beeton'" reinvestigates the notorious mid-Victorian preoccupation with etiquette in a detailed analysis of Mrs. Beeton's popular and indeed seminal *Book of Household Management* of 1861. A text that recognizes the contradictions involved in managing bourgeois culture, it is also keenly aware of its indigestion, as it were. Day speaks of the "indigestible economies of the Victorian bourgeoisie." Using a möbius construction as a model of simultaneous stability, flux and interpermeability, Day compellingly disengages Victorian middle-class self-definition from conceptualizations of dichotomies and dualities. Like production and consumption, their many presumed dialectics were part of a möbial strip rather than containable through juxtaposition. While Day's essay thus explores the making of British middle-class domesticity through household management, Christine Rinne reads the representative figure of the maidservant in nineteenth-century Central Europe. "Consuming the Maidservant" argues that the often single maidservant employed by bourgeois families in Austria and Germany were a culturally important, yet rarely analyzed, part of the newly emerging nuclear family. Unlike in Western Europe, the majority of middle-class households could only afford the so-called "girl for everything" (*Mädchen für alles*). In addition to serving within the confines of the household, the maidservant was also a representative of her employer to the public sphere. The girl's liminal position, Rinne shows in her reading of literature exclusively for servants (*Dienstbotenzeitungen*), was critical to the bourgeoisie's self-conception and -understanding, and that this was why her own consumption became a popular site of exhibiting control and exercising punishment. Regulating and monitoring the maidservant's own consumption was a desired site of punishment for poor representation or the potential threat of it.

The consequent fictional investment in the regulation and monitoring of consumption already indicates the representative significance of spectacle in the display of food (as representation of the power to consume) for the peculiarly bourgeois modernity that arose in the nineteenth century in, as we shall see, different parts of Europe as well as (former) colonies. Focusing on different spectacles of consumption, the essays collected in Part II seek to illustrate this very pervasiveness as well as the significantly diverse, and yet equally ideologically marked, functions. Thus, in "Pot-Bellied Salt-Cellars and Talking Plates: Fetishism and Signification in *Our Mutual Friend*," Andy Williams addresses the uses of cultural display and consumption on two different levels. While the critique of consumerism that propels Dickens's last finished novel, *Our Mutual Friend* of 1865, indisputably offers the most explicit assessment of Victorian commodity culture to be found in any of Dickens's novels, the work itself also formed a cultural event, meant to be consumed as part of a growing output of products, at the time of its publication. Reading the novel alongside its accompanying advertisements, the "Our Mutual Friend Advertiser," provides new insight into the burgeoning consumer culture in which Dickens wrote.

With Helen Pike Bauer's essay, "Eating in the Contact Zone: Food and Identity in Anglo-India," the study then moves into colonial consumption, addressing the functions of "exotic" luxury products, "other" consumption patterns, and the consuming (incorporation) of alterity from their representation abroad. Among the many adjustments demanded of the British when they went out to India, Bauer argues, was an acclimation to new food and new methods of preparation. In many literary works, both fiction and non-fiction, one can see the cultural function of the attempt to import English ideals of food and drink, to train servants to reproduce English manners and recipes. Bauer looks at little explored novels such as Flora Annie Steel's *On the Face of the Waters* and Sara Jeannette Duncan's *Set in Authority* and *The Simple Adventures of a Memsahib* as well as *The Complete Indian Housekeeper and Cook*, written by Steel and Grace Gardiner, an omnibus guide to establishing and running a household in India, to trace the creation of a new identity, the Anglo-Indian, through the amalgamation of cuisines. Adele Wessell's "Between Alimentary Products and the Art of Cooking: The Industrialisation of Eating at the World Fairs–1888/1893" similarly explores how it was significantly in the heyday of nationalist renaissances that Australia and the United States both commemorated anniversaries prompted by colonialism and did so through consumption on a spectacular scale at the

Melbourne International Exhibition and the Chicago World's Fair, in 1888 and 1893 respectively. By the 1890s, displays of industrial achievement and archaeological and ethnographic exhibitions had indeed become established as traditions of the world fairs. The industrialization of food production, processing and supply on display at the world fairs, supported the industrialization of eating itself. Excess was intended to invoke a sense of wonder to call attention to what was new or different in the modern period.

By contrast, at home in Britain, excess was increasingly policed. Especially as a growing vice of modern working man, it was conceived as a threat, needing middle-class management. In a pointed analysis of a very different form of alterity, Tamara Ketabgian's "Foreign Tastes and 'Manchester Tea-Parties': Eating and Drinking with the Victorian Lower Orders" traces domestic social discourses on the "stimulating" liquid tea in the last few decades of the East India Company's existence (roughly 1832-1848). An industrial rhetoric of production, consumption, and addiction essentially articulated a new preoccupation with the industrialization of the human body. But what is more, when Victorian novelists described a working class devoted to suspect and prophylactic stimulants–both in pennyworths of tea and in acts of consumption as wasteful as they are exciting–this "improvident" habit allied workers with fantasies of industrial discipline colored by orientalist overtones. If factory hands might indulge a taste for Eastern luxuries, so might they impersonate colonial servility in their workaday lives–as obedient "menials" serving a "gentle genii" of steam. Ketabgian reads Elizabeth Gaskell's *Mary Barton* (1848) and Charles Dickens's *Hard Times* (1854) not only as seminal social-problems-novels that view tea-drinking as a domestic ritual that enables potent modes of working-class expression, but also as texts that heighten a controversial Victorian affiliation between foreign tastes, mechanical labor, and the industrial habits of the body.

In a similar vein, Tara Moore reads both Dickens's *A Christmas Carol*, as undoubtedly the best known example of the occasional literature sensation that followed the 1840s cultural fascination with the "new" Christmas, and lesser known Christmas fiction such as Catherine Gore's *The Snow Storm* (1845) or Dickens's own "A Christmas Pudding" (1851) newly to dissect the construction of national identity through the fictional representation of Victorian Christmas food. Christmas fiction, Moore argues, constructs the illusion that consuming traditional festive food—especially through the double consumption of virtually evoked feasts in fiction as a consumable product itself—allows a specifically English national identity to be imbibed that moreover includes a sense of imperial superiority. By contrast, Hawthorne's "The Christmas Banquet" (1844), the next essay shows, expresses a very different attitude to the consumption of Christmas cuisine in Old or New England.

In fact, while Ketabgian and Moore underline the domestic reconstruction of imperialist discourses in dissections of alterity at home, and Bauer and Wessell are interested in self-consciously colonial explorations of national and other forms of identity in the Anglo-Indian community as well as in Australia, the final two contributions to this section focus on the "re-presentation" of food—including representative food of Old England—in nineteenth-century American popular fiction. In "Rewriting the Puritan Past: Food and Illicit Desires in Hawthorne's Fiction," Monika Elbert compellingly argues that when Hawthorne rewrites the history of his Puritan forebears, he imagines their extravagance, or excesses in passion, and sinfulness (often narcissism) in terms of their attitudes towards food. While Elbert draws on various of Hawthorne's writing, including "Egotism; or, the Bosom Serpent" and "The Christmas Banquet," her main focus rests on the food dynamics of *The House of the Seven Gables* (1851). The novel indeed revolves around spiritual love and illicit passions as it expresses tensions between the values of New England and Old England. The frame is not so much a house, but a cornucopia of food.

Alice Jenkins takes a similar approach in her reading of what have become American children's classics: best-selling novels for girls from 1865-1900, including *Little Women* and *What Katy Did*. Exploring the discourses of consumption and nutrition that surrounded images of girls reading in American writing for juveniles during the middle and late nineteenth century, Jenkins suggests a linkage of eating and reading that engendered binary tropes contrasting wholesome food with poison and healthy appetite with jaded palates. As Katy Carr's consumption of apples in an imposition of dietary restrictions on her family as a result of her unfettered reading of cookery books in *What Katy Did* poignantly throws up, discourses of food, consumption and hunger played a key part both in promoting and policing "wholesome" and "unhealthy" results of female literacy. Yet girls who eat and read at the same time are expressing an important independence from the familial context in which communal eating precludes reading. In this, Jenkins compellingly suggests, fictional girl readers may be developing an empowered attitude to themselves as interpreters of text which will eventually lead to a rejection of certain types of literary consumption. Still, excessive consumption of apples (or literary "poisons") conjure up fantasies of indigestion and regurgitation that indeed always formed the dark underbelly of modernity's interest in both spectacular and (the equally spectacular revelation of) secret consumption.

Part III: Blood, Blockage and Regurgitation: The Consumer's Modernity forms an attempt to highlight this largely obscured or elided part of the consuming fictions of modernity. Starting with Jim Chevallier's cultural analysis of "The Queen's Coffee and Casanova's Chocolate," this section reaches back furthest into the beginnings of modern consumption in order to trace patterns of embodiment and rejection, adulteration and expulsion, cultural and other forms of incorporation, the failure to digest, and the usefulness of such indigestion as a metaphor not merely in literature, but also in philosophy or popular representations of cultural icons. At the opening of "Kantstipation," Jason Peck and J.D. Mininger provocatively ask what Kant's dietary practices and digestive problems could possibly have to do with his writing. But what starts out as a deliberately startling invocation casts remarkable new light on the phenomenon of writers linking their intellectual to their digestive and excretory labors. Hence, the inability to produce writing can be viewed in metaphorical terms as a form of intellectual constipation, and Kant explicitly addressed the problem of a blockage in intellectual productivity as concomitant with complaints of poor digestion, constipation, and irritable bowels. A reading that renders his surprisingly consistent metaphors of indigestion prominent puts an important new spin on cultural history. Ilias Chrissochoidis's "A Chubby Orpheus: Handel's Corpulence as a Prerogative of Genius" similarly approaches the notoriety of Handel's corpulence through the pervasive, yet to an important extent, ambiguous and even embarrassed, cultural alignment of excessively producing genius, and exegetical efforts to sublimate physical corpulence. The representation of Handel at the time, Chrissochoidis suggests, strikingly exemplifies a bifurcated understanding of normative behavior that marked the beginning of biographical attitudes in music history where sensual excess is tolerated, if not expected, in those privileged to access the sublime realm of art.

Peculiarly provocative as these two essays may be, they articulate important shifts in aesthetic as well as cultural and social discourses in the eighteenth and nineteenth centuries. It is therefore of specific importance that the contribution in this section, as in this study at large, take evidence from various European countries as well as overseas. Kant and Handel may have both had a profound impact on cultural discourses in Victorian Britain, but most importantly, this very influence substantiates the interchange and reworking of aesthetics, ideologies, philosophies, and cultural productions (and their consumption) throughout eighteenth- and nineteenth-century Europe. Guilan Siassi's contribution, "The Insatiable I: Consumption and Desire in the Baudelairian Aesthetic," even more emphatically brings out seminal developments that so significantly shaped European aesthetic discourses. Charles Baudelaire's literary representations of intoxication and other "decadent" forms of consumption, Siassi argues, constitute a symptomatic response to an ineffable lack in the modern condition. Baudelaire places at the heart of his aesthetic vision an ideal of inebriation, by means of which "psychic scattering" and "self-disseminations" become both the primary modality and the end of modern art. His post-Romantic aesthetic gives expression to the temporal reconfigurations of desire that a dominant capitalist ethos and "consumer culture" both engender and promote.

Additionally to underscore the significance of trans-continentality, cultural and other forms of import and exchange for modernity's new consumer, and of the power of representation for the management of excess, the book ends with an analysis of breeding the foreign and the modern media in *Dracula*. Jared Green's "'No Mere Modernity': Biopolitics, Media, and the Breeding of the Modern Consumer in Bram Stoker's *Dracula*" situates Stoker's novel within the matrix of the late-nineteenth century's pseudo-scientific discourses of race and culture, of an evolving "morbid anthropology." Intriguingly read as a form of fictional ethnography, *Dracula* emerges as a transformative response to shifts in immigration and the production of new technologies as it figures forth modernity as a set of consuming practices that circulate around the use of specific transportation, communication, medical, and recording technologies. The foreign count's blood lust may be the ultimate expression of desire for excessive consumption, but the novel's emphasis on technology is perhaps less concerned with the atavism of the ethnographically captured foreigner as with the dehumanization of the "modern" consumer at home as well as abroad. Indisputably a source of anxieties, modernity's new consumer has, however, brought up a well of new plots that have indeed significantly reshaped the interest—as well as the consumption—of literary and cultural representation in the long nineteenth century. As the individual essays explore in detail the different aspects of consumer culture, and the consuming of culture, this collection also hopes to provide a new approach to the investigation both of consumption and its "re-presentation."

Notes

1. Jasper Fforde, *The Well of Lost Plots* (London: Hodder & Stoughton, 2003), 1-2.

2. Charlotte Brontë's *Jane Eyre* has, in fact, been the object of sequels and "revisions" ever since Jean Rhys's *Wide Sargasso Sea* (1966), which retold the story of Jane's double, her ethnic "other," from a postcolonial perspective. Compare Erin O'Connor, "Preface for a Post-Postcolonial Criticism," *Victorian Studies* 45.2 (2003), 219. Both Fforde's novels and Clare Boylan's completion of Brontë's fragments "Emma" and "Willie Ellin" in her recent novel *Emma Brown* (London: Little, Brown, 2003), however, show that Brontë's fiction lends itself to far different, and differently, postmodern sequels.

3. Fforde, *Lost Plots*, 1-2.

Part I

Production and Presentation: Making Food Fictions

Badly-Boiled Potatoes and Other Crises

Sumangala Bhattacharya

> "The cookery as it might, could, or should be, is misjudged for the
> cookery as it is. No notion exists of what might be gained in economy,
> in health, in morals, and in enjoyment by improved culinary skill."
> "The Mark-Lane Express on the Importance of Treating the Female
> Peasantry in Cookery," *London Times* (February 17, 1854)

By all accounts, the winter of 1853-54 was a severe one for Britain. It
was preceded and accompanied by considerable labor unrest and general
distress. Demonstrators in several counties broke into and looted bread
shops and bakeries. Poor relief systems in urban areas were overwhelmed by the numbers of applicants for relief.[1] In addition to the
worsening domestic situation, war with Russia seemed imminent as the
Crimean crisis was coming to a head. In the midst of all this, a growing
number of articles in newspapers and the periodical press drew attention
to a crisis of a different nature: the awful state of English cookery.

Editorials and essays on the topic of dismal English food (a recurrent
theme in the press in the 1850s) charged that bad cooking and its daily
consumption by the populace were insidious evils that threatened the
destruction of Britain, one household at a time. As asserted in the passage quoted in the epigraph above, bad cooking is no trivial matter af-
fecting just the unfortunate individual. The economic, physical, moral,
and emotional well-being of the entire nation is at stake as well. Physical
dissatisfaction with badly-cooked meals is projected into the political
sphere as social disaffection. In such reckoning, strikes, bread riots, social unrest, and other crises of industrial Britain are the indirect, far-flung
consequences of indigestion brought on by bad dinners. Although satirical, such editorials point up the Victorian ambivalence about industrial
culture and the stability of the bourgeois home. In these pieces, middle-

class families starve in the middle of plenty, as the abundance produced by industry is daily mismanaged and wasted by the ignorance and negligence of cooks and housewives. At a time when middle-class women were projecting an increased presence in the public sphere, as hostesses and as independent agents, the crisis of bad cookery required their return to the kitchen. In this essay I investigate how, in a number of periodical pieces from the 1850s and in Charles Dickens's *David Copperfield* (1850), middle-class anxieties about industrial culture and modernity are transmuted into fictions of bad English cookery.

The essay that appeared in the *Mark-Lane Express* struck a chord. It was rearticulated in the radical periodical, *The Examiner*, and that essay was reprinted in the *London Times* a week later. Similar essays appeared in *Blackwood's Edinburgh Magazine*. The opinions of an article intended for the small audience of a rural gazette was thus given a wide circulation among urban, middle-class readers, to whom the essay offered an appealing explanation for their own discontent.[2] The *Examiner* (in an ironic nod to its radical tradition) represents itself as voicing a neglected truth on behalf of "the people" in disseminating more widely the facts revealed by the "very sensible article" in the *Mark-Lane Express*, namely that "the female peasantry" of England are both ignorant of cookery and unconcerned about their ignorance. As a remedy, the author proposes establishing a canon of dishes, so that the women can be trained in a "common cookery like common sense."[3]

The common cookery outlined in the article takes the form of the standard fare of middle-class tables (not the likely diet of working-class households), which is contrasted as an elegant yet practical alternative to the gourmet fare of gentlemen's clubs and aristocratic tables. The training offered to the "female peasantry" need not encompass "the science of a Ude or Soyer" (both celebrated chefs in the nineteenth century) but need only ensure the acquisition of "sufficient skill to do a few common things well."[4] The list of "common things" that these cooks should learn constitutes a simple but satisfying three-course meal of "plain vegetable soup, a well-dressed mutton chop, and a well-boiled potato."[5] The list of dishes and the gendering of the cooks (women were more commonly employed as cooks in ordinary middle-class households) reveal that the issue here is not the state of working-class families but rather the well-being of the middle-class home. The merit of the imagined meal depends on the quality of the ingredients and the "common sense" skill of the ordinary British cook. The sauces and intricate preparations of gourmet cookery (the so-called "scientific" cuisine of celebrity chefs) are eschewed as impractical. Thus, the vegetable soup must be "plain" (not fussily enhanced with roux or flavorings), the meat "well-dressed," and the potato "well-boiled." Even as it decries the awful state of English cookery, the essay asserts the superiority of a middle-class aesthetic that is practical and British over an aristocratic aesthetic that is complicated, expensive, and cosmopolitan. The problem with the middle-class table is not that it is unaesthetic, but that its aesthetics are unrecognized.

The essay singles out the boiled potato—a choice laden with symbolic meaning—as an exemplar of British cooking. Boiling a potato is the simplest preparation of the tuber, one that leaves it closest to its natural state. Not only is the boiled potato a familiar feature of the working-class diet, it also frequently represents the food of starvation in the cultural imagination.[6] It is also an Irish food, an association that marks it as both ethnically and socially inferior. As Catherine Gallagher and Stephen Greenblatt observe in "The Potato in the Materialist Imagination," in nineteenth-century discussions of food, the difference between the potato and bread is not merely incommensurate but significant. Bread is the product of civilized and social labor, whereas the potato "represented a presocial state of isolation in which the poor were cut off from civilization and undifferentiated both from each other and from nature."[7] The essay rescues the potato from its ethnic and working-class associations by identifying it throughout the essay as the "well-boiled" potato. Shedding its disreputable origins through slow simmering, the well-boiled potato becomes as much a product of civilization as bread.

The well-boiled potato, the well-bred relative of the common boiled potato, is distanced from its degraded connections by becoming associated with an idealized past: "The last [well-boiled potato] is at present a thing purely ideal—it has never come out of the pot in the experience of living men. Do not be rash; do not say you have seen, much less eaten one, for it is because you do not know what it is, or what it should be like, that you imagine you have done so."[8] Unlike the ideal boiled potatoes of the past, the contemporary boiled potato tends to be "crude in the centre," or "pulp" or "watery."[9] In other words, the contemporary boiled potato is vulgar, unrefined, and without character, the converse of everything that the well-boiled potato represents. An emphasis on the aesthetics of this very simply prepared food helps to solidify the slippery boundary between the urban middle classes and their working-class (or lower middle-class) counterparts. The working-class boiled potato is mere nutrition. The "well-boiled" potato of the middle-class table, on the other hand, is a sign of gentility and indicates the possession of a refined palate as well as a well-trained cook.

The task of transforming the potato from its raw tuberous form into the aesthetic symbol of bourgeois prosperity devolves on working-class Englishwomen employed as cooks in middle-class homes. The crisis of

English cookery is the consequence of their failure. Such women are unable to accomplish regularly the desired transformation of the potato because they lack patience. The products of an industrial culture, these women are trained for work that can be done quickly, efficiently, and without independent judgment. The well-boiled potato requires a different kind of mindset altogether, one that combines solicitude and expert judgment. The proper boiling of a potato is a craft. Where the industrial discipline of the English working classes fail, the pre-industrial Irish laborer can succeed through native talent: "The Irish are said to be the only people competent to this performance, perhaps because it involves a practical bull, inasmuch as the first care in boiling a potato should be to prevent the boiling of the potato."[10] These directions distinguish the well-boiled potato (in contrast to its hastily-boiled vulgar cousin) as a food whose preparation and consumption bespeak a leisurely way of life.

In a similar vein, an essay printed in *Household Words* a few years prior to the one above complains of how English cooks ruin good cuts of meat through boring preparations and poor cooking techniques. The author of "A Good Plain Cook" (1850) complains that "Everything that is not roasted or fried, is boiled, "a gallop," till the quality of tenderness is consolidated to the consistency of a caoutchouc."[11] Citing essays that appeared in the *Examiner* and *Blackwood's Magazine* earlier in the year, the author of "A Good Plain Cook" presents a dismal comparison between English and Continental cooks. Despite the high quality of English meat and produce, English cooks invariably dish up tough meat and unappetizing vegetables: "in preparing butcher's meat for the table, the aim of foreign cookery is to make it tender, of English to make it hard . . . . Don't tell me the hardness is in the meat itself. Nothing of the kind; it's altogether an achievement of the English cuisine."[12] As with the badly-boiled potato, badly-stewed meat is the consequence of the cook's desire for haste, which leads her to boil meat at "a gallop" instead of with solicitous attention. Alternatively, the cook bores the diner by only serving meat that has been roasted or fried, both preparations requiring minimal labor. The English cook's Continental counterpart, faced with inferior materials, can turn out delicious meals because she is patient and creative (that is, less concerned with industrial efficiency and routine).

Letters from readers echoed the sentiments expressed in these and other similar essays. Reminiscing about his experiences in the military during the Napoleonic wars, the writer of a letter to the editor in the *London Times* (November 10, 1855) recalls picking up culinary tips from French prisoners. Ordinary French soldiers (working-class men, not cooks) knew that they could make a "good 'stodgy' savoury mess, fit to stick to a fellow's ribs" by throwing "whatever they had in the way of meat" and whatever they could forage into a communal pot. English soldiers, in contrast, were both too individualistic and too unskilled to eat well, with each man roasting his own ration of meat over a campfire "till all the fat and goodness of it frizzled out into the fire, and he got nothing most times but a black dry bit of stuff hardly fit for a dog to eat." A letter writer to the *London Times* (March 10, 1858) indignant on behalf of the soldiers garrisoned in Crimea points to "the invariable 'boiled beef' of the barrack mess, with its inevitable consequence—a disgust at the very sight of food thus served up, for I cannot say cooked." The author contends that "well-boiled meat ought to be as savoury as if roasted" but that the "soldiers suffer, not because their meat is boiled, but because it is ill-boiled." As in the other essays, haste, repetitive preparation, and culinary ignorance are to blame in this instance as well.

Individual displeasure induced by bad cookery multiplied throughout the nation becomes a national crisis. Reversing Thomas Carlyle's description of England as a nation suffering from spiritual dyspepsia, writers on this topic assert that physical dyspepsia is the root of the spiritual maladies of the nation.[13] The essay in the *Examiner* proclaims that the ramifications of the culinary crisis it has outlined affects the "economy, health, morals, and enjoyments" of all classes of society. Bad cookery wastes good resources, transforming abundance into lack. The impact on morals is especially striking, since different social classes are affected in a similar fashion: "A bad dinner in humble life has for its common consequence a quarrel with the wife, and recourse to the dram-bottle or the publichouse. The man disappointed of something to eat comforts himself with something to drink. . .Among the middle classes the evil is modified, but still of the same type."[14] Bad cookery leads to domestic violence and alcoholism among the lower and upper classes. In "A Good Plain Cook," contrasting post-dinner scenes are imagined as cautions to all classes. In upper- and middle-class households, the culinary "crimes" of the improperly-supervised working-class cook results in "Barmecide feasts—which disappoint the taste more because they have often a promising look to the eye." Husbands in such families may not beat their wives as a consequence, but they abandon the home for clubs and other masculine haunts: they "prefer the better fare at their clubs; and escape the Scylla of bad digestion, to be wrecked on the Charybdis of domestic discord." In poorer households, the post-dinner scene is "a spectacle of discomfort, waste, ill-temper, and consequently ill-conduct." Voyeuristically participating in the imagined post-dinner domestic crisis, the author (citing another author on the topic) writes: "If we could see. . .by the help of an Asmodeus what is going on at the dinner-hour of humbler of the middle class [sic]. . .The man quarrels with his wife because there is nothing he can eat, and he generally makes up in drink for the deficiencies in the article of food. Gin is the consolation to the spirits and the resource to the baulked appetite."[15]

While discussions abound of how bad cookery makes men bad husbands, fathers, and citizens, the effects on women never figure in the discourse. Women are imagined mainly as the producers, not consumers, of food. Heroines of Victorian novels, as Helena Michie observes, preside over dinners as angelic presences at the table, but are not diners themselves.[16] In the discourse of bad cookery, women's own appetites are rendered invisible, but the role of women in thwarting legitimate masculine appetites is underscored. The abundance and harmony of the bourgeois home are ruined by an implicit conspiracy between the working-class female cook and the socially ambitious middle-class wife who is ignorant of practical household matters. In "A Good Plain Cook," upper- and middle-class women are castigated for cultivating their knowledge of "all that pertains to personal blandishments."[17] Such women "keep a tight hand over their milliners and ladies' maids," but allow the "heinous offenses" of their cooks to continue without correction. In working-class families, where the cook and the wife are the same person, the problem is ignorance and contempt of culinary matters. Although the crisis of cookery and the instability of the bourgeois home are closely linked in these discussions, opinions differ on causality. While the above editorials point to a social pattern in which bad cooking leads to the disintegration of the home, other writers argue the opposite. In a short piece on the subject, "On Cookery" (1859), Harriet Martineau ascribes the crisis of cookery to the gradual undermining of the bourgeois home, until the domestic skills that were traditionally passed on from mother to daughter are virtually forgotten. In the absence of empirical knowledge, domestic skills such as cookery must be transmitted through formal pedagogy: "What is to be done, for cooking does not come by nature, nor even ordering a table by observation? The art must be learnt, like other arts, by proper instruction. We want, and we must have, schools of domestic management now that every home is not such a school."[18] Martineau's piece assumes an irreversible transformation of society: homes are not *now* as they once were. The homes of the idealized past were managed by women skilled in the domestic arts. Such women would never make the egregious and expensive mistakes made by the modern, urban housewife: "We have seen ladies buying pork under a sweltering summer sun, and inquiring for geese in January and July, and taking up with skinny rabbits in May."[19] Modernity has disrupted the transmission of these feminine skills and knowledge with consequences that can be felt in both the private and public spheres of life.

The moral lesson underscored in discussions of the state of English cookery is that bad cookery makes for domestic and national discord. This lesson finds a powerful literary articulation in the marital tensions of David and Dora in Charles Dickens's *David Copperfield*. In the novel (as in so many of the periodical press articles), masculine hunger disrupts the sanctity of the home and spills over into the public sphere. Faced with the prospect of going to work without a proper meal, a hungry and exasperated David reproaches his beloved "child-wife" Dora: "You know, my love, it's not exactly comfortable to go without dinner. Now, is it?"[20] David's hunger is not the result of poverty. David's income as a reporter, according to his own estimates, is well into three figures. The couple live in a newly-furnished "beautiful little house," enjoy extensive credit with the local shops, and have servants (613). Every aspect of David's life proclaims his moderate, steady success and marks his distance from Murdstone and Grinby's bottling warehouse. Yet David is often hungry.

Made irritable by a chronic state of hunger that arises paradoxically from abundance rather than from scarcity, David takes Dora to task for failing to order the household properly. He lists a series of "uncomfortable" meals he has had to endure since his marriage:

> "Now, my own Dora," said I, "you are very childish, and are talking nonsense. You must remember, I am sure, that I was obliged to go out yesterday when dinner was half over; and that, the day before, I was made quite unwell by being obliged to eat underdone veal in a hurry; to-day, I don't dine at all—and I am afraid to say how long we waited for breakfast—and *then* the water didn't boil. I don't mean to reproach you, my dear, but this isn't comfortable." (620)

Deprived of well-cooked and punctually-served meals at home because of the couple's "scrambling household arrangements," David suffers from a nagging sense of discomfort that is both physical and emotional (630). In his view, the trouble lies in Dora's inability to function as a prudent bourgeois housewife. Yet, as Dora timidly but repeatedly points out in her own defense, she has never pretended to possess any such skills. David's complaint is laced with his frustration that the gendered division of labor that conventionally structures middle-class households such as his has failed. While he is doing his bit as head of the household in the public sphere, Dora is unable to do her bit as head of the household in the private, domestic sphere. As a result, David's capital is squandered and his diligence in the workplace rewarded with off-and-on hunger. While prizing Dora as an ornamental wife whose beauty and gentility reflect his upward social mobility, he regrets that she is not a trustworthy manager of the fruits of his industry.

David's attempts at transforming Dora into a model housewife start during their engagement. He tries to introduce her to the "theory" of household management by giving her "the Cookery Book" as a present and offering occasional lessons in domestic accounting. Aware of Dora's resistance to the idea, he resorts to attractive packaging: "I got it *prettily* bound, first, to make it look less dry and more inviting. . . I showed her an old housekeeping-book of my aunt's, and gave her a set of tablets, and a *pretty* little pencil case and box of leads, to practise housekeeping with" (589; my emphasis). The subterfuge does not succeed. Pitting her own prettiness against the superficial allure of the binding and the toy-like implements with which David had hoped to delude her into an interest in household management, Dora uses the cookbook and the pencil case as props to exhibit her lapdog's cuteness instead: "the principal use to which the Cookery Book was devoted, was being put down in the corner for Jip to stand upon it without offering to come off, and at the same time to hold the pencil case in his mouth" (589). When David catechizes Dora by asking "what she would do" if he were to request "a nice Irish stew" for dinner once they were married, Dora's response defeats him by revealing the fallacies of his expectations: "she replied that she would tell the servant to make it; and then clapped her little hands together across my arm, and laughed in such a charming manner that she was more delightful than ever" (589). Dora is accustomed to the well-trained servants who realize her wishes without active supervision from the mistress of the household. While this exchange captures their different expectations of life, it also highlights David's determined blindness. Expecting his comforts to be ensured by a wife who is a "little housekeeper," as Agnes Wickfield is in her father's household (217), David refuses to see that Dora does not understand a model of domestic life in which the wife fulfills the duties of an upper servant.

The servants employed by David and Dora resemble neither the efficient servants of wealthy, upper-class families (such as the Spenlows) nor dedicated feudal servitors (such as Clara Peggotty). The Copperfields' servants are members of the urban proletariat, more accustomed to the demands of industrial labor than to the domestic tasks of the bourgeois home. They are driven by economic considerations, not by loyalty to employers. As a result, David never achieves his desired goal of a comfortable home—that is, a home whose comforts are characterized by the middle-class values (such as, efficiency, punctuality, and thrift) that have allowed him to prosper. David describes the domestic trials of his married life as the "Ordeal of Servants" (623), implying that the discomfort of which he complains is an ordeal inflicted upon the Copperfields by incompetent and delinquent servants. However, he clearly believes that the ordeal is brought upon them by Dora's inability to assert herself as a domestic authority over servants and tradesmen.

The incident which provokes David into remonstrating with Dora is precipitated by the egregious delinquencies of their cook, named (with exquisite irony) Mary Anne Paragon. Assuming that Dora's gentility endows her with the authority and ability to manage servants, David exhorts her to reprimand Paragon. More clear-sighted than he is, Dora refuses on the grounds that her authority as mistress of the house is hopelessly compromised by her inexperience: "'Oh, because I'm such a little goose,' said Dora, 'and she knows I am'" (619). David is himself intimidated by Paragon, whom he describes as "a remorseless woman" who "preyed on our minds dreadfully" (618). His cowardice is revealed in his decision to "reason with" Dora (a term that Dora shrewdly points out is his euphemism for scolding her) rather than "reasoning with" Paragon directly. While David feels his household is hostage to Paragon, fate intervenes. The Copperfields are freed from Paragon's thrall after the arrest of her "cousin" allows David to muster up the courage to act: "This nerved me to get rid of Mary Anne, who went so mildly, on receipt of wages, that I was surprised" (623).[21]

The members of the urban working class with whom David and Dora come into contact regard the Copperfields solely as purchasers of goods and services and feel justified in taking advantage of the couple's ignorance and inexperience of the marketplace. On the other hand, the Copperfields treat the servants and tradespeople as objects hardly worth any notice unless they prove to be troublesome. David and Dora know nothing of the antecedents of the servants they hire, except by means of vague references. Paragon's replacement, an old charwoman named Mrs. Kidgerbury, is too frail to undertake the physical labor of housekeeping (especially for such a disorganized home). While Mrs. Kidgerbury is at least dignified by a name and the vestiges of personality, those who succeed her are described merely as "a long line of Incapables" who demonstrated "an average equality of failure" (623). These servants are only minimally skilled at the intricate and unstructured work involved in maintaining a comfortable bourgeois household. Not only are they unsatisfactory workers, they are also indistinguishable and replaceable, like mass-produced commodities.

As middle-class householders, David and Dora feel that they are in the power of their servants and tradespeople. The city, with its multiplicity of legitimate and illegitimate occupations, offers the working class many alternatives to domestic employment, thus generating a shortage of

suitable help. Small tradesmen in the city do not depend for their liveli-
hood primarily on the patronage of a few local families (as in the country), and they are not willing to forgo immediate profit in favor of establishing a long-standing relationship. As David discovers, gentility is
irrelevant in such a milieu and is even a source of vulnerability. While
Paragon clearly believes in the philosophy of *caveat emptor* with regard
to her services, neither David nor Dora can bear the thought of an open
confrontation with her. Like Paragon, all other members of the working
class with whom David and Dora "had anything to do" (623) believe in
the doctrine of *caveat emptor*. David reluctantly comes to understand
that he and Dora are "two young birds" utterly at the mercy of the preda-
tory working class: "Everybody we had anything to do with seemed to
cheat us" (618). While David tries to sustain a misplaced belief that gentility (that is, a sensibility that shrinks from open confrontation and the
open negotiation of value) can prevail in the urban marketplace, Dora
accepts the fact that in dealing with Paragon and her ilk, she is indeed a
"little goose" for the plucking (619). When David's faith in gentility is
undercut by experience, he tries to hold on to yet another illusion: that
someone else, preferably his wife or aunt, can perform the disagreeable
task of dealing with the servants and tradespeople. Having escaped the
proletarian labor of transcribing Parliamentary sessions by becoming a
successful author, David believed he was "reasonably entitled to escape
from the dreary debates" that occur in Parliamentary speeches and in the
dealings of private life (670). However, his dealings with Paragon and
her successors prove that bourgeois home is a part of, and not a sanctuary
from, the market forces that structure society.

David's physical hunger is especially troublesome to him because he
is baffled by the economics of the situation. His hunger seems to arise in
the midst of an abundance that takes on a fabulous aspect, reminiscent of
the "baleful fiat of enchantment" which Carlyle had believed was an apt
description of the paradoxical simultaneity of wealth and scarcity in England.[22] David's household is not simply stocked with food and other
goods as any ordinary middle-class home might be; instead, it is a kind
of Eldorado of food. David tries to understand his hunger in the rational
and quantitative terms of accounts and bills, but his imagination conjures
up for him fairytale visions of abundance, such as a cellar paved entirely
with butter and the consumption of such immense quantities of pepper
that sets off a national scarcity: "It appeared to me, on looking over the
tradesmen's books, as if we might have kept the basement story paved
with butter . . . I don't know whether the Excise returns of the period
may have exhibited any increase in the demand for pepper; but if our
performances did not affect the market, I should say several families

must have left off using it" (624). These ironic exaggerations are focused on items that are adjuncts to the regular contents of the pantry rather than on items that would be the main ingredients of meals, so that butter and pepper take the place of meat and bread. David succinctly sums up the paradox of going hungry despite being able to command in the market such enormous quantities of goods: "And the most wonderful fact of all was, that we never had anything in the house" (624)!

David's industry produces a chimerical abundance that is analogous to the Barmecide feasts served up to the hypothetical middle-class husbands in "A Good Plain Cook." He takes refuge in the language of political economy: "I had reason to believe that in accomplishing these failures we incurred a far greater expense than if we had achieved a series of triumphs" (624). Yet eliminating wastefulness seems neither possible nor sufficient to allay his discomfiture with his domestic life. His troubles seem to him to transcend the economic and rational realm and verge upon the supernatural. Even the Cookery Book, which he had hoped would transform Dora, fails him even when he takes a personal hand in applying theory to practice: "In search of the principle on which joints ought to be roasted, to be roasted enough, and not too much, I myself referred to the Cookery Book. . .But the principle always failed us by some curious fatality, and we never could hit any medium between redness and cinders" (624). His hunger is a kind of curse, a "curious fatality," caused not by a dearth of joints to be roasted, but by the inexplicable intransigence of joints and other foods, which seem to resist consumption even as they tempt it. Conspiring with the intransigence of commodities is an intransigent proletarian work force, whose members know more about machine-made cotton than homemade bread, and understand the cash-nexus more thoroughly than the feudal values of fealty and service. David worries that the "want of system and management" in their household is a "contagion" that affects the servants and tradespeople who come into contact with them, as he tries to explain to Dora: "'The fact is, my dear,' I began, 'there is a contagion in us. We infect every one about us.'" (674) Seeing himself as both cursed and diseased, David surrenders to a perpetual state of indefinable discontent: "I was happy; but the happiness I had vaguely anticipated, once, was not the happiness I enjoyed, and there was always something wanting" (678).

In editorials and essays in the periodical press, as in *David Copperfield*, middle-class households seemed to suffer from a hunger that was both physical and spiritual, and that was a result of prosperity rather than scarcity. This perceived hunger appears as the peculiar product of industrial production and modern social relations, which replaces with efficiency and utilitarianism the older values of pleasure and communal life.

The cultural discomfiture with industrial modernity found expression in criticisms of the skills of British cooks and housewives. The domestic space, which was the purview of cooks and housewives, seemed both in dire need of the imposition of an industrial ethos and highly vulnerable to the ill effects of such an ethos. In *David Copperfield*, David wishes his household could be more organized and cost-effective; yet he is also distressed at the intrusion of the values of the market in his dealings with servants and tradespeople. In the editorials and essays, efficiency and routinization feature as the root causes of the decline of British cookery. Through either too much efficiency or too little, the wealth of resources that the middle-class households are able to command is transformed into Barmecide feasts and uncongenial surroundings that frustrate rather than satisfy desire. The crisis of cookery gave voice to the fear that the prosperity gained by industrial modernity might indeed be what David comes to believe is true in his case: cursed, diseased, and always something wanting.[23]

Notes

1. Throughout January and February of 1854, the *London Times* carried reports that rioters in Exeter, Nottingham, and Devonshire broke into and looted bread shops. More riots occurred in the following months and there were reports of occasional riots in London and Liverpool the following year. See also Gareth Stedman Jones, *Outcast London: A Study in the Relationship between Classes in Victorian Society* (Oxford: Clarendon, 1971), 1-17.

2. The recycling of essays on this topic in periodicals and newspapers primarily targeting a middle class readership suggests that the ideas referenced a familiar experience and therefore had a ready currency. A number of letters to the editor picked up on topic as well. No piece, to my knowledge, defended English cooking. The following articles, among others, developed the theme, often with extensive citations from each other: "Cookery" (*Examiner*, February 9, 1850), "Cookery and Civilisation" (*Blackwood's Edinburgh Magazine* August 1846), "A Good Plain Cook" (*Household Words* May 4, 1850), and "Thoughts upon Dinners" (Blackwood's Edinburgh Magazine June 1852).

3. "The *Mark-Lane Express* on the Importance of Treating the Female Peasantry in Cookery." Rpt. *London Times* February 17, 1854, 7.

4. "The *Mark-Lane Express* on Cookery," 7.

5. "The *Mark-Lane Express* on Cookery," 7. While the implication is that these items constitute staple elements of the working-class diet, the mutton chop alerts against such an assumption. Although working-class life in the 1850s showed some improvement from the desperate conditions of the previous decade, working-class and poor families were unlikely to afford what amounts to a three-course meal, featuring a good cut of meat. Citing Dr. Edward Smith's Report to the Privy Council on the Food of the Poorer Labouring Classes (1863), historian John Burnett points out: "It is clear that the diet of these numerically

large classes was as bad in 1863 as it had been at any time earlier in the century" (129). According to Burnett, the meats consumed by the poor constituted bacon and other low-quality meats, such as dried or salted beef (called "hamburg beef" from Germany). Mutton chops would appear too rarely in working-class meals for their proper preparation to be considered "common cookery." For further details, see Burnett, *Plenty and Want: A Social History of Diet in England from 1815 to the Present Day* (London: Scolar Press, 1979).

6. While the most famous food of starvation in literature is gruel (see Charles Dickens's *Oliver Twist*), the boiled potato (especially when cold) features as the food of starvation in social problem novels of the 1840s, such as Benjamin Disraeli's *Sybil, or the Two Nations* (1845) and Elizabeth Gaskell's *Mary Barton* (1848).

7. Catherine Gallagher and Stephen Greenblatt, *Practising New Historicism* (Chicago: U of Chicago P, 2000), 114.

8. "*Mark-Lane Express* on Cookery," 7.

9. "The *Mark-Lane Express* on Cookery," 7.

10. "The *Mark-Lane Express* on Cookery," 7.

11. *Household Words* May 4, 1850: 139.

12. "Good Plain Cook," 139.

13. Thomas Carlyle, "Characteristics," *A Carlyle Reader: Selections from the Writings of Thomas Carlyle*. Ed. G. B. Tennyson (New York: Modern Library, 1969), 27.

14. "*Mark Lane Express* on Cookery," 7.

15. "Good Plain Cook," 140.

16. Helena Michie argues that in such representations, "The delicate woman who does not assert her physical needs serves to recuperate the Fall and to reestablish lost innocence" (23). While ordinary physical hunger in women was held as indelicate, starvation seemed especially feminine. Narratives of starving widows and seamstresses flourished in literature, art, and the popular imagination. For further details, see Michie, *Flesh Made Word: Women's Figures, Women's Bodies* (Oxford: Oxford U P, 1987).

17. "Good Plain Cook," 140.

18. Martineau, 6.

19. Martineau, 6.

20. Charles Dickens, *David Copperfield* (Oxford: Oxford U P, 1997), 619. Hereafter cited parenthetically.

21. Chris R. Vanden Bossche argues that Dora's failure as a housekeeper is due to her upbringing within an aristocratic, rather than middle-class, economy. Whereas David decries wastefulness and idleness, Dora values leisure, genteel accomplishments, and an oblivious attitude to pecuniary considerations. For futher details, see Vanden Bossche, "Cookery, not Rookery: Family and Class in *David Copperfield*" *Dickens Studies Annual* 15 (1986): 94-98.

22. See "Midas" in *Past and Present*. Ed. Richard Altick (New York: New York U P, 1965), 7.

23. This essay would not be possible without the encouragement of my parents, Professor Sushil Kumar Bhattacharya and Mrs. Gitanjali Bhattacharya. I

would also like to acknowledge all the patience and craft of my dear friend, Dr. Sharilyn Nakata (who would never boil a potato badly or miss a typographical or grammatical error) and the support of my colleagues Dr. Harriet Linkin and Elizabeth Schirmer.

Vegetable Fictions in the "Kingdom of Roast Beef": Representing the Vegetarian in Victorian Literature

James Gregory

In nineteenth-century Britain consumption of meat signified status, roast beef remained powerfully associated with national identity, and a mixed diet was considered essential for a healthy existence. Yet Britain was the birthplace of the modern Western vegetarian movement. This essay examines vegetarianism's cultural meanings through its fictional representation. Whilst frequently being, as the *Westminster Review* noted in 1852, a "small recurring topic"—in newspapers, quarterly journals, and satirical magazines—vegetarianism's depiction in works of fiction has had little attention.[1] This is despite the vegetarian characters created by, amongst others, George Gissing, Charles Kingsley, Eliza Lynn Linton, George Meredith, Mrs. Oliphant, Mrs. Humphry Ward, and H. G. Wells. From Richard Feverel's youthful experience in Meredith's novel, to the fruitarian socialists of Wells's *Ann Veronica*, vegetarians had a presence which went beyond the few appearances noted in Carol Adams' groundbreaking *Sexual Politics of Meat*.[2]

Apart from demonstrating the presence of food reformers or faddists in the literature of the time, this essay shows that the treatment of dietetic nonconformity in these works exemplifies fiction's role in defining cultural norms. The vegetarian-teetotal character, frequently depicted as combining dietary "ism" with other "progressive" enthusiasms, played a satirical role, either in condemning social ills, or in caricaturing social purity crusades or advanced reform movements of the period. Dietetic difference often indicated more serious transgressions, and revealed connections between the materiality of food and the spiritual/ moral world.

Yet Victorian fascination with "eccentricity" also reveals itself through the treatment of vegetarians.

This literary representation reveals the varied associations made between "modernity" and the movement. Critics might present it as a fad, implying its transience as the next "new" cause; or discuss it as a manifestation of Western or British decadence.[3] Its supporters, concerned with the reputation of the reform and its propagandising organisations, argued for its antiquity and presented it as the "herald of a golden age." Given the privileged position of meat in Victorian culture, vegetarians struggled to convert the nation. But novelty or oddity value, and its association with similar "progressive" movements, generated discussion about vegetarianism in the press during its infancy, and in a period of growth during the *fin de siècle*. This "dietetic discourse" revealed relationships between dietary reform and a variety of subjects from race and imperialism to concerns about atheism, faddism and "sentimentalism."

Vegetarianism and Modernity

An exploration of fictional representation needs to be prefaced by a sketch of the vegetarian movement's complicated relationship with "modernity." Part of the complication no doubt lies in the fact that as a concept, modernity has "shifting and frequently contradictory meanings."[4] Furthermore, there was no monolithic "vegetarianism," for it comprised people with various motivations (hygienic, economic, religious, ethical); and presented itself to the public in various ways: as a "return to nature," as a movement towards a new golden age, and a progressive reaction to contemporary material and moral problems.

Vegetarianism seems to fit characterisations of Victorian "modernity"—as a response to industrialisation, urbanisation and separation from natural world— and the few scholarly historians of vegetarianism have been keen to relate their subject to modernity.[5] Contemporaries appreciated its modernity (or novelty), though they were aware of its classical antecedents and prevalence in the non-European world. Anglo-American commentators in that period of "new reforms" in the 1840s and 1850s described vegetarians as a "precious class of New Reformers" who adopted a "new-fangled system." Significantly, a pioneering vegetarian journals was entitled *The New Age* ("old things are passed away; behold all things are become new").[6] The movement collapsed temporarily—for various reasons—in the 1860s; in its revival and new recruits in the late-nineteenth century it was able to appear a youthful cause in that second era of newness, the *fin de siècle*. Historians of this self-consciously "modern" epoch have occasionally alluded to vegetarianism.[7]

In an age which perceived itself as one of unparalleled material and technological progress, apologists across the western world presented vegetarianism as in the vanguard of social, moral and hygienic reform.[8] Vegetarians (in common with many reformers) identified themselves with a general questioning of traditions.[9] Vegetarians looked to future vindication and seized on verdicts which acknowledged their inevitability: thus the American writer Henry Thoreau's view "that it [was] part of the destiny of the human race, in its gradual improvement, to leave off eating animals," the Russian scholar A. N. Beketov's description of it as the "food of the future," and the scientist Rudolf Virchow's assertion that the "future is with the vegetarians," were publicised by British vegetarians.[10] This belief in future vindication was trumpeted by the *Vegetarian*, the organ of the late-Victorian movement in London, which was advertised with the slogan "Vegetarianism is the coming subject" and described as pointing "to that Ideal Future."

The movement was also "modern" in its ambivalent relationship to science. Early-Victorian vegetarians exploited the scientist Justus von Liebig's new chemistry and the science of nutrition, some later polemicists found support in the theory of evolution.[11] As one prominent vegetarian, the humanitarian Henry Salt, noted, "it has been reserved to modern times to demonstrate the philosophic and scientific truth."[12] For dietary and other purposes (since vegetarianism, though primarily stressing dietary aspects in this period, could encompass a concern about animal-derived materials in general) vegetarians endorsed new vegetarian substitutes, and hoped for technological alternatives to animal exploitation. But they also included many, such as the physician and mystic Anna Kingsford, hostile to vivisection and anti-vaccination and critical of a "new priesthood" of science. Vegetarianism was thus one manifestation of that wider anti-materialism and anti-positivism in Victorian culture. The association of vegetarianism with communitarianism in the 1840s, and the "simple life" and "back to the land" tendencies of the *fin de siècle*, also revealed the unsympathetic response to aspects of modernity which the "primitive diet" might entail.

The association between vegetarian diet and progress was contentious. Its significance as a "sign of the times" when it emerged in the 1840s-1850s was debated. Did it represent advance or decline? Often belittled as faddish by those endorsing medical orthodoxy, critics hoped it would fade away as science exploded its claims. It was viewed as retrograde: as a cause which would endanger man's evolution (or the security of the nation) by limiting food resources and encouraging a race of puny and effeminate sentimentalists.[13] Others could describe it as something for the distant millennium.[14] Its reputation as a novel, marginal, visionary and contested cause was apparent in its fictional representations throughout the period. Literature reflected the movement's status as emblematic of modernity and anti-modernity.

Vegetarian Fictions

A number of representations of vegetarianism appeared in short stories and novels, some of which, attracting a mass readership, thus offered another opportunity for Victorians to encounter representation and discussion of the reform.[15] A more extensive treatment would have to consider the treatment of "vegetable diet" in eighteenth-century literature and in Romantic literature.[16] Not surprisingly perhaps, given the influence of Shelley, a number of poets tried vegetarianism: and poetry is a minor location for allusions to it.[17] Vegetarianism's unworldly reputation drew on this connection between diet and poetic dreamer.

Carol Adams's canon of feminist-vegetarian works of fiction from *Frankenstein* to the present-day neglects many Victorian instances, and she cites Isabel Colegate's modern (albeit Edwardian era-located) *The Shooting Party* instead.[18] Further research reveals fictional representation by a few obscure British vegetarian authors in the 1840s and 1850s (Elizabeth Blackwell, Fanny Lacy, James Duncan, Sarah Clubb).[19] From the 1870s, propaganda appeared in fiction and poetry produced by vegetarians such as the mystic Anna Kingsford, the temperance author Harriet Beavan, the millionaire shipbuilder Arnold Hills and the journalist J. A. Parker.[20] But it is representation in mainstream fiction, rather than the fiction produced for the movement, which is the focus here.[21]

In *Household Words* in 1851, Charles Dickens identified vegetarianism with teetotalism and pacifism as modern organised extremism.[22] Although his own fictional representation of the diet—David Copperfield's brief contemplation of the vegetable diet—is a reminder of youthful dalliance with dietetic unorthodoxy in literary circles (often, as in the cases of Robert Browning and G. H. Lewes, inspired by Shelley), the vegetarian movement's partial origins in a wider temperance movement meant that novelists wishing to condemn teetotal extremism might also, like Thackeray or Bulwer-Lytton, allude to it.[23]

A broader ultra-progressive world of competing or affiliated "*isms*" (as they were often dismissively referred to) provided the setting for fictional treatment of the dietetic heretic. Vegetarians appeared in the context of novels containing moral or social reform themes, a habit exemplified by Charles Kingsley's idealistic chartist tailor John Crossthwaite in *Alton Locke*. Small, pale, weak and prematurely aged, his diet explained a "great deal of the almost preternatural clearness, volubility, and sensitiveness of his mind."[24] The pioneer vegetarian community of "sacred socialists" at Ham Common in Surrey, appeared in thinly-veiled form in Mary Kelty's *Visiting My Relations*.[25] The association of perfectionist communitarianism and diet also surfaces in Margaret Oliphant's *Zaidee: A Romance* of 1851, in the figure of the philosopher and reformer and follower of Charles Fourier, Mr. Cumberland, dedicated to "Nature," eating "suaer-kraut and radishes" and attempting the "conversion of the world by vegetable diet."[26] Oliphant's novel first appeared in *Blackwood's Edinburgh Magazine*, where a couple of other works of fiction also fleetingly located vegetarians amongst progressive enthusiasts such as Quaker pacifists: Bulwer-Lytton's popular *My Novel; or, Varieties in English Life* and William Aytoun's "The Congress and the Agapedome."[27]

Such representations were an acknowledgment that vegetarianism was a component, if exceptional, of modern life. The figure of the vegetarian was not, however, confined to British literature. Although modern western vegetarianism was first organised in Britain, it found powerful stimulus in earlier and parallel American reform movements.[28] Showing her historical accuracy, George Eliot's recreation of provincial life in the era of the Reform Act made reference to establishing "a Pythagorean [i.e. vegetarian] community in the [American] backwoods."[29] Depicting transcendentalist-inspired vegetarianism and community experience in the same period were several American novels or short stories: Bayard Taylor's story set in a vegetarian community in 1845,[30] Orestes Brownson's *The Spirit-Rapper* (1854),[31] and a fictionalised account of a socialist community, *The Philosophers of Foufouville*. These works accurately reflected such communities' transatlanticism by including British characters.[32] Probably the presence or reference to vegetarianism was more prominent in American literature because of America's status as the destination for communitarian experiments. The earlier existence of Grahamism—a mass health reform movement which included vegetarianism—the vigour of temperance, women's suffrage and spiritualism; combined with these reforms' association with the American Whigs, explain frequent vegetarian allusions in mid-century American fiction.[33]

The revival of organised British vegetarianism from the 1860s was reflected in the appearance of vegetarians, cast as advanced reformers, in late-Victorian fictions by George Meredith, William Barry, Mary Ward, and Eliza Lynn Linton. Unusually, two leading characters in Meredith's *Beauchamp's Career* (1875) draw on Meredith's friendship with the radical Frederick Maxse, whose influence led Meredith to experiment with the diet for health reasons.[34] Nevil Beauchamp—opponent of hedonism, "flunkeyism," middle-class cowardice and apathy, and the vested interests of drink trade, Church, the Landed and the Law—is described by an opponent as a supporter of "pimping Republicanism and capsizing everything in. . .Old England." A protégé of the vegetarian Dr. Shrapnel, Beauchamp's austere altruism leads one character, Cecilia, to investigate vegetarianism, which leads to a "ludicrous-terrific" vision of human bloodlust, "in the shape of an entire community pursuing countless herds of poor scampering animal life for blood: she meanwhile, with Nevil and Dr. Shrapnel, stood apart contemning. For those who do not partake of flesh in this kingdom of roast beef must be of the sparse number of Nevil's execrated minority in politics."[35]

Linton's autobiographic *Christopher Kirkland* (1885) similarly portrayed dietary asceticism in the context of social regeneration, in the Lambert family.[36] Linton describes the mother, an ultra-radical reformer, as "one of those ascetic Bohemians who frankly prefer poverty and disorder to sufficiency and regularity. . . she would rather have a dish of herbs on a bare table than a stalled ox with glass and silver and damask as the adjuncts."[37] In Mr. Dalrymple, is depicted an eccentric, effeminate and sinister character, "in his way a clever as well as an eccentric man, at once charming and less than charming."[38] Dalrymple is a teetotal-vegetarian and occultist, an accurate reflection of the link between food reform and the occult/mystic tendency of late-Victorian modernity (although Kirkland's encounter with the Dalrymples is set in the early-Victorian period). But he is also an eater of opium, hashish and tobacco smoker, which would have been anathema for most vegetarians, associated as they were with the anti-narcotics movements.

These two works by Meredith and Linton were commercial failures by leading novelists. As the journalist Justin McCarthy observed of the "prose Browning," Meredith's work had probably not been read by "one in every thousand novel-readers."[39] But another novel depicting an advanced reformer who was dietetically unorthodox, the Catholic writer William Barry's *The New Antigone* (1887) was a very popular novel of ideas.[40]

Mary Ward's depiction of English vegetarianism c.1870 in the best-selling *History of David Grieve* (1892), picked up vegetarian propagandists' themes of increasing life-span and material advancement, and accurately located the movement in the North and Midlands of England. Adrian Lomax becomes vegetarian in a radical Leicestershire milieu of secularism, socialism and anti-vaccination; but is dismissed from his post on the *Penny Banner* for attacking carnivorism. Mancunian vegetarianism (centred on Lomax's "Fruit and Flowers Parlour") is briefly portrayed; its appeal attributed to the stresses and strains of modern life offering opportunities to any with novel solutions to "those daily needs which both goad and fetter the struggling multitude at every step."[41] Ward was a successful novelist: as an American journalist observed, a book by her was "an event in the literary world." Yet if the depiction of the whimsical "Parlour" consequently had many readers, reviewers ignored the vegetarian episode, except to include it among the irrelevant passages in an overlong work.[42]

Sherlock Holmes's journey past a vegetarian restaurant in "The Redheaded League" symbolises vegetarianism's presence in *fin de siècle* London.[43] It was a presence prominently featured in Edwardian works by two authors who were associated with the "advanced" milieu they were satirising: H. G. Wells and the largely forgotten Harold Begbie. A character in Wells's autobiographical *Love and Mr. Lewisham*, which was first printed serially in 1899, had spoken disparagingly of teetotal-vegetarianism. The fraudulent medium Mr Chaffery condemned the "Dissenter, the Nonconformist Conscience, the Puritan, you know, the Vegetarian and Total Abstainer, and all that sort of thing. . .I have cleared my mind of cant and formulae."[44] More substantially, Wells depicted food, dress and feminist reforms in his controversial *Ann Veronica*, published 1909. Through the characters Mr. and Mrs. Goopes, "the oddest little couple conceivable," these are presented as theoretically right but practically absurd: Wells has fun presenting an earnest discussion revolving around substitute lard as an "exceptionally purifying influence on the mind."

The Goopes, childless and servantless followers of the "simple life," live in the Tottenham Court Road where Mrs. Goopes, in between writing columns for *New Ideas* ranging in their themes from vegetarian cookery and vivisection, to degeneration and "Higher Thought," helps in a fruit shop. The diminutive and reserved Mr. Goopes, "with a large inflexible-looking convex forehead," teaches mathematics. At home they wear reformed clothing, Mr. Goopes dressed "in a pajama-shaped suit of canvas sacking tied with brown ribbons, while his wife wore a purple *djibbah* with a richly embroidered yoke." They hold a little gathering every Saturday "from nine till the small hours, just talk and perhaps reading aloud and fruitarian refreshments—chestnut sandwiches buttered with nuttose, and so forth—and lemonade and unfermented wine."[45]

The supporters of vegetarianism and other reforms are described as unattached youths, young artists and writers, self-supporting women or female students. They are washed-out and represent the "spectacle of failure protecting itself from abjection by the glamour of its own assertions." Here, Wells accurately identified important constituents and tendencies of the *fin de siècle* including that symbol of modernity, the self-supporting woman. His dislike of vegetarians, possibly due to his association of dietary abstinence with celibacy, was expressed in a number of characters and references in later works.[46]

An open-minded baronet is imperilled by metropolitan radicalism in Begbie's satire on various dietetic, religious, political and social "isms."[47] It was a world the author knew well, as a former vegetarian. His position as a renegade lampooning ultra-reform repeated what the horticulturalist James Shirley Hibberd, active in early London vegetarianism, had done in a short story of 1886.[48] Professions of ultra-humaneness are, as in many depictions of the vegetarian, contrasted with character flaws and shown to be impractical.

This depiction of vegetarians as comic was encouraged by popular satirical journals such as *Punch*. When Meredith charted the romance of a vegetarian drinker and a teetotal omnivore in *One of Our Conquerors* (1892) he exploited the comic potential of opposites and extremes attracting.[49] Stage farce, such as the popular *Follies of the Day* of 1851, similarly treated vegetarianism as comic.[50] Viewed as a modern fad along with interest in Eastern religions or spiritualism, vegetarianism remained a target for humourists such as E. F. Benson in the early-twentieth century.[51]

In 1897 the *Newcastle Leader* asked why "none of our realistic novelists have ever painted the dread monotony of the vegetarian life."[52] The only author dealing with the unglamorous thrift aspect was George Gissing, whose several vegetarian characters were inspired by his experience. The vegetarianism of shabby-genteel Virginia Madden in *The Odd Women* (1893) and Tymperly in "A Poor Gentleman," conceal their poverty. Henry Ryecroft, eponymous hero of Gissing's most popular work, senses "an odd pathos in the literature of vegetarianism," recalling his study of the periodicals and pamphlets "with all the zest of hunger and poverty, vigorously seeking to persuade myself that flesh was an altogether superfluous, and even repulsive, food."[53] Gissing captures the atmosphere of vegetarian restaurants and one strand of vegetarian propaganda, appealing to the economic needs of the new class of white-collar workers via sixpenny dinners: "poor clerks and shop boys, bloodless girls and women of many sorts—all endeavoring to find a relish in lentil soup and haricot something or other. It was a grotesquely heart-breaking sight."[54] But even Gissing had characters who were vegetarian on moral grounds or who were involved in communitarian schemes.[55]

One early critic described vegetarians as "one of the choicer specimens of the Utopian family" and food reform's association with community experiments throughout the period gave credence to the frequent label of utopianism.[56] This examination of fictional vegetarianism concludes with a brief consideration of literature which was clearly a response to modernity: utopian and scientific romance. Although vegetarianism has been a noted presence in utopian fictions of the Romantic period, the dietetic ambitions of early-nineteenth century social reformers had often involved *increasing* the population's consumption of meat, for instance in utterances by Chartist agitators and in fictions such as Douglas Jerrold's *Chronicles of Clovernook* which presented a future of abundant beef.[57] But vegetarianism frequently appeared in the imagined futures of late-Victorians. Some, like Bulwer-Lytton's *Coming Race*, Samuel Butler's *Erewhon*, H. G. Wells's *Time Machine*, being best-sellers.[58]

If contemporary circumstances often proved discouraging for Victorian vegetarians, such literary references were eagerly noted by them either as clear endorsement or as evidence that their cause was being debated. Evolution, according to Bulwer-Lytton, Robert Buchanan and others, would mean that the race of the future was vegetarian.[59] If the Eloi's degeneration was marked by their vegetable diet in Wells's scientific romance, for Bulwer-Lytton's supermen, the Vril-ya, bloodless diet signified a higher state of development. As they inform the novel's American hero, after studying his teeth the sages were "divided in opinion whether you were a harmless or an obnoxious animal. . .Carnivorous animals of your size are always destroyed, as being of savage and dangerous nature." Their own teeth were "modified by hereditary transmission," and even the barbarians of the underworld do not eat flesh.[60] The vegetarianism of the "coming race" was lost on the manufacturers of one beef extract who named their product "Bovril" in response to the novel's popularity.

Conclusion

Vegetarians had a presence in Victorian fictions, but their rarity reflected their limited numbers in society. Where they featured, vegetarians were associated with radicalism in politics and personal lifestyle in a milieu of "Bohemian humanitary," to use Henry James's phrase.[61] Dietetic nonconformity could then contribute to a satirical treatment of *soi disant* progressives or moral reformers whose solutions to modern ills, or exaggerated modernity, were treated as ridiculous.

These representations of "movement culture" or restaurant clientele—by Wells, Begbie and others—might be exaggerated but they often expressed sociological truths and accurately summarised vegetarian propaganda. The actuality of youthful experimentation was also expressed in dietetic reform as a phase for characters such as Meredith's Richard Feverel, the hero of the vegetarian George Bernard Shaw's novel *Immaturity*, or Christina in Ella Hepworth Dixon's *My Flirtation*.[62] Dietetic differences were recognised forms of "eccentricity" in a culture fascinated with eccentrics.[63] Obviously the appearance of a vegetarian might represent the arrival of an odd and therefore memorable character. Thus Crowl, the feisty character in Zangwill's locked-room mystery. was a republican vegetarian and the Edwardian "railway detective" Thorpe Hazell was a health food enthusiast.[64]

The perceived strangeness of vegetarianism allowed authors to indicate the otherness of characters, as with Rider Haggard's terrible Ayesha in his bestselling *She*; or the serial killer Sleuth, based on Jack the Ripper, in Belloc Lowndes' Edwardian chiller, *The Lodger* (1913).[65] The violence of these characters represented a denial of the pacific claims advanced by vegetarian advocates. That Ayesha was an ancient Greek and Sleuth a man obsessed with the Bible, was also indicative of the complicated relationship of vegetarianism to its contemporaries. The Victorian era was an age of plural and competing modernities. Vegetarianism, with its classical roots and novel status, its puritanical, mystical, utopian and other aspects, all dimensions expressed in fictional representations, reflected this.

Notes

1. [Samuel Brown], 'Physical Puritanism,' *Westminster Review*, April 1852: 405-442 [407].

2. Carol J. Adams, *The Sexual Politics of Meat: A feminist-vegetarian critical theory* (New York and London: Polity/ Continuum, 1990; reprinted 2000).

3. See [George W. Steevens], "The New Humanitarianism," *Blackwood's Edinburgh Magazine* 163 (January 1898): 98- 106.

4. Martin. J. Daunton and Bernhard Rieger, eds., *Meanings of Modernity: Britain from the late-Victorian Era to World War II* (Oxford: Berg, 2001), 3. See Susan S. Friedman, "Definitional Excursus: The Meanings of Modern/ Modernity/ Modernism," *Modernism/ Modernity* 8, no.3 (2001): 499- 513; and Marshall Berman, *All that is Solid Melts into Air: The Experience of Modernity* (1982; Harmondsworth: Penguin Books: 1988).

5. See James R. T. E. Gregory, "The Vegetarian Movement in Britain, c.1840-1901: A Study of its Development, Personnel and Wider Connections" (Ph.D. diss., University of Southampton, 2002). See also Julia M. Twigg, "The

Vegetarian Movement in England from 1847-1981: A Study of the Structure of its Ideology" (Ph.D. diss., London School of Economics, 1982); Colin Spencer, *The Heretics Feast: A History of Vegetarianism* (London: Fourth Estate, 1993), republished (2001) as *Vegetarianism: A History*; Keith Thomas, *Man and the Natural World: Changing Attitudes in England, 1500-1800* (London: Allen Lane, 1983); James Turner, *Reckoning with the Beast: Animals, Pain and Humanity in the Victorian Mind* (London: Johns Hopkins University Press, 1980); and Hilda Kean, *Animal Rights: Political and Social Change in Britain since 1800* (London: Reaktion, 1998).

6. *The New Age and Concordium Gazette and Temperance Advocate* (1843-1844). A brilliant examination of the "sacred socialist" community which produced this paper is provided by Jackie E. M. Latham, *Search for a New Eden: James Pierrepont Greaves (1777-1842), The Sacred Socialist and His Followers* (London: Associated University Presses, 1999).

7. For instance, Jan M. Romein, *The Watershed of Two Eras: Europe in 1900*, trans. Arnold. J. Pomeran (Middleton, Connecticut: Wesleyan University Press, 1978).

8. See Josiah Oldfield, "Vegetarian Still," *The Nineteenth Century* 44, no. 158 (August 1898): 246-52 for a treatment of vegetarians as progressives.

9. See, for instance, Charles Lane, *Dietetics: An Endeavour to Ascertain the Laws of Human Development* (London: Whittaker, 1849), 39.

10. Henry S. Salt, *A Plea for Vegetarianism Vegetarianism and Other Essays* (Manchester: Vegetarian Society, 1886).

11. For instance, Alfred T. Wintle identified the vegetarian movement's rise with evolution in his tract *The Dietary of Troops* (London: The "Vegetarian" office, 1892), iii.

12. Henry S. Salt, "Food Reform," *Westminster Review* 126, no.252 (October 1886): 483-99.

13. T. P. Smith, "Vegetarianism," *Fortnightly Review* 58, no. 347 (November 1895): 752-64 [763]; Henry Thompson, "Why 'Vegetarian'?" *The Nineteenth Century* 43, no.254 (April 1898): 556-69 [569].

14. George W. Foote, "The Secularist View: The Kinship of Life," in Henry S. Salt, ed., *The New Charter. A Discussion of the Rights of Man and the Rights of Animals* (London: George Bell and Sons, 1896), 122- 3.

15. Keyword searchable databases, such as Literature Online, Victorian Women Writers, Wright American Fiction, 1851-1875, The Making of America, and ILEJ have been used (see Bibliography for further details). The absence of a database of English novels comparable to American collections means that the references that can be picked up in obscurer fictions is not possible; although the Literature Online database does have a good coverage of English works of fiction, prose, poetry and dramatic.

16. On Romantic vegetarianism see Timothy Morton, *Shelley and the Revolution in Taste: The Body and the Natural World* (Cambridge: Cambridge University Press, 1994). See also Onno Oerlemans, "Shelley's Ideal Body: Vege-

tarianism and Nature," *Studies in Romanticism* 34:4 (winter 1995): 531- 52; and Bouthaina Shaaban, "Shelley and the Barmbys," *Keats-Shelley Journal* 41 (1992): 122- 38.

17. On Mary M. Singleton ("Violet Fane") see Jeremy Mason, *Oscar Wilde on Vegetarianism. An Unpublished Letter to Violet Fane with an Introduction and Notes* (Edinburgh: Tragara Press, 1991) and "A Fable," from Mary M. Singleton, *Poems by Violet Fane*, 2 vols. (London: J. C. Nimmo 1892). Edward Fitzgerald's vegetarian ditty appears in *The Vegetarian*, 15 January 1898: 41; see Alfred M. Terhune and Annabella B. Terhune, eds., *The Letters of Edward Fitzgerald* (Princeton, New Jersey: Princeton University Press, 1980), 2: 690, letter from Thomas Carlyle to Fitzgerald, December 1850, on a dinner of herbs suiting a passing "abstemious philosopher." Alfred Tennyson's verse "To E. Fitzgerald," in *Tiresias and Other Poems* (London: Macmillan, 1885), 2, records trial vegetarianism. According to David A. Wilson, *Carlyle on Cromwell and Others* (London: Kegan Paul, Trench, Trubner, 1925): 169, Tennyson was temporarily converted by Bronson Alcott in 1842. LeeAnne M. Richardson, "Naturally Radical: The Subversive Poetics of Dollie Radford," *Victorian Poetry* 38, no.1 (2000): 109- 24 [121: footnote 1]. Vegetarianism also features in verse by George Meredith (in "Jump-to-Glory Jane," 1889); F. W. O. Ward (in *'Twixt Kiss and Lip*, 1890) and William Allingham ("Blackberries," 1890).

18. Isabel Colegate, *The Shooting Party* (London: H. Hamilton, 1980); Carol J. Adams, *The Sexual Politics of Meat*: 105- 7; 127- 9. Other attempts to create such a canon focus on Americans such as the Grimke sisters, see Josephine Donovan, "Animal Rights and Feminist Theory," *Signs* 15, no.2 (winter 1990): 350- 75,and a critique by Kathryn George, "Should Feminists be Vegetarians?" *Signs* 19, no. 2 (winter 1994): 405-434.

19. Elizabeth Blackwell, *Ellen Braye: or, The Fortune-Teller* (London: 2 vols., Saunders and Otley, 1841); "Edward Noble," in James Elmzlie Duncan, *Flowers and Fruits: or, Poetry, Philosophy and Science* (London: Printed for the Author, 1843); Fanny E. Lacy, "The Vegetarian; or, a Visit to Aunt Primitive," *The Metropolitan Magazine*, April 1847: 403-13; Sarah A. Clubb, *Good Influence: A Tale for the Young, who are Willing to Seek the Stepping Stone to Health, Intelligence and Happiness* (London: Frederick Pitman, 1854).

20. See the following: Charles O. Groom-Napier, *Tommy Try* (London: Chapman and Hall, 1869), "Colossa" (Anna Kingsford) *In My Lady's Chamber: A Speculative Romance, Touching a Few Questions of the Day* (London: James Burns, 1873), first appearing in Kingsford's *Lady's Own Paper*, 1872; Kingsford's "The Turquoise Ring," *Tinsley's Magazine*, February 1871; and Edward Maitland, ed., *Dreams and Dream Stories* (1888); Harriet Beavan, *Lil Grey, or Arthur Chester's Courtship* (London: S.W. Partridge, 1879); Arnold F. Hills, *Sunshine and Shadows* (serialized in *The Vegetarian*, republished 1893); J. A. Parker, *Ernest England* (London: Leadenhall Press, 1895). Vegetarian poetry included Robert Sargeant, *The Revenge of the Beasts and other Vegetarian and Humanitarian Verses* (London: Nichols and Co., 1881); and [Harold Begbie?]

Odd Rhymes, Verses, Imitations, Jingles (London: Ideal Publishing Company, 1899) and verse in Maude Egerton King, *My Book of Songs and Sonnets* (London: Percival, 1893).

21. On temperance fiction, see Carol Mattingly, *Well-tempered Women: Nineteenth Century Temperance Rhetoric* (Carbondale, Illinois: Southern Illinois University Press, 1998), ch.7. Mattingly stresses, 125, that this literature was widely disseminated through popular magazines, tracts and novels, and Sunday School libraries. Perhaps some temperance novels- apart from Harriet Beavan's- featured vegetarian characters or discussion.

22. Charles Dickens, *The Personal History of David Copperfield* (1849-50), ch.36, "A Little Cold Water." *The Posthumous Papers of the Pickwick Club* (1837; Oxford, Clarendon Press, 1986) had featured, ch.20: 293, "an elderly pimply-faced, vegetable-diet sort of man." See Dickens, "Whole Hogs," *Household Words* 2, no.74 (23 August 1851): 505- 507; and *American Notes* (1842; London: Macmillan, 1925), ch.12: 146, "From Cincinnati to Louisville" on the Kentucky giant who looked as if he was "rather inclining to milk and vegetable diet."

23. See W. M. Thackeray, *The Virginians* (1858), 1: 243, defending "we modest Oenophilists"; Edward Bulwer-Lytton, *Kenelm Chillingley: His Adventures and Opinions* (Leipzig: Bernhard Tauchnitz, 1873), 1: 154. For connections between vegetarianism and temperance see J. R. T. E. Gregory, "The Vegetarian Movement in Victorian Britain and its Relationship with Temperance," *The Social History of Alcohol Review. The Journal of the Alcohol and Temperance History Group* 16, nos.1-4 (fall 2001/ spring 2002): 14-34.

24. Charles Kingsley, *Alton Locke: Tailor and Poet. An Autobiography* (1850; London: Macmillan, 1878), 28.

25. Mary A. Kelty, *Visiting My Relations, and Its Results: A Series of Small Episodes in the Life of a Recluse* (London: William Pickering, 1851). See Latham, *Search for a New Eden*.

26. See [Eliza Lynn Linton] "Zaidee: A Romance," *Blackwood's Edinburgh Magazine* 77, no.476 (June 1855): 680. *Zaidee* was published as a book in 1856.

27. [W. E. Aytoun], "The Congress and the Agapedome," *Blackwood's Edinburgh Magazine* 70, no.431 (September 1851): 359- 378; "Pisistratus Caxton" [Edward Bulwer-Lytton], "My Novel; or Varieties in English Life," *Blackwood's Edinburgh Magazine* 70: 433 (November 1851): 573.

28. See Frank Thistlewaite, *America and the Atlantic Community: Anglo-American Aspects, 1790-1850* (New York and Evanston: Harper Torchbooks, 1963). See also Robert H. Abzug, *Cosmos Crumbling: American Reform and the Religious Imagination* (Oxford: Oxford University Press, 1994); Stephen Nissenbaum, *Sex, Diet and Debility in Jacksonian America: Sylvester Graham and Health Reform* (Westport, Connecticut: Greenwood Press, 1980); Gerald Carson, *Cornflake Crusade* (London: Gollancz, 1959); Claudia Nelson, "Care in feeding: vegetarianism and social reform in Alcott's America," in Claudia Nelson and Lynne Vallone, eds., *The Girls Own. Cultural Histories of the Anglo-American*

Girl, 1830-1915 (Athens, Georgia: University of Georgia Press, 1994), 11- 33; James C. Whorton, *Crusaders for Fitness: The History of American Health Reformers* (Princeton, New Jersey: Princeton University Press, 1982); Susan E. Cayleff, *Wash and Be Healed: The Water Cure Movement and Women's Health* (Philadelphia: Temple University Press, 1987); and Russell Hickman, "The Vegetarian and Octagon Settlement Companies," *Kansas Historical Quarterly* 2, no.4 (1933): 377-85.

29. George Eliot, *Middlemarch. A Study of Provincial Life*, (serialised, 1871-72; London: Penguin, 1965), 203. The character Trawley is hot on the "French social systems," but decides instead to be a hydropath. A vegetarian American prophet figures in "A Minor Prophet," in George Eliot, *The Legend of Jubal, and Other Poems* (London and Edinburgh: W. Blackwood, 1874). The *North American Review* considered this the "gem" of the collection, October 1874: 486. Eliot read Samuel Brown's "admirable article" before it was published in the *Westminster Review* in April 1852, see Gordon S. Haight, ed., *The George Eliot Letters* (London: Oxford University Press; New Haven: Yale University Press, 1954), 2: 6.

30. "The Experiences of the A.C.," in Bayard Taylor, *Beauty and the Beast and Tales of Home* (New York: G. P. Putnam, 1872). Comments on vegetarianism appear in *Hannah Thurston. A Story of American Life* (New York: G. P. Putnam, 1863), 125, 136. The social reformer Lydia Maria Child indicated her pro-vegetarian sentiments in the characters of Paralus and Anaxagoras, in her Athenian *Philothea. A Romance* (Boston: Otis, Broader and Co., 1836), 13, 119. Louisa May Alcott drew on childhood experience of her father and Charles Lane's communitarian experiment for her story "Transcendental Wild Oats" (1873), reprinted in *Alternative Alcott. Louisa May Alcott, ed., with an Introduction by Elaine Showalter* (New Brunswick, New Jersey: Rutgers University Press, 1988), 364-379.

31. See Orestes A. Brownson, *The Spirit-Rapper* (Boston: Little, Brown, 1854), ch.8: "A Lesson in World Reform", 98 (Mr Long: "an Englishman just arrived in the country and announced as the Prophet of Newness" possibly echoes the reformer Charles Lane). Brownson was a leading figure in this milieu before converting to Catholicism.

32. "Radical Freelance," *The Philosophers of Foufouville* (New York: G.W. Carleton; London: Sampson Low, 1868), set in a community of Harmonians at New Jersey.

33. See "Whig Principles. What's Left of Them," *United States Democratic Review* 34, no.6 (December 1854): 465-77.

34. See S. M. Ellis, *George Meredith* (London: Grant Richards, 1920), 103 for discussion of the novel (started 1871, completed 1874), Meredith's favourite, and its echoing of correspondence with Maxse. On his vegetarianism see comments by Henry S. Salt, *The Vegetarian*, 1912: 37; Henry M. Hyndman, *The Records of an Adventurous Life* (London: Macmillan, 1911), 85- 86.

35. George Meredith, *Beauchamp's Career* (1875; London: A. Constable, 1902), 455- 56.

36. Eliza Lynn Linton, *The Autobiography of Christopher Kirkland* (London: Bentley, 1885), 3:19. See Herbert van Thal, *Eliza Lynn Linton. The Girl of the Period* (London: George Allen and Unwin, 1979), 142- 154; Nancy F. Anderson, *Woman against Women in Victorian England* (Bloomington and Indianapolis: Indiana University Press, 1987), 180. See Deborah T. Meem, ed., *The Rebel of the Family: A critical Edition* (Ontario: Broadview Literary Texts, 2002), 419, for Linton's disgust in 1891 at "Wild Women" involved in animal slaughter.

37. *Christopher Kirkland*, 3: 55.

38. *Christopher Kirkland*, 1: 191.

39. Justin McCarthy, "The Literature of the Victorian Reign," *Appletons' Journal: A Magazine of General Literature* (New York) 9, no.54 (December 1880): 541- 42.

40. William F. Barry, *The New Antigone* (1887): the character Mr Mardol. John Sutherland, *The Longman Companion to Victorian Fiction* (Harlow: Longmans, 1988), 459, characterises this as a "pro-Catholic novel of ideas." By 1906 it had reached its seventh edition. The American *Catholic World* 46, no.274 (January 1888), 531, described it as a "long and somewhat gloomy romance." Barry's essay attacking New Women, "The Strike of A Sex," *The Quarterly Review* 179 (1894): 289- 318, referred to Anna Kingsford the vegetarian.

41. Mrs Humphry Ward [Mary Ward], *The History of David Grieve* (London: Smith, Elder, 1892), 1: 338. See Enid H. Jones, *Mrs Humphry Ward* (London: Heinemann, 1973), 91- 7. *The Vegetarian Review*, 1897, 534, noted Ward's association with Mancunian vegetarians two or three years before. Her brother William Arnold was vegetarian whilst at Oxford and working on the *Manchester Guardian*.

42. See the American *Catholic World* 54, no.324 (March 1892): 918 for reference to the vegetarian section as contributing to its disjointedness; see "Book Reviews," *Overland Monthly and Out West Magazine* 42, no.142 (October 1894): 445- 448 [446] on Ward's literary fame. The *Overland Monthly*, in 20, no.118 (October 1892): 443, complained about the work's humourlessness.

43. Arthur Conan Doyle, "The Red-headed League," *The Strand Magazine* 2 (August 1891): 198-199. Trained as a physician, Doyle's autobiographical *The Stark Munro Letters* (New York: D. Appleton and Co., 1895), 124-25, includes a recommendation to one patient of vegetarianism. For another author's reference to the restaurants, see the "unsavoury and tasteless messes" at the "Currant Bush Restaurant" in the short story "Mr Dangle's Dilemma," in *Belgravia*, reprinted in *Littell's Living Age* 174, no.2255 (10 September 1887): 641- 704 [658].

44. H. G. Wells, *Love and Mrs Lewisham* (London: Harper, 1900; serialised in the *Weekly Times* in 1899), 196. Wells's Fabian associations brought contact

with several vegetarians: see Norman and Jeanne Mackenzie, *The Time Travel-ler: The Life of H. G. Wells* (London: Weidenfeld and Nicolson, 1973), 62, 102, 174. The Victorian puritanical tendency is sensitively discussed in Raphael Samuel, "The Discovery of Puritanism, 1820-1914: A Preliminary Sketch," in *Theatres of Memory*. Vol. 2. *Island Stories: Unravelling Britain*, posthumously edited by Alison Light with Sally Alexander and Gareth Stedman Jones (London: Verso, 1998), 276- 322.

45. H. G. Wells, *Ann Veronica: a Modern Love Story* (1909; London: Virago, 1980), 111.

46. See Peter Kemp, *H. G. Wells and the Culminating Ape: Biological Themes and Imaginative Obsessions* (London: Macmillan, 1982), 15- 17.

47. Harold Begbie, *The Curious and Diverting Adventures of Sir John Spar-row Bt., or, the Progress of an Open Mind* (London: Methuen, 1902).

48. James Shirley Hibberd, "Beans without Bacon: A Pythagorean Ro-mance," in *The Golden Gate and Silver Steps with Bits of Tinsel Round About It* (London: E.W. Allen, 1886).

49. George Meredith, *One of Our Conquerors* (London: Chapman and Hall, 1892), see 61, 70, 98, 122, 209, 414.

50. British Library, Additional Manuscripts, Lord Chancellor's Plays, vol. CLXXII and CLXXIII. "Bloomerism or Follies of the Day. A Farce. In one act," (performed Adelphi, 29 September 1851), 43037, ff.254-269. "Follies of the Day" was reviewed in *The Times*, 3 October 1851. See also Henry Walker, "The Vegetarian. A Serio-Comico-Semi Sentimental Song" (several editions 1859-1869).

51. See Edward F. Benson's *The Freaks of Mayfair* (London: T. N. Foulis, 1916), and *Paying Guests* (London: Hutchinson, 1929).

52. *The Vegetarian*, 2 October 1897.

53. In *Demos: A Story of English Socialism* (1886; London: Smith, Elder, 1897), 42: Mutimer's guides for life include vegetarian, malthusian, and free-thought works. See also *The Odd Women* (1893; London: Virago, 1980), ch.2 (8, 12, 19), ch.3 (23) and ch.4 (33); *The Crown of Life* (1899; London: Methuen, 1927), references to Otway's teetotal and vegetarian habits, in chapters 1 (4) and 7 (55); Tymperley in "A Poor Gentleman," (originally in *Pall Mall Gazette*, October 1899; reprinted in *The House of Cobwebs and Other Stories*, London: Constable, 1906); *The Private Papers of Henry Ryecroft*, (London: Constable, 1903), "Winter": ix: 245-7; and Sherwood and Milligan's projected Irish vege-tarian colony in *Will Warburton: A Romance of Real Life* (London: Constable, 1905), ch.3 (203-4) and ch.44 (307-8). On Gissing's vegetarianism see Paul Mattheisen, Arthur Young and Pierre Coustillas, eds., *The Collected Letters of George Gissing*, vol. 2 (Athens, Ohio: Ohio University Press, 1991), 356 and 358.

54. George Gissing, *The Private Papers of Henry Ryecroft* (1903; London: Constable, 1939), 231.

55. In May 1896 *The Idler* published a story, reprinted in *Harmsworth's Magazine*, December 1900 as "Vegetarianism vs Love," see Bouwe Postmus, "Mr Harmsworth's Blue Pencil: "Simple Simon" Revisited," *The Gissing Journal* 31, no.1 (January 1995), 1-10. A discussion of vegetarianism in *Life and Beauty*, August-September 1900 is reprinted in Matheisen, Young and Coustillas, *The Collected Letters of George Gissing* vol. 8 (Athens, Ohio: Ohio University Press, 1996). For echoes of the comments in Ryecroft see Jacob Korg, ed., *George Gissing's Commonplace Book* (New York: New York Public Library, 1962), 67.

56. "B.W.P." in *The British Controversialist* (1850), 309.

57. "Chronicles of Clovernook" appeared in *The Illuminated Magazine*, and was reprinted in 1846 (Offices of *Punch*). The Owenite John Francis Bray's *A Voyage from Utopia* (1842, see M. F. Lloyd-Prichard's edition, London: Lawrence and Wishart, 1957), 125 condemned the fact that the majority in Brydone (Britain) and Erino (Ireland) were restricted by poverty to a "chiefly vegetable diet."

58. Edward Bulwer-Lytton, *The Coming Race* (1871; London: Routledge, 1893); Samuel Butler, *Erewhon, or, Over the Range* (these chapters, 26 and 27, were additions to the first edition of 1872, when republished by Grant Richards, 1901). See Henry Festing Jones, *Samuel Butler, Author of Erewhon: A Memoir* (London: Macmillan, 1919), 2: 373- 74; and Henry Festing Jones, ed., *The Note-Books of Samuel Butler* (1921; London: John Cape, 1930), 361.

59. Other vegetarian utopias include [W. H. Hudson] *A Crystal Age* (London: T. Fisher Unwin, 1887); Edward Bellamy, *Equality* (London: Heinemann, 1897); Robert Buchanan, *The Reverend Annabel Lee: A Tale of To-morrow* (London: C. A. Pearson, 1898). Obscurer works include *Darkness and Dawn. The Peaceful Birth of a New Age* (London: Kegan Paul, Trench, 1884); *The Angel and the Idiot. A Story of the Next Century* (London: Stott, 1890).

60. *The Coming Race*, ch. 22: 111-112.

61. Henry James alludes to vegetarian-political connections in *The Bostonians* (1886; London: Penguin, 1966), where Basil Ransom assumes Miss Birdseye's circle are "mediums, communists, vegetarians" (ch.4: 29) and in ch.10 when discussing Verena Tarrant's background (63). James Snr. had been an acquaintance of a pioneer English vegetarian, Sophia Chichester.

62. George Meredith, *The Ordeal of Richard Feverel* (1859); George Bernard Shaw, *Immaturity* (1879; London: Constable, 1931), 55; "Margaret Wyman" [E. Hepworth Dixon] *My Flirtations* (1892; Philadelphia: J. B. Lippincott, 1893), 126.

63. Works of "eccentric biography" from the early-nineteenth century included diet reformers and should be seen as contributing to popular ideas on what was centric/ eccentric in diet, see "Roger Crab," in G. H. Wilson, *The Eccentric Mirror: Reflecting a Faithful and Interesting Delineation of Male and Female Characters* (London: J. Cundee, 1813) vol. 1, no.9.

64. "The Big Bow Mystery," reprinted in Israel Zangwill, *The Grey Wig or Stories and Novelettes* (London: Heinemann, 1903). Stories by Victor L. Whitechurch featuring Hazell appeared in *The Royal Magazine* in 1905, and were collected as *Stories of the Railway*, 1912.

65. Henry R. Haggard, *She: A History of Adventure* (1887, London: Longmans, Green, 1894), 137. *The Vegetarian* discussed the novel throughout 1889. Marie Belloc Lowndes' story was originally published in *Nash's Magazine*, January 1911.

"The Best Machine for Converting Herbage into Money": Romantic Cattle Culture

Ron Broglio

The Britishness of cattle should come as no surprise. Cattle are an important part of British advancements in agriculture. They serve as a means by which the British distinguish themselves from other nations with less robust cattle, and they indicate progress in agriculture toward increased national wealth and health. Records of cattle weighed at Smithfield Market make the point strikingly clear. A cattle carcass averaged 370 pounds in 1710. By 1795 the average weight of cattle to be slaughtered is 800 pounds yielding a carcass of 550 pounds.[1] In less then a century the eatable flesh of cattle had increased by almost one-third with most of this gain in the last half of the century. Such bounty became a point of pride for the British. The average Londoner is estimated as consuming almost a half pound of meat every day compared to the Parisian who eats 80 pounds per year. Meat becomes synonymous with prosperity. The opening page of William Youatt's 1864 *The Complete Grazier* proclaims "Of all the various sources from which the wealth of nations is derived, few have a superior claim to attention than the branch of rural economy which is the subject of the following pages."[2] The reference to Adam Smith's *Wealth of Nations* is no accident. Youatt goes on to quote Smith regarding the role of agriculture in accounting for the prosperity of Britain: "the capital employed in agriculture not only puts into motion a greater quantity of productive labour than any equal capital employed in manufactures, but also, in proportion to the quantity of productive labour which it employs, it adds a much greater value to the annual produce of the land and labour of the country, while it increases the real wealth and revenue of its inhabitants."[3] Youatt is fond of this passage in Smith and uses it in *Cattle* where he quotes Marshall's use of Smith in *Rural Econ-omy of the Midlands*.[4] Cattle breeding contributes to the wealth of Britain and, as seen in comparison to the amount of beef consumed in France, it makes Britain unique among nations.

Cattle are so valued that, for Thomas Bates writing in 1808, they are the answer to fears that a year or two of bad weather will diminish food supplies and force the nation to depend upon imported goods from other countries.[5] Bates's address to the Board of Agriculture and to the other agricultural societies of Britain is meant to show, as his pamphlet's lengthy title proclaims, "the merits of the different breeds of live-stock; pointing out the advantages that will accrue there from to the landed in-terest and the kingdom in general." Given the variety of new breeds and claims of merits for each, Bates calls for a means of judging these claims and advancing the breeding of those animals that will meet the demands and advance the economic ends of the nation. It is not just cattle in gen-eral, but "improved" breeds and new means of fattening them and quickly bringing them to market that make beef the pride of the nation for Bates and Youatt.[6] This essay sets out to explore how the changes manifest on the body of cattle—the very corporality of the animal—is constituted by the economic, political, artistic and decisively British cul-tural interests in beef. Furthermore, this essay considers how the ad-vances in beef become intertwined with shifts and "advances" in culture, politics, and economics. I will begin with the history of what was called "improved" cattle and the beefing up of beef. The discussion will then turn toward the culinary and cultural context of the late eighteenth and early nineteenth century, which situates and promotes the agricultural luxury of a beef culture.

The history of improved cattle breeding begins with Robert Bakewell in the 1760s. Bakewell rented land at Dishley Grange, located between Loughborough and Derby, where he meticulously created experiments in agriculture—canals for irrigating his fields, improved stalls for housing his animals, and, most notably, new practices for breeding cattle and sheep. As many historians of Bakewell observe, farmers and breeders are slow to change methods handed down to them over generations. There are understandable reasons for the slow innovations in farming. Adopting a new practice means risking crops or animals. The number of variables are often too complex for farmers to predict; what works well in one re-gion of the country or with one breed may not work well elsewhere or with other animals. Bakewell remains a remarkable figure in the history of agriculture because within his lifetime he was able to change the Brit-ish breeding practices that had remained the same for centuries. As an agricultural innovator, he focused on improving the form, flesh, and propensity for fattening of his beasts. Thus, animals would gain flesh and fat in less time and consequently increase the grazier's productivity and profits.

Traditionally farmers improved a herd by selecting females of the native stock and crossing them with males of another lineage or separate breed. In common practice no bull was used to breed in the same stock for more than three years since it was feared that more than this would weaken the generations of offspring. In breeding, it was held that the bulls served as the active source for variation in offspring while the cow remained the passive receptacle, although in some instances key characteristics might cross from the female to her offspring.[7] Improvement, then, depended upon selection of a fine male. Such breeding practices did not always yield the expected results and remained far from a predictable system for breeding. Breeding changed with Bakewell. As Youatt explains: "Mr. Bakewell's good sense led him to imagine that the object might be better accomplished by uniting the superior branches of the same breed, than by any mixture of foreign ones." This "good sense" was initially considered the breaking of a taboo, or as George Culley explains: "some have imbibed the prejudices against Bakewell's breeding practice so far as to think it is irreligious."[8] Bakewell developed "in-in" breeding of his cattle that is, he bred within the same family lineage. By mating close relations, he helped to insure the purity of the desired characteristics.[9] If an offspring did not meet his standards, it was eliminated from the breeding stock. Consequently having an ideal type to breed toward proved an important element of Bakewell's plan. It allowed him to read the body of the cattle and discern which characteristics were worthy of developing and which were to be eliminated. The success of his practice is chronicled in many eighteenth and early nineteenth century publications including Arthur Young's *The Farmer's Tour through the East of England* (1771), William Marshall's *Economy of the Midland Counties* (1796), George Culley's *Observations on Livestock* (1804), and William Youatt's *Cattle* (1834) which sites his predecessors observations in his own telling of the breeder's biography.

Bakewell began his breeding experiments by purchasing two longhorn heifers from Mr. Webster's Canley farm near his own. The superior quality of Webster's animals earned his cattle the name "Canley breed." Bakewell's bull came from Westmoreland. As Youatt chronicles "To these and their progeny he confined himself; coupling them as he thought he could best increase, or establish some excellent point, or speedily and effectually remove a fault."[10] From his Westmoreland bull and his heifer, Comely, came the bull Twopenny. Twopenny's offspring exemplify the in-in breeding for producing a well crafted animal . This particular lineage description ends with the notable animal Shakespeare. Agricultural essayists Marshall and Youatt each dedicate three pages to describing the finer points of Shakespeare, and Marshall hails him as "the best stock-getter the Midland district ever knew."[11] Just as the bard of England gave fame to British arts, so too the cattle by his name would serve as the ideal for British beef.

The success of Bakewell's cattle is evident in the rise in value and prominence of his longhorns. Formerly longhorn cattle were, according to the eighteenth century agriculturalist George Culley, too heavy of bone and too awkward in build to be of much notice. Furthermore, they were slow to mature and fatten for market. With more land being claimed for enclosures and crops, farmers had to find means for more quickly bringing their animals to market. Bakewell was able to fill out his cattle in the most desirable points and create quite large beasts in a relatively short amount of time. He even offered a wager that he could put fat on a cow's tail.[12] As Francois de la Rochefoucauld records in *A Frenchman in England* (1784), "All this is astonishing. I do not properly understand it, but I believe it as I believe in my religion—because I have been told what I ought to believe and because everyone believes in it."[13] Bakewell's corpulent cattle became renowned breeders that gave rise to famous offspring. One of his bulls was let out at the tremendous rate of 25 guineas per cow. In 1791 the bull Garrick was the first cattle sold with a documented pedigree. Bakewell's friend and close collaborator, John Fowler of Little Rollright in Oxfordshire, bred Garrick from a cow that was got by Bakewell's Hampshire Bull. Garrick was sold for £250. Two one-year olds by Garrick fetched over £150 each. These prices are quite large in comparison to 5 to 10 pounds for a common cow and 10 to 25 pounds for common stock when fattened.[14] With high profits, Bakewell prided in calling his animals "the best machine for converting herbage into money."[15] To insure his investment by keeping the lineage and character of his breed pure and to maintain high market prices, Bakewell founded the Dishley Society in 1783.[16] By the 1790s membership included prominent breeders from fifteen shires. By letting out his bulls, by putting his farm on display as a model for improvements, and by developing a local breeding society, Bakewell succeeded in replacing local cattle throughout the Midlands with his improved longhorn breed. Yet, despite the rapid growth of the breed, by the early 1800s the prominence of the longhorn had peaked. Breeding from coarse to increasingly finer bones with larger amounts of meat and fat produced misshapen animals that were overly fat and of poor health. Additionally, the longhorn was never well known for its milking qualities and the inbreeding continued to impoverish the milk yield. In place of the longhorn, a new breed would rise to fame and claim prominence throughout the nineteenth century.

As pupils of Bakewell, Robert and Charles Colling returned to their farms near Darlington and set to work on the local cattle breed—the shorthorn. Unlike the longhorn, both the large size and high milk yields of the shorthorns prepared the animals for their role as a pedigree breed. Additionally, the Collings included limited and highly selective cross breeding with Scotch cattle to ensure the durability of their stock's lineage. Art scholar Elspeth Moncrieff claims that it is the unimporoved Lincolnshire Shorthorn painted by George Stubbs in 1791 that was the first cattle of notoriety.[17] The ox belonged to John Bough who, as story has it, won the animal in a cockfight, as illustrated in Stubbs's painting (figure 2). The ox was cared for by John Gibbon who fattened it for show. Stubbs's inscription for his painting gives a brief and fabulous look at the history of the animal:

> To Sr. Joseph Banks Bart. President of the Royal Society. This print of the Lincolnshire ox, is humbly dedicated by his obedt. & devoted servt. Jno. Gibbons. This uncommon animal was fed (without oil cake) by Mr. John Gibbons, of Long Sutton in the county of Lincoln, and was carry'd to London in a machine, Feby. 1790, when he was exhibited by Gloucester, at his riding house, in Hyde Park, and then removed to the Lyceum in the Strand, where the exhibition of him still continues, & where this print was subscrib'd to by a great number of noblemen and gentlemen; all judges agree that the Lincolnshire ox, far exceeded any ever seen in size and fatness, being 19 hands in height and 3 feet & 4 inches across the hips. A wager of 400 pounds was offer'd that he would cut 9 10 11 & 12 inches think of solid fat upon the rib if slaughter'd in the spring of 1790.

The painting's dedication to Joseph Banks as president of the Royal Society indicates the scientific wonder provoked by the beast as well as Banks's land holdings in Lincolnshire. The Lincolnshire Ox was shown in the Lyceum alongside curiosities from the far reaches of the empire including a rhinoceros—also painted by Stubbs—and three ostriches.[18] Five hundred prints of George Stubbs's painting were made and sold at subscription. Among those who received a copy of the painting were Richard Payne Knight, Joseph Banks, and Arthur Young. These three men alone display the various forces at work on the body of the animal— the politics and landscape aesthetics of Knight, the science of Banks and the agricultural reform of Young. Constance-Anne Parker explains that Stubbs's print was used as part of a publicity campaign to promote the advancement of agriculture and the breeding of prize cattle.[19]

While the wondrously large Lincolnshire Ox made the shorthorns famous, it was the Colling brothers who advanced the breed as a whole and who successfully reared animals that far exceeded the weight of the Lincolnshire Ox. The Collings first found fame with their animal the Durham Ox who was bred from Charles Colling's bull Favourite. In 1801, Colling commissioned a portrait of the animal from George Cuitt and had the image engraved by Robert Pollard. The ox was sold by Colling to Mr. Bulmer for £140 who after only a month sold the ox to John Day for £250. Only a few weeks later Day was offered £2,000 for the Durham Ox. Realizing the animal's value was in the fees he garnered from exhibitions, Day refused to sell the beast and instead toured the Durham Ox at some two hundred venues throughout England, Wales, and Scotland from 1801 to 1807.[20] John Boultbee was commissioned to paint the ox for Day's first exhibition of the animal. This painting and its subsequent engraving by Whessel became the most famous cattle image of the nineteenth century. Over 2,000 copies of John Whessel's engraving were sold in the first year of its publication. The ox was later painted by George Garrard and Thomas Weaver. Its massive 133-inch girth and allegedly flawless quality made it the standard for the breed. Garrard even made a plaster model of the ox and exhibited the model as the ideal for what a shorthorn should look like. Garrad writes extensively on the animal's perfection in his *Description of Oxen*. While Colling had lost out on a money-making animal, the notoriety of the Durham Ox promoted Colling's breed and ensured that he would get high studding fees and high prices at market. In 1810, Colling got 1,000 guineas for his prize bull Comet. Later, with George Coates' *Herd Book* for Short Horn Cattle (1822), the shorthorns became the first cattle to have a published book of pedigree; consequently, the shorthorns became the benchmark for agriculture and for what was possible in British cattle breeding. Weighing in at nearly a ton each, these cattle were the pride of the nation.

By claiming that improved breeds advance the nation's wealth, breeders draw from the already close connection between the British people and their beef. Throughout the eighteenth and early nineteenth century a number of other activities allowed beef to play a prominent role in British culture. The political connection between beef and Britain is most evident in the political cartoons of the period. James Gillray's "Politness" serves as an example.[21] A stout Englishman sits with his pint of beer in his hand and his bulldog at his feet. Behind him hangs a large cut of red meat on a hook. He stares down a Frenchman seated to his side. In contrast to the beefy Englishman, the thin Frenchman wears refined clothes and a wig. The Frenchman holds a container of snuff in direct contrast to British beer. At his feet a mousy dog cowers from the growling British bull dog. Whereas the Englishman has large slabs of meat behind him, the Frenchman has two small frog's legs. The caption below the illustration reads:

With Porter, Roast Beef, & Plumb Pudding, well cramm'd
John English declares that Monsr. may be D__d,
The Soup Meager Frenchman such Language don't suit,
So he Grins Indignation and calls him a Brute.

Gillray contrasts the plain and simple fair of England and the plain speaking English yomen with the French fop and his elaborate soups and sauces. Through simple iconography and metonymy, the common food of Britain stands for its people and its politics.[22] Even before Gillray roast beef is tied to Englishness as evident in Joseph Addison's elaborate history of renowned beef eaters: King Arthur whose men sat down to whole roasted ox, Henry VIII's mythical knighting of a sirloin, the Order of Beef-Eaters who guard the king, and Queen Elizabeth's Maids of Honor who did not eat the dainty tea and buttered bread of the contemporary Maids but rather were given three rumps of beef for their breakfast.[23] As with Gillray's comic, Addison's essay from *The Tatler* is meant to contrast the stout English table with elaborate and unnatural French cooking which, as Addison tells it, allows nothing to be served in recognizable form or in its natural season. The English find suspect French cuisine's transformation of ingredients such that items are not identifiably related to how they appear in nature. French food changes nature into complex elements of culture. Gillray's overly refined Frenchman is an example of effeminate culture. In contrast, the English keep their food close to its natural state. By doing so, the Englishman is, as "Brute," a part of the nature he devours while he is also a masculine figure showing his dominance over the rest of nature.

The juxtaposition of the Frenchmen to English Roast Beef is clear in William Hogarth's *The Gate of Calais*. At the center of the painting a scrawny French cook bends under the weight of a hefty side of beef that is on its way to Madam Grandsire's, a local hotel owned by an Englishman. Next to the cook and the heavy roasted meat stands a thin and ragged French soldier holding a small pot of *soupe maigre* and looking longingly at the side of beef. As Ben Rogers notes in his history of beef in the eighteenth century, other political icons emerge from the painting as well. The sun shines just above the beef to highlight the English coat of arms at one the city's fortifications. A Scotsman cowers with his meager meal in a dark corner, having fled from the failed 1745 rebellion against the British crown. In another darkened corner three old women like witches huddle over a flatfish and, as Roger notes, they point "in superstitious ecstasy at the image of Christ they have detected in its features."[24] The side of beef serves as the central actor in this scene causing a variety of reactions by other characters all of whom show their politics and allegiances with their stomachs. Their impoverished meals remain in stark contrast to the hefty beef that is almost too much for a Frenchman to carry across the courtyard. The English admired Hogarth's painting for its "downright, fair play, John Bull" quality.[25] The painting is part of a much larger gastronomic and political allegiance in England that can be traced via Hogarth.

The Gate of Calais was one of Tobias Smollett's favorite prints and the author found various occasions to use it in his work. In *The Adventures of Ferdinand Count Fathom* the hero arrives in England to breath in "British freedom, opulence, and convenience."[26] No sooner has he taken in the view than he is speedily crammed into a coach and his small frame is crushed by the portly British who accompany him. One jolly dame tells "Monsieur" that "my corporation is made up of good, wholesome English fat; but you are puffed up with the wind of vanity and delusion."[27] Despite remonstrance she continues the insult in the manner of Hogarth's *Calais*: "What! I warrant you have an antipathy to flesh, because you yourself are nothing but skin and bone. I suppose you are some poor starv'd journeyman taylor come from France, where you have been learning to cabbage, and have not seen a good meal of victuals these seven years; you have been living upon rye-bread and soup maigre, and now you come over like a walking atomy, with a rat's tail at your wig, and a tinsey jacket; and so forsooth, you set up for a gentleman, and pretend to find fault with a surloin of roast beef."[28] Several years later, Smollett found the reference to roast beef appealing enough to include it in his comedy *The Reprisal* where the third scene opens with stage directions that look something like Hogarth's painting only it is now "four meager Frenchmen" required to shoulder the buttock of beef.[29]

William Hogarth's influence continued in one of the most curious of many eighteenth century social clubs, the Sublime Society of Beefsteaks, which he co-founded in 1735 with Henry Rich the harlequine and machinist of Covent Garden Theater and George Lambert a scene painter for Covent Garden. As Ben Rogers explains in his history of the Society, the group was formed by well known artists, writers, and actors who convened at Drury Lane to eat meat and talk shop each Saturday during theater season from October to June. At each meeting, the group sang Henry Fielding's *The Roast Beef of Old England* from his *Grub Street Opera*:

When mighty roast beef was the Englishman's food,
It ennobled our hearts, and enriched our blood,
Our soldier were brave, and our courtiers were good.
Oh the roast beef of England,
And old England's roast beef!

But since we have learnt from all-conquering France,
To eat their ragouts as well as to dance,
Oh what a fine figure we make in romance!
Oh the roast beef of England,
And old England's roast beef![30]

Later five extra stanzas were added by Richard Leveridge and in the revised version *The Ballad of Roast Beef* remained popular for over a century and a half.[31] In the 1760s Theodosius Forrest created a new Song of the Day specifically for the Society that included the stanza:

Throughout the realms where despots reign,
What tracks of glory now remain!
Their people, slaves of power and pride,
Fat Beef and Freedom are denied!
What realm, what state, can happy be,
Wanting our Beef and Liberty?[32]

This song replaced Fielding's and was sung at each meeting. After the Covent Garden burnt down in 1808, the meetings were held at the Old Lyceum beginning in 1809. Eighteen years after displaying the Lincolnshire Ox in the Lyceum as a scientific curiosity and hailed advancement in agriculture, The Sublime Society of Beefsteaks met in the same location to sing the praise of "Beef and Liberty" as proclaimed in their Song and on the Society's silver medal worn by members.

Further connecting beef and the kingdom, in the 1780s the Prince of Wales joined The Sublime Society and was followed in membership by his brothers. The Prince later became King George IV. His father, George III, had a great love for agricultural improvements in general. He set up model farms at Windsor, Kew, and Mortlake. At Kew, for example, the King had twenty-three acres set aside for experiments in growing turnips and buckwheat. As a follower of Arthur Young's *Annals of Agriculture*, he contributed a series of essays under the pseudonym of Ralph Robinson, the name of one of his Windsor shepherds.[33] He also set out to improve animal breed including cattle and imported Spanish Merino sheep. The King was captivated by Boultbee's famous paintings of Collings's Durham Ox. So, Farmer George, as the king styled himself, provided Boultbee with a house near the Cumberland Lodge and commissioned him to paint the Royal Herd of shorthorn cattle. With the paintings by Boultbee for the king, cattle became marked as national animals. Portraits of the Royal Herd create a fantastically nationalistic troupe almost as wondrous as Henry VIII's legendary knighting of a loin of beef as Sir Loin. Nor was Boultbee the only artist employed by George III. Boultbee's pupil, Thomas Weaver, was also commissioned to paint the Royal Herd as was Benjamin Marshall.[34]

Commissions by the King to a variety of artists who specialized in animal portraits point to the growth in this subgenre of painting. John Boultbee became known for his depiction of Bakewell's longhorn cattle. He also made a famous portrait of the portly Bakewell sitting on his horse and showing off his lands and cattle in the background. From Bakewell, the artist was recommended to Robert Fowler where Boultbee painted the Little Rollright herd including Garrick who fetched a record profit at market. Boultbee's apprentice, Thomas Weaver, became known for his depiction of shorthorns including Colling's famous White Heifer. Following the success of George Garrard's *Description of Oxen*, James Ward set out to make two hundred accurate drawings of British livestock for a project approved by the Board of Agriculture and to be financed and printed by Boydell. Unfortunately, despite Ward's labors, the Boydell firm had fallen from its successful print ventures of the early 1790s and was unable to complete the project. Among the many animal portrait artists, Ward was the only one not satisfied with his position as an animal painter. He continued to show landscape and historical paintings at the Royal Academy in the hopes of becoming recognized in a more prestigious genre. As an animal painter, Benjamin Marshall is unique in his ability to group animals and show them from more than right angles views. Consequently, the animals seem to fit more naturally into the landscape. Marshall's pallet harmonizes the colors of the cattle hide with the surrounding brownish green landscape to further suggest a unity between the animals and their environment. Quite a few other artists worked in the genera of animal portraiture during the Romantic period including Charles Towne, Henry Chalon, John Fernely, William and Henry Barraud, Daniel Clowes, John and David Dalby, and Abraham Cooper.[35] Most of these artists where aware of each other's work and all competed for the limited number of patrons seeking such portraits. Animal portraiture arose from a cultural love affair for beef and liberty. Artists in this genre used the picturesque as the form and technique for displaying the animals and drew from a growing industry of agricultural improvement to provide a market for and financing of their work. The result is a curious phenomenon in which the animal becomes both subject of and subjected to the ideals born out in paintings. The animal is captured and framed through domestication and breeding then through art which in turn fosters new methods of breeding and husbandry.

British tastes and tales shape cattle. The corporeal sense of the beast—the material or sensate sense—becomes 'improved" through a cultural sensibility in art, literature, drama, politics, agriculture, and economics. Cattle become cultured. Youatt explains that "Cattle are like most other animals, the creatures of education and circumstances. We educate them to give us milk, and to acquire flesh and fat. . . . when he receives a kind of culture at our hands, he seems to be enlightened." [36] As the pride of the nation, cultured cattle in turn effect human culture. From art to economics the British John Bull becomes beefier.

Notes

1. William Youatt, *The Complete Grazier and Farmer's and Cattlebreeder's Assistant: A Compendium of Husbandry* (London: Lockwood and Co, 1864), 257.

2. Youatt, *Grazier* 1.

3. Youatt, *Grazier* 1-2.

4. In *The Complete Grazier*, Youatt makes a point of showing how not just the farmer but also his cattle are "productive labourers" contributing to the stimulation of "industry" (1). He does so to counter claims by Malthus that "A fatted beast may in some respects be considered, in the language of the French economists, as an unproductive labourer: he has added nothing to the value of the raw produce that he has consumed" [Thomas Malthus, *An Essay on the Principle of Population* (London: J. Johnson, 1798), 100.]

5. Thomas Bates, *Address to the Board of Agriculture, and to the Other agricultural Societies of the Kingdom on the Importance of an Institution for ascertaining the Merits of the Different Breeds of Live-Stock; Pointing out the Advantages that will accure therefrom to the Landed Interest and the Kingdom in General* (Newcastle upon Tyne: Preston & Heaton, 1808), 6.

6. Such national pride is perhaps nowhere more evident than in the name of George Coates's improved ox—painted by Thomas Weaver and engraved by William Ward—the animal's name is quite simply "Patriot" [D. H Boalch, *Prints and Paintins of British Farm Livestock 1780-1910* (Harpenden: Rothamsted Experimental Station Library, 1958), 15.]

7. Harriet Ritvo, *The Platypus and the Mermaid* (Cambridge, MA: Harvard UP, 1997),107. Henry Cecil Pawson, *Robert Bakewell: Pioneer Livestock Breeder* (London: Crosby Lockwood and Son, 1957), 39.

8. Elspeth Moncrieff and Stephen and Iona Joseph, *Farm Animal Portraits* (Woodbridge, Suffolk: Antique Collector's Club, 1988), 168.

9. In chapter one of *The Animal Estate* Harriet Ritvo remarks on the parallels between inbreeding of prize cattle and the closed circle of aristocratic marriages. Harriet Ritvo, *The Animal Estate* (Cambridge, MA: Harvard UP), 1987.

10. William Youatt, *Cattle: Their Breeds, Management, and Diseases* (London: Baldwin and Cradock, 1834), 192.

11. Pawson, 54.

12. Francios de la Rochefoucauld, *A Frenchman in England*. 1784, ed. Jean Marchand (Cambridge: Cambridge UP, 1933), 201.

13. de la Rochefoucauld 201.

14. George Garrard, *Description of the different varieties of oxen, common in the British Isles* (London: J. Smeeton, 1800), "Long-Horned Cattle." There are no page numbers in the collection of verbal and visual text so I include the chapter headings instead.

15. Ritvo, 66.

16. Pawson, 93.

17. Moncrieff, 175.

18. Christopher Lennox-Boyd, Rob Dixon, and Tim Clayton. *George Stubbs: The Complete Engraved Works* (New York: Harper and Row, 1989) and Alistair Duckworth, "Jane Austen and George Stubbs: Two Speculations" *Eighteenth-Century Fiction* 13.1 (October 2000): 64. Lennox-Boyd also notes that the ox was intended to be slaughtered for the King's birthday celebration. An injury to its legs due to the obese weight of the beast and lack of exercise caused the animal to be put down earlier and served in honor of Princess Mary's birthday.

19. Constance-Anne Parker, *Mr. Stubbs the Horse Painter* (London: J. A. Allen, 1971), 90.

20. Moncrieff 26, 176.

21. For this illustration I am indebted to Ben Roger's fine book *Beef and Liberty* (London: Chatto and Windus, 2003). He provides detailed information on the growth of a beef culture in England in the eighteenth century. Other notable examples of Gillray illustrating British beef include *French Liberty. British Slavery* 21 December, 1792 and *Fat Cattle* 16 January, 1802 in Richard Godfrey's *James Gillray: The Art of Caricature*. Also see Gillray's *The British-Butcher, Supplying John-Bull with a Substitute for Bread* 1795 in Diana Donald's *The Age of Caricature: Satirical Prints in the Reign of George III*.

22. Hanna Glasse's *The Art of Cookery Made Plain and Easy* advances simple British fair in contrast to French cuisine nouvelle. Her introduction takes to task the fashion of having a French chief in British kitchens: "So much is the blind Folly of this Age, that they would rather be imposed on by a French Booby, than give Encouragement to a good English Cook." (Rogers 67) The third chapter of Glasse's *Cookery* elaborates on the wastefulness of French cooking "Chapter III. Read this Chapter, and you will find how expensive French Cook's Sauce is."

23. Joseph Addison, *Tatler* March 21, 1710, *The Works of Joseph Addison* (New York: Harper and Brothers, 1854), 44. For further discussion see Ben Roger's *Beef and Liberty*.

24. Rogers, 100.

25. Marjorie Bowen, *William Hogarth: the Cockney's Mirror* (New York: D. Appleton-Century, 1936), 74.

26. Tobias Smollett, *The Adventures of Ferdinand Count Fathom*, ed. Om Brack, Jr. (Athens, GA: University of Georgia Press, 1988), 128.

27. Smollett, 129.

28. Smollett, 130.

29. Roberth Etheridge Moore, *Hogarth's Literary Relationships* (New York: Octagon Books, 1969) 171.

30. Henry Fielding, *The Grub-Street Opera*, ed. Edgar V. Roberts (Lincoln: University of Nebraska Press, 1968), 54.

31. For details on the ballad see Ben Rogers, 78 and Edgar V. Roberts, "Henry Fielding and Richard Leveridge: Authorship of the 'Roast Beef of Old England'" *Huntington Library Quarterly* 27:2 (February 1964): 175-81. Forrest also penned a cantata about Hogarth's *Calais*, see Rogers, 102-03.

32. Walter Arnold, *The Life and Death of the Sublime Society of Beef Steaks* (London: Bradbury, Evans, & Co. 1871), 45.

33. His essays include discussion of the best means for crop rotation. George III. "To Arthur Young." January 1, 1787, *The Letters of King George III*, ed. Bonamy Dobree (London: Cassell, 1968), 207-08.

34. Moncrieff, 62 87, 91.

35. Moncrieff, 90.

36. Youatt, *Cattle* 4.

Möbial Consumption: Stability, Flux, and Interpermeability in 'Mrs Beeton'

Helen Day

Preoccupations with Food, Eating and Etiquette

During the mid-Victorian period there was a preoccupation with food, eating and etiquette and, according to social and culinary historians, this had particular significance for the bourgeoisie. These preoccupations were part of larger concerns about status and were related to relative economic and social instability. As Margaret Beetham explains, the bourgeoisie was neither "economically nor discursively monolithic" and financial and social ruin was a continual threat.[1] Rapid expansion and increasing urbanisation resulted in a huge number of rising industrialists and merchants jostling for position. Stephen Mennell claims that social competition was, in part, a result of intensified pressure "from below" as "the longer chains of social inter-dependence produced by state-formation and the division of labour tended to tilt the balance little by little towards the lower social groups."[2] The bourgeoisie was a heterogeneous group of individuals who sought a homogenous identity which protected them from the declining land-owning aristocracy and rising working classes, but who also desired the heterogeneity of individual status enhancement.

As the number of individuals attempting membership to the bourgeoisie increased, "the required outward manifestations of gentle status became more and more formalised and elaborate."[3] Status was not just about having wealth but knowing how to use it and display it to the best advantage: an individual required material wealth—cutlery, china, servants, flowers and food all had to be bought—but also the "taste" to spend this wealth appropriately. Dinner parties were one way in which the middle classes and those aspiring to bourgeois status could display their décor, food and servants to friends, neighbours, associates and competitors in an attempt to consolidate or raise their place in the hierarchy. Table manners, along with other social etiquettes, allowed the bourgeoisie to maintain the boundaries between themselves and the other classes as well as police the distinctions between individuals. Etiquette was a manifestation of both collective values and hierarchical differentiation.

Weber and Bataille's Modes of Consumption

Mrs. Beeton's *Book of Household Management* (1861) is a text that reflects and addresses these preoccupations with food, eating and etiquette. We cannot understand this book without emphasizing the importance of its presentation of alternative yet interdependent modes of consumption, modes which appear, and sometimes were, contradictory. Frequent fluctuations in the capitalist marketplace meant that there were no guarantees that the resources of the bourgeoisie were secure. In order that money should not be wasted, households had to balance conspicuous status-enhancing display with management and economy. Max Weber's notion of "Protestant Work Ethic and the Spirit of Capitalism," which encouraged the reinvestment of wealth and advocated frugality, self-denial, sobriety and a life devoid of excess can be used to explain one of the ways that resources were used and controlled.[4] For the bourgeois mistress, this was a mode of consumption that required economy and recycling: in practical terms this meant plain food and left-overs. There is no shortage of economic recipes, like "Bubble-and-Squeak," that used up leftover cold meat, in the *Book of Household Management*.[5]

What this mode of consumption did not account for was the need of the bourgeoisie to enhance their status by displaying power. George Bataille's theories of expenditure provide a useful way of understanding these motivations because he distinguishes between material utility and a more symbolic utility. While the former is concerned with "acquisition and conservation of goods," the latter involves "unproductive expenditures" such as luxury, and competitive spectacles, which represent a form of consumption that is productive and useful only in so far as it produces and demonstrates power and status for the individual concerned.[6] Since "wealth" was generated not only by work but also by status-enhancing consumption, competitive spectacles like dinner parties were vital constituents of the bourgeois economy. Like its readers, the *Book of Household Management* took this seriously recognising that "dining is the privilege of civilisation" and that "much depends on dinner." Mrs. Beeton even goes so far as to state that "the rank which a people occupy in the grand scale may be measured by their way of taking their meals."[7]

Bataille's theories, with their emphasis on the positivity of loss, demonstrate a series of economic, social and symbolic principles that appear to be at odds with the tenets of utility, rationality and parsimony often associated with Victorian modernity. On the one hand consumption was a useful and productive activity, part of a rational homogenous economy managed by a vigorous Protestant Work Ethic and strict patriarchal, scientific and moral definitions of what was natural for and necessary to the industrial, imperial, domestic and corporeal body. On the other hand consumption was wasteful, unproductive and heterogeneous. Nowhere were these intriguing oppositions, and the attempt to control or disguise them, so evident as in the discourses of the domestic economy. The bourgeois home was considered to be symbolically (and physically) separate from the wealth-producing workplace. It was a place where women were expected to be reproductively useful but appear economically idle and luxurious. The everyday food eaten by the family was consumed according to useful, healthy, moral principles (gluttony in the male, for example, was considered self-indulgent and wasteful) in strict contrast to the luxurious consumption expected for the symbolic status-enhancing dinner party.[8]

In the dynamic of capitalism expenditure and display were equally as important as saving and investment: the difficulty lay in negotiating and maintaining a successful balance between them. There were a number of cartoons and books like Charles Selby's *The Dinner Question* (1860) which satirized those living in stringent economic circumstances who tried to mimic higher class gestures. Lynette Hunter reproduces a cartoon from *Punch* (1867) called "Genteel poverty dining in state" which pictures a couple sitting at a plainly covered table with a wheat sheaf rather than flowers in the middle. The young servant boy presents a dish to his master but under the lifted dome is an empty plate.[9] The system of etiquette—serving and dining—is in place but there is no money left over for the actual food.

Mrs. Beeton offered practical solutions to a bourgeois economy of food usage that was concerned both with "gentility" and elegance and with recycling left-overs, and which promoted status enhancement while ensuring long-term economy. She argues that, while both the dinner party and the dinner at home have to be considered with a view to their nicety and enjoyment, the latter should be more concerned with economy.[10] Dishes for family meals were in direct contrast to those that were intended for serving in company. Peas could be used to make a soup that might last the household a couple of days or to make a side dish "Green Peas A La Francaise," which only served four.[11] The "Bills of Fare" offered at the end of the recipe section clearly reveal these differences. A "Plain Family Dinner in January" reveals that dishes served on Monday minimised waste by using up "the remains" from Sunday:

> *Sunday.* – 1. Codfish and oyster sauce, potatoes. 2. Joint of roast mutton, either leg, haunch or saddle; broccoli [*sic*] and potatoes, redcurrant jelly. 3. Apple tart and custards, cheese.
> *Monday.* – 1. The remains of the codfish picked from the bone, and warmed through in the oyster sauce. 2. Curried rabbit, with boiled rice served separately, cold mutton, mashed potatoes. 3. Somersetshire dumplings with wine sauce.

> A "Dinner for 12 Persons" in January however, consists of a First Course, Entrees, Second Course, Third Course and Desserts and Ices, each with between four and eight choices ranging from "Carrot Soup à la Crécy" to "Boiled Ham, garnished with Brussels Sprouts" and "Vol-au-Vent of Preserved Fruit."[12]

The fact that these different types of meal were often linked (leftovers from dinner parties could be used to feed the family later in the week) suggested that, rather than being contradictory, these two modes of consumption were being constantly negotiated.

Möbial Consumption

Considered separately Bataille's concept of unproductive expenditure and Weber's Protestant Work Ethic do not seem satisfactorily to explain the consumption practices of the mid-Victorian bourgeoisie. Placing these two concepts in negotiation allows us to interpret the bourgeois obsession with food, eating and etiquette and offer a hypothesis for the apparent contradictions implicit in a set of eating habits which simultaneously encouraged frugality and restraint *and* opulent and decadent display. We can attempt to model these complex concepts and practices by making use of the möbius strip. At each point on the möbius there is a precise opposition, an inside and an outside, yet if we follow the movement around the möbius strip at no point is it possible to determine when one changes into the other. The möbius construction is a model of simultaneous stability, flux and interpermeability, and as such, can be used to model systems both synchronically and diachronically. Modelling cultural and economic phenomena such as the two modes of mid-Victorian consumption möbially rather than dichotomously can explain why the bourgeois mistress could neither afford to save or expend too much. Eating too frugally could lead to the loss of one's place in the hierarchy while eating too luxuriously could lead to bankruptcy: both resulted in a loss of status, that all-important bourgeois commodity. Choices about consumption practices needed to be carefully controlled and negotiated over both time and space.

Understanding that the mid-Victorian bourgeoisie had to mediate between these möbial consumption practices goes some way to explain why they were so preoccupied with eating and table manners: food and etiquette had so much material and symbolic *work* to do. Along with the fairly straightforward choice about how much income to spend on dinner parties and luxurious expenditure and how much to use for everyday meals came a whole series of associated choices and negotiations. There was the matter of how to choose between the myriad new products of the capitalist market-place, of whether to make foods like bread and preserves at home or buy them from shops, of learning which foods were in season, and of how to tell if foods like meat and milk were past their best or even adulterated. Once these choices had been made there were further challenges such as the problem of how consumption could be controlled and appetites regulated in the face of new and frequent meal events. This, in turn, gave rise to concerns about how to cope with indigestion. Within the home there were difficulties arising from having to devise menus to impress and menus to use up left-overs. Women especially had to learn to deal with the surveillance of their bodies and their homes from both female friends during visiting hours and from invited dinner party guests. Indeed it was those bourgeois women who were expected to regulate this domestic economy who felt most keenly the social anxiety surrounding meals and eating events.

Attitudes towards bourgeois femininity, as well as the behaviours these attitudes encouraged often appeared contradictory. Anxieties about different modes of eating were expressed in etiquette books such as *The Bazar Book of Decorum* (1870) which criticised women for eating voraciously at "secret luncheons" where "she" would "swallow cream tarts by the dozen, and caramels and chocolate drops by the pound's weight" in order to appear properly feminine, her "gorge" rising before company at the sight of a single pea in front of other people at dinner.[13] Helena Michie maintains that bourgeois femininity was defined by negation: "Denial of food is an affirmation of a precarious class position." A lady was expected to eat very little because she didn't have "male desires" and did little to work up an appetite.[14] Joan Jacobs Brunning insists that anorexia nervosa was "latent in the economic and emotional milieu of the bourgeois family" as early as the 1850s and suggests that, rather than terming these "eating disorders" they might well be characterised as "consumption disorders" since they arose in response to certain aspects of capitalism which challenged conventional feminine roles.

> Formerly integral to their lives, the preparation and serving of which signified both their roles in the family and social structures and their commitments to and acquiescence in those roles, food was now becoming available in excess, in quantities and aesthetic appearances far exceeding women's own individual creations. Bourgeois women experienced the confusions and anxieties of changing social roles through the production and consumption of food.[15]

Hunter explains that technology, commerce, urbanisation and the industrial revolution combined to isolate the middle-class woman in the home, with servants to relieve her of much of the domestic labour and a husband who spent much of his time either at work or at his club. The housewife responded, she claims, "with a series of gestures related to food." Her life revolved around a proliferation of small meals (breakfast, nooning, afternoon tea, supper) that placed "enormous emphasis on the significance of food preparation and presentation."[16] Choosing and eating food became significant episodes around which women's time, energy and values could be consolidated.

Women were expected to regulate and control both their appetites and their body shape in the face of multiple meal events. In the 1860s and 1870s Sam Beeton's *Englishwoman's Domestic Magazine* ran a series of articles and letters addressing both the dangers of straight-lacing and the pleasure and pride that an hour-glass figure sometimes afforded women. The dual emphasis on women's reproductive health and status-enhancing femininity can be explained by the two modes of consumption mentioned earlier. Women were expected to have the curvaceous hips of a healthy, reproductively useful woman but also needed to display an excessively tiny waist. *The Young Ladies' Treasure Book* (c 1881-82) published an illustration of a woman's "Artificial Waist" alongside one of a "Natural Waist" to show how the internal organs were displaced by continuous tight-lacing.[17] Normal digestion would have been impossible and constipation and indigestion everyday occurrences. The corset literally moulded and figuratively encoded body shape by enhancing the "natural" difference of the female form: straight-lacing became a focus for debates about the health, beauty and eating habits of bourgeois women. Elsewhere I have argued that the contradictions involved in these consumption practices were expressed in the digestive illnesses that plagued affluent Victorians. "The indigestible economies of the Victorian bourgeoisie" is my term to explain these confusing and contradictory material and symbolic attitudes, behaviours, and preoccupations.[18]

The Importance of Being Beeton

The confusing and contradictory attitudes and behaviours required of bourgeois women in their everyday role caused literal and symbolic indigestion. What was needed was a guide that understood and "digested" these anxieties and offered easy and digestible advice on how to make the right choices. There were, of course, myriad magazines, etiquette books, cookery books and manuals available to women at this time, perhaps so many that deciding which one to buy and what advice to follow became yet another difficult choice for women. What made *The Book of Household Management* (1861) so popular and successful was a complex mixture of good marketing, timing, a sense of completeness, and the particularities of tone and form of address which offered inspiration to readers and understood their aspirational desires. "Mrs. Beeton" also fulfilled the need for a figure that was both authoritative and accessible.

Although Nicola Humble describes Isabella Beeton as "an unlikely arbiter of middle-class tastes and manners," she was, in many ways, ideally placed to become the oracle on household management during the 1860s for a number of reasons.[19] She was both alike and very different from most of her readers. Like them, she was the wife of a successful businessman who worked in the city and brought in a reasonable wage giving them an average standard of living in middle-class terms. As Margaret Beetham makes clear, she aimed her book at "the woman who employed servants."[20] Isabella Beeton had given birth to, and lost, a child, had her own home and servants and had to learn how to manage these without much in the way of maternal guidance. She was not a natural cook and Nancy Spain reports that Isabella was heard to vent her frustration at her lack of competence in household matters with the cry "Why has no-one written a book—a *good* book for brides? To help them learn these things?"[21]

Unlike the majority of her readers, Isabella was a working journalist, married to and supported by Sam Beeton, the publisher of the *Englishwoman's Domestic Magazine*, one of the most popular and innovative magazines for women of the time. Spain, in her biography of her great-aunt Isabella, describes the Beetons as a very "un-Victorian couple" and offers a portrait of a marriage based on complimentary skills and knowledge. Both parties were involved with their own writing projects and enjoyed frequent trips abroad where business was interspersed with sight-seeing.[22] One of the reasons Isabella Mayson may have chosen such a husband was her rather unconventional childhood. Her mother's remarriage to Henry Dorling, Clerk of Epsom Racecourse introduced Isabella to the world of the local aristocracy and gentry, but also meant that she became unpaid nurse-maid to her younger siblings and half-siblings in the rooms under the Grandstand when the house in Epsom High Street reaching bursting point.

Although most of the ideas and philosophies in the *Book of Household Management* were probably ones that Isabella believed in, the differences between the way of life of the "mistress" in "Chapter One" and that of Isabella as a working journalist, suggest that she was writing about the accepted domestic ideology of the time rather than living by it.[23] It is doubtful that Isabella, busily writing and researching for her magazine columns and book, testing recipes and visiting Paris to arrange fashion plates and paper-patterns, as well as spending time at Sam's offices in the Strand, could have had the time or energy to spend her days in the way she describes in *The Book of Household Management*. Despite returning from her German Finishing School as a "very passable imitation of [a lady]," having "strong notions about duty" and "no ambitions beyond marriage," Sarah Freeman challenges the notion of Isabella as a "perfect lady," claiming that this "popular image" existed only in literature, and that fundamentally Isabella was "nothing like her," since a perfect lady would not have written a cookery book nor contemplated being a popular journalist.[24]

When Isabella first took over the household and cookery columns of the *Englishwoman's Domestic Magazine* early in 1857 she was twenty-one, had only been a mistress of her own household for eight months and felt that her inexperience as a writer, as well as her ignorance of cooking, meant she was clearly unqualified for the job. Freeman maintains that the appearance of Isabella's first articles was preceded by "many weeks of studying cookery books" and "questioning her own cook" as well as "experimenting in her kitchen."[25] Like her readers, Isabella knew what it was like to pour over cookery books, negotiate with her cook and face the prospect of failure at the dinner table. Through the letter bags of the *Englishwoman's Domestic Magazine* she had also read countless accounts of women who were unsure about their domestic roles and wanted help and guidance from someone they could trust.

Once Isabella had decided to compile and edit a collection Sam put into action a utilitarian campaign to collect recipes from the "Housewives of Great Britain" by wooing them in the *Englishwoman's Domestic Magazine* with the promise that "the knowledge and skill of a few may be acquired by thousands." The recipes came pouring in with every post and a "terrifying process of sorting, classifying and duplicating (in addition to the testing) began." It was, Spain claims, one of the rules that "Nothing is to go into the book untried" and Isabella's half-sister Lucy remembers watching her "brilliant sister," "whirling about the place, beating eggs and mixing pastry: divinely dissatisfied with her efforts."[26]

It was partly Isabella's lack of knowledge about cooking and household matters that made her so successful as a writer. She was able to put herself in the place of anxious novices and anticipate what they wanted and needed to know. The other reason she was so popular was that she managed to convey to her readers that household management was much more than just a series of tasks. She guided them through the basics firmly and confidently yet impressed upon her readers that this required constant negotiation with others (servants, friends, guests, even one's husband). Mrs. Beeton "digested" both the concerns and anxieties of these women *and* the solutions to these problems, presenting them in a way that could be easily understood and which didn't challenge the more conventional notion of bourgeois femininity. *The Book of Household Management* was also more popular than other texts of the period that addressed a similar audience, most notably Eliza Acton's *Modern Cookery for Private Families* (1845) and Alexis Soyer's *The Modern Housewife* (1848).[27] This was partly because Mrs. Beeton addressed all aspects of household management, not just cookery, but also because she recognised, and to some extent, shared the anxieties and concerns, needs and desires of her readers. She chose to address them in two ways: as someone who understood the pressures they were under and as an as older, more matronly figure, a "universal mother."[28]

The editor-persona "Mrs. Beeton" inspired her readers and responded to their needs, addressing both the ideological functions and practical role of the mistress whilst helping to redefine the notion of the housewife as vital to the running of the home, family and nation. Freeman describes the opening chapter as "a concise but comprehensive essay on the art of being a lady" designed to "win over every woman in England."[29] Any women who felt her position to be unimportant and useless could be persuaded by the strength of Mrs. Beeton's rhetoric: the mistress is "the first and last, the Alpha and Omega in the government of her establishment" and "it is by her conduct that its whole internal policy is regulated."[30] In her opening sentence, Mrs. Beeton compares the mistress of the house to "a Commander of an Army" who attains the "highest rank" of the female character when she enters into knowledge of household duties.[31] In 1845, Florence Nightingale, writing a letter to a friend from Scutari, used the same military metaphor to compare her role as nurse and manager of a hospital to that of a domestic mistress. She declared that although she always expected to end her days as Hospital Matron she "never expected to be a Barrack Mistress."[32] Mary Poovey, in her thesis on the ideological work of gender in mid-Victorian England argues that these two narratives, the domestic narrative of maternal nurturing and self-sacrifice, and the military narrative of individual assertion and will, were constructed dialectically.[33] Nurturing and self-sacrifice were considered "natural" for women and were related to their reproductive usefulness: self-assertion and power in women however, were excessive, even luxurious. The möbial interplay of the seemingly contradictory forces of the passive domestic angel-in-the-house and the rather ruthless organisational principles of the successful military nurse found their exposition in the ideological work of the domestic ideal which both Nightingale and Mrs. Beeton, in their own ways, embodied.

Use and Luxury in *The Book of Household Management*

Mrs. Beeton made household management into both a science and an art. She educated her readers in a way that gave them credit for having inquiring minds but which assembled and organised a mass of information into "easily digestible nuggets."[34] By telling readers the "why" as well as the "how to" *The Book of Household Management* had similar objectives to those defined by Sam for the first issue of the *Englishwoman's Domestic Magazine* in 1852: the "improvement of the intellect, the cultivation of the morals, and the cherishing of domestic virtues," the adoption of a tone "free from severity" and the blending of "amusement with instruction."[35] This rather indulgent assumption of intellectual curiosity and desire for useful self-improvement exhibited in *The Book of Household Management* was a combination of the Beetons' shared belief in female education and the ethics of "self-culture, self-discipline, and self-control" fostered in texts like Samuel Smile's popular manual of self-improvement *Self-Help* (1859).

As well as the quotations and advice of literary and moral figures, the most obvious educational pointer is the additional information which accompanies many of the recipes. An advert for the second part of the serialised *Book of Household Management* defined this material as the "history, description, properties, and uses, of every article directly and indirectly connected with the Household."[36] It took the form of seemingly unformulated and disorganised mini-essays on subjects such as the natural history of the key ingredient, physical and scientific properties, culinary uses, nutrition, chemistry, geography, botany, horticulture, anthropology, myth and legend, fable, folk and literature. Some even made

use of relatively up-to-date scientific information and industrial manufacturing techniques as this accompaniment to Aunt Nelly's Pudding reveals:

TREACLE OR MOLASSES. – Treacle is the uncrystallizable part of
the saccharine juice drained from the Muscovado sugar, and is either
naturally so or rendered uncrystallizable through some defect in the
process of boiling. As it contains a large quantity of sweet or saccharine
principle and is cheap, it is of great use as an article of domestic economy. Children are especially fond of it: and it is accounted wholesome.
It is also useful for making beer, rum and the very dark syrups.[37]

The reader is informed how the culinary relates to history, culture,
literature, art, politics, geography, science and horticulture, although
there is little guidance about the ways in which this information should
be read and used. If it was intended as dinner party conversation, this
conflicted with the general insistence that girls should not talk about food.
If, as Newcomb insists in *Home and its Associations: A Book for Young
Ladies* (c1860), girls should not "make remarks respecting the food" or
"discuss the contents of [their] plate" then under what circumstances
could they make use of the excerpts they had read in *The Book of Household Management*?[38] Such information could be expended unproduc-
tively in order to maintain control over servants or to seduce a husband
with knowledge of domestic affairs. Equally, it could have been read for
the pleasure of learning, a luxury for women who spent most of their
time in the home. Perhaps the most important thing that Mrs Beeton did
for her readers was to show them that learning about all aspects of
household management could be enjoyable; that the duties of the mistress may not necessarily be "incompatible with the enjoyment of life."[39]
Out of the thousands of recipes in the book Isabella added "Author's
Recipe" to only a handful. Those for "The Baroness Pudding" and "Useful Soup for Benevolent Purposes" negotiate between the two modes of
consumption and suggest one way that Mrs. Beeton (as an editor and, I
think, as a person) wanted to be "read." The Baroness Pudding was
"kindly given to [Isabella's] family by a lady who bore the title here pre-
fixed to it" so, in fact, was not Isabella's recipe at all but gave her the
opportunity to flaunt her connections.[40] This cultural capital classified
Mrs. Beeton as having prestige, taste and distinction. "Taste" claims Pierre Bourdieu, "classifies, and it classifies the classifier."[41] By reproduc-
ing the Baroness' recipe in her own discursive formation Mrs. Beeton
appropriated the cultural capital for herself. Her readers, by making this
recipe themselves and presenting it as a named dish at a dinner party,
were also, to a lesser extent, demonstrating this cultural competency and
defining themselves as having "taste." Juxtaposed with this ostentation

was the "Useful Soup for Benevolent Purposes" which Mrs. Beeton noted was "used in the Winter of 1858 by the Editress, who made, each week, in her copper, 8 or 9 gallons of this soup for distribution amongst about a dozen families of the village near where she lives."[42] She clearly wanted to demonstrate that, as a privileged member of society, she had the time to partake in the bourgeois tradition of charity begun at home. Although her readers could have been inspired to try out such a recipe on their own local poor, the recipe was more useful to Mrs. Beeton because it produced and demonstrated her status.

The Need for Updating and Remarketing *The Book of Household Management* (1861)

Bourgeois preoccupations with food, eating and etiquette were clearly linked to anxieties about wealth. For the mid-Victorians, attitudes to wealth and how it should be consumed were complex, even contradictory. Mrs. Beeton had some understanding of this "indigestion" in the bourgeois system and used her role as an editor and journalist to advise women how to consume appropriately. At a time when having "taste" was vital in order to demonstrate class allegiance and to distinguish individual status *The Book of Household Management* "digested" both the concerns of her readers and the solutions to their problems.

Patterns of consumption and the relationship between the two modes of consumption I have outlined in this chapter did not remain the same throughout the nineteenth century. In order to appeal to different readers with a variety of levels of income and lifestyle, as well as to keep up with technological changes and commercial goods, Sam Beeton and the publishers Ward, Lock & Tyler constantly updated and remarketed the *Book of Household Management*.[43] The synchronic nature of the möbius construction helps explain why the 1861 version spoke to particular women at a particular time about modes of consumption they would have encountered in their everyday lives. The diachronic nature of the möbius allows us to model a system of change which explains that new editions and remarketed versions of the original *Book of Household Management* were needed to digest the seemingly indigestible concerns of the next generation of women readers.

Notes

1. Margaret Beetham, *A Magazine of Her Own? Domesticity and Desire in the Woman's Magazine, 1800-1914* (London: Routledge, 1996), 20.

2. Stephen Mennell, *All Manners of Food: Eating and Taste in England and France from the Middle Ages to the Present.* Second Edition (Urbana: University of Illinois Press, 1996), 32.

3. Mennell, All Manners, 208.

4. Max Weber, *The Protestant Work Ethic and the Spirit of Capitalism.* 1904-05. Translated by T. Parsons. (London: Routledge, 2002).

5. Mrs Isabella Beeton, ed. *Mrs Beeton's Book of Household Management* (London: S. O. Beeton, 1861), 287.

6. Georges Bataille, *The Bataille Reader*, edited by Fred Botting and Scott Wilson (Oxford: Blackwell, 1997).

7. Beeton, *Household Management*, 905.

8. Helen Day, "Waste Not Want Not: The Excesses of Gluttony in the Early to Mid-Victorian Period," Harlan Walker ed., *The Fat of the Land* (Bristol: Footwork, 2003), 56-76.

9. Lynette Hunter, "Proliferating Publications: the Progress of Victorian Cookery Literature." Pp. 51-70 in *Luncheon, Nuncheon and Other Meals: Eating with the Victorians.* ed. C. A. Wilson (Gloucestershire: Sutton, 1994), 64.

10. Beeton, *Household Management*, 16.

11. Beeton, *Household Management*, 580-81.

12. Beeton, *Household Management*, 913, 910.

13. Helena Michie, *The Flesh Made Word: Female Figures and Women's Bodies* (Oxford: Oxford University Press, 1987), 19.

14. Michie, *Flesh Made Word*, 17-18.

15. Deborah Thompson, "Anorexia as Lived Trope: Christina Rossetti's 'Goblin Market.'" *Mosaic* 24

(1991): 89-106, 99.

16. Hunter, "Proliferating Publications", 69.

17. John Gloag, *Victorian Comfort: A Social History of Design 1830-1900* (Newton Abbot: David & Charles, 1979), 94.

18. Helen Day, "The Indigestible Economies of the Victorian Bourgeoisie," in *Consuming for Pleasure: Selected Essays on Popular Fiction*, ed. Julia Hallam and Nickianne Moody (Liverpool: Liverpool John Moores University Press, 2000), 11-31.

19. Nicola Humble, "Introduction." in *Mrs Beeton's Book of Household Management*, ed. Isabella Beeton (Oxford: Oxford University Press, 2000), viii.

20. Beetham, *Magazine*, 63.

21. Nancy Spain, *Mrs Beeton and Her Husband* (London: Collins, 1948), 62.

22. Spain, *Mrs Beeton*, 62.

23. Kay Boardman, "The Ideology of Domesticity: The Regulation of the Household Economy in Victorian Women's Magazines." *Victorian Periodicals Review*, 3:2 (2000): 150-64. As Boardman persuasively argues, the "ideology of domesticity had become so pervasive in the Victorian period that by the 1850s debates about domestic ideology permeated literary and visual representational practices at every level," 15.

24. Sarah Freeman, *Isabella and Sam: The Story of Mrs Beeton* (London: Victor Gollancz, 1977), 19.

25. Freeman, Isabella and Sam, 133.

26. Spain, *Mrs Beeton*, 119-20.

27. Beeton *Household Management*, Title-page. For those unfamiliar with the original 1861 edition, *Mrs Beeton's Book of Household Management comprising information for the Mistress, Housekeeper, Cook, Kitchen maid, Butler, Footman, Coachman, valet, Upper and Under house-maid's, lady's maid, Maid-of-all-work, laundry-maid, Nurse and Nurse-maid, Monthly, Wet and Sick-nurse etc. Also sanitary, medical and Legal memoranda; with a history or the origin, properties, and uses of all things connected with home life and comfort, By Mrs Isabella Beeton* is essentially divided into four parts. The book opens with instructions to the mistress on the management of her household including chapters on the duties of the female staff at the top of the servant hierarchy, the housekeeper and cook and their helpers. This is succeeded by the recipes which make up by far the largest section, followed by information on the cleaning and serving duties of lower domestic servants, separated into male and female, and ending with childcare and occasional servants like the wet-nurse and male advisors of medicinal and legal disciplines.

28. Kathryn Hughes, "Introduction" in *Mrs Beeton's Book of Household Management* ed. Isabella Beeton. Facsimile of First Edition (London: Cassell, 2000), ii.

29. Freeman, *Isabella and Sam*, 187, 190.

30. Beeton, *Household Management*, 1.

31. Beeton, *Household Management*, 1.

32. Ernest Sanger, *Englishmen at War: A Social History in Letters 1450-1900* (Stroud: Sutton, 1993), 286.

33. Mary Poovey, *Uneven Developments: The Ideological Work of Gender in Mid-Victorian Britain* (London: Virago, 1989), 197.

34. Humble, "Introduction," xii.

35. Freeman, *Isabella and Sam*, 77.

36. Humble, "Introduction," xii.

37. Beeton, *Household Management*, 621.

38. Rev. Harvey Newcomb, *Home and Its Associations: A Book for Young Ladies* (Edinburgh: Gall & Inglis, c.1860), 71-72.

39. Beeton, *Household Management*, 2.

40. Beeton, *Household Management*, 630-31.

41. Pierre Bourdieu, *Distinction: A Social Critique of the Judgement of Taste*, trans. R. Nice (London: Routledge, 2002), 6.

42. Beeton, *Household Management*, 85.

43. As Isabella Beeton died in 1865 of puerperal fever following childbirth she did not have anything to do with versions of her book published after this date (except the *Dictionary of Cookery*, the proofs of which she was correcting shortly before her death).

Consuming the Maidservant

Christine Rinne

The nuclear family emerged in the eighteenth century as a result of the budding middle-class. Budde has outlined four results of this new structure: a more intense and intimate notion of marriage, the "discovery" of childhood and child-rearing, the removal of women and children from contributing to the family's income and a spatial and ideological distinction between the developing private and public spheres.[1] Servants, who had been integrated into the family they worked for during the previous centuries, were now excluded from this evolving notion, though many continued to reside with their employer. During this time the number of female servants rose dramatically compared to males, as industry grew and agriculture declined. In 1819 in Prussia 24.2 percent of all servants were male, but by 1882, only 3.2 percent of all German servants were men.[2]

Between 1840 and 1914, 68.9 percent of German bourgeois families employed one maidservant.[3] These domestic employees had immediate and necessary access to this emergent private sphere, yet under the new definition of the family unit they were not considered a member of it. They were essential to the maintenance of the household, the care of the children, as well as the formation and ideology of the family, though not as an accepted member. The maidservant was located within the domestic sphere but outside of the family's boundaries, a restricted member situated on numerous artificial borders. This fissure in the domestic constellation provided her with a rare position of privileged access and the possibility of both exposing and challenging its limitations; consequently she became a potential threat to the family's stability.[4]

The newly established institution of the nuclear family was vulnerable, and the state had "an interest in maintaining and protecting the family as one of its "basic props.""[5] The foundation of the family was located in the institution of marriage, which was codified in the Prussian Civil Code (*Allgemeines Landrecht für die Preußischen Staaten*) of 1794 as a life-long emotional relationship between two partners. The primary function of marriage is defined as having and raising children, and is given a prominent position in the first paragraph of the Code.[6] The fifth section of the Prussian Civil Code (*Gesindeordnung*) delineates the rights and duties of servants and their employers. Cases of improper behavior by maidservants, whether factual or fictional, occupied public debates and fantasies; consequently the state imposed regulations that did not allow these fears to be realized. In addition to the servants' occupational and moral obligations, the master and mistress were legally bound to serve as surrogate parents to their young employees; this role is reflected in the right to punish servants, including corporal punishment, and the demand for model behavior. A maidservant must have the opportunity to master her tasks in another's household; only then is she prepared to become a wife and mother. A maidservant's pregnancy, which in many versions of the law is grouped with contagious and disgusting (*ekelhaft*) illnesses, was grounds for immediate dismissal; marriage was one of the few reasons a servant could quit.[7] These laws were adopted throughout German-speaking areas and remained largely unchanged until 1918.

This essay will consider the maidservant's role in her employer's as well as her own food consumption. Many of her tasks involved representing her employer in and to the public, a contested yet seemingly unavoidable consequence of delegation; however, an inability to clearly define precarious binaries such as public and private, outsider and family, as well as emerging ideas of social and gender equality threatened bourgeois notions of identity and in fact its very foundation. The potentially destructive capabilities of the maidservant in her role as representative led to preventative punishment in her own consumption.

Production

Of the many tasks that maidservants were expected to complete, three key responsibilities revolved around the employer's meals, namely shopping, food preparation and serving. This in itself is not especially surprising, yet when one considers that this was presumably the most publicly visible example of the maidservant serving in the housewife's place, it becomes apparent why it was such a point of heated public debate. Many feared what the maidservant might do, whether knowingly or because of her ignorance. She could manipulate her role in food production to gain great favor, new freedoms or exact revenge. Meals were viewed as an opportunity for the housewife to demonstrate her skill, ability and creativity, yet realistically it displayed her capability to run her household, to organize and delegate the work.

Shopping

The nineteenth century brought a new responsibility to the German housewife, namely shopping. A majority of foodstuffs were previously homegrown and clothing was handmade; now, however, new technology allowed, and changing household structures often required, that many household necessities be purchased. Meyer argues that shopping is a result of the development of bourgeois society, as well as an integral component of its structure, and that this evolvement forced women to acquire new competence.[8] Despite what seems to have been a general sense of distrust on the part of the housewives for their live-in employees, they did entrust the everyday shopping to them. Handbooks suggest that housewives provide clear instructions regarding where, and what servants should buy as well as what the total expenditures should be; however, the degree to which housewives did so and to which maidservants chose to follow these instructions appears to have varied greatly.

The unique aspect of this arrangement is that the maidservant is sent with her employer's money to make purchases that she largely does not consume herself. In some cases she will use a small portion of the goods, such as foodstuffs, and in others she will use them to benefit her employer, such as cleaning products. In theory, maidservants did not need to make many purchases with their personal funds for their own consumption. As it was, they had very little disposable income of their own, since room and board composed a large portion of their total emolument, and much of the required clothing was either provided as part of the wage or given as a Christmas gift.[9] It was expected that a significant amount of their monetary earnings be put toward savings, and any remaining funds could be applied toward personal needs and entertainment, though such expenditures were discouraged and considered wasteful.

Servant newspapers (*Dienstbotenzeitungen*), which were published by various political, social and religious organizations, were the only leisure reading material addressed solely toward maidservants. Many of these newspapers were short lived; the unions that supported them often struggled and suffered from financial problems, however, advertisements offered an attractive method of augmenting income. Beginning in the 1870s, after the laws were made less restrictive, it became common practice for German newspapers of all sorts to receive a large portion (50-70% around turn of the twentieth century)[10] of their income from advertisements.[11]

The advertisements that appear in the servant newspapers can be categorized into four types.[12] The first group is composed of products that the maidservant would purchase with her own money, for her own consumption, and consists primarily of prefabricated clothing and personal hygiene products. Not surprisingly, many of the goods are various creams and tonics, results of wonderful new scientific advancements, which promise to miraculously take care of common ailments such as dry hands or freckles. The next grouping consists of occupational services. These are services that would have helped the young woman advance herself, such as schools that provided further instruction or job placement agencies.[13] The third type of advertisement offers various types of entertainment, including other reading material and social events. Because many of these servant newspapers were run by organizations or unions that represented servants, they also held social events in addition to regular meetings. The final category of advertisements, comprising about half, represents products that would have been used in the household in which the maidservant was employed, and unlike the previous products, paid for by the employer. These are, however, often products that the maidservant would have required to carry out her duties, such as cleaning or cooking; additionally, there are services and specific stores that advertise here. Because the maidservant generally lived in the same household as she worked, it is not plausible that she would be purchasing goods for her own home. However, it would not be surprising if these firms advertise here with the hope that these young women, once married, would continue to purchase these products, at the named stores, for use in her own home.

Advertisements are incorporated into the content of articles as well. The newspapers supported some of their advertisers by explicitly mentioning specific products or stores when answering reader's questions or making general household-related suggestions.[14] Whether or not further funds were exchanged for these gestures is unclear, and perhaps not important; more significant is how the newspapers support and manipulate the role of the maidservant as a representative consumer and aid in establishing the habits of a future housewife.

The two primary complaints by housewives about maidservants who were sent to make purchases on their behalf were firstly, that the maidservants stole, or rather, withheld some of the designated funds by lying about the prices or receiving a percentage back from the storeowner, and secondly, that they used this opportunity to gossip with others, often about their employers.[15] Not only was this seen as a waste of valuable time, but more importantly, there was a fear that this gossip would shed an unfavorable light on the employer. Consequently, handbooks often address these issues in an attempt to give inexperienced wives tips on how to properly instruct their maidservants as well as teach employees how to gain favor and maintain their virtue.

Henriette Davidis, one of the most popular cookbook and housewife handbook authors of the period, describes how she was personally swindled by a maidservant who retained money after each purchase. She implies that there is an irresistible temptation present in the stores, and when left alone, maidservants are incapable of withstanding it. It is not that the act itself has such substantial financial consequences, but rather the malicious, habitual repetition inherent in it and the deceptive, base motivations. Davidis does not suggest that the tradition of sending a maidservant to make the purchases be modified, rather she offers a method that would prohibit such behavior, namely checking all purchases and amounts spent immediately when the maidservant returns.[16] Gordon appeals to the maidservant's sense of morality, emphasizing loyalty and efficiency while shopping. Not only should the employee be cautious as to how she spends the shopping money, but she should also look for bargains.[17]

Margarete Michaelsen, under the pseudonym of Ernst Georgy, wrote the novel The Berlin Brats (Die Berliner Range), the second volume of which is a parody of maidservants and bourgeois culture in Berlin. It contains a passage that describes how Mr. Thiele, a storeowner, uses gifts to retain his young maidservant customers despite his high prices. "'You are always in such a hurry! How about a piece of chocolate?'—He held up a glass jar and she took a piece out for herself and acted coy.— 'But Miss, such a little morsel doesn't matter. I so enjoy watching you nibble with your white teeth! How is your rose soap?" —'Thank you Mr. Thiele, I still have some!'"[18] Mr. Thiele's flirtatious ways do result in financial gain, though eventually competing shop owners tell the young women that he is married, forcing him out of business. A similar situation is depicted in Clara Viebig's so-called servant novel (Dienstbotenroman), Daily Bread (Das tägliche Brot), in which a family owns a store, and the wife runs an employment agency for domestic servants. Using this position she attempts, often successfully, to persuade maidservants to shop at her store, as well as share their gossip, though her methods and attitude eventually cause the family's downfall.[19] These two literary examples illustrate the common "problem" of easily manipulated maidservants, who, when left unattended in the city, are unable to withstand seductive storefronts, flirtatious men, and gossiping women.

The maidservant, acting in her mistress's stead, is told where to make any necessary household purchases. Though there were perceived negative social consequences of this practice it persisted. Because it is the servant who ultimately decides what to purchase and where, she becomes the target of burgeoning industrial and capitalist advancements. The housewife's concern for gossip and stealing while the maidservant is shopping demonstrates that she had no right to the property of her employer, including his reputation, though she was expected to positively contribute to it. The crucial factor is her interaction with outsiders that is inherent in shopping, whether with a shop clerk or fellow shopper. These representatives of the public contribute to, and become agents of, the employee's feared betrayal. I do not mean to suggest that maidservants were innocent puppets duped by the mistress or the master. The fact that maidservants often augmented their income while shopping and used this opportunity to talk with others suggests that they too were aware that this situation afforded them some freedoms and room to negotiate.

Cooking

A majority of maidservants were involved in food preparation, some independently as cooks, and others as helpers to the housewife.[20] Food preparation, especially when guests were coming, was about much more than meeting nutritional needs; cooking is viewed as an art that should provide enjoyable meals that reflect the household's status. The potentially destructive power of a maidservant in the kitchen can be seen in an article about a supposed new sickness called "kitchen choler" (*Küchenkoller*), which appeared in the "German Medical Weekly" (*Deutsche Medizinische Wochenschrift*) on 8 March 1900. The illness, reportedly caused by working in a hot, poorly ventilated kitchen,[21] results in a hysterical, choleric condition and is described as follows: "A nervous affliction, but unfortunately to a large degree contagious. Yes, the contagion can spread from the girl of an affected household to the neighboring and bordering families, to an entire block and thereby take on the character of an epidemic."[22] The author and medical doctor Dr. Leopold F., is unable to provide the exact number of those who are afflicted, though he claims that approximately half of all who work in the kitchen are affected.[23] The doctor, however, admits his lack of methodology. He states that he cannot provide exact statistics and is basing his claims on experience from his practice and his own household, "in a way on my own body."[24] His statement is reflective of his own fears, when he feels threatened by his employee because she has invaded his physical space with her supposed hysteria. Though cooking occurs within the confines of the kitchen, generally without much interaction with others, its consequences can be public, in this case spreading beyond servants to include innocent neighboring families.

Serving

Serving the meal was the final phase of the maidservant's interaction with the foodstuffs she purchased. It was also another significant occasion when the maidservant interacted with people outside of the family, though this time within the confines of the home. Regardless of the degree to which a maidservant was directly responsible for food preparation, she was certainly involved in serving the dinner guests. While working, a maidservant was expected to maintain a certain appearance, and a crucial portion of her uniform was composed of an apron, which served to protect her dress. The nature of the work being performed determined the style and color of her apron; for example aprons for cooking were larger and made of dark material, while those for serving were smaller and of lighter material.[25]

The employers' desire to be able to distinguish maidservants led to the evolution of a uniform in urban regions by the 1860s.[26] Not only did an established type of clothing provide an immediate visual marker, but it also served to remind both employer and employee of the social hierarchy and their respective duties and responsibilities. A majority of the maidservants came from the countryside as the city alone was unable to provide the high number of servants demanded by the tremendous urban and bourgeois expansion, and this "uniform" was based on the clothing that the young women brought with them.[27]

While the apron initially served to protect one's clothing from dirt and wear, the white apron as discussed here took on a different role. It designates a readiness to serve, demonstrates the cleanliness and (sexual) purity of both the household and oneself, and finally, adds to the household's décor. Whereas dark aprons were meant to mask the consequences of heavy housework, white aprons were not primarily intended to protect, but rather to project the ideals of the bourgeois household. "White visualized cleanliness, spotlessness, purity, and unsoiledness not only on a hygienic, but especially on a moral level, in the sense of sexual innocence, but also obedience and finally prosperity."[28] Cleanliness is portrayed predominantly in the maidservant's characteristic white apron, which was reserved for such special occasions. When she was receiving the employer's guests or representing her employer in public while shopping, the girl in the white apron demonstrated physical cleanliness as well as moral and sexual purity. The use of white clothing to adorn, in the form of apron, bonnet, and gloves, provide a visible outer layer of cleanliness, despite the apron's origin as a means to absorb dirt and protect the clothing underneath.

Her physical appearance, together with her reserved and contained behavior, led to the desired effect of disguise, of blending into the background. Gordon elaborates:

> Aprons are a thoroughly necessary article, not only to protect clothing (for this the wide, well-covering, actual work aprons serve), rather also, in order to lend a pretty, delicate appearance while going out. For work, during which one gets dirty especially easily, such as when washing dishes, it is a good idea to keep an over-apron ready that is easy to wash and can quickly be removed when one is called away from such work. It not only protects the apron, but the girl can also appear cleaner in front of the employer or guests. To go out lighter, if not white aprons, are worn, as well as when a girl must serve at the table.[29]

The author makes distinctions between types of aprons, namely work aprons and over-aprons (*Überschürze*), both as a means to protect the decorative apron, referred to simply as an apron. The primary function mentioned here is to adorn and enhance, to make the maidservant presentable not only to her employer, but to those outside of the household. This is the case both for the guests who may enter the private realm, as well as when the maidservant leaves the confines of the house.

Good manners were key to impressing one's guests, and because many maidservants were young country girls with little or no formal training, much less exposure to such events, housewives were advised to provide careful instructions beforehand in order to prevent embarrassing mishaps. Serving requires attention and overview; one should have a detailed plan beforehand, and discuss every detail with the servant(s).[30] One word that appears frequently is noiseless. Regardless of whether a maidservant was serving food or beverage, or waiting for her next task, she was not to be heard. After providing details about from which direction what is served, Grauenhorst continues: "All work, also coming and going, shutting the door, etc. should occur as quietly as possible. The girl serving should not take or show any interest in the gathering and their discussions."[31] In addition to silence, there is also an emphasis on not directly touching anything being served. Platters and dishes mediate between the gloved maidservant and the consuming employer and guests. For example, if silverware is being handed to the guests, a plate should be used.[32] The maidservant has a necessary function, but her goal should be to remain unnoticed, to blend into the background rather than becoming incorporated into the dinner party. Yet, her clothing inherently contradicts this dictate, as it in fact conjures up notions of sexuality and does little to detract from her presence.

Despite the many warnings about excess and suggested definitions of appropriateness, sexuality was inherently tied to the white apron through its form and appearance. Aprons were often made of the same material as undergarments, as were their adornment.[33] Surely the similarities between the two were not lost on admirers, and served to heighten the woman's appeal. Gaugele provides a description of the apron's allure and similarities to undergarments, especially a petticoat or slip.

> The sensuous qualities of apron and undergarment material, with their softness, delicateness and decoration, aided in characterizing the polarization of the sexes as a sign of femininity and the essence of feminine eroticism.... The large bow in the back of every woman in a white apron repeats the delight in the "freeing" of a corseted body. The trapezoid and v-shaped apron bib reflect the inner shape of the corset and outwardly reflect these forms through material. As outer underwear, the white apron reflects bodily intimacy onto the clothing's covering, through to the small decorative aprons, which are interspersed with lace and have ruched hems that not only emphasized the female genitalia, but also represented them in their cut, which has persisted until today in waitress aprons.[34]

Though the body is further concealed by an apron, the shape and material are reminiscent of what is under her outer layer, hence more arousing, especially since this clothing appeared on the only woman in the household who was allowed to possess or exude any sexuality. Grauenhorst also underscores this theme, by tying sweet, decorative and insubstantial desserts to young girls in small aprons. "Many believe that when a young girl in a small white apron mixes a few sweet dishes together, maybe even rolled pralines, she has sufficient training!"[35] The diminutive underscores the need for practical rather than decorative cooking skills, through the need for a practical rather than decorative apron.

In 1781 Johann Rautenstrauch published his treatise "About the Chambermaids in Vienna," which sought to explain firstly, why maidservants are so seductive and dangerous and secondly, why a majority serve as lovers to married men. The text led to at least three published rebuttals and one defense, which suggest that interest in the topic was abundant.[36] Rautenstrauch's proposed source of the maidservant's attraction is her clothing. "The cause of her dangerous appeal is clearly located in her clothing. It is the most advantageous and attractive for the female body; it puts the forms of all limbs in its true light; it splendidly outlines the thighs and hips–in short, it charms the eye."[37] He finds their clothing too formfitting, and suggests that men cannot help but be attracted to them. The author continues by warning that because other women augment their natural body shape with "frightening" means such as whalebone, iron wire and horsehair, admirers are no longer able to distinguish between the natural and the artificial.[38] This is the question that was still on the minds of many a century later, namely what is really under those coverings.

First published in 1898, Gerhart Hauptmann's play "Führmann Henschel" takes place in the 1860s and tells the story of Henschel's family and its slow demise, which is brought on by their maidservant Hanne. When the story begins, Henschel's wife is sick and once she dies her fear is realized; he marries Hanne. At key points in the play, Hanne's apron is an important visual symbol. The first mention is found early in the story, when Henschel returns from a trip and brings an apron for her back with him. Throughout the play, solely in the stage directions however, the apron reappears. The first time it appears she holds it in front of her face when she fears she might lose her job; in the second she triumphantly pulls it off because she knows Henschel is going to propose marriage; in the third she holds it in front of her face when she is accused of killing his wife; and the fourth time she stuffs it in her mouth when she thinks he is accusing her of killing his son.[39] The apron serves as a means of protection for Hanne when she fears rejection; she employs this symbol of servitude to hide her face, her eyes, and her mouth. She draws it in front of her, a visible reminder of her position, whether actual or imagined, within the house, with the hope that subservience will bring a reprieve from accusations; when she expects a marriage proposal, she victoriously throws down her sign of maidhood. Here her apron functions in a more traditional role, namely to remind those of her supposed position, to reclaim innocence.

When serving, a maidservant represents her employer to outsiders who have entered the home, though in this case her mistress and master are also present; she is constantly monitored by both employer and outsider. Her uniform provides a visual marker of her position, setting her apart from her surroundings, yet at the same time, she is expected to blend in, to act more like a decoration than a part of the entertainment. Her attire however, while signifying numerous representative bourgeois values such as cleanliness, also has sexual connotations that draw the eye toward her rather than away, only highlighting the tension that often existed between the housewife and the maidservant.

Consumption

The fifth section of the Prussian Civil Code, which governs servitude, states that servants must be sufficiently fed, but nothing about the quality, frequency or type of food. And though employers generally recognized that the servants needed (and deserved) regular, balanced and edible meals, it was agreed that the employees did not have an inherent right to the same quality of food as their betters. Many critics during this period attributed the maidservant's snacking to the lack of sufficient nourishment and the intentional withholding of any extras.[40] For households in which there were multiple servants, it was common practice that a separate meal was prepared for them; however, in most households the extra effort was not worth it. In these cases the women generally received the same food their employers ate, though in controlled portions and often in the form of leftovers.[41]

Davidis addresses both sides of this debate, beginning with an attempt to set a standard for what maidservants should eat. She recognizes that some housewives, out of a desire not to be wasteful, will include spoiled meat or fat in the meals for the servants but argues that the nature of a maidservant's work requires hardier portions, and that is one of the key reasons why better food is required. Davidis then appeals to the housewife's, namely her attentiveness and efficiency, by saying that food, which some carelessly designate as feasible for maidservants to eat, should have in fact never have been allowed to get so far.[42] This does not, however, mean that employees should be permitted to eat whatever they please.

While the position of the housewife was validated in their handbooks, maidservants were told to be thankful for whatever they might receive, as it is the employer who is giving part of his own hard-earned bread to the employee. "Don't forget, others also work for us, therefore we must also gladly work for them."[43] This quote illustrates a common theme, still prevalent today, namely that housework is of secondary importance to other types of work. Though servants are integral to the well being of the family and the state of the household, their work frequently goes unrecognized and has little, if any, monetary value. Guidebooks that provide a typical day of a maidservant, in an attempt to teach time management skills, do not mention eating meals.[44] Perhaps most disturbing are some accounts that appeared in the servant newspapers about substandard food. For example "Our Page" (*Unser Blatt*) describes so-called "servant coffee" that was made from various leftover coffee beans (and dust or whatever else might be in the corners of the bins) and "servant soup" that was made from sausage casings.[45] There was also a court case in which a woman was convicted because she fed her maidservant spoiled meat that was being sold as dog food.[46]

Maidservants were responsible for purchasing and often preparing what they ate, yet the quality and quantity was dictated by their employer. Many housewives, taught the necessity of frugality, saw an easy way to save, despite calls for social equality or at least decency. Outdated, vague laws and conflicting social norms allowed this to become a popular site of punishment for actual, perceived and feared misrepresentation. Though not the only site of punishment, meals offered a frequent and consistent reminder of one's position within the delicate construction of the family, and an effective means to remind the employee of her duties as such.

Conclusion

Maidservants are located between the privacy of the nuclear family and the public sphere that surrounds and continuously threatens it. These women have responsibilities to maintain its stability and coherency even as they represent a potentially destructive access to this intimate unit. In many capacities, the maidservant serves as substitute for the housewife and a representative for the family to the public, making her position all the more precarious. The multitude of treatises, investigations, as well as fiction on the position of the maidservant around the turn of the twentieth century indicates that the issue entered a new phase in the public mind. Politicians, historians and social activists began addressing the issues surrounding the working and living conditions of maidservants more fervently. Though there were few immediate changes as a result, modernity clearly left its mark on servitude. The maidservant's increasing subjectivity, expanding notions of equality, fragile binaries and abundant paradox all led the bourgeoisie to take further measures to secure its tenuous foundation and status.

Notes

1. Gunilla-Friederike Budde, *Auf dem Weg ins Bürgerleben: Kindheit und Erziehung in deutschen und englischen Bürgerfamilien 1840-1914* (Göttingen: Vandenhoeck & Ruprecht, 1994), 25.

2. Rolf Engelsing, *Zur Sozialgeschichte deutscher Mittel- und Unterschichten* (Göttingen: Vandenhoeck & Ruprecht, 1973), 231-32.

3. Budde, *Auf dem Weg*, 276. Unlike in nearby countries, the German-speaking areas were generally poorer and therefore had fewer servants per household. I will discuss only female servants in this essay, as they were the ones who worked primarily in the home and formed a considerable percentage of the serving population.

4. This unique position of the maidservant is by no means limited to the German-speaking world. Scholars such as Jane Gallop in *The Daughter's Seduction* and Anne McClintock in *Imperial Leather*, as well as numerous others, have addressed this constellation.

5. Ute Frevert, *Women in German History. From Bourgeois Emancipation to Sexual Liberation,* trans. Stuart McKinnon-Evans (Oxford: Berg, 1989), 64.

6. Budde, *Auf dem Weg,* 25-26.

7. Wilhelm Kähler, *Gesindewesen und Gesinderecht in Deutschland* (Jena: Verlag von Gustav Fischer, 1896), 170, 176; *Allgemeines Landrecht für die Preußischen Staaten von 1794* (Frankfurt/Main: Alfred Metzner Verlag, 1970), 419-26.

8. Sibylle Meyer, *Das Theater mit der Hausarbeit. bürgerliche Representation in der Familie der wilhelminischen Zeit* (Frankfurt: Campus, 1982), 127-28.

9. Anabella Weismann, *Froh erfülle Deine Pflicht! Die Entwicklung des modernen Hausfrauenleitbildes im Spiegel trivialer Massenmedien in der Zeit zwischen Reichsgründung und Weltwirtschaftskrise* (Berlin: Schelzky & Jeep, 1989), 56-57.

10. Dirk Reinhardt, *Von der Reklame zum Marketing. Geschichte der Wirtschaftswerbung in Deutschland* (Berlin: Akademie Verlag, 1993), 180.

11. Christiane Lamberty, *Reklame in Deutschland 1890-1914. Wahrnehmung, Professionalisierung und Kritik der Wirtschaftswerbung* (Berlin: Duncker and Humbolt, 2000), 168.

12. My findings are based on the following newspapers: *Deutsche Dienstboten-Zeitung*; *Das Hauspersonal. Erstes Fachblatt für den häuslichen Beruf*; *Berliner Dienstboten-Zeitung. Zeitschrift für die Interessen des gesamten Gesindestandes*; *Im deutschen Haus*; *Unser Blatt. Zentral-Organ für die Gesamtinteressen der Angestellten des Hauses*; *Zentralorgan des Verbandes der Hausangestellten Deutschlands.* A small percentage of readers were male, but because these newspapers were for urban areas and for servants working in households, a large majority of the readers were women. The advertisements are very simple, generally consisting of the product's name and a brief description or claim about its results; if there is a picture, it is usually a small sketch of the product or someone holding it.

13. It was common for maidservants to change jobs multiple times a year. There were a large number of available jobs, and it was also common for employers to fire maidservants before going away during the summer or Christmas as a means to save money. Gertraud Zull, *Das Bild vom Dienstmädchen um die Jahrhundertwende. Eine Untersuchung der stereotypen Vorstellungen über den Charakter und die soziale Lage des städtischen weiblichen Hauspersonals* (Munich: tuduv-Verlagsgesellschaft, 1984), 149.

14. For example, in an issue of "Our Page" (*Unser Blatt*) there is an article entitled "How should our food be prepared? A Presentation by the editor Mr. Perlmann to the Aid Club for Female House Personnel." (Wie soll unsere Nahrung beschaffen sein? Vortrag des Herrn Redakteur Perlmann im Hilfsverein für weibliches Hauspersonal.) In it, he includes an extensive advertisement for various Maggi cooking products. *Unser Blatt. Zentral-Organ für die Gesamt interessen der Angestellten des Hauses. Nachrichtenblatt für alle Vereine der Dienenden.* 11 February 1900, 45.

15. Henriette Davidis, *Die Hausfrau. Praktische Anleitung zur selbständigen und sparsamen Führung des Haushalts. Eine Mitgabe für angehende Hausfrauen von Henriette Davidis*, 2nd edition (Leipzig: E. U. Seemann, 1863), 168. Maidservants were generally given only two Sundays a month off and occasionally one evening a week. This, coupled with the fact that a majority of the young women were from the countryside and new to the city, meant that they had few if any friends or acquaintances, and shopping was one of few times they had to converse with others; gossip was indubitably exchanged.

16. Henriette Davidis, *Die Hausfrau. Praktische Anleitung zur selbständigen und sparsamen Führung des Haushaltes. Eine Mitgabe für angehende Hausfrauen von Henriette Davidis. Neue vollständig durchgearbeitete Ausgabe von Elisabeth Schmitz*, 2nd edition (Regensburg: Verlag von J. Habbel, 1911), 64-65. It is interesting to note that this comment is not present in the 1863 edition, which implies that this "problem" became more prevalent during the second half of the nineteenth century.

17. Emy Gordon, *Die Pflichten eines Dienstmädchens, oder: Das A-B-C des Haushaltes* (Donauwörth: L. Auer, 1893), 18.

18. Ernst Georgy, *Über die Berliner Dienstboten*, volume 2 in *Die Berliner Range* (Berlin: Verlag von Rich. Bong, 1900), 57. All translations are my own.

19. Clara Viebig, *Das tägliche Brot* (Berlin: Egon Fleischel & Co., 1904).

20. Gordon, *Die Pflichten*, 13.

21. Though the stove's heat is listed as the primary cause, later in the article he includes others that indicate that the servant, and possibly the housewife, is also at fault. Dr. F's almost laughable list of causes includes premenopause, unhappy love affairs, and the constantly changing desires of the housewife, as well as the standing and eating habits associated with the profession. "Der Küchenkoller. Eine sozial-medicinische Studie von Dr. Leopold F. in Berlin." *Deutsche Medizinische Wochenschrift. Mit Berücksichtigung des deutschen Medicinalwe-*

sens nach amtlichen Mittheilungen, der öffentlichen Gesundheitspflege und der Interessen des ärztlichen Standes, 26, no. 10 (March 1900): 168.

22. "Der Küchenkoller," 167.

23. The doctor does not give his full name, though this does not seem to have been common practice in this journal.

24. "Der Küchenkoller," 167.

25. In contemporary American culture the figure of the sexy French maid is still prevalent, as can be seen in anything from television advertisements to women's lingerie; she wears a modified version of this same uniform.

26. Elke Gaugele and Susanne Helitosch, "Weiß beschürzt. Zur Sprache der Dienstmädchenkleidung," in Gut behütet, streng bewacht. Tübinger Dienstmädchen nach der Jahrhundertwende, eds. Karin Priem and Edda Rosenfeld (Tübingen: Kulturamt, 1992), 110.

27. Gaugele and Heliotsch, "Weiß beschürzt," 111.

28. Gaugele and Heliotsch, "Weiß beschürzt," 115-117.

29. Gordon, Die Pflichten, 104.

30. Sophie Scheibler, Allgemeines deutsches Kochbuch für alle Stände. Ein entbehrliches Handbuch für Hausfrauen, Haushälterinnen und Köchinnen, 38th edition, (Leipzig: C.F. Amelangs Verlag, 1903), 536.

31. Grauenhorst, Katechismus, 20-21.

32. Scheibler, Allgemeines deutsches Kochbuch, 536; Gordon, Die Pflichten, 48.

33. Gaugele and Heliotsch, "Weiß beschürzt," 120.

34. Elke Gaugele, Schurz und Schürze. Kleidung als Medium der Geschlechterkonstruktion (Köln: Böhlau Verlag, 2002), 207.

35. Erna Grauenhorst, Katechismus für das feine Haus- und Stubenmädchen. Ein Lehrbuch in Fragen und Antworten über sämtliche Arbeiten im herrschaftlichen Haushalte von Frau Erna Grauenhorst, Vorsteherin der Hausmädchenschule des Fröbel-Oberlin-Vereins in Berlin (Berlin: Fröbel-Oberlin-Verlag, 1910), 69.

36. The following are located in the Austrian National Library: Der Spennadelstich eines Stubenmädchens an den Verfasser der Schrift über die Stubenmädchen in Wien. (Prague: bei Johann Ferdinand Edlen von Schönfeld, 1781); Dem Verfasser des Büchels über die Stubenmädchen: Etwas auf die Nase. Von Theresia W. einem Stübenmädchen in Wien. (Vienna: in der von Ghelenschen Buchhandlung, 1781); Ein Stubenmädchen als Strafpredigerin des Autors über die Stubenmädchen in Wien. (Vienna: Gerold. Buchhandlung, 1781); Johann Rautenstrauch, Schutzschrift der gekränkten Stubenmädchen in Wien. Vienna: Hartl, 1781).

37. Rautenstrauch, Johann. Über die Stubenmädchen in Wien (Vienna: Sebastian Hartl, 1781), 7.

38. Rautenstrauch, Über die Stubenmädchen, 7-8.

39. Gerhart Hauptmann, "Führmann Henschel" in volume 1 of *Sämtliche Werke*, ed. Hans-Egon Hass (Frankfurt/Main: Verlag Ullstein, 1966), 918, 930, 982, 986.

40. Snacking (*naschen*) had been considered a bad habit amongst maidservants for centuries. In Viebig's novel there is a scene in which a maidservant is caught by the son of the family breaking into a cabinet where leftovers are stored because she is underfed; he demands sex for his silence. Viebig, *Das tägliche Brot*, 196-98.

41. Gertraud Zull, *Das Bild vom Dienstmädchen*, 163-64.

42. Davidis, *Die Hausfrau*, 181.

43. Joseph Drieselmann, *Das goldene A, B, C. Ein Wegweiser für angehende Dienstmädchen zu einem nützlichen, zufriedenen und glücklichen Leben. Ein Anhang zu jedem Lesebuch für Oberklassen der Volksmädchenschulen, und ein Schriftchen zur Vertheilung an angehende Dienstmädchen* (Erfurt: Verlag von G. W. Körner, 1852), 8.

44. Grauenhorst, *Katechismus*, 66; *Das tüchtige Dienstmädchen gute Führung und Leistung im Hause* (Berlin: Verlag der Hauswirtschaftlichen Volksbibliothek, 1896), 45.

45. *Unser Blatt. Zentral-Organ für die gesamt Interessen der Angestellten des Hauses. Nachrichtenblatt für alle Vereine der Dienenden*, 13 May 1900, 148. The report is based on recipe requests from housewives that appeared in the newspaper "For the House" (*Fürs Haus*) a few weeks previous.

46. *Zentralorgan des Verbandes der Hausangestellten Deutschlands* 7, no. 5 (May 1915): 17. This appears to be one of the few times that the courts stepped in, and also occurred after some areas had begun to change the laws governing servitude.

Part II

Victorian Spectacles of Consumption

Pot-Bellied Salt-Cellars and Talking Plates:
Fetishism and Signification in *Our Mutual Friend*

Andy Williams

The opulent abodes of the "society" characters that make up the social circle of the nouveau-riche Veneerings in *Our Mutual Friend* are as much shrines to the commodity fetish as they are places of residence. In the bazaars and emporia of mid-century London, the arrangement and display of commodities was becoming increasingly important. Images of commodities, and the spectacle of their display, were becoming equally, if not more, significant than their use values. In the novel the Veneering house is often described as a business, and the Veneerings as the owners of an 'establishment'.[1] They are disdainfully treated as landlord and landlady by those who consume at their expense, but the way that their guests see them and their house also evokes the growing fashion for visiting the new stores to take in the displays of novelty and luxury goods. This sense is emphasized by Veneering's self-conscious display of his 'bran-new' commodities. When the geriatric Lady Tippins is canvassing support for Veneering's impending entry into Parliament (he buys membership of the Commons in the same way that he buys his belongings and the social status they connote), it is fitting that she describes him with reference to the tasteless opulence of his interior décor. As if inviting her friend to take a turn in a fashionable shop, she urges her to dine with the Veneerings in order to experience his displays of tasteless consumer goods: "'Come and dine with 'em,' she implores, 'you really ought to see their gold and silver camels. I call their dinner-table, the Caravan'."[2]

Early in the novel the Veneerings are introduced in terms of a description of their house and a list of their belongings, rather than with any real reference to their human traits.

> All their furniture was new, all their friends were new, all their servants were new, their plate was new, their carriage was new, their harness was new, their horses were new, their pictures were new, they themselves were new, they were as newly married as was lawfully compatible with their having a bran-new baby, and if they had set up a great-grandfather, he would have come home in matting from the Pantechnicon, without a scratch upon him, French polished to the crown of his head.[3]

The mention of the Pantechnicon, a Belgravia bazaar that sold all manner of fashionable consumer goods, draws a parallel between the Veneerings' Stucconia residence and the popular palaces of consumption. Even more consequential is the rhetorical slippage between the commodities and the human beings listed here. In the same list the reader encounters not only furniture, plate, a carriage, and pictures, but also servants, friends, a baby, and the Veneerings themselves. This is the first paragraph in which the reader encounters the Veneerings, and it introduces a textual strategy that recurs throughout the novel. In the playful prose that describes the society characters, humans are frequently described as though they were inanimate objects, and commodities are often figured as living things.

This textual tactic is clearest in this passage when the hypothetical great-grandfather is evoked. Its proximity in the text to the bran-new baby suggests that the great-grandfather might well be someone the pair had considered "setting up" in order to lend gravity to the family scene that they had fabricated. The Veneering baby is used by its parents as little more than a prop in their dealings with society. The cultural sign of their parenthood, it is often used by Mrs Veneering to cultivate a vacuous image of herself as a loving parent.[4] This function is emphasized by the fact that it remains unnamed throughout. When it is not being referred to simply as "baby", it is ironically objectified by the narrator, who describes it as an "article."[5] It is entirely within the Veneerings' capability to employ an elderly man whom they could produce at dinner parties in much the same way that Mrs Veneering uses her baby to gain emotional capital in conversations with guests. The curious mixture of animate and inanimate in this list, however, makes it impossible to tell whether the text is referring to a person or a grandfather clock (an item which could have been plausibly bought in the Pantechnicon).

This ambiguity creates the impression that within the Veneering establishment, humans occupy the same textual space and fulfill the same function as signifying commodities. The hybrid object/subject status of the French-polished great-grandfather retrospectively commodifies the other people on the list, be they friends, servants, or the baby. Shortly after this passage, one encounters an extension of this textual play: "There was an innocent piece of dinner-furniture that went upon easy castors and was kept over a livery stable-yard in Duke Street, Saint James's, when not in use [. . .]. The name of this article was Twemlow."[6] Fulfilling a similar position to the great-grandfather, Twemlow is explicitly figured as a piece of furniture. Like the dinner set made in the shape of a train of gold and silver camels that treks across the Veneering dinner table, he is little more than an object[7] to be displayed to connote the status of his hosts. Twemlow, continues the narrator, "being first cousin to Lord Snigsworth,[. . .] was in frequent requisition, and [. . .] might be said to represent the dining-table in its normal state":

> Mr and Mrs Veneering, [when] arranging a dinner, habitually started with Twemlow, and then put leaves in him, or added guests to him. Sometimes, the table consisted of Twemlow and half a dozen leaves; sometimes, of Twemlow and a dozen leaves; sometimes, Twemlow was pulled out to his utmost extent of twenty leaves.[8]

The narrator here avoids metaphor, preferring instead a form of proto-surreal reification. The minor aristocrat actually becomes part of the Veneerings' highly significant furniture. He circulates as a value in the Veneering household, one commodity among many.

Twemlow is not the only character to receive such treatment. Georgiana Podsnap, the daughter of the self-important Mr. Podsnap, is treated much like a commodity in that she is only wanted by the scheming Lammles for her value in exchange, when she is on the brink of "being sold into wretchedness for life" to the unscrupulous Fledgeby.[9] To her father she is just one possession amongst many, who can be "put away like the plate, brought out like the plate, polished like the plate, counted, weighed and valued like the plate".[10] Almost all of those who enter the Veneerings' sphere of influence are objectified and commodified in similar ways. By the end of the novel Veneering's "intimate friends" are not even introduced by name. "These friends, like astronomical distances, are only to be spoken of in the very largest figures".[11] One is a contractor who "gives employment, directly and indirectly, to five hundred thousand men"; another is a chairman who works on so many boards that "he never travels less by railway than three thousand miles a week"; another is a speculator in shares who has made "three hundred and seventy-five thousand pounds" in eighteen months.[12] These characters exist in the Veneering dinner parties with no other identity than a figure which connotes their economic value. Stripped of their individual histories, they too circulate as abstract values.

The ghoulish old Lady Tippins comes in for similar treatment. She is a woman almost entirely composed of expensive millinery and beauty products. As she turns up at the Lammles' wedding, it is said of her:

> Whereabout in the bonnet and drapery announced by her name, any fragment of the real woman may be concealed, is perhaps known to her maid; but you could easily buy all you see of her, in Bond Street; or you might scalp her, and peel her, and scrape her, and make two Lady Tippinses out of her, and yet not penetrate to the genuine article.[13]

Any "genuine" self or "fragment of the real" that might still exist is lost beneath the layers of commodities that constitute her. It is unsurprising that, when a Veneering party is seen through her eyes, she is only able to account for the guests with reference to the clothes and accessories they wear. Her description of the wedding reads like the contemporary catalogues of goods used by the shops to advertise their wares.

> Bride; five-and-forty if a day, thirty shillings a yard, veil fifteen pound, pocket handkerchief a present. Bridesmaids; kept down for fear of outshining bride, consequently not girls, twelve and sixpence a yard, Veneering's flowers, snub-nosed one rather pretty but too conscious of her stockings, bonnets three pound ten.[. . .] Mrs Veneering; never saw such velvet, say two thousand pounds as she stands, absolute jeweler's window, father must have been a pawnbroker, or how could these people do it?[14]

These people are seen to live out their lives and their relations with each other in terms of the signifying commodity form. This anatomy of Victorian consumer-bodies is another instance of the way that wealthy characters are objectified and commodified in the novel.

Further, *Our Mutual Friend* is a novel that is full of animated consumer goods. The houses of the "society" characters are full of objects that seem to come alive. In fact, it could be said that one of the novel's organizing tropes is that the people are commodified and objectified, while the commodities that surround them are described as if they were living, acting, subjects. The first such case is the example of Mr. Podsnap's plate. The first time Mr. Podsnap is introduced, the reader is given more information about his "hideously solid" plate than about the man himself. His ugly crockery is even given a voice of its own. "Everything said boastfully, "here you have as much of me in my ugliness as if I were only lead; but I am so many ounces of precious metal worth so much an ounce; – wouldn't you like to melt me down?[15] This, however, is just the beginning of its anthropomorphic adventure. As Podsnap's guests sit around the dinner-table talking their usual mix of inane nonsense and mindless gossip, the dinner set holds an alternative parallel dinner party. A "corpulent straddling epergne" takes the role of the host, and is clearly meant to resemble the portly Podsnap. "Blotched all over as if it had broken out in an eruption rather than been ornamented," this hideous plate boasts about how much it is worth "from an unsightly silver platform in the centre of the table." The next humanized accoutrements to be described are "four silver wine-coolers, each furnished with four staring heads, each head obtrusively carrying a big silver ring in each of its ears." These ornate "dinner guests" serve the purpose of conveying the sentiments of the large plate "up and down the table," and handing them on to the "pot-bellied silver salt-cellars." The salt-cellars in turn pass on the message to the enormous silver cutlery, which "widened the mouths of the company expressly for the purpose of thrusting the sentiment down their throats with every morsel they ate." This small scene, in which household items come alive in order to hold forth to each other, and to the real dinner guests, on their value as commodities, is important for the way that it incorporates both of the textual phenomena I have identified. Consumer objects are quite clearly animated here, in order to satirize middle-class consumer culture. But also, by inviting the comparison between these objects and the people they mimic, the human characters (all bourgeois consumers) are objectified. A little later we read that, "The majority of the guests were like the plate, and included several heavy articles weighing ever so much."[16] I should stress that this is just one of many such instances that occur regularly, in different ways, throughout the novel.

As well as not being unique in *Our Mutual Friend*, this kind of response to Victorian commodity culture is certainly not unique amongst contemporary texts. Just two years after this serialized novel was concluded, in 1867, perhaps the most influential commentator on Victorian capitalism was to explicate his theory of the commodity with a remarkably similar textual strategy. Karl Marx, writing from his base in the same bourgeois London milieu as Dickens, began *Capital* with a description of Victorian society as "an immense accumulation of commodities."[17] Immediately one imagines the crammed shelves of the proto-department stores enticing the consumers with the spectacle of their display. This visual image is only reinforced when the text goes on to theorize the commodity more closely. "A commodity appears, at first sight, a very trivial thing, and easily understood," but "its analysis shows that it is, in reality, a very queer thing, abounding in metaphysical subtleties and theological niceties".[18] What should be a very mundane object is figured as possessing semi-religious, mystical powers. On its own, the object should not seem anything other than it is—an inanimate thing composed of the sum of its constituent parts. "It is as clear as noon-day," Marx states, "that man, in his industry, changes the forms of the materials furnished by Nature, in such a way as to make them useful to him."[19] A table is made out of wood, just like a silver epergne is made out of silver. The form of the wood or of the silver is altered, but the end product is still composed of the very same material that was there at the start of its manufacture. As soon as the product enters the marketplace, however, this is forgotten, states Marx. Talking of the table, he continues:

> So soon as it steps forth as a commodity, it is changed into something transcendent. It not only stands with its feet on the ground, but, in relation to all other commodities, it stands on its head, and evolves out of its wooden brain grotesque ideas, far more wonderful than "table turning" ever was.[20]

Like Podsnap's plate, and so many of the other animated commodities in *Our Mutual Friend*, Marx's table appears as an autonomous actor. When faced with a culture in which commodities, and representations of commodities, circulate to such an unprecedented extent, Marx's response is to argue that objects are falsely invested with a fetish value. The line of reasoning which led him to this conclusion is complex, and is worth glossing. In developed capitalist economies, argues Marx, workers are forced to sell their labor as a commodity on the market (they are literally commodified). This modern process of production alienates people from the products that they manufacture. The fragmentation in the market leads to a fragmentation in the subject. The worker is no longer the objective master of the process of production, and is, instead, a mechanical part incorporated into a dehumanized system. This not only describes the actual experience of work, but also the relationship between workers and the products of their labor. The thing that comes off the end of the assembly line feels truly alien. Likewise, in the marketplace, all the products that meet our gaze in shops, in advertisements and in other people's possession seem to gain a magical character, a life of their own.

The "mystical" or "enigmatical" character of commodities appears when a culture loses sight of the origin of these objects in human labor. "The social character of men's labour appears to them as an objective character stamped upon the product of that labour."[21] A process familiar to readers of Dickens can be discerned, then, in which humans (productive workers) are reified or commodified (as they sell their labor power), and the products of their work (commodities) appear strangely animated. As Marx put it, "a definite social relation between men [. . .] assumes [. . . the fantastic form of a relation between things." [22] Commodity fetishism, the impression that commodities are endowed with a life independent of the social process of their production, it should be emphasized, has nothing to do with what Marx calls an item's use value. An object's material qualities are unimportant. A commodity only seems to be an autonomous actor when it becomes an object of economic exchange.[23]

The shared metaphorical and rhetorical vocabularies between the Marxian and Dickensian text are striking. But can the theory of commodity fetishism be read alongside *Our Mutual Friend* in order to more fully understand its response to Victorian consumer capitalism? In a sense, both books can be seen to offer textually striking, but now fairly conventional, critiques of their commodity culture. Marx's text uses the trope of commodity-come-alive and the human-become-thing in order to lament the alienation of workers from the products of their labor and their essential humanity. Dickens's uses the same trope to criticize bourgeois consumers who were alienated from their essential humanity so much that they express their own identities, and live out their relations with each other, only through the objects that they buy and display. Marx is concerned with criticizing the realm of production, and Dickens that of consumption. Both texts go beyond the personal, and level systemic critiques at a society in which the commodity has become God. Aside from this, however, I believe that an understanding of the machinations of commodity fetishism can lead to an understanding of another, more radical, element to the novel's social analysis.

In order to tease out this other dimension of the criticism that *Our Mutual Friend* levels at commodity culture, I would like to turn briefly to another examination of Victorian fetishism. The article "Fetishes" appeared in Dickens's weekly journal *All the Year Round* in July 1864, the week before the fourth part of *Our Mutual Friend* was released, and three years before *Capital* was published. In a move similar to that of Marx, the piece starts by inverting the colonial logic of the fetish by applying it to aspects of British culture.

> What is a fetish? Generally a bundle of rags, a mass of rubbish, a muttered charm [. . . .] Out of these materials the poor benighted savages, on whom we spend millions to bring them a clearer sense of truth, make a something which thenceforth rules their lives and determines their actions [. . . .] We laugh at their fetishes, but are our own much better? Analyze them, and I think we shall come to rags, rubbish [*and*] a muttered charm of words [. . .] as making up most of them.[24]

It then turns to a number of spheres of nineteenth-century bourgeois life to examine examples of very British fetishes. By far the largest portion of these concerns examples from the world of fashion and consumer culture. "Why must my wife spend a sum of pounds upon a length of silk which she puts over her gown proper, behind, and which the great art is to let trail on the ground like a Peacock's tail?", he asks. And "why should she uncover those dear old shoulders of hers to the pitiless light of day and the more pitiless eyes of the court? Why must she run the risk of catching cold by changing her comfortable ribbed merino stockings and rational hose boots, for the thinnest silk and satin?" He continues:

> What inherent virtue is there in one cut of cloth more than in another? [. . .] Imagine Aspasia in ionic chiton and graceful, saffron coloured peplum falling to her heels, walking down Pall Mall with head uncovered and rosy feet—a trifle spread, we should say—shod in sandals! What would all the clubs say to this rebel against the ruling fetish? There are men in those clubs who would face a Balaclava charge without wincing, but I doubt if any one among them would give Aspasia his arm. Still less would he give it to the noblest woman now living on this earth, if she had made herself up in a tunic and "pantalets", and walked abroad as a full-fledged Bloomer, disdainful of lengths of silk.[25]

So what is a fetish for the narrator of this article? As it is for Marx, it is an object bestowed with strange powers of fascination which are not integral to it, and have nothing to do with the materials of which it was composed. It is also a manufactured item, an article of consumption. Its perceived powers, however, do not have their origins in any alienation from the object during production. They are on the surface of the object, and their purpose is to perpetuate cycles of consumption and display.

The narrator of this article states that a fetish consists of the material object, plus "a muttered charm."[26] Its fetish character rests on the shared *meanings* associated with material objects. "Fetishes" states the speaker in the article, "are all ordinations [. . .] which are assumed to make a man better than before. Not by virtue of his truth and goodness [. . .] but by virtue of the charm − by the grace of a *verbal* fetish."[27] The daring Aspasia would be an outcast because her outlandish dress does not *signify* her femininity in an acceptable way. The "powers" bestowed upon objects, according to this article, have everything to do with how and what they *mean* within systems of signification. Crinolines are only the "right" thing to wear, implies this piece, because the indigenous dress of the "savage" and the shocking bloomers of the proto-feminist are not. In this respect, this theory of fetishism has more in common with that of the twentieth century philosopher of consumerism Jean Baudrillard than it does with that of Karl Marx.

For Baudrillard, Marx's theory of fetishism has to be questioned because it leaves no room for the way commodities circulate as signs as well as economic values. Calling it a "metaphysic of alienated essence," he takes issue with the way Marx ties fetishism only to exchange value, preserving use value as the true, natural, objective state of the object.[28] He argues that Marx's argument is validated by the latent essentialism involved in the naturalization of use value. For Marx, he states, "utility as such escapes the historical definition of class. It represents an objective, final relation of intrinsic purpose [. . .] whose transparency, as form, defies history."[29] The emphasis on exchange is also seen to highlight a false emphasis on the mode of production as the determining force within capitalist society, at the expense of an adequate theory of consumption.

> What else is intended by the concept of "commodity fetishism", if not the notion of a false consciousness? [. . .] All of this presupposes the existence, somewhere, of a non-alienated consciousness of an object in some "true", objective state: its use value? [. . .] The fetishistic theory of infrastructure and superstructure must be exploded.[30]

The critic here sees the use/exchange value relation as analogous to the crude Marxist interpretation of the base/superstructure model, in which all that is cultural (and therefore linked with signification) is seen as directly determined by an economic base at the heart of capitalism.[31]

From here he sets about the task of dismantling what he sees as "the conceptual fetish of a vulgar social thought", and highlighting what he sees as missing from Marx's concept of commodity fetishism.[32] He starts this with an appeal to the etymology of the word fetish. Today, and since Marx, he argues, "it refers to a force, a supernatural quality in the object" that is divorced from human influence.[33] The word originally came from the Portuguese *feitiço*, which meant "artificial." The primary sense of this was "to do," or "to make," which itself was derived from the Latin *facticius*. This attention to the historical significance of the word allows him to argue that in various languages, and from its earliest usage, the word has always connoted artifice and fabrication—in other words, he states, "a labour of appearances and signs." It is this second, older, meaning that forms the basis of his argument that a "theory of fetishism as *"the manipulation of forces"* should be substituted for one of *"a manipulation of signs,"* and a magical economy of transfer of signifieds for a regulated play of signifiers."[34] If fetishism exists, he argues, "it is a fetishism of the signifier."[35] The Marxist model of explaining the commodity fetish, then, gets in the way of understanding how objects, as they appear in commodity cultures, are conduits for the free flow of signification. Baudrillard argues that in the Marxist model an ideology of false consciousness extends through the commodity form, allowing a falsely stable and monolithic utility to act as an ideological prop, letting products circulate unhindered. However, Baudrillard argues that use value is itself produced as a sign (and is not a fundamental truth) to help keep consumption going and the consumer society in business. In the fetishized realm of consumption objects are misrecognized everywhere as being endowed with forces, like "happiness, health, security, etc."[36] We see this so much that we forget that "what we are dealing with first is signs: a generalized code of signs, a totally arbitrary code of differences, *and it is on this basis, and not on account of their use values or their innate "virtues," that objects exercise their fascination.*"[37]

Whilst *Our Mutual Friend*'s treatment of the society characters and their belongings, and of commodity culture more generally, might display some signs of a will to unmask an "alienated essence" behind the frenzy of consumption, there is no doubt that it is also aware of the systematic nature of the way commodities *signify*. When people are figured as commodities, or things seem to have strange powers in this text, there often seems to be a strange form of fetishism at work. This textual strategy often displays the way that the signifier is at work on the surface of the commodity as much as it laments the passing of an age in which human relations did not have to be mediated through consumer objects. To illustrate this I would like to return one last time to the Veneering table. A section of the text that describes the very first Veneering dinner demonstrates many of the points that I have made so far.

> The great looking-glass above the sideboard, reflects the table and the company. Reflects the new Veneering crest, in gold and eke in silver, frosted and also thawed, a camel of all work [. . .] and a caravan of camels take charge of the fruits and flowers and candles, and kneel down to be loaded with the salt. Reflects Veneering; forty, wavy-haired, dark, tending to corpulence, sly, mysterious, filmy – a kind of sufficiently well-looking veiled prophet, not prophesying. Reflects Mrs. Veneering; fair, aquiline-nosed and fingered, not so much light hair as she might have, gorgeous in raiment and jewels, enthusiastic, propitiatory, conscious that a corner of her husband's veil is over herself. Reflects Podsnap; prosperously feeding, two light-coloured wiry wings, one on either side of his else bald head, looking as like his hairbrushes as his hair, dissolving view of red beads on his forehead, large allowance of crumpled shirt-collar up behind. Reflects Mrs. Podsnap; fine woman for Professor Owen, quantity of bone, neck and nostrils like a rocking horse, hard features, majestic head-dress in which Podsnap has

hung golden offerings. Reflects Twemlow; grey, dry, polite, susceptible
to east wind, First-Gentleman-in-Europe collar and cravat [. . .]. Reflects mature young lady; raven locks, and a complexion that lights up
well when powdered – as it is – carrying on considerably in the captiva-
tion of mature young gentleman; with too much rose in his face, too
much ginger in his whiskers, too much torso in his waistcoat, too much
sparkle in his studs, his eyes, his buttons, his talk, his teeth. Reflects
charming old Lady Tippins on Veneering's right; with an immense ob-
tuse drab oblong face, like a face in a tablespoon, and a dyed long walk
up the top of her head, as a convenient public approach to the bunch of
false air behind.[38]

I quote this passage at length and uninterrupted so that its sheer scale can
be fully appreciated. It starts with some familiar animated fetishized objects, as the train of camels is brought to life, trekking across the over-
sized table, stooping to pick up food along the way. This soon blends
into more reification of the human as almost every character is frag-
mented, objectified and commodified as they form part of a seemingly
endless list. Human sweat is figured as jewelry, hair as hairbrushes, buttons and studs melt into the same list as teeth and eyes, a fanciful passing
description of a woman's bone structure transforms her first into dino-
saur skeleton, and then into a rocking horse. Indeed the very form and
mode of address of the passage reminds one as much of advertisements
as it does novels. This is a list, but not the kind of list that a reader of
novels usually expects. It borrows heavily from the convention of cataloguing goods that one finds so often in Victorian advertising (examples
of which abound in the "Our Mutual Friend Advertiser," the sizeable
advertising supplement that accompanied each monthly serial edition of
the novel as it was first published).

At times it is difficult to tell where the objects which adorn the people end, and the actual human subjects begin. When one reads of Lady
Tippins' false hair, Twemlow's collar and cravat, Mr. Lammle's studs
and Mrs. Veneering's jewelry, it is truly difficult to tell whether they are
the prosthetic extensions of their wearers, or whether the metonymic
process turns the people into the prostheses of the commodities. The
commodities and the people gain value as part of this differential system
of signification. Mrs. Veneering's jewels are valuable – but only in comparison with the golden offerings hung in Mrs. Podsnap's head-dress,
and the showy studs worn by Mr. Lammle.

Even the people, when described unproblematically as such, are not
truly people, but reflections of themselves, symbols in a system of symbols. They too take on value not from any essential characteristics, but
only from their relations with each other. Mrs. Veneering garners her

value from the (itself insubstantial) reflected glory of her spouse, who in turn is rendered valuable through his perceived relations with Twemlow and the obnoxious Podsnap. This passage is a perfect example of the novel's rendering of commodity fetishism. It is not simply a fetishism of alienated essence, however, it is one of the proliferation of signifiers and objects. The reader is given the sense of a virtual world of multiple and multiplying animated commodity signs as images of people and objects reflect in the mirror, and off each other, in a relay of differential play.

Notes

1. Charles Dickens, *Our Mutual Friend* (London: Penguin, 1997), 17.

2. Charles Dickens, *Our Mutual Friend*, 249.

3. Charles Dickens, *Our Mutual Friend*, 17.

4. Charles Dickens, *Our Mutual Friend*, 19, 120, 123, 248, 253, and 611.

5. Charles Dickens, *Our Mutual Friend*, 19.

6. Charles Dickens, *Our Mutual Friend*, 17.

7. Charles Dickens, *Our Mutual Friend*, 17.

8. Charles Dickens, *Our Mutual Friend*, 17.

9. Charles Dickens, *Our Mutual Friend*, 409.

10. Charles Dickens, *Our Mutual Friend*, 146.

11. Charles Dickens, *Our Mutual Friend*, 610.

12. Charles Dickens, *Our Mutual Friend*, 610.

13. Charles Dickens, *Our Mutual Friend*, 122.

14. Charles Dickens, *Our Mutual Friend*, 123.

15. Charles Dickens, *Our Mutual Friend*, 135.

16. Charles Dickens, *Our Mutual Friend*, 135.

17. Karl Marx, *Capital, Volume One*, in *The Marx-Engels Reader*, ed. Robert C Tucker (New York: Norton, 1978), 302-3.

18. Karl Marx, *Capital*, 319.

19. Karl Marx, *Capital*, 319-20.

20. Karl Marx, *Capital*, 320.

21. Karl Marx, *Capital*, 320.

22. Karl Marx, *Capital*, 321.

23. Karl Marx, *Capital*, 322.

24. 'Fetishes', *All The Year Round*, 11 (1864): 569.

25. 'Fetishes', 571.

26. 'Fetishes', 569.

27. 'Fetishes', 572 (my emphasis).

28. Jean Baudrillard, *For a Critique of the Political Economy of the Sign*, trans. Charles Levin (St Louis: Telos, 1981), 91.

29. Jean Baudrillard, *Critique*, 130.

30. Jean Baudrillard, *Critique*, 89-90.

31. It could be argued that what Baudrillard is doing here, in trying to solve the base/superstructure problem, is merely extending the superstructure all the way down, and completely excising the economic last instance in the process. Due to the parallels between political economy and signification, this would have alarming ramifications on his theory of representation, amounting to a denial of any materially existing real world at all. This is not, however, what he is doing. His attention to signs and the signifier does not equate to a denial of materiality. On the contrary, he would want to view the 'representational', or the 'ideological' sphere of signification, as a material productive force. Instead of doing away with the material, and arguing that signs are all that there is, he wants to argue for the materiality of the signifier itself.

32. Jean Baudrillard, *Critique*, 88.

33. Jean Baudrillard, *Critique*, 91.

34. Jean Baudrillard, *Critique*, 91. Again, I would like to caution against Baudrillard's use of the term 'signified' in this context, and suggest instead its substitution for the term 'referent'. I believe that at times Baudrillard confuses the difference between these two terms, often to the extent of using them interchangeably.

35. Jean Baudrillard, *Critique*, 92.

36. Jean Baudrillard, *Critique*, 91.

37. Jean Baudrillard, *Critique*, 91. There is a sense in which Baudrillard's dismissal of Marx is sometimes a little too vehement. At various points in his analysis he seems to rebuke the Victorian thinker for not being poststructuralist enough, not theorizing the sign, and not concentrating on the importance of consumption enough, all of which seem a little unfair. If one filters out these vehement rhetorical flourishes, it is possible to see Baudrillard's engagement with Marx as a fruitful and nuanced dialogue rather than a simple blustering dismissal.

38. Charles Dickens, *Our Mutual Friend*, 21.

Eating in the Contact Zone: Food and Identity in Anglo-India

Helen Pike Bauer

Among the many adjustments demanded of the English when they went out to India was their acclimation to new foods and new methods of preparation. In both their resistance to and adoption of new culinary norms, one can see the struggles of these men and women to construct an Anglo-Indian identity. Food may begin as a form of security; consuming the familiar reinforces one's sense of a persistent personality and set of values. But replicating an English diet and pattern of meals often proved both difficult and unhealthy. Those Anglo-Indians who learned to prefer fresh local ingredients to tinned imports from England, who learned about the herbs available in the bazaar, about the advantages of keeping their own animals for meat and milk developed a diet that was neither English nor Indian, but Anglo-Indian. Food became a means of both ethnographic education and self-definition. One can trace in the cookbooks, fiction, and diaries of the late nineteenth- and early twentieth-centuries the struggles of Anglo-Indians to develop a knowledge of the indigenous culture and to maintain, at the same time, a sense of self.

Many Anglo-Indians seemed loath to give up their old eating habits. But the environmental conditions demanded adjustments, and the cookbooks of the period served a function beyond that of merely providing recipes. They take a stance toward Anglo-Indian culture, educating and advising their readers about food, its preparation, its service, the staff that buys and cooks it, the prices of food and the wages expected, and move on to the refinements of class distinctions and race relations. Issues of food may be central, but their significance widens in these books. To be sure, the power created by a knowledge of local material life can become a way of defining oneself as different and superior. In a very few cases, however, the familiarity with both Indian custom and the economic conditions and spiritual practices that give rise to it becomes an entrance into a wider knowledge that is more than just an assertion of distinction. Constructing the Anglo-Indian diet, then, becomes a method of creating an identity and a critical stage in the larger education demanded of the English in India.

As David Burton, in *The Raj at Table: A Culinary History of the British in India*, points out, nineteenth-century Anglo-Indians differed from their predecessors in important ways.[1] The earliest English settlers, members of the East India Company, had become increasingly at home in India as their wealth and power grew. They had arrived alone, without wives or families, and, in time, their radical social independence allowed them to assimilate more easily to Indian life. They wore Indian-style clothes at home, took Indian mistresses and ate Indian food. By the beginning of the nineteenth century, however, political pressures drew many back to an English way of life. The Governor-General, Lord Wellesley, who assumed office in 1794, was more socially conservative and expected the same attitude from his countrymen. And the Indian Mutiny of 1857 and the subsequent rule of India directly by the Queen and her representatives profoundly altered the relationship between Indians and Anglo-Indians. The revolt and the reprisals created a keener sense of solidarity among the Anglo-Indians and rigidified their sense of superiority over Indians. English women were encouraged to travel to India either to marry or to join their husbands; the larger presence of Anglo-Indian women created a deeper family structure and further altered the social dynamic.[2]

Many of the mid-century arrivals tried to affirm their Englishness by replicating their familiar English diet. And novels set in mid-century are filled with descriptions of the kinds of meals consumed. Flora Annie Steel's *On the Face of the Waters*, published in 1896, is set during the Mutiny. Even though her anti-heroine, Alice Gissing, prefers to live in a style in which "there was no cult of England,"[3] she still serves English meals. "It had been one of those heavy luncheons, beginning with many meats and much bottled beer, ending with much Madeira and many cigars, which sent the insurance rate for India up to war risks in those days."[4]

Indeed as the century progressed, numerous Anglo-Indian cookbooks were published with directions for procuring and cooking familiar food. Alice Gissing's menu is given material detail. In the fifth edition of the charmingly titled *Madras Cookery Book by An Old Lady-Resident*, we are told that the book, first published in 1847, has been entirely rewritten. Even the new edition, published in 1919, however, shows the kind of heavy diet that remained customary for many. Meat dominates: duck, beef, lamb, and chicken. Even "cheese macaroni" calls for beef gravy. And a sausage machine seems a necessary kitchen tool.[5] Mrs. John Gilpin's *Pakwan-ki-Kitab; Memsahib's Guide to Cookery in India*, published in 1914, presents recipes and menus that are meat-driven. Mrs. Gilpin gives ninety days of menus. Breakfasts typically have fish, meat, and cheese courses. Lunches have meat, vegetable, cheese, and dessert courses. Dinners have soup, fish, often two meat, savory, and dessert courses.[6] The fact that beef was forbidden to Hindus and that much of India was vegetarian seems inconsequential to these cookbook writers. Burton asserts that most cooks in Anglo-Indian homes were Muslim, but pork and especially bacon were common fare.[7]

But looking more closely at some of the cookbooks of the period reveals a tension between the kinds of advice given and the majority of the recipes provided. Although there is some growth in the number of recipes for what may be considered Indian food, it is the tone of the introductory essays that best reveals the complex relationship in these books between the writer and the reader. Increasingly, cookbooks and, in general, books on household management, addressed as they are to women newly arrived in India, help fashion an attitude to the domestic life, of which meal preparation becomes only the starting point. These cookbooks were written by experienced Anglo-Indians, usually, though not exclusively, women. They are introductions to the life and culture of India, to the information that novices must absorb, the appearance and the contents of the cookhouse, the servants who prepare and serve food, the kinds of food available, and the appropriate relationship between a mistress and her servants. Many contain not just a descriptive but a hortatory tone. The cookbook comes to function as a conduct manual.

In the late eighteenth and early nineteenth centuries, the Anglo-Indian woman had little direct involvement in the kitchen. She saw her role as supervisory. J. K. Stanford writes in *Ladies in the Sun: The Memsahibs' India, 1790-1860*, that in the late eighteenth- and early nineteenth-centuries, "No lady ever demeaned herself to visit the bazaar and buy her own food. She left that entirely to her native cook, for to enter and bargain in the meat or fish stall, quite apart from the smell, was 'bad for the prestige.' . . . Nor did they ever enter their back premises, the 'cook houses' in which their viands were prepared."[8] Anglo-Indian women took little control over the kitchen's sanitation. As Stanford concludes about the relationship between the mistress and the cook, "No mem-sahib ever poked her nose too closely into his methods and it was folly to be too wise about them."[9]

But as the nineteenth century progressed, and the number of memsahibs grew, they were encouraged to know more about how their households were run and to take more direct responsibility for the products that emerged from the kitchen. The anonymous author of *Dainty Dishes for Indian Tables* maintains that the second edition of her book, published in 1881, will contain two new chapters, one on curries, one on pelaus, suggesting some new interests of her readers, though most of the recipes are for English or French food, for roast meats, sauced vegetables, and chilled desserts. But her advice to women supervising kitchens introduces the delicate questions of dealing with servants. You may find that your cook will make some extra money for himself, she says, by buying the full amount of the ingredients needed for a dish but using only half. This is a problem that needs tact; it is best not to confront the cook and create domestic dissension. Give him more money than is needed for his shopping. "It will be wise to allow him a certain latitude in the matter of prices, which will leave him at liberty to do justice to the recipe."[10] Many of these cookbooks balance the injunction to supervise the household staff with the necessity for tolerant management, for making allowances for Indian custom or for acknowledging the poverty of a servant's family. Anglo-Indian women unused to Indian culture need guidance in the ways of behaving in that most immediate site of the complexity of race relations, the kitchen.

Colonel Arthur Robert Kenney-Herbert, under the pen name "Wyvern," wrote cooking columns for the *Madras Atheneum* and the *Daily News*. In 1878, Kenney-Herbert published his work in book form, titling it *Culinary Jottings for Madras, or a Treatise in Thirty Chapters on Reformed Cookery for Anglo-Indian Exiles*. Kenney-Herbert believes he is giving not merely cooking advice, but advice on how to live. "Unless amicable relations exist between the cook and his mistress or master, the work will never be carried out satisfactorily."[11] He addresses the placement of the kitchen, the kinds of utensils needed and the treatment of the staff. These are not technical matters. "Giving us a clear, nicely equipped room for the preparation of our food, and a kitchen, entirely separated from godowns and stabling, easily accessible from the house, and consequently continually subject to scrutiny and wholesome discipline, I think that the backbone of the evils I have spoken of would be broken, ladies would find the supervision of their domestic economy a pleasure rather than a penance, and we should be able to congratulate ourselves upon having really laid the foundation-stone of true reform at last."[12]

It is reform that many late nineteenth-century Anglo-Indian cookbooks urge. Memsahibs must take responsibility for the food being prepared, for its wholesomeness, for the balance of the diet, but must do so without being overbearing. Anglo-Indian women are being tutored in the choreography of responsibility, a complex art that many had not needed to master before they arrived in India. But now these young women must first ensure that the kitchens were clean. In *The Mem Sahibs' Book of Cookery*, A.C.S. [Angela C. Spry] writes, "A dirty kitchen is a disgrace, so let every *mem-sahib* have this part of her establishment well under her surveillance, and though her too frequent presence in the kitchen is unnecessary, yet she should make a point of visiting it periodically to see that it is kept clean and orderly."[13]

In her essay "Feeding the Imperial Appetite: Imperial Knowledge and Anglo-Indian Domesticity," Mary Procida argues that Anglo-Indian women well into the twentieth century, resisted involving themselves too closely in kitchen matters. Procida sees that refusal as a political gesture. It allowed women to assert control over the kitchen without delving too deeply into its daily work. Allowing the memsahib to supervise without participation permitted her both a distance from and a power over the work of the kitchen. Procida maintains, "The Anglo-Indian bungalow was an important site for cultural appropriation and transformation. . . . The hybrid Anglo-Indian domestic culture was intended to demonstrate the colonizers' mastery and dominance in the private arena of the empire as in the public sphere."[14] Procida argues persuasively about the balancing of roles and powers, but the cookbooks of the period, with their exhortative tone, suggests that women were being urged in a different direction, to become more knowledgeable about the minutiae of food and its preparation, and the period's literature supports this more complex picture.

In 1889, Flora Annie Steel and Grace Gardiner collaborated on an omnibus guide to establishing and running a household in India, *The Complete Indian Housekeeper and Cook*. Steel and Gardiner, two prominent and highly respected memsahibs who had made what they considered a thoroughly successful adjustment to life in India, are attempting to reproduce versions of themselves, efficient, knowledgeable women who can train and supervise an Indian staff to shop, cook, and serve meals; who can grow vegetables, keep cattle, move a household to the hills in hot weather, or, should they prefer, live bearably in the plains through scorching heat. The volume also contains over a hundred pages of recipes. And its tone suggests an uneasy mix of Empire building and respect for indigenous knowledge. The analogy between running a household and running an empire is announced early and articulates an attitude that pervades much of the literature, even if it often remains unsaid.[15]

Steel and Gardiner regularly elevate the role of the mistress and demean that of Indian servants. But relying on their Indian servants and assuming that their readers will as well, they encourage, nevertheless, a much greater intervention in kitchen matters than Procida presents as the norm. They hold high standards for the mistress and for her direct responsibility in the household. She should learn Hindustani; Anglo-Indian women were frequently criticized for their ignorance of the language. She should be familiar with the Indian names for food, herbs, and medicine. Steel and Gardiner, like many late nineteenth-century cookbook writers, provide English and Hindustani names for ingredients, cooking utensils, and weights and measures.

Moreover they recommend to the mistress that there is much to be learned from Indian culture, its intelligence in dealing with its own world, particularly the heat, and they lodge an indirect, sometimes direct, series of criticisms against English practice. It is not the Indian climate, they argue, that is to blame for newcomers' discomfort and illness; it is the English lack of common sense, their neglect of a healthy diet, appropriate dress, and moderate exercise. "We blame India for all our ailments, forgetting to accommodate our habits to its climate.[16]

Although many complain about the hygiene of the kitchen, Steel and Gardiner find that, here too, the memsahib has something to learn from the Indian. "There can be little doubt that the complicated ceremonies which ensure a certain isolation and technical purity to the high-caste natives at meal times are based on the hygienic benefit of a scrupulous horror of contamination. The Westerners might well follow the East in this respect."[17] The authors ignore the religious beliefs that command such distinctions, but they acknowledge in their very limited way, the superiority of Indian culture.

They also mock Anglo-Indian practices. They emphasize the deleterious effects of heavy eating; they poke fun at those who ask their servants to create fantastic ice-cream confections in an environment where the result cannot gel. They urge memsahibs to use the fresh ingredients available in the bazaar, in fact, to visit the bazaar and become acquainted with its offerings, to keep their own cows in order to insure fresh milk and their own poultry for fresh eggs.

This complex work, promoting the Raj and recognizing, sometimes grudgingly, the worth of the people it rules, was a direct challenge to Anglo-Indian women. The successful housewife in India must have not only intelligence, organizational skill, and resourcefulness; she must have local knowledge and tact. And the arena where many of these strengths are developed and tested is the kitchen. In devising a diet for her family, supervising, and, at times, taking part in the buying or raising of the ingredients, in monitoring the preparation and service, the memsahib must take direct participatory responsibility. Cooking and eating become methods of identity building.

In their recipes these cookbooks take one of two approaches toward incorporating Indian food into the diet. Some address the issue directly, extolling the benefits of fresh fish and vegetables, giving advice about the kinds of fish available in India, for example, or the Indian names for familiar food. In some cases, Indian names are used exclusively, as if the memsahib is already familiar with the words. Steel and Gardiner begin a chapter on fish recipes with an admonition, "There are many good Indian fishes, so it is a mistake to despise them."[18] They classify the fish and give numerous recipes for their use. They encourage their readers to learn to cook Indian vegetables and fruits, using methods of preparation appropriate to these new foods. "Indian vegetables are often called insipid, but the fault lies chiefly in the disgraceful way in which they are cooked," that is, they are all boiled together instead of separately.[19]

Kenney-Herbert considers the issue of salads, a course that was just becoming popular in England. "There can be no doubt whatsoever that this method of dressing raw vegetables, if correctly done, is wholesome, and a singularly commendable staple for people who live in hot climates."[20] He suggests a variety of salad ingredients, supplementing the familiar lettuce, onions, and tomatoes with Indian vegetables "young brinjals, the molley-keeray, bandicai."[21] And he summarizes his approach,; "a careful study, then, of what we can do in India in this branch of cookery, is worthy of everyman's attention."[22]

But often these cookbooks simply add indigenous ingredients without comment, quietly mixing such English recipes as those for roast duck, lamb, and chicken with those for hump, the salted hump of an Indian ox.[23] One cookbook urges the reader to make sure ingredients are fresh, and lists cocoanuts, green chilies, green ginger, and limes as examples.[24] Another gives a long list of different curry mixes, for example Madras Dry Curry, Fish Curry, Beef Curry, without any suggestion that these are not ingredients in a daily diet.[25] In *Pakwan-ki-kitab*, Mrs. Gilpin states her principle, "to use the materials at hand."[26] This recognition of the ready availability of fresh food and the explication of the ways it can be incorporated into a meal demonstrate the subtle movement of the Anglo-Indian diet from the familiar to a taste for new ingredients.

It is perhaps in the fiction of the period that we best see the tensions between the different roles the memsahib must play, the different demands on her ingenuity, and the different responses engendered. Irony can play lightly over reported dialogue, and the presence of a narrator, who is often herself a memsahib, adds a further voice, perspective, and complexity. Cookbooks can give advice, and their tone can suggest how deeply this advice is needed, but fiction, imaginatively recreating the disputes, is revealing, especially when it is written by an Anglo-Indian woman.

One such writer is Sara Jeannette Duncan; in *Set in Authority*, she depicts the lives of early twentieth-century Anglo-Indians in a provincial town in the plains. Many of the scenes take place at private dinners, public receptions, domestic breakfasts, at places where food is consumed and often spoken of. As the women gather at the close of a dinner party, the conversation ranges from their children sent abroad to the price of a saddle of mutton. These women complain about what their cooks claim to pay at the market, but they themselves will not go to bargain, and they look with some distaste at anyone who does. If encouraged to do so, they recoil. One woman, not present, claims to pay far less than they. She is quoted. " 'My dear,' she said, 'it's simple *robbery*. All I ask you to do is to go one day to the market yourself—I'll take you—and we'll get the best saddle in Pilaghur for seven-eight.' Well, I suppose I was lazy but we never went.'"[27] Such conversations, about the price and quality of food, about the advisability of intervening in the cook's domain, of mixing too freely in the Indian markets, are common in the novels.

Duncan's novel *The Simple Adventures of a Memsahib* gives a rich portrait of the education of an English bride just arrived in India. Helen Browne's attempts to manage her household, its furnishings, its servants, its meals, becomes her method of learning the cultural norms of her new home. Helen's husband gives her advice about where and where not to buy their tinned food. In her travels with George to the hills, Helen learns the culinary frugalities of camp life. But her first experience in her new home is to be introduced to the servants. And it is in her dealings with her cook that Helen develops a knowledge of the intricacies of running a household and creates her new persona of a memsahib. She inspect the cookhouse, criticizing its lack of cleanliness. She protests against what she considers an exorbitant price for eggs. Finally, she visits the bazaar, becomes acquainted with its practices, asserts her knowledge of appropriate prices, and, in general, establishes her domestic authority through her knowledge of local culture. But Helen never fully succeeds in mastering her household. She never learns Hindustani and cannot speak with her servants, so when great difficulties arise, she turns them over to her husband.[28]

The intricate details of food and drink, however, portray the experiences of a young woman learning the life of her new home yet desiring to replicate elements of her old. What makes this novel particularly remarkable, however, is its lightly fictionalized narrator, an older, accomplished memsahib on the verge of retiring to England. She looks affectionately at Helen who is trying to negotiate an identity in this new world.

But the narrator sees the limitations and false steps. Helen and George arrive by train in Lucknow, once the scene of the great siege during the Mutiny. But the Brownes are annoyed because there is no ice for their drinks. The narrator remarks, "Lucknow, with her tragedy still upon her lips . . . —and the Brownes' bitter complaint of Lucknow was that they found no ice there! Ah, little Brownes! I write this of you more in sorrow than in anger."[29]

But the Brownes do learn some of the material manifestations of the spiritual beliefs of Indians. Traveling up through the hills on ponies, they stop at a little village to eat the lunch they had brought along, but must ask for milk. Milk is readily available, but the Brownes cannot be allowed to drink from the cups of the villagers. To allow a Christian to do so would be to defile the cups. "The outcast sahib bought a new little earthen pot for a pice, breaking it solemnly on a stone when they had finished; and even mixed with the taste of fired mud the buffaloes' milk was ambrosial."[30]

Helen Browne must learn not only those Indian ingredients that she can use, not only to supervise a cooking staff, that is, not only how to appropriate Indian food for her own use; she must learn the prohibitions of the indigenous culture, the ways in which she cannot consume, either literally or figuratively, the world she has entered. Such attention to, respect for Hindu or Muslim beliefs and practices is rare in the fiction of the late nineteenth- and early twentieth-centuries. Duncan allows us a few moments in her novels when her more sensitive characters become aware that, in their thoughtless eating and drinking, they are on the verge of moral violation.

Such a lesson was difficult for Anglo-Indians to learn. Even when they understood the caste structure, they could rarely accept it as they easily did the class structure in England. In 1883, Nora Scott went to Bombay to join her husband, who had recently been appointed to the High Court of Bombay. Over the next six years, she wrote a daily journal which she would send as a letter each week to her parents in England; they shared it with other family members and friends. Scott's journal was written as an immediate reflection on the day's activities but was also written to those for whom her life was distant and strange. This mixed composition, a diary and a letter, written soon after the day's events and read months later, devised in the intimate style of a journal and yet destined to be read by many others, presents Scott's education in Indian culture. She was no novice to living abroad; she had spent the preceding ten years in Egypt, where her husband had served as a judge.[31]

But Scott finds India more difficult to understand than Egypt. Her journal reveals an intelligent, experienced woman who still struggles with her new life. Much of the journal dwells not on the food she eats at home but on her visits to take meals in Indian households. With tact and a sense of humor, she reports the bafflement and unease she frequently experiences, particularly over caste strictures about eating food prepared by others.

She recounts a conversation between a friend, Mr. Ruith, and one of his servants. They are discussing two acquaintances. "He asked his servant what caste one of them was—'Oh, he is low caste, he will eat meat.' 'What is that man?' said Mr. Ruith, pointing to the other. 'Oh, he is very low—lowest of all.' 'What does he eat then?' 'Oh, he eats what the sahib does,' indicating Mr. Ruith himself!" (4). Ruith's consternation and Scott's bemusement are both apparent.[32] Scott herself experiences on a number of occasions, however, the effects of caste. She comes to the aid of a young Indian girl who has been beaten. "She was trembling all over, but able to walk and speak to us. Pedro [Scott's servant] has given her some food, and she has cooked it for herself. When I offered her some tea, she shook her head. She could not drink or eat anything prepared by our hand—she was too high caste for that."[33] Scott's journal, in numerous small anecdotes, demonstrates the other side of adjusting to food in India. The Anglo-Indian must learn the customs, the spiritual restrictions, that create prohibitions, that diminish the sense of superiority bred in the Anglo-Indian community and accept, for a moment at least, his or her place in the Indian structure.

But there are few scenes such as this in Anglo-Indian writing, whether journals, fiction, or cookbooks. The English in India assumed their superiority, and their identity was ratified continually by both the public and private world of the Raj. And yet they were forced to make adjustments, and in time they acclimated themselves to new customs and to new food. Cookbooks often functioned to show them the way. Fiction dramatizes the stages of their struggle to integrate themselves without losing their difference from the larger Indian world, without being consumed by the culture they had come to rule. By appropriating indigenous food to their own ends, Anglo-Indians could assert their power. But their position was as hybrid as the name they gave themselves. Their diet, finally, became a mark of their never fully successful adjustment.

Notes

1. David Burton, *The Raj at Table: A Culinary History of the British in India* (London: Faber and Faber, 1992), 1-3.

2. Among the many studies of British social life in India during the eighteenth and nineteenth centuries, some pay particular attention to women. See especially Hilton Brown, *The Sahibs: The Life and Ways of the British in India as Recorded by Themselves* (London: W. Hodge, 1948). Dennis Kincaid, *British Social Life in India* (London: Routledge, 1938). Margaret Macmillan, *Women of the Raj* (London: Thames and Hudson, 1988). Neville Pran, *Rare Glimpses of the Raj* (Mumbai: Somaiya Publications, 1998). J. K. Stanford, *Ladies in the Sun: The Memsahibs' India, 1790-1860* (London: Galley Press, 1962).

3. Flora Annie Steel, *On the Face of the Waters* (New Delhi: Arnold-Heinemann, 1985), 47-48.

4. Steel, 48.

5. *The Madras Cookery Book by an Old Lady-Resident*, 6th ed. (Madras and Bangalore: Higginbotham, Ltd., 1919).

6. Mrs. John Gilpin, *Pakwan-ki-Kitab; Memsahib's Guide to Cookery in India* (Bombay: A. J. Combridge & Co., 1914).

7. Burton, 140.

8. Stanford, 69.

9. Stanford, 69-70.

10. *Dainty Dishes for Indian Tables*, 2nd ed. (Calcutta: W. Newman & Co., 1881), iv-v.

11. Arthur Robert Kenney-Herbert, *Culinary Jottings for Madras, or a Treatise in Thirty Chapters on Reformed Cookery for Anglo-Indian Exiles* (Totnes, Devon: Prospect Books, 1994), 12.

12. Kenney-Herbert, 513.

13. A. C. S. [Angela C. Spry], *The Mem Sahibs' Book of Cookery*, 2nd ed. (Calcutta: n.p., 1894), 3.

14. Mary Procida, "Feeding the Imperial Appetite: Imperial Knowledge and Anglo-Indian Domesticity," *Journal of Women's History* 15, issue 2 (Summer 2003), 14.

15. Flora Annie Steel and Grace Gardiner, *The Complete Indian Housekeeper and Cook* (London: William Heinemann, 1898).

16. Steel and Gardiner, 196.

17. Steel and Gardiner, 243.

18. Steel and Gardiner, 259.

19. Steel and Gardiner, 295.

20. Kenney-Herbert, 203.

21. Kenney-Herbert, 204.

22. Kenney-Herbert, 203.

23. Kenney-Herbert, 115.

24. *Madras Cookery Book*, 1.

25. Spry, 60.

26. Gilpin, 1.

27. Sara Jeannette Duncan, *Set in Authority*, ed. Germaine Warkentin (Peterborough, Ontario: Broadview Press, 1996), 27.

28. Sara Jeannette Duncan, *The Simple Adventures of a Memsahib*, ed. Thomas Tausky (Ottawa, Ontario: Tecumseh Press, 1986).

29. Duncan, *Simple Adventures*, 265.

30. Duncan, *Simple Adventures,* 283-84.

31. Nora Scott, *An Indian Journal*, ed. John Radford (London: The Radcliffe Press, 1994).

32. Scott, 4.

33. Scott, 157.

Between Alimentary Products and the Art of Cooking: The Industrialisation of Eating at the World Fairs – 1888/1893

Adele Wessell

[W]here life is active, where the thousand anxieties of industry and business consume a man's spirit, there cannot be a life of luxury. Usually, the need for nutrition seems, to people driven by the whirlwind of business, no longer a pleasure but a burden; they consider the time spent at the dinner table as lost, and they demand of those charged with serving them that they are never left waiting. . . cooking without ceasing to be an art, will become scientific and will be elaborate in formulas, in the service too often of a method and a precision which leaves nothing to chance.[1]

Writing at the turn of the nineteenth century, Auguste Escoffier, one of the most famous chefs of the period, anticipates the impact of the industrialisation of food on the art of cooking. His account is testimony to the way food traverses the boundaries between production and consumption; its preparation and ingestion are a "practice of everyday creativity."[2] Food culture is not just conditioned by what ingredients are produced and available. Methods of preparation and consumption are also revealing of inspiration, of taste and cuisine at a particular moment of history. The industrialisation of eating was a critical phase in the transformation of food at the end of the nineteenth century, when production, processing and distribution had all undergone dramatic change to shape and influence what ends up on our plates. The nineteenth century World Fairs were at once pedagogic and promotional of this shift in the culture of eating and their audience was unprecedented. The Chicago

World Fair in 1893 heralded the advent of the consumer-based society and celebrated the industrialisation of the food business. Curiosity about other peoples and new foods, mediated by the terms of the marketplace, produced an early form of touristic consumption. "Alimentary Products" on display at the Melbourne Centennial Exhibition in 1888 demonstrate the sense of promise industrialisation held for overcoming the tyranny of distance white Australians felt at that moment. In this essay I will consider the impact of technology on culinary culture, how this can also be linked to lifestyle, to knowledge and information shared or imposed, to the influence of particular authorities.

International exhibitions provide important evidence of the practices and discourses with which food is infused. The way people eat relates to how they apply ideas and influences to the material resources and knowledge they have. International exhibitions provide important evidence of the practices and discourses by which knowledge and cultures were exhibited. By the 1890s, displays of industrial achievement and archaeological and ethnographic exhibitions were established as traditions of the World Fairs, intended for instruction as well as entertainment. The nineteenth century World Fairs reinforced contemporary pedagogical theory; this emphasised learning through observation, comparison and classification. As one Melbourne journalist remarked 'In an exhibition such as ours we not only see but are seen.'[3] Consistent with the emergence of the museum, the art gallery, the diorama, the cyclorama and the *tableau vivant*, in the same century, the exhibitions were divided into classes of exhibits for learning through looking. According to contemporary industrialist Joseph Bostito,

> One of the greatest things to be expected from an International Exhibition in Melbourne was that it would give the working classes of this colony an improved technical education. They had only to walk from one court to another in order to go, as it were, from one country to another, and see the proficiency which technical art had attained amongst other nations as compared with what was the case here.[4]

The relationship between education and culture reflected in the international exhibitions extended beyond pedagogy as a classroom practice to the pedagogy of cultural practices. This intersection of interests, however, occurred at a particular moment of time and space, and in an institutional context with an investment in the dissemination and production of knowledge. The business of international exhibitions was essentially symbolic, although they conformed to the requirements of an industrial, commercial, material culture.

The Melbourne International Exhibition in 1888 and the World's Columbian Exposition five years later commemorated the anniversaries of the arrival of the First Fleet in Australia and the Spanish Caravels to the Americas, although *progress* appears to have been the dominant cause for celebration. The past constructed around Columbus and the First Fleet became reference points from which the present could be defined and a very different future imagined.[5] Although commemorating events that occurred three hundred years apart, the anniversaries themselves share a moment of historical specificity, and exhibited similarities produced by their conjunction and the cultural and historical affinities the two societies share. The Fairs showed off the cultural strengths of the nation and developed markets for goods. The differences between the two countries are plainly exposed; the Columbian Fair marked the coming of age for the United States as a political and industrial power and developed international markets for manufactured goods. Conversely, the Melbourne exhibition represented the movement from colonial to national politics and was used to extend markets for its primary products. As expressed by the Royal Commission for the Melbourne Exhibition, "new countries" have raw materials to sell and require in exchange for those 'commodities older countries are best able to provide. In these respects [exhibitions] fulfil uses and ends beyond those they would in Europe.'[6] World Fairs and Exhibitions were a visible manifestation of the importance of commerce and the notions of progress and history with which it was imbued that dominated the period.

The first international exposition, in London's Crystal Palace in 1851, placed emphasis on material culture and celebrated colonial appropriation of raw materials. The exposition thus served the interests of the Empire, and the industrialists and entrepreneurs whose projects were seen to promote progress, and who largely made up the corporate boards that directed and administered the fairs. As a result of such activities businessmen were able to extend their role to cultural arbiters. World Fairs thereby escalated the merging of state and corporate culture.[7] The 1851 exposition became what one author described, as the first 'stocktakings' of the world, the purpose being 'to show us where we are.'[8] The Columbian World Fair and Melbourne International Exhibition also provided occasions to reassess the past in order to determine progress.

The growing importance of Chicago as an urban centre was reinforced by staging the Columbian Fair in 1893, and was well established in the early part of the next century. As James Gilbert has written of Chicago in the 1890s 'it might be said with some truth, that [it] could imagine itself as a prototype for the emerging urban culture of modern America.'[9] Melbourne rivalled Sydney in terms of population and means when plans got underway to hold a centennial exhibition. New South Wales had already rejected the suggestion that the first colony follow a convention becoming established in anniversaries.[10] Grand exhibitions marking the material progress of nations had become accepted fare of centennials, and their significance in new world societies had been given expression in the Philadelphia Centennial Exhibition in 1876. This was promoted as particularly important in the Australian context. As the report of the Royal Commission for the International Centennial Exhibition put it, 'In the new countries and especially where so far from centres of European skills and industry as are the settlements of Australia, the value of international exhibitions is particularly great. Indeed almost essential to their development.'[11]

The Melbourne exhibition in 1888 was preceded by the first international exhibition eight years earlier, reflecting the self-confidence of the younger colony and the importance it attached to exhibitions as well as its claim to national prestige. Both the Melbourne Exhibition and the Columbian World Fair can be placed in the context of their application in the process of city building.[12] But neither city was isolated from international conventions, and often drew on international influence and standards by which to confirm their own distinctiveness as well as affirm their global importance.

The Anthropological Building, the live outdoor ethnographic exhibits adjacent to it and the Midway Plaisance exhibits of the Columbian World Fair, were part of a tradition of human display initiated at the Paris Exposition in 1889, which introduced ethnographic villages as a central component of the world fair. The Midway Plaisance was a commercially sponsored self-contained amusement area in which a series of model villages abounded in food and dance. Visitors could sit in German beer gardens, eat Swiss cheese and enjoy the most modern, newly carbonated soft drink, first enjoyed at the fair. The emphasis of industrialising nations was on the symbolic dimensions of ethnicity, lifestyle and cultural aspects such as dance, dress, food and language, which were ideal forms to extend to an Exhibition; the display of people was prominent in other nation's exhibits. Here they could all be packaged, regulated, circulated and consumed. Bringing food, rides, music and theatre into one complex was immensely popular and another important legacy of the Fair, inspiring the permanent amusement and theme park. The corporate-designed amusements and mix of product with entertainment reverberates in the late twentieth-century fascination with Disneyland and McDonalds Happy Meals.

The practice of displaying human groups, particularly indigenous peoples, for profit, entertainment or public edification, however, has a longer history. Cultural critic and artist Coco Fusco has traced this history to the display of Arawak people who were brought by Columbus to the Spanish Court after his first voyage.[13] In Fusco's judgement,

> Designed to provide opportunities for aesthetic contemplation, scientific analysis, and entertainment for Europeans and North Americans, these exhibits were a critical component of a burgeoning mass culture whose development coincided with the growth of urban centers and populations, European colonialism, and American expansionism.[14]

Such exhibits were intended to reinforce the superiority of European worldviews. As Curtis M. Hinsley has confirmed, the use of ethnographic displays became a central component of world's fairs and usually incorporated elements of contemporary anthropology as well as the Barnum-type sideshow of human freaks and oddities.[15]

What each society understands as food can be interpreted through ethnographical observation, as Levi-Strauss reminds us and the Fair was a forum for putting this on display. The domestic arrangements of people living on the Midway were put on display, providing further opportunity for edification and amazement according to the former Governor of Virginia:

> in each establishment something may be learned from the ingenious devices by which sterile resources are made to yield sustenance and even comfort. Open for inspection are the kitchens of the Turks and Chinese, where the modes of preparing food, and some of the material which enters into the composition of it, will furnish occasion for surprise. Or if one prefers a glimpse at more primitive conditions of existence, he may profitably spend an hour or two in the tents of the nomads, among the princes of the Bedouins who, with their families, cling to the Gipsy fashions of their desert life under the shadows of the palaces which line the shore of Lake Michigan. In the huts of the Nubians there is a craving for meat which seems insatiable; while a little way down the street, in the Joss-house of the Chinese, delectable soup made from gelatinous bird's nests is served in dainty cups of grotesquely figured porcelain.[16]

The conditions under which people performed on the Midway, and the impact of the commodification of their culture was not acknowledged publicly, by Frederick Ward Putnam or many of the contemporary observers, to have any effect on the reproduction of rituals or the culture of those exotic Others who performed. The distinction between "real life" and the simulation of the rituals was obscured by the claim to authenticity, which ignored the cultural dynamic of the day to day existence of groups living on the Midway having any affect on the experience. One New Zealand visitor to the fair, G. W. S. Patterson, for example, declared that 'The Street of Cairo was truly Egyptian.'[17]

The Fair focussed the urge to consume, from the food on display to the consumption of foreign cultures on the Midway. Amusement as well as instruction could be obtained in the consumption of these images in the context of the marketplace, which conditioned their meaning, as described by Walter Benjamin:

> The world exhibitions glorify the exchange-value of commodities. They create a framework in which commodities' intrinsic value is eclipsed. They open up a phantasmagoria that people enter in order to be amused. The entertainment industry facilitates this by elevating people to the level of commodities. They submit to being manipulated while enjoying their alienation from themselves and from others.[18]

Material success was a dominant theme in the Melbourne Exhibition and the Chicago World Fair, progress being measured against the standards set by other nations. As a book published by the authority of the NSW Commissioners for the Columbian Exhibition declared, 'if Australians, combined with the venturous energy, had the hopeful industry of the Americans and the thrifty temperance of the Canadians, Australasia, with her vast natural resources, might soon be made the centre of Greater Britain.'[19] Overshadowing the ambiguous civic themes of liberty and equality in the case of the United States, material resources dominated the Australian exhibits in Melbourne, but an art gallery and musical concerts accompanied these for the first time in an Australian exhibition. The relationship between cultural pursuits and commercial interests was explained by the *Argus*:

> In a nation's history, intellectual and artistic culture come last. First there is the stern necessity of manual work, then the adoption of every invention that renders labour more economical and more valuable, and in the end the production of a specific art and literature.[20]

'Culture', in this sense was the end result of material progress. The United States, on the other hand, had moved from a producer to consumer society.

The Midway represented the consumption of culture through simulations of social identities in the context of amusement. Entrance fees were charged into the sideshows of the Midway, collectively described as a 'bazaar of all nations.'[21] In reference to its meaning as a public market or street of shops 'bazaar' described very well the cultural supermarket that legitimated the success of American capitalism at the fair. Conversely the marketplace resolved the distinctions between the values of American culture and exotic peoples and furthermore, provided a sign of power presumed universal. After all, as one observer commented, the greatest power visible in the World's Fair was 'naturally' that of money.[22] The image of exotic peoples making money for themselves impressed Hubert Howe Bancroft and submerged their culture into the free market trade that the fair celebrated. In a revealing statement in the opening pages of *The Book of the Fair*, Bancroft asserts the value of the marketplace in negating the boundaries between cultures otherwise necessary for their presence to have meaning: 'Of all the distinguishing features which separate mankind from the brute creation, perhaps there are none more noticeable than that man is a trading animal.'[23] Edward Farrington, the Chemist of the Agricultural Exhibition, went further in universalising the value of the market and its functions:

No people are above wanting a currency which they can take home, no matter where they live, and find it to be as good there as here. . . . There may have been minor influences at work, such as pride of nationality and of personal strength, but to be fed, clothed, sheltered, and mounted, and to be able to save a little something to take back, were the prime inducements. In like manner the people of the nations, and frequently the invasion of one nation by another, are the result of needs.[24]

Those people prepared to authenticate their cultures within the terms of the marketplace provided reassuring images to some American publics. Yet participants also had their own economic motives to perform, according to Edward Farrington, and these were not connected with either the cause of Eurocentric human sciences or public education that the World's Fair also promoted. That the reception of the Midway by nineteenth century audiences was accompanied by wonder as much as faith in the nation and economy reflects the ambiguity of representational practice.

As Hinsley has stated, the exhibition of humans was related to material progress in the context of the ideology of the nineteenth century industrial age.

As a collective phenomenon the industrial exposition celebrated the ascension of civilised power over nature and primitives. Exhibition techniques tended to represent those peoples as raw materials; within the regnant progressivist ideology they occupied the same category.[25]

Represented graphically at the Melbourne Exhibition, the dominance of the white *man* was portrayed as no more or less than the coming of civilisation. The South Australian gallery in Melbourne included two tableaux; one representing the 'noble savage in his native state'; and the other 'the civilised man in the act of driving the savage out.'[26] The colonial is imagined here as both a gendered and ethnic subject, united inseparably in the idea of civilisation, the Aboriginal unsullied by European cultural influences. The material progress made since taking possession was portrayed in wheat fields and seen in the distance, a spacious city with its gleaming spires.

In such a configuration, culture is defined in opposition to nature. What is edible, however, is determined by the symbolic function of different foodstuffs; how the food is positioned within broader cultural differentiations. The cultivation of exotic foods in Australia, like wheat, sheep and cattle, was crucial in establishing a familiar and long-term food supply to reaffirm the cultural and historical bonds that sustained a sense of British identity. Native produce was, by necessity, an important part of the diet for many colonialists during the nineteenth century, although by 1900 interest had dissolved. The Department of Public Instruction in Sydney included a table of 'Substances used as Food Chiefly by the Aborigines of NSW' in their Court at Chicago, with a description of the economic application of the products.[27] No one seems to have heeded their advice and for many years indigenous produce, like macadamia nuts, were overlooked in Australia but exploited elsewhere. The appeal of such binary constructions as nature and culture, however, extended beyond Australia and was crucial in international exhibitions in giving form to the myth of modernity. Symbolic displays of industrial and cultural achievement marked a coming of age as a political and industrial power. The World Fairs represented the movement from a predominantly agricultural nation towards a modern urban industrial society.

The official goals of the Columbian World Fair, to provide stability in the face of great change, to encourage American unity, to celebrate technology and commerce, and to encourage popular education underpinned all the exhibits. The excess of the fair was intended to invoke a sense of wonder in its audience, whether from the marvels of industry and science or human display, it called attention to what was new or different in the modern period. Despite the publicity which preceded its opening, it still managed to amaze and inspire its audience.

On the opening day of the fair, on the 1st of May 1893, President Cleveland addressed a crowd estimated to be of more than 300,000 people, before applying pressure to an ivory button that set the machinery of the fair in motion:

As by a touch the machinery that gives life to this vast Exposition is now set in motion, so at the same instant let our hopes and aspirations awaken forces which in all time to come shall influence the welfare, the dignity, and the freedom of mankind.[28]

In one flick of a switch the Fair gave a new focus to technology, and opened the age of electricity. As Judith Adams writes, 'most of all, the Columbian Exposition was a spectacle for the emerging technology that would power and transform the coming new century—electricity.'[29] By the 1890s electricity had become the icon of technological advance. The gas lighting installed for the Melbourne 1880 exhibition was replaced at great cost eight years later to allow for nighttime opening. Electricity was becoming an increasingly important aspect of business and consumption and the Fairs provided it with a new identity as a sign of progress and modernity and a vehicle for the hopes and dreams of a modern future. The celebration of electricity promoted at the fair, along with the consumer and corporate symbolism illuminated the path to modernity, industrial growth and economic power.

The overriding theme of the World Fairs was progress, in which the host nation was constantly moving forward and upward, the belief that life would get better with hard work, technology and healthy living. Faith in technology was coupled with an enthusiasm for improvements in society and human prospects, despite, or perhaps because of the obvious and disparate effects of the Depression. Author John Habberton predicted that temperance legislation would be a dead issue in 1993; 'Proper cooking and improved physical habits will have neutralized the desire for stimulants' he argued.[30] Columnist Bill Nye agreed that less attention would be paid to temperance legislation and more to the human stomach. Bad cooking, he explained, 'especially as we find it in poor hotels or on the road, is the parent of many drunkards.'[31] Electrical engineer John J. Carty predicted the immense changes the use of electricity would bring to the domestic economy. Kansas representative, Mary E. Lease went further to proclaim the benefits of electricity on agriculture:

Science will take in condensed form from the rich loam of the earth, the life force or germs now found in the heart of corn, in the kernel of wheat, and in the luscious juice of the fruits. A small phial of this life from that fertile bosom of Mother Earth will furnish man with subsistence for days. And thus the problems of cookery will be solved.[32]

What resonates throughout many commentaries on the Fair is their extraordinary optimism, bolstered by modernist assumptions and rationalities about the authority of science and technology and a teleological and totalising view of progress.

The World Fairs became an important forum for popularising the new domestic science. The impact of the application of principles of chemistry to the "science of cookery" gave birth to the home economics movement. Ellen Swallow Richards, the first woman student of the Massachusetts Institute of Technology, where she taught sanitary chemistry, set up the Rumford Kitchen in Chicago with the Bureau of Hygiene and Sanitation. The Board of Lady Managers was disappointed, having hoped to secure a scientific restaurant under Richards' direction in the Woman's Building.[33] Their model kitchen was constructed in the Woman's Building while the Rumford Kitchen was located in the Liberal Arts and then the Anthropological Building. The food in the Kitchen was served in portions containing a fixed amount of nutrition, and the menu card on each table gave the requirement for one-fourth of one day's ration, with the weight and composition of each dish composing the meal. To reduce the expenses of the exhibit the food cooked was sold under a concession from the administration of the Exposition. The World Fairs themselves were never designed to make a profit. They were, rather, elaborately choreographed cultural exercises, dedicated to advancing scientific and educational objectives. The Massachusetts Board of World's Fair Managers outlined the intentions of the exhibit in their 1894 Report:

> to illustrate the present state of knowledge in regard to the composition of materials for human food, the means of making these materials most available for nutrition, and the quantity of each necessary for a working ration. It was also in part intended as a centennial celebration of the services to humanity of a man of Massachusetts birth and parentage, Benjamin Thompson, Count Rumford of Bavaria, the first to apply the term "science of nutrition" to the study of human food, and the first to apply science to the preparation of food materials. Not the least valuable part of the exhibit consisted of the series of pamphlets prepared for the Rumford Kitchen by authorities in the several departments of science which relate to human food and nutrition. That such men . . . were willing to prepare these scientific papers shows a great step toward placing this branch of sanitary science in its rightful place.[34]

Concern with safety and predictability accompanied industrial-scale food production. The rhetoric of purity 'untouched by human hand' neutralized mechanization. Henry J. Heinz embodied the spirit of the Chicago Fair. He was the 'Cleanliness King of the late nineteenth century'.[35] Heinz began producing pickles in the 1870s and expanded into canning to build up one of the biggest businesses in Pittsburgh, the capital of the U.S. steel industry. Heinz used packaging and advertising to become one of industrial foods biggest moguls.[36] The famous "pickle pin," designed as a give-away was introduced at the Columbian Fair, accessorising the company's logo.

The World Fair provided important grounding for the mass marketing, packaging, advertising and consumption of the twentieth century. Exposition wits told amusing stories about the crowds that surged towards the Agriculture Building as lunchtime approached, to consume the specialties of food and drink companies exhibited for advertising purposes.[37] In the 1880s and 90s, food companies like Heinz, Nabisco, Kellogg and Campbell were among the largest American firms and agribusiness dominated U.S. industry. Chicago was the venue for the launch of the hamburger and the debut of many processed food products; Cracker Jacks, Aunt Jemima Syrup, Cream of Wheat, Shredded Wheat, Pabst Beer, Juicy Fruit chewing gum made by Chicago industrialist Wrigley. Both Wrigley and Heinz emulated classical Greek and Roman styles in their factory designs and collected an impressive number of art works, bestowing social cache on the industrialists. In the language of the Fair, the United States would survive its current troubles and prosper in the future 'through a corporate alliance of business, culture, and the state.'[38] A nation's self-presentation at these fairs can be seen as a reflection of their drive towards a modern consumer image. While product and meal introductions were important aspects of the fair it was the idea that consumption was in itself an act of pleasure that was its most lasting legacy. Lifestyle, not meat and bread, became commodified in the hamburger.

The hamburger was publicly launched at the Chicago World Fair in 1893, cementing its association with the United States and modernity, although it took until the second half of the 20th century before it became internationalised. The hamburger has a history of its own that incorporates U.S. immigrant culture.[39] Its success, however, is emblematic of the industrialisation of eating. It could appeal to a new industrial aesthetic that completed the industrialization of food; a regular, machined form, an unmistakable uniformity and a predictability of consistency and taste. Hamburgers can also be eaten quickly and on the move, features of Americans' relationship to food often acknowledged by Europeans.[40]

By the end of the nineteenth century meat had become relatively cheap and abundant in the industrial world; a product of colonial markets and the technology for industrial freezing. Owing to the enterprise of Thomas Sutcliffe Mort, Australia had a large frozen meat trade. The first shipment of frozen Australian meat was made to England in 1877.[41] Industrialists looked to Chicago for knowledge on meat preservation—

dustrialists looked to Chicago for knowledge on meat preservation—canning, chilling, smoking, dry and wet salting.[42] Chicago was the principal meatpacking and shipment centre in the US in the late nineteenth century. By the 1870s Australian canned meat accounted for 7 percent of England's meat supply.[43] Changes in transport, industry and technology are illustrated in the availability of different ingredients and new methods of food preparation, an increasing variety of chilled foods and meals that can be kept for a period of time. "Fast food" originated in the United States and is most commonly associated with US culture, as the literature attests.[44] The term didn't appear until the 20th century, but the century before witnessed the evolution of desire for what the Fast Food Society declare as 'today's need for speed,' produced by a perceived lack of time and need for efficiency.[45]

"Housekeeping is getting to be ready made, as well as clothing," one woman commented in *Good Housekeeping* in 1887.[46] Food preparation was simplified by both ready to eat meals and reliable guidance. In the latter half of the nineteenth century, magazines and almanacs offering household advice became increasingly popular. During the 1880s, cookbooks began to appear in abundance for the first time, serving a number of functions. In addition to food samples, a free souvenir book entitled *Recipes Used in Illinois Corn Exhibit Model Kitchen* was given to visitors of the model kitchen in the Women's Building, promoting the consumption of corn. *Favorite Dishes*, a collection of autographed recipes compiled for the Columbian Exposition, shares many features with charitable cookbooks that began after the Civil War. Carrie Shuman hoped the book would appeal to women of limited means, who would 'dream longingly and hopelessly of the Exposition.'[47] The dominance of women in cookbooks throughout the period attested to the strength of the concept of separate spheres, but the consequences of this are ambiguous. From the growth in publications dealing with "women's topics" also emerged a forum for women's voices. The growth of the genre relates to changes in domestic life, but they are equally important in producing culinary culture. The food consumed at the World Fairs provides a useful glimpse into some of the main developments in food history that remain a potent legacy, as well as a record of changing tastes.

Food presented at the nineteenth century World Fairs is evidence of the paradigm shift accompanying industrialisation in that century. A number of different themes emerge:

> growing rates of literacy facilitating the growth of an industry in cookbooks;
> an increasing emphasis on economy, hygiene, scientific management and organization;

the relationship forged between food reform and civic life;
the evolution of promotional literature produced by food and kitchen companies;
the rising influence of technology;
emergent interest in the cuisines of other cultures;
changes in ingredients and preparation and presentation;
diversification in the social class of consumers.

It is necessary to place such changes in a more general historical context. Social and political change, changes in social values, structures and beliefs are reflected in culinary culture. While meals may be limited by the availability of particular foods, changes are often independent of supply and are central to the issue of food and culture.

As food gets faster and cooks 'assemble' rather than create dishes the industrialisation of eating attracts more vocal critics. Food history alerts us to the way that culture operates at a number of different levels inclusive of ways of life and practices. Culture in this way relates more broadly to the social and political context in which practices manifest themselves and meanings are made. As aspects of the processes of nation-building the convergence between national and international fields enacted in expositions also confirms the wider context in which such ideas were developed or reinforced. While national identity may have been a compelling experiential framework in Australia and the United States in the nineteenth century, changes in industry, technology, food production and consumption were closely related and in a sense reinforced the dilution of national differences upon which this depended. The legacy of this period is ambiguous. While not wanting to return to the hunger that characterised past times, it may be worth questioning the pastimes we pursue with all the extra time industrial food gives us.
The role of the next revolution in food history will be to subvert the last.[48]

Notes

1. Auguste Escoffier, "Auguste Escoffier on the Art of Cooking in Modern Society" [1907] in *Choice Cuts: A Savory Selection of Food Writing from Around the World and Throughout History* ed. Mark Kurlansky (New York: Ballantine Books, 2002), 25-26. Escoffier is perhaps best known for his "Epicurean dinner," a French meal served to hundreds of people simultaneously in thirty-seven cities throughout Europe.

2. See Michel de Certeau, *The Practice of Everyday Life* (Berkeley: University of California Press, 1984) xi-xxiv.

3. *Argus* 4 August 1888.

4. *Victorian Parliamentary Debates* vol. 55, 1887, p. 551. Joseph Bostito is best recognised for his contribution to the thriving commercial trade in eucalyptus. He began distilling oil from eucalyptus leaves for medicinal purposes in 1851 and recognised the economic value of the oil during a period in which Australian trees were held of comparative little value in the country. Bostito was therefore particularly sensitive to the benefits of international comparisons and exchange.

5. In the context of the popularity of World Fairs in the nineteenth century, an attempt to understand the meanings of these events does however seem appropriate. As John Bodnar has remarked, events such as the Philadelphia Centennial Exposition (1876), the Chicago World Fair, the Pan American Exposition in Buffalo (1901), and the St. Louis World Fair (1904), did contain evidence of the ways in which the past was interpreted, and were themselves often organised around commemorative dates. Bodnar has claimed that the relationship between the past and the present expressed to visitors of the fairs served the interests of cultural leaders. *Remaking America: Public Memory, Commemoration, and Patriotism in the Twentieth Century* (Princeton: Princeton University Press, 1992).

6. *Report of the Royal Commission for the Melbourne Centennial International Exhibition of 1888 to the Queen's Most Excellent Majesty* (London: Eyre and Spottiswoode, 1889) 25.

7. See Alan Trachtenberg on this subject in relation to the Columbian World Fair specifically. *The Incorporation of America: Culture and Society in the Gilded Age* (New York: Hill & Wang, 1982).

8. Mrs. Cashel Hoey, "Philanthropic Work of Women in British Colonies and the East" in Baroness Burdett-Coutts (ed), *Woman's Mission: Collection of Papers on the Philanthropic Work of Women Prepared for the Royal British Commissioners of the World's Columbian Exposition* (London: Sampson Low Marsten Ltd, 1893), 334. [Title page torn in half, title from binder's title]

9. James Gilbert in James Gilbert, Amy Gilman, Donald M. Scott and Joan W. Scott, *The Mythmaking Frame of Mind: Social Imagination and American Culture* (Belmont: Wadsworth, 1993) 135.

10. Against a popular trend, Sir Henry Parkes proclaimed in NSW Parliament that an exhibition "was not a fitting way to celebrate a colony's birthday." *New South Wales Parliamentary Debates* (Vict. 50 & 51, vol. 28, 1887): 869.

11. *Report of the Royal Commission for the Melbourne Centennial International Exhibition of 1888 to the Queen's Most Excellent Majesty* (London: Eyre and Spottiswoode, 1889), 25.

12. The decision to hold the World Fair in Chicago was the triumph of a particular group of urban elites wanting to further their own collective and individual interests. Interurban rivalry between New York City and Chicago was a significant aspect of the history of the event. See Badger R. Reid, *The Great American Fair* (Chicago: Nelson Hall, 1979); for an analysis of the city politics

of the Chicago World's Columbian Fair.

13. Coco Fusco, *English is Broken Here: Notes on Cultural Fusion in the Americas* (New York: The New Press, 1995), 40. In 1992 Coco Fusco and Guillermo Gómez-Peña toured throughout the United States in a cage performing the role of a 'noble savage' on display *'Two Undiscovered Amerindians Visit. . . .* The performance also went to Madrid, London, Sydney and Buenos Aires. Coco Fusco describes and reflects on this experience in Part I: "The Other History of Intercultural Performance," pages 37-63.

14. Fusco, *English is Broken*, 40.

15. C. M. Hinsley, "The World as Marketplace: Commodification of the Exotic at the World's Columbian Exposition, Chicago, 1893" in *The Poetics and Politics of Museum Display* eds. I. Karp and S. D. Lavine (Washington DC: Smithsonian Institute Press, 1991), 344-365.

16. William E. Cameron, *History of the World's Columbian Exposition* (Chicago: Columbian History Company, 1893), 321.

17. G. W. S. Patterson, *The World's Fair and My Trip Around the World: A Description of Cities Visited and Scenes and Scenery Witnessed in Some of the Chief Cities and Countries of the Old and New World* (Auckland: H. Brett, 1894) 64.

18. Walter Benjamin, *Reflections: Essays, Aphorisms, Autobiographical Writings* ed. Peter Demetz, trans. Edmund Jephcott (New York: Harcourt Brace Jovanovich, 1978), 152.

19. Edward Dowling, *Australia and America in 1892: A Contrast* (Sydney: Charles Potter, Government Printer, 1893), viii.

20. Cited in Graeme Davison in *Australians 1888: A Historical Library* eds. Graeme Davison, J. W. McCarty, Ailsa McLearly (Sydney: Fairfax, Syme and Weldon, 1987), 25.

21. Hubert Howe Bancroft *The Book of the Fair: An Historical and Descriptive Presentation of the World's Science, Art and Industry, as Viewed through the Columbian Exposition at Chicago in 1893* (Chicago: Bancroft Co., 1893), 62. Bancroft claims that revenue from the Midway Plaisance alone exceeded four million dollars, six times more than was gained from all sources of the Paris exposition, p. 881.

22. Edward H. Farrington, scrapbook referring to the Chicago World's Fair, 1893, *Edward H. Farrington Papers* State Historical Society of Wisconsin (Madison) Box 3, vol. 1, 1887-1936.

23. Bancroft, *Book of the Fair*, preface.

24. *Edward H. Farrington Papers*, Box 3, vol. 1, 1887-1936, State Historical Society of Wisconsin (Madison).Box 3, vol. 1, 1897-1936.

25. Hinsley "World as Marketplace," 345.

26. *Popular Guide to the Centennial Exhibition with which is incorporated the Stranger's Guide to Melbourne with Plans Compiled from Various Sources* (Melbourne: W. H. Williams, 1888), 116.

27. *World's Columbian Exposition, Chicago, 1893 Catalogue of the Exhibits in the New South Wales Courts* (Sydney: Charles Potter, Government Printer, 1893), 1205.

28. Bancroft, *Book of the Fair*, 96.

29. Judith Adams, "The Promotion of New Technology Through Fun and Spectacle" *Journal of American Culture.* 18:45-55 (Summer 1995): 47.

30. In Dave Walter, *Today Then: America's Best Minds Look 100 years into the Future on the occasion of the 1893 World's Columbian Exposition* (Helena: American and World Geographic Publishing, 1992), 155.

31. Edgar Wilson "Bill" Nye in Walter, *Today Then*, 39. Prohibition was also a preoccupation of the French in their assessment of American food. In 1938 *Larousse Gastronomique* declared that 'good food can only be appreciated accompanied by good wine.' "*Larousse Gastronomique* on American Food" in *Choice Cuts: A Savory Selection of Food Writing from Around the World and Throughout History* ed. Mark Kurlansky (New York: Ballantine Books, 2002), 410.

32. Mary E. Lease, in Walter, *Today Then*, 177-78.

33. Jeanne Madeline Weimann *The Fair Women: The Story of the Women's Building World's Columbian Exposition Chicago 1893* (Chicago: Academy Chicago, 1981), 462.

34. The Rumford Kitchen Exhibit at World's Columbian Exposition, Chicago, 1893," Excerpts from *Report of the Massachusetts Board of World's Fair Managers* Boston, 1894, *http://libraries.mit.edu/archives/exhibits/esr/esr-rumford.html* (18 December 2004).

35. Felipe Fernandez-Armesto *Food: A History* (London: Macmillan, 2001) 244.

36. Heinz used the World's Fairs to advertise the industrialization of production, processing and eating. In the "Heinz Dome" of 1939 New York World's Fair Heinz demonstrated hydroponic cultivation in the Garden of the Future. An animated stage show dramatized "the story of strained baby food." Another animated character, "Aristocrat Tomato Man," sang and danced and smacked his lips. A series of six plaques depicted the company's progress in food preparation.

37. Bancroft, *Book of the Fair*, 396.

38. Trachtenberg, *Gilded Age*, 217.

39. See Evan Jones, *American Food: The Gastronomic Story* 2nd ed. (New York: Random House, 1981); Ronald McDonald, *The Complete Hamburger* (Secaucus: Carol Publishing, 1997).

40. See for example, Claude Fischler "The McDonaldization of Culture" in *Food: A Culinary History* ed. Albert Sonnenfeld, under direction of Jean-Louis Flandrin and Massimo Montanari (New York: Columbia University Press, 1999), 530-547.

41. Thomas Sutcliffe Mort's vision for the industrialisation and preservation of dairy produce and meat was largely unrealised before his death, but the first successful consignment of frozen meat by a Scottish firm used the process he

developed. His engineer, Eugene Nicolle, introduced the modern refrigeration process of liquefied ammonia in 1867. His estate at Bodalla was the first to make use of a mechanical cream separator imported in 1881.

42. See Edward Dowling *Australia and America in 1892: A Contrast* (Sydney: Charles Potter, Government Printer, 1893), 100.

43. Historic Houses Trust of NSW, *Colonial Food and Drink, 1788-1901* (Sydney: Historic Houses Trust, 1985), 20.

44. See for example: John Mariani, *America Eats Out* (New York: Wm Morrow, 1991); Joe Schlosser, *Fast Food Nation* (New York: Houghton Mifflin, 2002); George Ritzer, *The McDonaldization of Society. An Investigation into the Changing Character of Contemporary Social Life* (Pine Forge: Sage, 1996).

45. Fast Food Society website *http://www.fast-food-society.de/*, (15 October 2001).

46. Cited in Carl Degler *Out of Our Past* (New York: Harper & Row, 1959), 359.

47. Cited in Weimann, *Fair Women*, 469.

48. Fernandez-Armesto, *Food: A History*, 251.

Foreign Tastes and "Manchester Tea-Parties:" Eating and Drinking with the Victorian Lower Orders

Tamara Ketabgian

In the preface to her novel *Mary Barton* (1848), Elizabeth Gaskell claims that she seeks to portray "the state of feeling among. . .many of the factory-people in Manchester."[1] Not surprisingly, in the chapters that follow we hear plenty about Victorian working-class rage, middle-class ignorance, and the generally unhappy state of labor relations. We also, however, encounter a number of "Manchester tea-parties," to use Gaskell's term for the domestic gatherings that populate her text in great detail. Many modern critics view these scenes as either disengaged from or implicitly hostile to the more politically fraught world of the factory.[2] Yet, as this essay will show, Gaskell's juxtaposition of tea drinking and industrial life is far from coincidental. For Gaskell and her contemporaries, tea inseparably belonged to the scene of industrial production and consumption. In *Mary Barton, Hard Times* (1854) and early Victorian works of social investigation, this stimulating liquid addressed the emergence of foreign and specifically classed forms of affect and appetite. Whether faulted or celebrated for its "exciting" effects, tea crowned an industrial rhetoric of consumption and showed how this rhetoric—like the British factory itself—was deeply tinged by Orientalist fantasies of social and political order. For, just as factory hands might indulge a taste for Eastern luxuries, so might they impersonate colonial servility in their workaday lives—as obedient "menials" serving a "gentle genii"[3] of steam.

Rivaling beer and gin as the "condiment" of choice among Lancashire's proletarian masses, tea infused working-class domestic ritual with remarkably comforting connotations. In addition, however, it inspired searching questions about industrial pleasure, labor, sociality, and waste—questions properly belonging to the realm of political economy. For Gaskell and her contemporaries, tea drinking resonated with both work *and* play: this "regular" habit sought to recreate a sense of the continuous and intense "excitement" allied with machine culture. Thus preoccupied by the industrialization of the human body, Victorians sketched a working class devoted to foreign and prophylactic stimulants—both in pennyworths of tea and in acts of consumption as wasteful as they were exciting.

Tea Ceremonies

As critic Elizabeth Kowaleski-Wallace has shown, waste was one of the primary criticisms leveled against tea drinking in the eighteenth century.[4] Victorians invoked a similar rhetoric in their own gender and class-inflected critiques of "improvident" domesticity. Charles Dickens parodies this form of admonition in *Hard Times*, which describes an impromptu "tea party" in the barren apartment of Stephen Blackpool, an unemployed power-loom weaver in the industrial center of Coketown:

> [Stephen] lighted a candle, set out his little tea board, got hot water from below, and brought on small portions of tea and sugar, a loaf and some butter from the nearest shop. The bread was new and crusty, the butter fresh, and the sugar lump, of course in fulfillment of the standard testimony of the Coketown magnates, that these people lived like princes. . . . It was the first glimpse of sociality the host had had for many days. He too . . . enjoyed the meal—again in corroboration of magnates, as exemplifying the utter want of calculation on the part of these people, Sir.[5]

As a novel painted in broad and fairly schematic strokes, *Hard Times* contains few scenes that focus so closely upon working-class domestic practice. Stephen, the narrator implies, can only afford to buy very small quantities of sugar and tea. For Blackpool and his guests, fresh butter and new bread are unusual treats, and white "lump" sugar—the more highly refined sugar of the middle class—is shockingly luxurious, especially for a man with such poor future prospects. Anticipating the criticism of industrialists and political economists, Dickens dwells on the powerful symbolic and emotional significance of these expenditures.

Stephen's modest gathering resembles many meals in *Mary Barton*, a text that, like *Hard Times*, never retires the interpretive lens of economics. In one such scene, Gaskell carefully recounts the hospitality of Alice Wilson, a poor washerwoman living in a damp cellar room. Closely following Alice's movements as she prepares for her guests, we learn that "[h]alf an ounce of tea and a quarter of a pound of butter went far to absorb her morning's wages" (29-30). Gaskell adds, however, that this party is an "an unusual occasion" (30), and one that offers abundant emotional recompense for its cost. "Can you fancy," Gaskell asks, "the bustle of Alice to make the tea, to pour it out, and sweeten it to their liking, to help and help again to clap-bread and bread-and-butter? Can you fancy the delight with which she watched [her guests]?" (30). Both simple *and* luxurious, the domestic ritual of tea drinking here enables potent modes of working-class expression and consolation. Like Stephen's own modest meal, Alice's tea party conveys a profound sense of warmth, "comfort" (66), and sociality. Far from merely "improvident" or "uncalculating," these two gatherings support an alternate economy of pleasure—a gift economy in which ceremonial acts of waste convey specific working-class values of comfort, community, and home.[6]

Just as Dickens and Gaskell stress the charged emotional aspects of tea for its working-class consumers, so do both authors follow early Victorian critics in treating this beverage as the industrial "meal" *par excellence*. As Elizabeth Gaskell's distant relation Peter Gaskell notes in *Artisans and Machinery* (1836),[1] his medical study of Lancashire factory hands, "the staple [diet]" for such workers "is tea and bread. Little trouble is required in preparing them for use; and this circumstance, joined to the want of proper domestic arrangements, favours their extensive use amongst a class so improvident and careless as the mill artisans."[7] Viewed as morally suspect, this easy poverty-line diet signaled the absence of domestic economy among mill workers. Like other contemporaries who faulted tea's wasteful and "comparatively innutritious"[8] nature, Dr. Gaskell allies this taste with the rhythms of a degrading industrial lifestyle. Replacing the milk and porridge of the rural districts, and the home-brewed beer extolled by William Cobbett, tea and bread were popular convenience foods for the industrial masses, which might easily buy these items from the corner chandler's shop and supplement them with small quantities of sugar and butter.[9] As historians Sidney Mintz and John Burnett observe, this development is not surprising when we consider the expensive tax on malt, the high cost of milk for most urbanites, and the relative affordability of tea in the nineteenth century, due to its ability to support a high degree of dilution and to market factors such as lower trade duties, adulteration, and the export of cheaper tea leaves from India.[10] While maligned as a habit leading to idleness and emasculation, tea thus emerged as the "last resource" of the industrial poor, only one crucial step away from meals of mere "bread and water."[11]

A signifier for both early Victorian working-class waste and want, tea drinking occupied the psychologically freighted space between luxury and necessity. As sociologist Jack Goody claims, "the revolutionary potential of food [concerns]. . . differences in access to luxury foods, associated with those in power."[12] If we recall tea's historic evolution from rarity (in 1650) to luxury (in 1750) to necessity (in 1850) (Mintz, 148), it is no surprise that tea gained an especially potent ceremonial meaning among Victorian working classes, which often invoked its aura of privilege in economies of great scarcity. According to William Alcott, whose book on tea and coffee went through four British editions, the poor "will sooner go without their food than their tea, thousands will tell us, even when they use no milk, nor cream, nor sugar in it."[13] Certainly the sheer minimalism of this diet—sometimes solely consisting of tea—made little nutritional or economic sense. Why, after all, would the poor insist so strongly upon tea when they might instead buy some "real" food—some more bread, porridge, or potatoes? The answer to this question transcends mere economy and dietetics, since tea drinking clearly served other important ritual and symbolic functions. Tea transformed cold and meager purchases into "a hot meal" (Burnett, 37-38), and usually required lighting the domestic hearth.[14] Cobbett, for instance, claims that "in the course of the year 200 fires [are] made that would not be made, were it not for tea drinking" (14). And, as Alice Wilson shows when she visits the Barton family for tea, warmth forms an integral part of tea's ceremonial value: upon entry, Alice immediately detects "the delicious glow of the fire" and "the comfortable sounds of a boiling kettle" (E. Gaskell, 18).

Like the tea drinkers discussed by Alcott, Alice and the Bartons belong to a universe in which the same urges support both luxurious excess and life itself. In this respect, the characters of *Mary Barton* reproduce mythic narratives of improvidence posed most fantastically by *Hard Times*'s industrialist Mr. Bounderby. Bounderby defines *all* working-class desire as a uniform hunger for luxury—for lavish objects of appetite that nonetheless address simple, instinctive states of comfort and satiety. "There's not," he claims, "a Hand in this town, Sir, man, woman, or child, but has one ultimate object in life. That object is, to be fed on turtle soup and venison with a gold spoon" (96). In Bounderby's sweeping vision of Coketown, the hunger for luxury is more than an apt metaphor for desire; it is the *only* material form that desire assumes, whether voiced by labor agitators, by Stephen Blackpool in his wish for a better home life, or by Bounderby's own discontented wife, Louisa. According to Bounderby, any claim made within the sphere of the emotions—whether of uncertainty, discontent, or sheer abstract longing—boils down to the same restrictive edible formula. Indeed, as a particularly admonitory form of the middle-class economic imagination, this formula realizes unexpected symbolic and emotional effects. With its emphasis on the insatiable drives of the industrial body, orthodox economic rhetoric thus created new forms of meaning within the most humble of daily practices—such as taking tea. Parodied by Bounderby's "turtle soup" refrain, this economic calculus endowed acts of working-class waste and "luxury" with a deeply weighted sense of subjective, ceremonial, and transgressive expression—expression rooted both within and beyond physical appetite.

Elizabeth Gaskell is, of course, no Bounderby. Like him, however, she laments habits of luxury and waste among *Mary Barton*'s working people. Gaskell peppers her text with remarks faulting the Bartons for their "extravagance" and "child-like improvidence" (22, 24). Yet while interpreters sometimes claim that these remarks show a defensive conformity to middle-class economic doctrine,[15] *Mary Barton* also mines the hidden affective dimensions of this doctrine in its detailed accounts of tea-drinking and industrial sociality.

Headed by a folk ballad urging "Polly" to "put the kettle on,/ And let's have tea" (13), Gaskell's second chapter dwells extensively on a tea party hosted by the Barton family. After a "long whispering, and chinking of money," Mr. and Mrs. Barton instruct their daughter to "[r]un. . .just round the corner" and buy some unusual items—eggs and ham—and some more predictable, but certainly no less enjoyable, staples—"a pennyworth of milk," "a loaf of bread," and, most notably, "[a] sixpennyworth of rum, to warm the tea" (16). As I have noted elsewhere, Gaskell here offers an intricately textured account of working-class consumption, in which the bulk, quantity, and expense of food blends inextricably with the generous and sociable aura of the event as a whole. Sketching acts that are both financially ruinous and ritually dignifying, this scene exploits the psychic aspects of popular economic rhetoric, as it sought to distinguish between waste and want, desire and need, "economic" and "noneconomic" actions.[16] At the same time, then, that Gaskell faults the distressing "improvidence" of the Bartons, who exhaust almost all of their savings on a single indulgent meal, she also shows how political economy—with its porous distinction between need and desire—supplied working people with a site for profoundly expressive acts of waste and consumption.[17]

Industrial Habits

While early and mid-Victorian critics paired tea with lamentable working-class waste, they also recognized that it sustained habits of great industrial efficiency. Already an object of luxurious domestic ceremony,
tea served a pivotal role among the everyday practices that constituted
Victorian industrial labor.[18] Manchester social investigators Peter
Gaskell and James Kay both mark the uniformity with which workers
consumed tea and bread during factory shifts or work breaks. Dr. Gaskell
claims that, whether for breakfast or the evening meal, tea is "almost
universally taken in the mill," sometimes even while the machinery is
still going (116-17). Tea was thus first associated not with home but with
work—and especially with an industrial arena that stressed the importance of time efficiency (Mintz, 130-32). As noted in an 1861 study of
public diet, tea was "the drink for light meals that are meant to restore
without fatiguing and without interrupting thought or business."[19] Cheap,
convenient, and energizing, this beverage seemed ideally suited to the
short work breaks of nineteenth-century machine culture.

As a mode and object of working-class consumption, tea revealed a
controversial affiliation between mechanical labor and the industrial habits of the body. In their studies of Lancashire in the 1830s and 40s, critics
such as Kay describe factory hands struggling to match "the mathematical precision, the incessant motion, and the exhaustless power of the machine" (Kay, 25). Held to a demanding standard of mechanical performance, such workers accelerated and intensified their actions in an endless
attempt to keep "up to speed." Fatiguing and overstimulating, this labor
also yielded a notoriously painful deficit of stimulus *outside* of the factory. For, if laborers emulated the machine's "incessant motion" and
"exhaustless power" during the working day, after work they faced a related problem: how to replenish the massive amount of energy consumed
by industrial labor.

For Kay and Dr. Gaskell, the solution to working-class fatigue un-
cannily mirrored its industrial origins. Both critics sketch people who, in
their moments of recreation, seek to remedy fatigue by mimicking the
machine with habits of "exciting," repetitive, and "extravagant" consumption. Unable "to resist the seductions of appetite," they pursue substances and experiences promising "false excitement" (Kay, 33, 26) and
"temporary relief" (P. Gaskell, 221). Whether factory workers, former
factory workers, or general inhabitants of the industrial milieu, these
people remake their own anatomies through habits that reprise mechanical models of speed, intensity, and efficiency. Kay, for instance, claims
the very bodies of workers display signs of this intensive acceleration:

"industrial artisans," he notes, "are frequently subject to a disease, in which the sensibility of the stomach and bowels is morbidly excited; the alvine secretions are deranged and the appetite impaired" (26). Like other industrial "stimulants" such as alcohol, coffee, tobacco, and opium,[20] tea provoked similarly "quickening" symptoms—symptoms that viewers repeatedly compared to the physical and emotional effects of factory work. Thus, in both the bodies of "improvident" consumers and the realm of working-class social ritual, mechanized labor shaped an influential language of industrial habit, affect, and consumption.

Always seeking "excitement," Victorian mill workers consumed tea and other stimulants in ways that established a close fusion between them. Compared to "a weaker kind of laudanum" (Cobbett, 14), and even more frequently to alcohol, tea yielded results that supposedly differed "very little" from those of other companion drugs (Alcott, 18). Like the Bartons' gathering, in which rum is purchased "to warm the tea," industrial accounts often document the mixing of tea and spirits by mill workers: in "universal breakfast[s]" of the drink "flavoured. . .with gin or other stimulants" (P. Gaskell, 116) and in evening meals of it "mingled with spirits accompanied by a little bread" (Kay, 24). Certainly many Victorians extolled tea as a "temperance" beverage. However period critics also invoked the rhetoric of temperance to decry the amoral drive for stimulus promoting the consumption of both tea *and* alcohol. As William Alcott insists in his screed against tea, this drink might result in "increased energy of the system," but it is a "fictitious strength—a strength without strength" (18). "[S]o far," Alcott reflects, "as [tea] excites or exhilarates us at all, [it] does it by operating on the nervous system. . .in nearly the same way with alcoholic and fermented drinks, and opium, and tobacco" (9-10). For Alcott, tea *itself*—rather than labor or environment—single-handedly fuels "the causes of an unnatural thirst and an undue fondness for excitement" (174). In this way, Alcott returns us full circle to questions surrounding industrial labor, working-class leisure, and—of course—causation. Serving a consolatory and prophylactic role, the stimulus of tea at least briefly "corrected" states of industrial deficiency. Yet in doing so, tea shifted readily between cause and effect, since its short-lived results also supported the very forms of industrial excitement that they sought to remedy.

Eastern Tastes

As one substance among a pantheon of popular food substitutes, tea captured the expressive ritual aspects of Victorian working-class production and consumption. Moreover, from its historical alliance with the East India Company and developing British national identity,[21] this drink supported crucial cultural and metaphorical relays between industrial labor, foreign tastes, and "exciting" habits. As Sidney Mintz has observed, tea—along with West Indian sugar—reveals "the intimacy of links between colony and metropolis" and between industrial and colonial forms of power (116, 138). In this context, tea drinking offered Victorians a powerfully specular emblem for the relation between the British factory system and the East India trade, which possessed its own "factors" and "factories."

While working-class tea parties sustained Eastern trade and empire, the notion of the "factory" also evolved with the administration of the East India Company in the seventeenth century. Before assuming its later meaning as a site for the production of goods, the term "factory" defined "[a]n establishment for traders carrying on business in a foreign country[,] a merchant company's trading station," and "[t]he employment, office, or position of a factor" or agent.[22] As a commodity from China and India that such factors would have exported,[23] tea thus shows how both the early "factory" and its later, presumably more indigenous British form were shot through by exciting habits and tastes from abroad. Indeed, when we recall the factory's imperial origins, it—like tea—reveals a mercantile and fantastically Eastern logic present at the heart of modern industrial discipline. Certainly tea drinking was a practice specifically shaped by the culture of the Victorian factory. Yet, at the same time, the very *concept* of the factory—as a network of systemic production and distribution—drew crucially from these same foreign and "luxurious" practices: the consumption and exchange of tea and other Eastern commodities. Starting with tea or ending with it, these two genealogies of consumption treat the Victorian factory as a figuratively, if not literally, colonial venture.

For Victorians, then, tea not only simulated the "exciting" effects of industrial discipline; it also framed this discipline as a contested field of signification, shaded by overtones of legendary Eastern coercion. With its twinned images of Orientalizing labor and consumption, tea resonated with popular period metaphors of the factory as a realm of "enslaving" and mythically Eastern rule.[24] Combining references to the Near and Far East, to Arabian fable and Asiatic despotism, such fantasies of untroubled technological governance appeared in a number of early Victorian texts, but most conspicuously in works by novelist (and later prime minister) Benjamin Disraeli, industrial apologist Andrew Ure, and social investigator William Cooke Taylor.[25] Through their mythic and often antimodern scenes of industrial concord, these texts promoted a vision of working-class machine culture that was intensely—if not ironically—infused by legends of Eastern grandeur, tyranny, and servility.

Disraeli's novel *Coningsby* (1844) stresses the exotic nature of an industry that also supported powerful strains of British national triumphalism. When he visits Manchester, Disraeli's eponymous hero confronts a factory scene that blends the foreign, the fantastical, and the mechanical:

> He entered chambers vaster than are told of in Arabian fable, and peopled with habitants more wondrous than Afrite or Peri. For there he beheld, in long-continued ranks, those mysterious forms full of existence without life, that perform with facility, and in an instant, what man can fulfill only with difficulty and in days. A machine is a slave that neither brings nor bears degradation; it is a being endowed with the greatest degree of energy, and acting under the greatest degree of excitement, yet free at the same time from all passion and emotion. It is, therefore, not only a slave, but a supernatural slave.[26]

With its references to mysterious slaves, genii, and Arabian fable, *Coningsby* portrays an industrial identification with despotic forms of Eastern social order.[27] Disraeli's idealized mechanical slaves represent power relations that challenge the nature and discernability of submission in both humans and machines, in both Britain's exterior colonies and its interior ones. By featuring such mechanical marvels, *Coningsby* encourages its readers to mythologize forms of coercion that enlightened Western practices also presumably sought to curb. Yet, while Disraeli clearly fantasizes about the presence of such uncomplaining and unrebellious slaves, he nonetheless seeks to remove any trace of the "degradation" or coercion that we might naturally associate with despotism. Human workers are conveniently absent from this mythic scene, and, Disraeli insists, we need not worry about unfeeling machines—however "excitable" they may seem. In his vision of supernatural docility and efficiency, Disraeli solves the problem of corrupting power relations by appearing to dispense with volition itself.

But, as a perfectly automated system, *Coningsby*'s factory is still indebted to a symbolic form of Asiatic despotism. Although Disraeli's remarks literally concern only demons, spirits, and machines, in a figurative sense they support a fantasy of servile and enslaved labor—whether human, subhuman, or superhuman. And, as the narrator shows when he excludes "excitement" from "passion and emotion," he perhaps too readily discounts mechanical forms of affect specific to Victorian working-class culture. Disraeli uses the term "excitement" to describe a mechanical condition remarkably similar to the stimulus and excitement that period critics also credited to *human* industrial labor and consumption. Both restrictively physical and potentially emotional, working-class "excitement" thus challenges the utopian premises of Disraeli's system of mechanical "slavery."

Whereas *Coningsby* seeks to maintain an important distinction between human and mechanical oppression, Ure and Taylor treat this difference as largely irrelevant in their earlier industrial accounts. For instance, in *The Philosophy of Manufactures* (1835), his paean to the "factory system," Ure imagines both workers and machines as ideal colonial subjects. In the mill's "spacious halls," Ure notes,

> the benignant power of steam summons around him his myriads of willing menials, and assigns to each the regulated task, ... demanding in return only attention and dexterity. . . [From] the gentle docility of this moving force . . . magnificent edifices [have risen], surpassing far in number, value, usefulness, and ingenuity of construction, the boasted monuments of Asiatic, Egyptian and Roman despotism within the short period of fifty years. (18)

Here Ure views the British industrial juggernaut as a system of mystified and "benignant" order modeled after—but also transcending—the vast public works of ancient despotic empires.[28] In his sketch of interchangeable human and technological obedience, the factory's central steam engine serves both as a despot *itself*—summoning other workers and machines as its willing "menials"—and as an obedient subject *of* despotism, displaying an unmistakably "gentle docility."[29] Like Ure, Taylor defines the smooth operations of the mill as a complex of extreme and untenable power relations. In his *Notes of a Tour in the Manufacturing Districts of Lancashire* (1842), he too poses a scenario of willing slavery: a "strange . . . combination of perfect despotism with perfect freedom."[30]

By comparing industrial progress to practices of barbaric foreign rule, both Taylor and Ure "look backward" to systems of government that, for many Victorians, were renowned for their cultural stasis and mystification of power relations. As Karl Marx was later to note in the case of the "Asiatic mode of production," this model of a vast, despotic society relied upon forms of labor whose very communal and cooperative nature tended to obscure any awareness of a direct relation between worker and landowner, between those who labor and those who alienate labor.[31] Particularly for Victorian observers of China and India, despotism entailed the machinations not only of a lone, tyrannical ruler, but also—and perhaps even more significantly—the populace's own powerful, collective identification with state and community. If, for such a populace, coercive labor relations still existed, they also assumed a more generalized form.[32]

Because it would be performed for one's own community, individual labor would thus *seem*, to all extents and purposes, voluntary.

Taylor's model of British industrial "despotism" seeks to sustain precisely this illusion of consent. In his portrait of impressive mechanized order, emphasis shifts back and forth from an insistence on freedom to an exaggerated language of submission and constraint. In the factory, Taylor notes, "human agents work with all the exactness of machinery... These operatives are thus stringently ruled by their own consent: they feel that the government they are under works in all its parts for the promotion of their own interests; their obedience is complete" (123-24). Fusing images of machinery and "complete obedience" with claims of voluntarism, Taylor in effect reproduces the diffused and mystifying effects of authority considered typical of despotism: with the millowner—or despot—nowhere to be found, the factory poses forms of "stringent authority" to which workers submit both automatically and of their own accord.

Such parallels aside, Taylor's emphasis on consent jars markedly with his period's understanding of despotism, as a system of rule premised upon coercion. The formulation of despotism offered by Charles Montesquieu in the eighteenth century still remained influential for Victorians. In this system, Montesquieu found that "the goods and the lives of. . .subjects are always at the sovereign's disposition, exposed to all the caprices and untamed whims of a tyrant."[33] Referring particularly to China, Montesquieu described a form of government that inspired obedience largely through the fear of violence. The Chinese people, he remarked, "can be made to do nothing without beatings."[34] For not only Montesquieu but also James Mill in his *History of India* (1818), such forms of threat had definite consequences within the realm of affect.[35] Both writers traced an extreme servility of temperament to the severe conditions of subjection faced by a conquered people.

When compared to political systems notorious for their coercion and dissimulation, the factory's "perfect" docility appeared questionable, if not ethically suspect. Yet, even if Victorian industrial myths failed to provoke skepticism due to their authoritarian content, their narrative style no doubt would: Taylor, Ure, and Disraeli all praised the mill's "gentle" and "automatic" despotism in tones so extreme as to approach self-parody. Their exaggerated claims certainly fueled technological enthusiasm, but they also revealed the latently insecure aspects of industrial triumphalism. Premised upon Eastern models of potentially violent tyranny and implausible obedience, these texts imagined a world of mechanical intensity that was simultaneously regressive and utopian. Their sketches of industrial regularity defined a symbolic economy in which fantasies of foreign rule and labor efficiency found their complement in anxieties about equally intense and accelerated habits of consumption. Modern, despotic, and in every sense extreme, the factory thus casts new light on the Manchester tea-party, as a scene in which mechanistic systems of production reappear in the exciting tastes of the working-class body.

Whether in the realm of labor or leisure, of mill work or tea-drinking, Victorian industrial texts repeatedly focused on the contested relation between mechanical automatism and volitional feeling. How, then, should we interpret such diverse and pervasive accounts of "excitement"? I have suggested that—as a British fantasy of extreme Eastern discipline—the factory trained its workers to live and consume in particularly regular and intense ways. In many period texts, the working class's taste for "exciting" stimulants consistently mirrored the rhythms of efficient industrial production. Yet, as figured by both tea-drinking and the mill's own myths of extreme tyranny and servility, this "excitement" also exceeded the limits of industrial and economic efficiency, to convey alternate forms of cultural power and subjective expression. Forming the stuff of Arabian legend and industrial habit, this condition provided a distinctly mechanical language for working-class varieties of affect, ritual, and community. For, like other habits of consumption, tea-drinking not only registered the effects and conditions of machine work; it also commented on and made sense of this work. In this respect, tea offered working people a consolatory fantasy of industrial control and extravagance, exercised among their own bodies, economies, and communities.

Much like Ure's and Disraeli's Eastern legends, these tea-parties served a mythic representational function. Through daily practice, they allowed the factory's "willing" slaves to reverse the logic of their despotic order: to consume in its image the products of *other* Eastern factories and thus to participate in a symbolic economy mingling highly freighted imperial, ceremonial, and labor roles. As a habit poised between industrial and recreational modes of excitement, tea thereby forged powerful links between the world of the factory and the East Indian factor, between mythic and equally mechanistic forms of Victorian working-class labor, appetite, expression, and excess.

Notes

1. Elizabeth Gaskell, *Mary Barton: A Tale of Manchester Life* (Harmondsworth: Penguin Books, 1970), 4.

2. Catherine Gallagher, for instance, argues that such scenes ultimately neglect the world of the factory for more pastoral scenes of private human experience, at best expressing "simultaneous impulses to associate and to dissociate" social and domestic realms. See *The Industrial Reformation of English Fiction, 1832-1867* (Chicago: University of Chicago Press, 1985), 114; also Raymond Williams, *Culture and Society, 1780-1950* (New York: Columbia University Press, 1983), 109; and Arnold Kettle, "The Early Victorian Social-Problem Novel," *The Pelican Guide to English Literature: From Dickens to Hardy*, Vol. 6, ed. Boris Ford (Baltimore: Johns Hopkins University Press, 1973), 169-87.

3. Andrew Ure, *The Philosophy of Manufactures* (London: Frank Cass, 1967), 18.

4. Elizabeth Kowaleski-Wallace, "Tea, Gender, and Domesticity in Eighteenth-Century England." *Studies in Eighteenth-Century Culture*, Vol. 23 (1994), 131-45. I thank Professor Kowaleski-Wallace for her comments on this essay.

5. Charles Dickens, *Hard Times*, ed. George Ford and Sylvère Monod (New York: W. W. Norton, 1966), 117-18.

6. On the gift and gift economies, see Marcel Mauss, *The Gift: Forms and Functions of Exchange in Archaic Societies*, trans. Ian Cunnison (New York: W. W. Norton, 1967) and Georges Bataille, *The Accursed Share: An Essay on General Economy*, Vols. 1-3, trans. Robert Hurley (New York: Zone Books, 1993).

7. Peter Gaskell, Artisans and Machinery: The Moral and Physical Condition of the Manufacturing Population Considered with Reference to Mechanical Substitutes for Human Labour (London: Frank Cass, 1968), 119.

8. James Phillips Kay[-Shuttleworth], *The Moral and Physical Condition of the Working Classes Employed in the Cotton Manufacture in Manchester* (London: Frank Cass, 1970), 24. William Cobbett offers an earlier and more emphatic critique of tea in *Cottage Economy* (London: Peter Davies, 1926).

9. Sidney W. Mintz, *Sweetness and Power: The Place of Sugar in Modern History* (New York: Penguin Books, 1985), 128-30. For more on the great popularity of this trio—tea, sugar, and bread—among Victorian working classes, see John Burnett, *Plenty and Want: A Social History of Diet in England from 1815 to the Present Day* (London: Thomas Nelson, 1966) and Wolfgang Schivelbusch, *Tastes of Paradise: A Social History of Spices, Stimulants, and Intoxicants*, trans. David Jacobson (New York: Pantheon Books, 1992).

10. Before 1840, tea was primarily exported from China. In addition, tea was more accessible to the lower classes after the 1784 Commutation Act, which repealed existing English duties on tea from approximately 119% to 12.5%. Tea sales leapt from 5 million pounds to 13 million in the year after the

repeal. For more specific figures from 1814 to 1832, particularly when compared to population growth, see Peter Gaskell, 118 fn.

11. David Davies, *The Case of Labourers in Husbandry* (London: G. G. and J. Robinson, 1795), 39, 37.

12. Jack Goody, *Cooking, Cuisine, and Class: A Study in Comparative Sociology* (Cambridge: Cambridge University Press, 1982), 149.

13. William A. Alcott, *Tea and Coffee* (Boston: George W. Light, 1839), 159. British editions were published in 1855 (Manchester), 1859 (London), and well into the 1870s.

14. All the tea parties featured in *Mary Barton* include the lighting of a domestic hearth. In *Hard Times*, however, Stephen Blackpool acquires hot water from elsewhere.

15. See Rosemarie Bodenheimer, "Private Grief and Public Acts in *Mary Barton*," *Dickens Studies Annual: Essays on Victorian Fiction*, Vol. 9, ed. Michael Timko, Fred Kaplan, and Edward Guiliano (New York: AMS Press, 1981), 199-200; Deborah Epstein Nord, *Walking the Victorian Streets: Women, Representation, and the City* (Ithaca: Cornell University Press, 1995), 148; and Coral Lansbury, *Elizabeth Gaskell: The Novel of Social Crisis* (New York: Barnes and Noble, 1975), 25. For a more approving treatment of Gaskell's shifting tone, see Deirdre D'Albertis, *Dissembling Fictions: Elizabeth Gaskell and the Victorian Social Text* (New York: St. Martin's Press, 1997).

16. Jean Baudrillard, "The Ideological Genesis of Needs," *For a Critique of the Political Economy of the Sign*, trans. Charles Levin (New York: Telos Press, 1981), 73.

17. See Tamara Ketabgian, *The Lives of Machines: The Industrial Imaginary in Victorian Literature and Culture*, forthcoming.

18. On daily and bodily practice, see Michel de Certeau, *The Practice of Everyday Life*, trans. Steven Rendall (Berkeley: University of California Press, 1984) and Pierre Bourdieu, *The Logic of Practice*, trans. Richard Nice (Stanford: Stanford University Press, 1990).

19. Jamie Shalleck, *Tea* (New York: Viking Press, 1972), 51; cf. Eugène and Auguste Pelletier, *Le Thé et le Chocolat dans l'Alimentation Publique* (Paris: Eugène and Auguste Pelletier, 1861), 127.

20. Unlike later views of alcohol and opium as depressants, Gaskell and Kay—like many other early Victorian physicians—largely defined them as stimulants. See P. Gaskell, 220-21.

21. On the nationalistic rhetoric surrounding tea cultivation and consumption, see Julie Ellen Fromer, *A Necessary Luxury: Tea in Victorian Fiction and Culture* (Ph.D. diss., University of Wisconsin-Madison, 2002) and Suzanne Daly, *What Came Back: The Material Culture of India in Mid-Victorian Novels* (Ph.D. diss., Columbia University, 2002).

22. *Oxford English Dictionary*, ed. J. A. Simpson and E. S. C. Weiner (Oxford: Clarendon Press, 1989). The *OED* traces the first usage of the term to the later sixteenth century.

23. For a study of the consumption of tea and Chinese culture in the early modern period, see David Porter, *Ideographia: The Chinese Cipher in Early Modern Europe* (Stanford: Stanford University Press, 2001).

24. On Orientalizing industrial rhetoric in *Hard Times*, see Tamara Ketabgian, "'Melancholy Mad Elephants': Affect and the Animal Machine in *Hard Times*." *Victorian Studies*, Vol. 45, No. 4 (Summer 2003) 650-76.

25. For a discussion of Ure and Cooke Taylor in the context of early Victorian nationalist and pro-industrial rhetoric, see Joseph Bizup, *Manufacturing Culture: Vindications of Early Victorian Industry* (Charlottesville: University of Virginia Press, 2003).

26. Benjamin Disraeli, *Coningsby* (Harmondsworth: Penguin, 1989), 170-80.

27. Critics have viewed this vision of Manchester as a sign of Disraeli's literary inability to accommodate the newness and strangeness of industrialism. See Steven Marcus, *Engels, Manchester, and the Working Class* (New York: W. W. Norton, 1974) 40-45. One exception is Mary Poovey, *Making a Social Body: British Cultural Formation 1830-1864* (Chicago: University of Chicago Press, 1995).

28. In this passage, Ure also treats the British industrial system as a benevolent spiritual and imperial project. Through its updated technology of rule, it seeks both to "meliorate the condition of its citizens" and "to diffuse along with its commerce, the life-blood of science and religion to myriads of people still lying 'in the region and shadow of death'" (18-19).

29. On other contradictory aspects of Ure's claims regarding human and mechanical power, see Karl Marx, *Capital: A Critique of Political Economy*, Vol. 1, trans. Ben Fowkes (Harmondsworth: Penguin, 1976), 544.

30. W. Cooke Taylor, *Notes of a Tour in the Manufacturing Distrincts of Lancashire* (New York: Augustus M. Kelly, 1968), 124.

31. Karl Marx, "The British Rule in India," *On Colonialism* (Moscow: Foreign Languages Pub. House, 1960), 35-41.

32. Li Jun, "In defence of the Asiatic mode of production," *History of European Ideas*, Vol. 21, No. 2 (May 1995), 344-45.

33. Charles de Secondat Montesquieu, "Geographica," *Oeuvres complètes de Montesquieu* (Paris, Editions Nagel: 1955), 2. 934-37, cf. Jonathan Spence, *The Chan's Great Continent: China in Western Minds* (New York: W. W. Norton, 1998), 90.

34. Charles de Secondat Montesquieu, *The Spirit of the Laws*, trans. Anne M. Cohler, Basia Carolyn Miller, and Harold Samuel Stone (Cambridge: Cambridge University Press, 1994) 126-27.

35. James Mill, *The History of British India*, Vol. 2 (New York: Chelsea House Publishers, 1968) 324.

National Identity and Victorian Christmas Foods

Tara Moore

The December 16, 1854 issue of *Punch* includes an illustration "The Theatre of War. A Private Box for England's Dear Boys Before Sebastopol!" In the sketch, five English soldiers crowd around a newly opened crate. The tattered, disheveled men have just disemboweled the crate so that onions, a wrapped fowl, liquors, hot pickle, wine, cigars, and a boar's head litter the foreground. One soldier holds a letter he has just taken from the box. This soldier's eyes meet those of the viewer, and his hand waves a greeting from across the distance of the inert narrative as if sending a message of Christmas thanks from the Crimea. His fellows, enraptured with the contents of the box, focus their attention on the Christmas fare. One soldier in a patched uniform lifts a toasting grate out of the box while another blissfully smokes a cigar. A third has already opened a tin and begun to taste a familiar delicacy. The fifth figure reverently lifts an enormous plum pudding from the box as he kneels before it. Through the open tent flap, one can see more tents and a line of sentries which stretches into the distance below a mountain landscape, reminding the viewer that these soldiers have only temporarily paused in their labor.

The pun in the title of this tableau, "A Private Box," implies a metaphor of performance in this frontline scene. *Punch* contributors express the voyeuristic interest the British at home felt toward events in the Crimea. After all, by this date the newspaper reports of the Charge of the

Light Brigade on 25 October had gained the nation's attention. *Punch* projects a home fascination with the war onto the frontline soldiers. Of course, their private box is not a theater box, but a crate containing a cornucopia of traditional Christmas foods. The spaces usually attributed to spectator and performer are renegotiated in this scene of consumption. Instead of belonging to an audience, these soldiers crowded around a "private box" perform a ritual of English Christmas consumption for the reading audience back in Britain.

Modern readers and contemporary reviewers alike respond strongly to the performative feasting scenes in the Victorian Christmas literature. Who does not recall with satisfaction Scrooge's gift of the prize turkey, "the one as big as me?"[1] *A Christmas Carol* is only one of many examples of the occasional literature sensation that followed the 1840s cultural fascination with the "new" Christmas. The wealth of Christmas books, Christmas numbers of periodicals, and nonfiction pieces on the "history" of Christmas served as forms of advertisement for the national Christmas foods that had never been entirely forgotten but which had begun to be touted with the revitalization of the Victorian Christmas from the 1840s on. Through the Christmas book market, the Victorian reader participated in a double consumption; she consumed the bound book and, within that text, she became witness to a more tacitly engaging and "natural" form of consumption: that of English Christmas fare and feasts.

The depiction of articles of food in "The Theatre of War" raises two questions that pertain to much of Victorian Christmas literature: how does it contribute to the construction of a national identity? In what ways does Christmas food define boundaries between the self and Other? I will focus on the ways in which the English employed Christmas food to help establish boundaries of identity, an ideology which is, after all, a performance. Christmas fiction constructs an illusion that consuming traditional festive foods allows the celebrant to imbibe English national identity, including a sense of colonizing superiority. I will follow a foundation of food theory with a consideration of the importance of plum pudding in mid-century texts by Charles Dickens, Thomas K. Hervey, *Punch*, and others.

Christmas historians like J. A. R. Pimlott, J. Golby and A. Purdue, and Mark Connelly all agree that the Victorians changed Christmas from an excuse for raucous revels into a celebration of the family. Golby and Purdue argue that the Victorians "reinterpreted [Christmas] in light of their own preoccupations" which included the growing importance of the family space as a place of retreat and privacy.[2] By shrinking Christmas's stage to the intimate family setting, the Victorians created an ideological feasting paradox: they delighted in descriptions and illustrations of interclass feasts in the baronial hall, but they refocused their energies on the ritual of the sober, domestic Christmas table with an obligatory social consciousness. Because the Victorians continued to idealize a fantasy version of the Stuart Christmas, one in which feasting played a very large role, eating became a way of connecting with an otherwise unattainable nostalgia.[3] The scopaphilic joy of feasting in the baronial hall becomes most clear in Hervey's early nonfiction work, *The Book of Christmas*. While subsequent Christmas books place feasting in far more modest settings, bountiful provisions are never far away.

Food theory offers a particularly fitting inroad into decoding Englishness in feast-filled Christmas literature, especially since the 1990s flood of studies on food and identity. Mary Douglas's trailblazing and formalistic essay "Deciphering a Meal" instructs readers to think of food as a language or code.[4] In "Meals, Food Narratives, and Sentiments of Belonging in Past and Present," an informative overview of the history of food studies, Peter Scholliers traces the increasing emphasis his field has put on identity research since the 1980s when identity was "directly and intimately linked to food."[5] Food theorists have come to expand food's identity-building context beyond simple consumption to the processes of preparation, maintenance of taboos, and eating rituals. These food rituals allow eating to become a socially-charged activity, one used to draw boundaries of exclusion and inclusion.[6] Douglas and Scholliers both warn against seeking a universal food language, but rather emphasize the need to read each code inside its specific context.[7] The fictional Christmas context offers signs of heightened national identity since leisure time and conspicuous consumption combine to reveal the Victorians at their self-fashioned best.[8]

Within the context of Victorian fiction, Christmas is a national narrative, and objects of food within the Christmas tradition take on a role of embedded texts. As such, this language of encoded Englishness can be decoded and read as English fears of the colonized Other. Roland Barthes's *Mythologies* found not only the sign, but the national myth in food, as Barthes argued that wine is a "totem-drink" for the French and that steak possesses a morality while being both patriotic and nostalgic.[9] Cultural history can even be read in codes of eating: David Bell and Gill Valentine write, "[t]he history of any nation's diet is the history of the nation itself, with food fashions, fads and fancies mapping episodes of colonialism and migration, trade and exploration, cultural exchange and boundary-making."[10] Bell and Valentine remind us that the idea of a "*national* foods" is a fiction, that the national diet is "a feast of imagined commensality."[11] After all, how can a particular food item, whether "natural" or processed, belong to one nationality as opposed to another?

In the chapter devoted to the American Christmas dinner in Louisa May Alcott's *Eight Cousins*, the narrator omits a detailed description of the upper middle-class feast, saying, "Every body knows what a Christmas dinner is, so we need waste no words in describing this one."[12] Alcott's reticence contrasts sharply with the typically abundant descriptions of Christmas feasts in Victorian Christmas books, but her sentiment resembles these British texts ideologically by supporting the myth of a national knowledge of a proper Christmas meal. The idea of a national food exists in the fantasy of a shared tradition within a geographic boundary.

Individual foodstuffs can be used to express affiliation with certain groups, and Victorian authors repeatedly use Christmas foods to construct a view of the Other. In the autobiography of his Victorian childhood, Edmund Gosse recalls how the maids secretly fed him plum pudding one Christmas because "the poor dear child ought to have a bit, anyhow."[13] To his father, the dissenting Philip Gosse, the plum pudding had become "an idolatrous confectionary," a sign of Catholicism and, therefore, "the flesh offered to idols."[14] The maids rebelliously overruled the father's ban against Christmas fare because they believed that an English child needed to participate in the consumption of Christmas ritual. By infiltrating his body with a mainstream signifier of Englishness, the maids probably hoped to convert the young Gosse from his father's zealous morality. They attempt to colonize his body by marking it with a signifier of their dominant mainstream culture.

Hervey and Dickens both refer to Christmas-pudding as an emblem of English colonial dominance. *The Book of Christmas* was published just as the Victorian period, and its still-famous commercialization of Christmas, was getting underway. Hervey's depiction of Christmas pudding only begins to suggest the extremes to which Dickens will later take this emblem. Hervey writes, "[Plum-pudding] is a blackamoor, and derives his extraction from the spice lands. His Oriental properties have however received an English education and taken an English form, and he has long ago been adopted into the family of Father Christmas."[15] Hervey's illustrator personifies Plum-pudding as a portly figure in medieval dress with a spherical, black head. Here Hervey draws lines between English identity and the foreign Other. Plum-pudding is also "a truly national dish, and refuses to flourish out of England."[16] In this Christmas narrative, Plum-pudding cannot thrive in the lands that produce its raw ingredients; the Asian locations do not appreciate the apparent cultural "superiority" of an English Christian Christmas. Hervey's text suggests that as readers perform the Christmas narrative in which he instructs them—when they eat plum-pudding—they consume not only the product of a spice trade, but also an emblem of English cultural dominance and colonial economic exploitation.

The plum-pudding evolved through many centuries of English history. One nineteenth-century historian notes that "the plum-porridge was the progenitor of the pride and glory of an English Christmas."[17] The plum-pudding itself emerged sometime in the seventeenth or eighteenth centuries and was set apart from its forebear as a dessert. It gained heightened Christmas prominence during the Victorian revival of Christmas.[18] By the 1850s, fictional descriptions of Christmas meals most often highlighted the plum-pudding as the focal dish. The roast beef, the goose, and the newly imported turkey also figured in expectations of the popular Christmas meal, but the standardization of these meats were in flux depending on the trade situation of the times.[19] Plum-pudding remained current throughout the nineteenth-century, and it captured the national imagination as a signifier of how one celebrated the English Christmas. Print material then spread instructions about the culinary performance of the English Christmas to an eager audience, and the middle class proved itself able to participate in the purchase and consumption of the many ingredients required in the time-consuming dish.

In *A Christmas Carol*, an extremely food-oriented text, Scrooge suggests that the Christmas celebrant should be boiled along with the pudding and "buried with a stake of holly through his heart."[20] The metaphor turns the celebrant, by extension the consummate Englishman, into the plum pudding itself. Nearly a decade late, Dickens explores Empire through plum-pudding in his 1850 piece "A Christmas Pudding," printed in his Christmas number of *Household Words*. Here Dickens uses the "emblem of our commercial eminence" to narrate specifically English trade relations.[21] Mr. Oldknow falls asleep on Christmas Eve and dreams of interacting with figures that represent the different colonies that provide ingredients to the English dish. For example, he argues with an Andalusian Arab, the Genius of the Raisin, about how English trade practices would improve the lazy native industry. The Arab figment defends his right to trade isolation, but Oldknow discounts this entirely, later suggesting that "the end of commerce is not to make individuals rich [. . .] but to diffuse all the productions of nature and art, amongst all the inhabitants of the globe."[22] Dickens's pro-English propaganda not only identifies the commercial weaknesses of other nations, but also conceals a more accurate impetus of informal Empire: the accumulation of English wealth and power through the dogma of free trade.[23] Dickens's narrative paints England as pursuing charity on an international scale by bringing English porcelain to the huts of Andalusia.[24] Later the narrator extols the egg collectors of Cork to direct their energy to trade, to "rely upon industry, and not upon agitation!"[25] It is not enough to purify the objects of trade through consumption; the laborers who produce them for an English consumption must be converted to English trade practices and, above all, a realization of English supremacy.

English supremacy is again represented by the plum-pudding in *Punch's* 1848 "John Bull Showing the Foreign Powers How to Make a Constitutional Plum-Pudding." John Bull sits proudly behind the Magna Charta rolled out like a table cloth, with a plum pudding inscribed with English values such as "Liberty of the Press," "Common Sense," "Order," "Trial by Jury," "Religion," and "True Liberty of the Subject."[26] Crowned European and Asian rulers look on, scratching their heads over this English ingenuity. In this political setting, the plum pudding takes on the role of a globe. With his knife and fork in hand, John Bull testifies to his right and ability to carve up the globe while the foreign Others powerlessly watch. Similarly, an 1852 cartoon spoofs the insult taken by foreigners who viewed their defeated flags displayed as trophies at the Duke of Wellington's lying in state. Here an English cook quickly removes the roast beef and plum-pudding from his window display because "It hurts the feelings of the foreign gents as they walk by!"[27] The Christmas fare, like the captured flags, is made to symbolize English dominance so blatantly that it offends outsiders.

Food theorists agree that food is used to draw boundaries, but food also serves as a liminal object that passes from, and forces us to note the difference between, the outside and the inside. Lupton claims that food's liminal qualities also allow it to bridge a gap between nature and culture.[28] Bakhtin includes this argument in his discourse about the grotesque body, and how we eat the world, in fact we "[rend] the world apart" and take joy in the fact that we can in this way triumph over the world: man "devours it without being devoured himself."[29] This pertains to Hervey and Dickens's deep satisfaction in consuming the globe-shaped Christmas pudding: they are consuming the products of a global Empire, expressing their own survival at the oppression and destruction of foreign cultures. They eat without being eaten.

Plum-pudding represents idealization of an English identity through Christmas, but, most importantly, it signifies a celebration and clear consumption of Empire. In Dickens's "Christmas Pudding," the figments of Empire—the Genius of the Raisin, the Cork egg-collector—relate to how the Englishman sees himself. In the conclusion of the dream narrative, Dickens introduces a *"power-loom weaver"* to represent English might.[30] This last figure masterfully steps into the picture with the pudding cloth, the material that binds all of the ingredients of Empire together. The choice of a power-loom weaver signifies a technological advancement in England's recent past. In the same way Charlotte Brontë

England's recent past. In the same way Charlotte Brontë turned to the Luddite rebellion in the face of mid-century Chartist debates, Dickens calls upon the earlier technology to efface more contemporary controversies. After the weaver binds together all the ingredients and ethnicities in his cloth of English technology, Oldknow elatedly cries "We, in our united interests, well bound together, produce Christmas-pudding."[31] English interests blot out individual colonial interests, as far as Dickens is concerned. This Christmas writing teaches English readers to consume a version of English-ified Empire along with their Christmas pudding.

The liminal quality of food also raises questions of its purity. Bell and Valentine note the fear of unknown, potentially unclean foods.[32] Cooking cleanses the potential bodily pollution the unclean foods threaten, but it does not entirely remove the anxiety about taking contaminated food into "me." The same argument can be made when considering the coded language of food: how does a Victorian English person cleanse a product they understand to represent foreign, ethnically and culturally "contaminated" foodstuff? Hervey and Dickens symbolically "cook" the colonial ingredients with their rhetoric: they, like Hervey's blackamoor Plum Pudding, have "received an English education and taken an English form."[33] In Dickens's piece, the power-loom weaver performs the "cooking" process by wrapping the ingredients in the English cloth. Language is needed to cleanse the code of food, to make it palatable and even nationally sustaining for the English diet.

An 1856 *Punch* illustration reinforces the plum-pudding as a signifier of British global dominance. A sketch shows the emblematic figures Britannia and the American Jonathan sitting down to a plum-pudding while Mr. Punch condescendingly pats Jonathan on the back. The cartoon commemorates the American government's return of the British exploration ship, the *Resolute*. Abandoned during an exploration of the north pole, the *Resolute* was found by an American commercial ship and obtained by the American government who presented it to Britain as a goodwill offering. In the image, the central plum-pudding is topped with a miniature ship with holly sprouting from its mast. White sauce covers the top of the sphere, suggesting the north pole, and the effect most clearly exhibits the British construction of their national dish as a globe. In the sketch, titled "Britannia and Jonathan—Mother and Child are Doing Well," Britannia and Mr. Punch both patronize the "good Boy" Jonathan, who has recognized the duty he owes his "Mother." However, a tension of global dominance underlies the image of Christmas affability. British and American flags have been stuck into the makeshift globe on opposite sides of the pudding's north pole. The globe-shaped dish is an English one, and Jonathan appears as a obedient guest at the queenly Britannia's table. The British lion smiles smugly from its position at Britannia's feet. The illustration stacks the table in favor of Britannia's power and clout, presenting an image that shrinks the appearance of American power.

Not only food, but ways of consuming become a path toward ethnic identity. In her housekeeping instruction manual, Isabella Beeton works on the assumption that English ways of eating prove the nation's superior destiny: "The rank which a people occupy in the grand scale may be measured by their way of taking their meals, as well as by their way of treating their women. The nation which knows how to dine has learnt the leading lesson of progress. It implies both the will and the skill to reduce to order, and surround with idealisms and graces, the more material conditions of human existence; and wherever that will and that skill exist, life cannot be wholly ignoble."[34] The following examples exhibit how habits of Christmas dining also serve to educate a nation in its national identity.

Reviewers of Christmas literature are often distracted by scenes of Christmas fare. The reviews become a text of food once removed from the original novel. In a review of the Christmas books of 1846 season, a anonymous reviewer in the *Dublin University Magazine* first quotes the plum-pudding scene from *A Christmas Carol* before introducing the topic at hand: a review of Dickens'ss current Christmas book, *The Battle of Life*. When William M. Thackeray reviewed the Christmas books for 1845, he praised the feasting passages in Catherine Gore's *The Snow Storm* as the work's "best piece of writing" and is "exceedingly luscious and agreeable."[35] Of all the scenes in the text, why do eight pages about a well-stocked, traditional farmhouse Christmas feast stand out? Throughout Gore's text, the author sets up a preference for rural or local commodities by contrasting the merry Christmas scene in a farmer's cottage over the sculpted feast in the estate house. The narrator belittles the baronet who imports French chefs to make Christmas pastries. Gore's fictional feast is specifically Yorkshire in composition, and, while the cottager hosts lack a plum-pudding, they are able to offer the wassail bowl:

> "A genuine wassail-bowl for Christmas Eve!" cried Shoreham,—sniffing the rich aroma of cinnamon and cloves it diffused through the room.
> "And of the finest old Japan china!"—added Lady Charles, rendering homage due to a certain curious old punch-bowl, which had graced the buffet of Bush Farm nearly a century before,—a gift to old Welland's grandfather, from the skipper of a Hull Indiaman.[36]

The simple Yorkshire feast concludes with this symbol of English Empire, and the foreign-made bowl transports and translates the English traditional spiced punch. Later in the narrative the long-lost heir returns from the sub-continent with a fortune and a developed policy of Empire. Like many Christmas books, *The Snow Storm*'s happy conclusion depends on the near-miraculous return of an uncle from India; the uncle is able to reestablish the English home with wealth taken from Empire. The Wellands' eighteenth-century china bowl prefigures the Indian wealth by containing the signifier of English community and custom. The shared wassail punch and the bowl that contains it both become signifiers of ideal English community and affiliation. The Japan china's Asian origins add a layer of English pride in commercial trade authority to a seemingly rustic event taking place in the metropolitan culture.

The rhetoric of Empire in the bowl's designation points to a domestic Orientalism of the imported commodity. Elizabeth Kowaleski-Wallace traces the workings of Empire in English-owned china as she traces the object's etymology of china and finds that the term summarizes the history of trade and the power of a Western market on the Eastern state.[37] The Wellands, however, own a piece of *Japan* china, a doubly layered acknowledgement for the way that distant nations are boiled down and represented by the objects they produce. The bowl is "curious," but it evidences the presence of a century-old image of Orientalism in the idealized rural English home that Gore's text suggests is on the verge of extinction. By drinking to English community out of an object made precious as a symbol of commercial superiority, the characters of this Christmas novel build the metropolis on relics of the periphery.

Authors continued to use Christmas foods as sites of cultural dis-ease long after the initial wave of Victorian Christmas had been marketed and consumed. "Alien Cheer" appeared in *Punch* on Christmas Day, 1907. In this satirical sketch the artist depicts a doleful John Bull character mourning over his plate of traditional English roast beef.[38] This meat has been "Killed and Chilled in Chicago," much to the Englishman's disdain.[39] Christmas fare has entirely turned the tables: the meal that was once celebrated as free trade superiority has become a disgusting complaint against modernized trade systems and technology.

Conclusions: Consumption and Impregnation

William M. Thackeray crafted his review of the 1847 Christmas books to include a defense of what he considered the object of this developing genre: "I doubt, after all, if there is any need for an artist to make his portraits like. What you want is not to be struck by the resemblance, but to be impregnated with the idea."[40] Impregnation certainly seems a shocking verb for the action of reading; it is, however, an accurate metaphor for the function of Christmas food in the construction of Englishness. Scholliers develops ideas of identity out of the fact that consumers actually ingest and absorb food, thereby making it a part of themselves and using the foods' signs to "demarcate their own and the other group."[41] By eating the Christmas pudding, Charles Dickens's Mr. Oldknow builds up his flesh upon the sign of Empire, and can he possibly continue unchanged from consuming such food? As food theorists do not tire of saying, "you are what you eat."

Artists of Christmas fiction, both visual and verbal, are ensuring the continuity of their offspring, Christmas print matter, by investing the reader with a national identity and a desire to re-establish this identity annually by consuming Christmas literature: Christmas books, seasonal periodicals, and nonfiction histories. Such texts impregnate the reader with an alternative image, a reflection of an unrealistic ideal. Thackeray voices an odd corporeal metaphor for the work of literature on the occasional reader. They consume Christmas narratives of Englishness and demonstrate their own change in a very visible way: they give birth to their own adaptation of the narrative by performing it themselves.

A growing readership found instruction for Christmas consumption and English identity in Christmas literature. Homi K. Bhabha writes that the "perspective of nation as narration will establish the cultural boundaries of the nation so that they may be acknowledged as containing 'thresholds' of meaning that must be crossed, erased, and translate in the process of cultural production."[42] Narrative portrayals of Christmas food reveal mid-century Anglo-Saxon preoccupations with thresholds of Englishness being infiltrated through empire and trade. A sense of insecure boundaries with the racial Other caused the English to retreat into a rhetoric of supremacy. The plum-pudding often carries the sign of colonial authority, and plum-puddings created by Hervey, Dickens, and *Punch* all open the Victorian Christmas food to a colonial discourse analysis. Not only particular dishes, but also ratified styles of eating lend themselves to the dialogue between Christmas foods and English national identity. Evidence of emigrant English people carrying on the culinary signs of Englishness despite the challenges of climate further attests to the strength of this food's association to an ethnic identity by the latter half of the nineteenth century.

I started this chapter with a description of "The Theatre of War," an illustration punning on the performative nature of war, and one in which I read the performative nature of English Christmas foods. In the *Punch* illustration, the 1854 audience saw their frontline soldiers being re-stocked with elements that they believed contributed to English national identity. The Christmas box signifies an outpost of Englishness in an otherwise foreign and unknown terrain. This portrayal of pre-packaged Englishness naturally raises questions about how colonial forces were supposed to maintain their English identity while cut off geographically from the source of their food rituals and celebration traditions. In the is-sue following the one containing "The Theatre of War," *Punch* sings "A Christmas Carol for the Crimea" to "ye lion-hearted men" who hold only meager feasts that holiday: "But not a man amongst you can more heart-ily desire/ Here with his friends that he could be beside a blazing fire,/ Than we do, safe at home, who eat our pudding and our beef/ In peace—thank you, and such as you brave fellows and your chief."[43] Here the pudding again represents English solidarity, but the poet also employs beef, the pre-Victorian celebratory fare which had been replaced with an emphasis on poultry by the 1850s. The symbol of English beef calls upon a nostalgic, sentimental portrayal of nation.

"A Christmas Carol for the Crimea" constructs a sense of the boundaries of Englishness patrolled by the men who are absent for the 1854 Christmas dinner. The reference to "lion-hearted men" even sug-gests a connection to that earlier, romanticized imperialism of Richard the Lion-hearted and the crusades. *Punch* is entirely supportive of the troops during the first year of the Crimea campaign, and in this patriotic poem the writer references the meager Christmas feasts that the soldiers will enjoy, feasts that do not adequately express the heights of English identity being otherwise performed by these men abroad. Knowable Christmas traditions in the British camps, slender though they be, con-trast with the unknown traditions of the Russians' Christmas. Once again, the artist uses food to construct boundaries to the illusory implication of nation.

Notes

1. Charles Dickens, *A Christmas Carol* (Peterborough: Broadview Press, Ltd., 2003), 119. Harry Stone reads this and other turkey-child comparisons as examples of Dickens'ss dark side, situating it within an argument about Dick-ens'ss obsession with cannibalistic images. *The Night Side of Dickens: Canni-balism, Passion, Necessity* (Columbus: Ohio State University Press, 1994), 85.

2. J. Golby and A. Purdue, *The Making of the Modern Christmas* (London: Batsford, 1986), 49-51.

3. Walter Benjamin explains the process of conveniently historicizing the past by seeing "a past charged with the time of the now" which one might "[blast] out of the continuum of history" in *Illuminations* (New York: Schocken Books, 1986), 261.

4. Mary Douglas, "Deciphering a Meal" *Food and Culture: A Reader* Eds. Carole Counihan and Penny van Esterik (New York: Routledge, l997), 36.

5. Peter Scholliers's "Meals, Food Narratives, and Sentiments of Belonging in Past and Present," in *Food, Drink, and Identity: Cooking, Eating, and Drinking in Europe Since the Middle Ages*, ed. Peter Scholliers (New York: Berg, 2001), 7.

6. Deborah Lupton, *Food, the Body and the Self* (London: Sage Publications, 1996), 1-2.

7. Douglas, "Deciphering," 37; Scholliers, "Meals," 17.

8. Studies of the cultural mainstream Victorian Christmas allow scholars to follow the ethnic portrayal of a white Englishness, something that Patrick Williams and Laura Chrisman encourage as a development in colonial discourse analysis: "The power, valorization and experience of 'whiteness' as a form of contemporary ethnicity needs serious theoretical and critical attention." Introduction. *Colonial Discourse and Post-Colonial Theory: A Reader,* eds. Patrick Williams and Laura Chrisman (New York: Columbia University Press, 1994), 17.

9. Roland Barthes, *Mythologies*. Trans. Annette Lavers (New York: Hill and Wang, 1972), 58, 63.

10. David Bell and Gill Valentine, *Consuming Geographies: We Are Where We Eat* (New York: Routledge, 1997), 168-9.

11. Bell and Valentine, *Consuming Geographies*, 169.

12. Louisa May Alcott, *Eight Cousins* (Boston: Little Brown, and Company, 1927), 232.

13. Edmund Gosse, *Father and Son* (London: Penguin Books, 1989), 111.

14. Gosse, *Father and Son*, 112, 111.

15. Thomas K. Hervey, *The Book of Christmas* (1837) (London: Wordsworth Editions, 2000), 75.

16. Hervey, *Book of Christmas*, 106.

17. Robert Chambers, *Chambers' Book of Days* (Edinburgh: W. & R. Chambers, 1869). *Hillman's Hyperlinked and Searchable* Chambers' Book of Days. Ed. Michael Hillman. *www.thebookofdays.com*.

18. Tanya Gulerich, *Encyclopedia of Christmas* (Detroit: Omnigraphics, Inc., 2000) 471.

19. While roast beef continued to be referenced as the traditional meat dish at Christmas, this did not translate to roast beef's actual appearance on every Christmas table. By the 1860s, turkeys were the vogue, and the *Times* estimated that more than ten thousand were shipped from the country to London for the Christmas season.

20. Dickens, *Christmas Carol*, 42. *The Muppets' Christmas Carol*, with its talking vegetables and child-friendly use of food to represent benevolence, most palpably represents Dickens'ss original food-centered narrative.

21. Charles Dickens, "A Christmas Pudding," *Household Words* 1:39 (21 Dec. 1850): 301.

22. Dickens, "Christmas Pudding," 303.

23. The years between 1830 and 1850 saw the end of Britain's "ancien regime" and the shift to a free trade argument for Empire, according to Andrew Porter. Introduction. *The Oxford History of the British Empire* vol. 3 ed. Andrew Porter (New York: Oxford University Press, 1999), 26. Martin Lynn notes Britain's gains from the free trade stance of colonization and informal colonization in that 1. it made Britain the "workshop of the world" and 2. it deployed "capitalism as a moral force" which taught enterprise and a British work ethic. Martin Lynn "Policy, Trade, and Informal Empire in the Mid-Nineteenth Century," in *The Oxford History of the British Empire,* vol. 3, ed. Andrew Porter (New York: Oxford University Press, 1999), 103.

24. Dickens, "Christmas Pudding," 301.

25. Dickens, "Christmas Pudding," 303.

26. "John Bull Showing the Foreign Powers How to Make a Constitutional Plum-Pudding," *Punch* 15 (Dec. 1848): 267.

27. "Too Civil by Half!" *Punch* 23 (1852): 226.

28. Lupton, *Food, the Body and the Self,* 17.

29. Mikhail Bakhtin, *Rabelais and His World* (Bloomington: Indiana University Press, 1984), 281.

30. Dickens, "Christmas Pudding," 303.

31. Dickens, "Christmas Pudding," 303.

32. Gill and Valentine, *Consuming*, 48-49.

33. Hervey, *Book of Christmas*, 75.

34. Isabella Beeton, *Mrs Beeton's Book of Household Management* (Oxford: Oxford University Press, 2000), 363.

35. William M. Thackeray, "Christmas Books" in *Contributions to the Morning Chronicle* (Urbana: University of Illinois Press, 1955), 106.

36. Catherine Gore, *The Snow Storm* (1845) (New York: Kiggins and Kellogg, Publishers, nd.), 141.

37. Elizabeth Kowaleski-Wallace, *Consuming Subjects* (New York: Columbia University Press, 1997), 58.

38. The roast beef Christmas meal predates the Victorian switch to goose and then turkey.

39. "Alien Cheer," *Punch* 133 (25 Dec. 1907): 461.

40. William M. Thackeray "A Grumble About the Christmas-Books" *Fraser's Magazine* 35 (Jan. 1847): 117.

41. Scholliers, "Meal," 8.

42. Homi K. Bhabha, *Nation and Narration* (New York: Routledge, 1990), 4.

43. "A Christmas Carol for the Crimea" *Punch* 27 (23 Dec. 1854): 255.

Rewriting the Puritan Past: Food and Illicit Desires in Hawthorne's Fiction

Monika Elbert

In a most curious scene in Hawthorne's *The Scarlet Letter,* the minister Dimmesdale, in a manic mood after his forest encounter with Hester (who has just let her hair down), comes back into the civilized Puritan community with sin on his mind. He has an inclination to whisper wild and impure thoughts to a passing maiden, "as fair and pure as a lily that had bloomed in Paradise."[1] Shortly thereafter, he has another evil impulse to "teach some very wicked words" (220) to a group of Puritan children. Ultimately, he returns home safely, but before writing his (confessional) Election Sermon, he is overcome with hunger and eats "with ravenous appetite" the food he requests from the servant (225). He flings the earlier version of the solemn sermon into the fire, and after gorging himself with food, he writes the confessional sermon that will reveal his sinful identity to the crowds. This disjunction between the material and the spiritual realms (with its ensuing hypocrisy among the Puritans) is often explored by Hawthorne in his excursions and digressions about food.

This large unseemly appetite, so incongruous with the higher spiritual character of the minister, Dimmesdale, shows the raw passion which had been initially unleashed by Hester. Many times in Hawthorne's fiction, forbidden sexual desire or material ambition is juxtaposed with an inordinate desire for food. Although recent historians, like Richard Godbeer, have shown that Puritans were not opposed to sexual passion—it was readily acceptable within the confines of marriage—it had to be controlled: "Puritans sought not to repress their sexual instincts but to keep them within ordained borders."[2] As one Puritan worthy, Thomas Hooker, put it (in terms of food imagery!), "I know there is wild love and joy enough in the world as there is wild thyme and other herbs, but we would have garden joy and garden love, of God's own planting."[3]

When Hawthorne rewrites the history of his Puritan forebears, he imagines their extravagance, or excesses in passion, and sinfulness (often narcissism) in terms of their attitudes towards food. In looking at the food imagery in several Hawthorne stories, like "Egotism; or, the Bosom Serpent" (1843, rpt. in *Mosses* 1846) and "The Christmas Banquet" (1844, rpt. in *Mosses* 1846), one notes how the characters are consumed, literally, by their sense of ego—through their relationship to food. In "The Bosom Serpent," for example, Roderick, the protagonist, has swallowed a snake which "gnaws" at him (passim, 269, 270, 273),[4] driving him almost mad, until he finds an antidote in his beloved Rosina. Indeed, her has tried to starve the snake out of his system, but to no avail: "while the wretched man was on the point of famishing, the monster seemed to feed upon his heart and to thrive and wax gamesome, as if it were his sweetest and most congenial diet" (279). Self-consumption (egotism) and consumption are often identical in the Hawthorne canon. Similarly, in "The Christmas Banquet," the misanthropic guests who come together every Christmas to complain of their lot in life do so as they are presented with a sumptuous feast, which is described in as great a detail as their litany of sins. For Hawthorne, communal charity is of utmost importance, and the dinner guests' chary views of mankind make them miserable guests; the hypochondriac wishes the malcontent to indulge in "yonder tureen of viper soup . . . a fricassee of scorpions . . . the apples of Sodom" (290). Hawthorne obviously draws from allegory in some of his "food" tales to describe various sins—related to the egocentricity of protagonists, who often happen to be wealthy or upstanding citizens.[5]

In *The House of the Seven Gables* (1851), however, the entire framework seems to revolve around the desire for food, that is, for love, and for money. There are two food-related themes that converge in this novel: Hawthorne's critique of the rigid Puritan code that has created the Maule-Pyncheon feud (and that has left vestiges of class tension in the nineteenth century) and Hawthorne's exploration of woman's increasing independence (manifest in their relationship to food) in the nineteenth century. In the latter case, the juxtaposition of domestic meals (and the rhetoric of cookbooks) and the selling of material goods (food) in Hepzibah's cent shop makes sense because the novel represents Hawthorne's experiment with the sentimental mode—as he combines the discourse of domesticity with the marketplace. For example, in one long passage, in chapter seven, Hepzibah, the fallen aristocrat (heir to the Puritan Pyncheon curse), who tries her hand in the cent-shop by selling gingerbread cookies, also attempts to win the favor of her returning brother,

Clifford (incarcerated unjustly for many years). In trying to gain his affection, she attempts to prepare a meal, with the aid of a fine English "Cookery Book":

> If any volume could have manifested its essential wisdom, in the mode suggested, it would certainly have been the one now in Hepzibah's hand; and the kitchen, in such an event, would forthwith have steamed with the fragrance of venison, turkeys, capons, lauded partridges, puddings, cakes, and Christmas pies, in all manner of elaborate mixture and concoction. (98).

Though she desires to cook up a "nimble little tidbit" for breakfast, her resources, as a fallen New England aristocrat, are limited, and she puts away "the savory volume" as she inquires from her young, pure, and quintessentially American cousin Phoebe (on a visit to the Seven Gables) what food is in stock—whether the chickens have laid eggs. But the chickens have been delinquent, and Hepzibah is forced to bargain with the fishdealer, selling his wares from door to door, for some mackerel. Her ideas about aristocratic dishes from English cookbooks deteriorate into modest New England fare.

There were several old English cookbooks widely circulated in America that Hepzibah might have been using as her "Cookery" book. Eliza Smith's *The Compleat Housewife: Or Accomplished Gentlewoman's Companion* (1742), written in England but widely circulated in the colonies, or Susannah Carter's *The Frugal Housewife or Complete Woman Cook* (1772) also written in England but republished in America, might have been the treatise from which Hepzibah initially tries to draw her recipes, ill suited to the American scene.[6] In fact, Hawthorne might be making a statement about the need for America to have its own cuisine, just as American Romantics, Hawthorne among them, were making a literary declaration of independence through their writing. Hawthorne is more likely thinking about Lydia Maria Child's best-selling *The American Frugal Housewife,* "Dedicated to Those Who Are Not Ashamed of Economy" (Boston, first edition, 1829), which was specifically meant to stand in opposition to the British cookbook of the same name. In fact, in her dedication alone, Child clearly states that her audience must be modest (in terms of domestic economy), and she prefaces the book by stating, "It has become necessary to change the title of this work to the '*American* Frugal Housewife,' because there is an *English* work of the same name, not adapted to the wants of this country" (frontispiece, emphasis Child's).[7] Child adopts some of Franklin's ideas about frugality and writes a domestic philosophy for American women; as she asserts, "Books of this kind have usually been written for the wealthy; I have written for the poor. I have said nothing about *rich* cooking; those who can afford to be epicures will find information in the 'Seventy-five Receipts'." Child explains that economy is mistakenly confused with "avarice" regarded as "ungenerous and selfish," but she pronounces that economy is a saving grace, "The man who is truly economical, is laying up for himself the permanent power of being useful and generous."[8] Hawthorne's novel obviously shows Hepzibah's move from indigence to economy/frugality and then to usefulness, the kind of lesson Child was trying to impress upon her female readers.

Cooking, or a revolution in cooking, becomes a central metaphor for loving, as Hepzibah tries her best to placate her voracious brother Clifford, just returned from a wrongful stay in prison, where one can imagine the prison fare scanty at best. However, Hepzibah, with her privileged past, has few cooking or nurturing skills: she has "no natural turn for cookery" (216). However, she has an inclination to please her brother's palate upon his return from prison: "She watched the fish with as much tender care, and minuteness of attention . . . as if her own heart were on the gridiron" (100). Meanwhile, the pure-hearted Phoebe is the cook par excellence, because she has learned the art of cookery from her mother in the countryside. And since her mother is not a genteel Pyncheon, but rather a common woman, the modest Phoebe becomes the icon of American democratic cuisine—which will finally prove to be the antidote to the class discord (between the aristocratic Pyncheons and democratic Maules) in the novel. Interestingly, Phoebe's housewifely abilities are described as witchlike—an anthem in terms of the Puritan discourse framing the story. Her housekeeping is described as a king of "natural magic" (71) and a kind of "homely witchcraft" (72), which also allies her with the magical powers of Holgrave. And like Holgrave, she has had a middle-class, rather than aristocratic, upbringing; as she announces to Hepzibah, "I mean to earn my bread. You know, I have not been brought up a Pyncheon. A girl learns many things in a New England village" (74). Phoebe has much common sense and thus can manage the cent-shop (and turn a profit) as adroitly as she can churn butter or clean the house and manage the garden, which have fallen into shambles under Hepzibah's lack of housekeeping skills.

Much extravagant description is given to Hepzibah's and Phoebe's preparations for Clifford—the cooking styles of the women are quite divergent. Phoebe, who ultimately offers the key to the Maule/Pyncheon feud through her loving nature, is obviously the "Angel of the Household," and though not born a lady, she is gentrified though her domestic abilities. Indeed, Hepzibah even recognizes her as an angel (82), and the narrator confirms, "Angels do not toil, but let their works grow out of them; and so did Phoebe" (82). Uncle Venner perceives her as "one of God's angels" (82, 221) and the convalescent Clifford feels he is under the care of an angel (142).[9] By contrast, as mistress of the household and as businesswoman, Hepzibah shows little talent. Yet, cousin Phoebe from the country, who is a natural cook, is also a wonderful business-woman in the cent-shop: Phoebe herself asserts that she is a natural "housewife" as well as "saleswoman" (78). She describes her role as economist in her parents' household as well as vendor in the marketplace: "Oh, I have done the shopping for the family, at our village-store . . . And I have had a table at a fancy fair, and made better sales than anyone" (78). Clearly, Phoebe is the type of woman who epitomizes Child's ideal woman as being nurturing, but also frugal and useful.[10] Hepzibah, aw-estruck by Phoebe's talents, cannot comprehend how Phoebe can be a Pyncheon, as she is aware "of this native inapplicability . . of the Pyncheons to any useful purpose" (77). Much is made of Phoebe's an-cestry—that her talents come from her mother's side, a non-Pyncheon and a commoner. This reliance upon "her mother's blood," as Phoebe maintains, allows her a type of freedom to transgress class and gender boundaries—to move from the democratic to gentrified settings, from country to city, and from the woman's domestic sphere to the man's marketplace. She has the Midas touch (a Pyncheon trait, but softened), as shown in her marketing skill in the cent-shop, and as ascribed to her cooking for the just-returned Clifford, who savors Phoebe's cooking over his own sister's culinary talent: "Phoebe's Indian cakes were the sweetest offering of all—in their hue, befitting the rustic altars of the innocent and golden age—or, so brightly yellow were they, resembling some of bread which was changed to *gold*, when *Midas* tried to eat it" (100, emphasis mine). Not surprisingly, the virtue of Indian cakes was lauded in Lydia Maria Child's *The American Frugal Housewife* as a cheap but savory cake: "Indian cake, or bannock, is sweet and cheap food."[11] Child's popular recipe for Indian cake, significantly, is taken from the indigenous people who use American food resources. And this recipe is what Hawthorne uses as Phoebe's claim to culinary fame (her "Indian cakes") in *The House of the Seven Gables*. She is clearly the emerging American woman who reigns over the domestic household but who also has a voice in the marketplace as family economist.

Though Phoebe and Hepzibah are different in their temperaments and origins, the kitchen and the cent-shop bring them together as partners. The women's food preparation for Clifford is a veritable offering of love, but from the portrait of the Puritan forebear, old Colonel Pyncheon, one finds only disapproval: "the Puritan's face scowled down out of the pic-ture, as if nothing on the table pleased his appetite" (101). Still, the women's offerings are blessed by the womenfolk of the past, as the ghosts of the past converge with the women of the present in the rivalry to cook up the best meal. In this Gothic domestic novel, it is refreshing to find that the ghosts do not simply return in the shape of persecuting patriarchs but in competitive women cooks: "Perchance . . . the ghosts of departed cook-maids looked wonderingly on, or peeped down the great breadth of the flue, despising the simplicity of the projected meal, yet ineffectually pining to thrust their shadowy hands into each inchoate dish" (99).[12] Interestingly, Clifford, the man who has been wrongly imprisoned and repressed (like Dimmesdale in *The Scarlet Letter*), has a ravenous appetite: "He ate food with what might almost be termed voracity, and seemed to forget himself, Hepzibah, the young girl, and everything else around him, in the sensual enjoyment which the bountifully spread table afforded" (107). Although the coffee Phoebe offers him seems to bring a "spiritual gleam" to his otherwise "animal being," it is a faint light at best, as he clamors for "More, more! . . . This is what I need! Give me more!" (107). With his almost bestial appetite, Clifford also represents the repression he has endured in the prison, tantamount to the Puritan severity of the past, as he manifests a great eye for sensual beauty; though he dislikes the sight of the aged, crooked Hepzibah, he clamors for the presence of the lovely, young Phoebe. Yet Hepzibah tries her best to make the dismal house a home as she offers him the fruits of her kitchen labors: "There is nothing but love here, Clifford . . . nothing but love. You are at home!" (107).

This seventh chapter ("The Guest") is the most protracted food-centered chapter in the book, as it distinguishes between the cuisine of the past and the present, and as it illustrates Clifford's almost childlike delight in eating. However, there are many more chapters (and instances), where food and passions are aligned and where Hawthorne continues to attack the improper attitudes towards food, especially in relationship to the criminal and aristocratic Pyncheon lineage. It should be noted that both the progenitor Puritan Pyncheon, Colonel Pyncheon, and the ancestor who resembles him the most, the current-day Judge Jaffrey Pyncheon both die by choking to death on their own blood—in fits of apoplexy. The wronged original "wizard" Maule had cursed the Pyncheons, with his dying words, "God will give him [Colonel Pyncheon] blood to drink" (8). Moreover, after the original Matthew Maule is executed as a witch, not only do the tyrannical male Pyncheons succumb to apoplexy, but the "the water of Maule's Well . . . grew hard and brackish" and it was rumored that the water produced "intestinal mischief to those who quench[ed] their thirst there" (10). Holgrave insists that the water is "bewitched" (94). Interestingly, only Phoebe, of mixed Pyncheon blood, and with her nurturing and cooking talents, can bring back a semblance of order to the garden, wholesomeness to the house, and purity to the tainted water. And even the infertile chickens, who feed off the snails in the brackish well water, regain their fertility under the auspices of Phoebe's loving presence.

If one looks at the dying scenes of both Colonel and Judge Pyncheon, there is a striking similarity in the parallelism of the chapters. Both of them die, with the image of sumptuous banquets and festivity on their mind—and with blood in their mouth. In the first case, Colonel Pyncheon is celebrating the completion of the ill-fated House of the Seven Gables, built by Thomas Maule, the son of the "wizard" Matthew Maule, persecuted by the Pyncheons, who wrested his land away. The doomed celebration of the completion of the house was to be executed in pomp and merriment, but also with solemnity. We hear that the "Puritan magnate [Colonel Pyncheon] bade all the town to be his guests. A ceremony of consecration, festive, as well as religious, was now to be performed" (21). The prayer and dedication were carried out by the Reverend Higginson, and ironically, the narrator makes the point that the spirituality needed to be balanced by physical release, in terms of food: "A psalm from the general throat of the community" (ironic in light of the fact that Pyncheon dies a few pages later of choking to death, by apoplexy) was "to be made acceptable to the grosser sense by ale, cider, wine, and brandy, in copious effusion . . . and by an ox roasted whole, or, at least by the weight and substance of an ox, in more manageable joints and sirloins" (11). In addition, there is a profusion of other foods served:

> The carcass of a dear . . . had supplied material for the vast circumference of a pasty. A cod-fish of sixty pounds, caught in the bay, had been dissolved into the rich liquid of a chowder. The chimney of the new house, in short, belching forth its kitchen-smoke, impregnated the whole air with the scent of meats, fowls, and fishes, spicily concocted with odoriferous herbs, and onions in abundance. The mere smell of such festivity, making its way to everybody's nostrils, was at once an invitation and an appetite. (11)

The reader, too, imbibes this picturesque scene and can almost smell the intoxicating aromas. The communal festivity is attended by the clergy, the aristocracy, as well as the "plebeian classes" (12). Though the housewarming would seem to present the occasion for a merging of the classes, the narrator clearly distinguishes the classes through their clothes. The Lieutenant-Governor, feeling rebuffed that Colonel Pyncheon does not greet him, barges into his study and discovers Pyncheon's corpse:

"The iron-hearted Puritan—the relentless persecutor—the grasping and strong-willed man—was dead!" (15). There is a strange juxtaposition between the feasting guests and the deceased Pyncheon, with "blood on his ruff" and saturating his beard (15). It is almost as if the excess of food represents his own excessive ambition to seize and possess land illegally. And such ambition is finally seen as dark and sinful, akin to the dark powers of witchcraft—as the narrator comments about Judge Pyncheon's zeal, "ambition is a far more powerful talisman than witchcraft" (274).

All of the Pyncheons seem to be cursed with this excessive appetite.[13] Even the more gentle Clifford, as we have seen, had a "coarser expression" and "a look of appetite": "In his natural system, though high-wrought and delicately refined, a sensibility to the delights of the palate was inherent" (207).[14] He shares the same acquisitive, grasping spirit of his forebears, although he is not guilty of the crime that sent him to prison—the murder of his uncle, who actually died in the typical Pyncheon manner, by an attack of apoplexy. The Pyncheon who most resembles the old Puritan patriarch is the modern-day Judge Jaffrey Pyncheon: in an almost heavy-handed manner, Hawthorne often makes the comparison between the appearance of the present-day Judge and that of the Colonel, whose sinister portrait hangs in the parlor, where both Colonel and Judge Pyncheon die, appropriately enough. The modern Judge Jaffrey Pyncheon, uncharitable in his attitudes towards community and eager to find the old Indian deed to claim more land, dies, fittingly enough, alone in the parlor of the House of the Seven Gables, with the Puritan ancestor in the portrait, "with all his English beef about him," looking down upon him. Moreover, like the tormented Roderick who suffers from indigestion in "The Bosom Serpent," Judge Pyncheon has a disease associated with choking, in this case apoplexy, which kills him. The pure-hearted Phoebe had recoiled at first meeting the Judge as she heard the gurgling in his throat, a sign of the Maule curse upon the Pyncheons that they would choke on their own blood. In the Judge's protracted death scene, there is "a disagreeable choking, or stifling, or gurgling, or bubbling, in the region of the thorax, as the anatomists say" (272). The narrator tauntingly gibes, as he focuses upon the corpse, "look at your watch, now! . . . It is within ten minutes of the dinner-hour! It surely cannot have slipt your memory, that the dinner of to-day, is to be the most important . . . of all the dinners you ever ate" (273). And the narrator evokes a sumptuous spread and banquet (a description which resonates on three pages!) that coincides with the imagined nomination of the now-deceased Pyncheon to the Governorship. In this surreal chapter, the dead Judge Pyncheon (through the voice of the taunting narrator) imagines the gubernatorial nomination and speech and fantasizes about the food he is missing: "Real turtle, we understand, English mutton, good roast-beef, or dainties of that serious kind, fit for substantial country-gentlemen, as these honorable persons mostly are" (273). He cannot imagine it will be as delicious as "French cookery, but an excellent dinner, nevertheless" (273). No simple Indian cakes cooked by Phoebe would appear at this table!

Several pages after Pyncheon imagines the wine-drinking and conversation with the statesmen, he goes back to the idea of the food he is missing, almost compulsively so. Again, these scenarios are created by the narrator looking down at corpse of Pyncheon in the parlor, so Hawthorne's irony cannot be mistaken. At the moment of expiration, Pyncheon is still thinking about ambition, greed, and food. The litany of food and delicacies is impressive: "Turtle, salmon, tautog [a type of oysterfish and a delicacy], woodcock, boiled turkey, Southern mutton, pig, roast-beef" (275). There is a sense of regret as Pyncheon realizes he has missed the spread: "for once, the Judge is entirely too late for dinner" (275). In an excursive passage, the narrator reinforces the image of Judge Pyncheon, in terms of his appetite, as brutal and bestial:

> The Judge, had he done nothing else, would have achieved wonders with his knife and fork. It was he, you know, of whom it used to be said, in reference to his ogre-like appetite, that his Creator made him a great animal, but that the dinner-hour made him a great beast. Persons of his large sensual endowments must claim indulgence, at their feeding time. (275)

This image of Pyncheon, as both monster, and as animal feeding at a trough, will be juxtaposed shortly with the simple but venerable Uncle Venner, who, though indigent, knows how to value food—and eats in moderation. Indeed, the pig Venner feeds from scraps of housewives' alms is more like the Judge than poor Venner himself. The narrator further taunts the dead Pyncheon by alluding to his soiled bloody shirt: "Neither would it be seemly in Judge Pyncheon, generally so scrupulous in his attire, to show himself at a dinner table with that crimson stain upon his shirt-bosom" (275). But the image of food torments him to the last: Pyncheon feels he should make haste to go home, after noticing the indiscreet stain, and "There, after a lass of brandy and water, and a mutton-chop, a beef-steak, a broiled fowl, or some such hasty little dinner and supper, all in one, he had better spend the evening by the fireside" (275). With his epicurean tastes, Pyncheon is obviously as cursed as any protagonist in Hawthorne's Puritan spectacles; this type of hedonism reflects a self-centeredness and neglect of one's civic duties.

Juxtaposed with the fantasy about the evening banquet is Judge Pyncheon's earlier thought, before the long food excursion, that he has been negligent (and indeed, he has): he has wanted to fix the headstone of his wife's grave, which has fallen for some time now, and he thinks about aiding the impoverished widow of a childhood friend, but his intentions are not really sincere, as the narrator show: the "decayed widow" had "laid her case of destitution before him, in a very moving letter. She and her fair daughter have scarcely bread to eat. He *partly* intends to call on her, to-day—perhaps not—accordingly as he may happen to have leisure, and a small bank-note" (272). As a man without leisure and without generosity, Judge Pyncheon will not be truly charitable, even on his dying day—and his friend's wife will still have "scarcely bread to eat." His acts of munificence, like those of his predecessor, Colonel Pyncheon are mere show.

Unlike the Pyncheons, Holgrave, the descendant of the Maules, has the proper attitude towards food—and women. Colonel Pyncheon and Judge Pyncheon have both had voracious appetites—and have destroyed the women in their lives along the way. Indeed, Colonel Pyncheon wears out three wives before he meets his own demise. And Judge Pyncheon, though he only had one wife, seemed to be her undoing, through his tyrannical posture: "the lady got her death-blow in the honey-moon, and never smiled again, because her husband compelled her to serve him with coffee, every morning, at his bedside, in token of fealty to her liege-lord and master" (123). But Holgrave is egalitarian and the perfect mate for Phoebe, as he knows how to cultivate a garden. In fact, he asks her, in this symbiotic relationship, to care for the flowers, as he tends to the vegetable garden. Early in the narrative, Hepzibah warns Phoebe of the eccentric Holgrave, insisting that he has "a law of his own" (85) and that he belongs to a group of radicals (reformers and philanthropists among them) who "ate no solid food, but lived on the scent of other people's cookery, and turned up their noses at their fare" (84). Though Holgrave is not so magical that he can avoid food (Hepzibah's prejudice is unfounded), he is stoical, and indeed, he can thrive on a vegetarian diet, unlike the beef-eating, gout-ridden Pyncheons. He mocks the Pyncheon chickens for being infertile as a result of their "aristocratic lineage" (90), though as we later see, under Phoebe's care, the chickens thrive and lay eggs (a propitious sign for the Phoebe-Holgrave mating). Like a good Transcendentalist, Holgrave prefers more spiritual fare than the heavy Pyncheon meats, and in veiled sexual discourse, asks Phoebe for a blossom of her flowers now and then "exchange for all the good, honest kitchen vegetables with which I propose to enrich Miss Hepzibah's table" (93). In some ways, the couple, even in the courtship stage, reminds one of the "New Adam and Eve" theme that so attracted Hawthorne. (Indeed, Hawthorne's story of the same title, "The New Adam and Eve" was published in 1843.) Holgrave imagines a type of utopian existence with Phoebe, which will permit them to be "fellow-laborers, somewhat on the community-system" (93). Though finally, their life together will be more middle-class and domestic than utopian/communal, this new way of tending the earth is refreshing, considering that land was the basis upon which the feud was waged between Maules and Pyncheons.[15]

The women in the text, as well as Uncle Venner, are the real nurturers and providers. Uncle Venner attempts to bridge the gap between the poor (the newly impoverished, like Hepzibah, along with the poor street person, like himself) and the well-to-do with his almost Fourierist dreams of an almshouse that would equalize everyone. When Hepzibah opens the cent-shop, he is the first to congratulate her for her labors: "I'm glad to see you beginning to do your work, Miss Hepzibah" (62). Rather than relying upon the almshouse, he trusts upon the collective charity of the town—to give him scraps for sustenance, in return for performing odd jobs around the yard or in the house. In discussing his future plans, he alludes to the "brick-house" or "work-house," actually the Salem almshouse, where he means to retire only after he has completed his work, in three or four years' time, to "be idle and enjoy" himself (62). Whether Venner owns a pig or not, he collects scraps for the mythical pig, he says he will slaughter when he has become sufficiently stuffed, so that he can offer a communal feast. This, in opposition to the Pyncheon show of food, is what Hawthorne imagines as a true charitable gesture. Uncle Venner, the poor homeless beggar, though charitable in his impulses, wants to make a pig roast for the community when he retires: "he would make a feast of the portly grunter, and invite all his neighbors to partake of the joints and spare-ribs they had helped to fatten"(286). Almost a perfect likeness of Child's vision of the frugal economist, Uncle Venner knows how to make the best of his situation, collecting "cabbage-leaves, turnip-tops, potato-skins, and the miscellaneous refuse of the dinner-pot, which the thrifty housewives of the neighborhood . . . were accustomed to set aside" (186). In Lydia Maria Child's chapter, "How to Endure Poverty," she expresses the sentiment that one could retain one's dignity even if forced to succumb to alms[16]; Venner illustrates this principle perfectly. He himself pokes fun at the simpleton or village idiot in the almshouse who got there because he could not become useful, in the Yankee vein—such a type remains idle because not even "our busy Yankees have [n]ever found out how to put him to any use?"(64). A combination of street poet and pragmatic philosopher, Uncle Venner gives Hepzibah sound advice about marketing "stale" food in her cent-shop: "A stale article, if you dip it in a good, warm, sunny smile, will go off better than a fresh one that you've scowled upon" (66). He also reminds her that it is dangerous to give credit and advises her to be self-reliant: "Brew your own yeast, and make your own ginger-beer" (66).

Though Hepzibah has no animus towards Uncle Venner, as his age alone makes him venerable, she has had to eradicate her sense of superiority—by throwing aside her English Cookery book and also by accepting the democratic masses who visit her cent-shop. Truly, she has become "useful" and modest, to use positive terms from Child's view of the virtues of economy. Initially, she has viewed her customers as dirty and proletarian, and notes their callous ways or drunken breath, even if they at times give her sound advice, "A cent-shop, and no yeast! . . . That will never do!" (53-54). Yet at times, she is overly compassionate, as she refuses to take money from a fragile-looking housewife, who appears to be the victim of a brutal husband. Finally, she feels derisive of the aristocratic class: feeling " a sentiment of virulence . . towards the idle aristocracy to which it had so recently been her pride to belong" (55). Hepzibah condemns one of the wealthy would-be customers, who enters the shop merely to gawk at the fallen aristocrat: "Must the whole world toil, that the palms of her hands be kept white and delicate? (55). Thus, she is transformed from useless and idle to useful and frugal—in a narrative which continuously scorns idleness. Almost in fear of the masses, she initially gives Ned Higgins, the little boy who clamors for and devours gingerbread cookies, one Jim Crow cookie for free, but then she thinks better of her own need and asks him to pay for the second one.[17] Yet, a true feeling of charity overcomes Hepzibah, in the final chapter, as she gives Ned enough silver to satisfy the bottomless pit of his belly with an adequate supply of cookies. In some ways, the appetites of the new up-and-coming underclass are as ravenous as those of the Pyncheon upper class; capitalism has whetted everyone's appetite for more.

The novel also ends with an image, ostensibly (but not entirely) positive, of a "gingerbread house" in the country, which the newly betrothed Phoebe and Holgrave, as new owners of the Pyncheon country estate, plan to bestow upon Uncle Venner. Indeed, all the inhabitants of the old Pyncheon estate, the House of the Seven Gables, make a mass exodus to the country estate, as the deceased Judge Pyncheon's money and land go to the surviving Pyncheons. Phoebe promises to fix up for Uncle Venner a cottage on their estate, "the prettiest little, yellowish-brown cottage you eve saw . . . for it looks just as if it were made of gingerbread"(371).[18] It is not clear whether Hawthorne's attitude is disingenuous or sincere, as the image of gingerbread cottage seems too cloyingly sweet and domestic. In fact, the vision that is more satisfying belongs to Uncle Venner himself, who agrees to company the family, but who imagines himself as a "Roxbury russet," a hardy type of apple indigenous to New England; as he describes himself, "a great deal the better, the longer I can be kept" (318).[19] And he prides himself on his wisdom, which he likens to "golden dandelions . . .which never grow in the hot months, but may be seen glistening among the withered grass, and under the dry leaves as late as December" (318). This final image of a sustaining but simple food is more in keeping with both Lydia Maria Child's and Hawthorne's notion of New England cookery and economy.[20] From start to finish, the food dynamics in Hawthorne's *The House of the Seven Gables* revolve around spiritual love and illicit passions (and ambitions)—between the spiritual and the material—and around class feuds (between the underclass and aristocracy), as it explores the tensions between the values of New England and Old England. The frame is not so much a house, but a cornucopia of food—and an invitation to sample the food that only Phoebe and Holgrave can provide.[21]

Notes

1. Nathaniel Hawthorne, *The Scarlet Letter*, Centenary ed., vol.I (Columbus: Ohio State Univ. Press, 1962), 219. Further references to the Hawthorne texts are to the authoritative Centenary editions of his works: Nathaniel Hawthorne, *Mosses from an Old Manse*, Centenary, vol. X (Columbus: Ohio State UP, 1965) and Nathaniel Hawthorne, *The House of the Seven Gables*, Centenary ed., vol II (Columbus: Ohio State UP, 1965).

2. Richard Godbeer, *Sexual Revolution in Early America* (Baltimore: Johns Hopkins UP, 2002), 55. Godbeer, who focuses on the Puritans' "eroticization of the spirtual" notes the Puritans' ambivalence towards sex: "Puritans were both exuberantly permissive and vehemently restrictive" (55). Recently, other historians have acknowledged the bawdy side of Puritans. See also, James Deetz and Patricia Scott Deetz, who assert, "The seventeenth century was a time of robust interactions between the sexes. It was commonly supposed that when a man and woman were alone together they would be involved in sexual activity of some sort or another, and the laws that governed sexual behavior are to be seen against this background" (*The Times of their Lives: Life, Love, and Death in Plymouth Colony* [N.Y.: W. H. Freeman and Co., 2000], 133).

On the other hand, women were always penalized more for exhibiting sexuality, and this idea enters Hawthorne's texts. According to Else L. Hambledon, "Marriage, which would have served a rehabilitative function, and which was, moreover, a woman's only 'career option' in the seventeenth century, became difficult for women branded as sexual transgressors" ("The Regulation of Sex in

Seventeenth-Century Massachusetts," in *Sex and Sexuality in Early America*, ed. Merril D. Smith [NY: NYU Press, 1998], 111.

Hawthorne's ideal of womanhood embodied in Phoebe corresponds more to the idea of nineteenth-century True Womanhood. I believe that Hawthorne is relating his notion of Puritan sexuality to the same regulatory system or surveillance of nineteenth-century bourgeois sexuality, as examined by Michel Foucault in *The History of Sexuality*.

3. Godbeer, 55.

4. As in the case of the Pyncheon ancestral disease, Roderick's bosom serpent is hereditary: Roderick asserts that the snake "once crept into the vitals of my great-grandfather, and dwelt there many years, tormenting the old gentleman beyond mortal endurance. In short, it is a family peculiarity" (282). Phoebe, in *House*, imagines a likeness to a serpent in Judge Pyncheon's physical attributes (119).

5. The view that Puritans equated sexuality and economics (as power) is promoted by Boris Vejdovsky, in his discussion of Mather's *Wonders of the Invisible World*, which, he feels, "relays the anxiety of Puritan men—husbands, brothers, planters—under the weight of patriarchal demand, and it expresses their fear in images where sex, economies—monetary as well as semiotic—and politics reflect one another" ("'Remember Me': The Wonders of the Invisible World –Sex, Patriarch, and Paranoia in Early America," in *The Puritan Origins of American Sex: Religion, Sexuality, and National Identity in American Literature*, eds. Tracy Fessenden, Nicholas F. Radel, and Magdalena J. Zaborowska [N.Y.: Routledge, 2001], 66).

6. For a discussion of early American cookbooks, see Julie A. Matthaei, *An Economic History of Women in America: Women's Work, the Sexual Division of Labor, and the Development of Capitalism* (N.Y.: Schocken, 1982), 40-50.

7. Lydia Maria Child, *The American Frugal Housewife:* "Dedicated to Those Who are Not Afraid of Economy," (Bedford, Mass.: Applewood Books, Rpt of Boston: Carter, Hendee, and Co., 1833 edition), frontispiece.

8. Child, *American Frugal Housewife*, 6, 7.

9. Joel Pfister maintains that Hawthorne uses Phoebe as a way to display "the cultural uses of and need for a distinctively middle-class femininity" ("Cleaning House: From the Gothic to the Middle-Class World Order," in his *The Production of Personal Life: Class, Gender, and the Psychological in Hawthorne's Fiction*. [Stanford, Calif.: Stanford UP, 1991], 149). Gillian Brown feels that Phoebe, as "true woman," represents "domesticity as a welcome change that relieves the effects of other changes" ("Women's Work and Bodies in *The House of the Seven Gables*," in her *Domestic Individualism: Imagining Self in Nineteenth-Century America* [Berkeley: Univ. of Ca. P, 1990], 94).

10. See Hildegard Hoeller's enlightening essay about Lydia Maria Child's famous cookbook: "A Quilt for Life: Lydia Maria Child's *The American Frugal Housewife,*" *American Transcendental Quarterly* 13, no. 2 (1999): 89-104. Through what seemed like sentimental and domestic discourse, Child was able to be transgressive as well. Child depicted woman not simply as a moral force,

the traditional "angel of the household," but also as an economic force in the household, thus merging the gender spheres of home and marketplace.

11. Child, *The American Frugal Housewife,* 75. The entire recipe for Child's rendition of "Indian cakes" can be found in *The American Frugal Housewife,* 75-76.

12. Colonial women were far less free than nineteenth-century women in their "lives and work choices," as they came under their husbands' jurisdiction. Matthaei shows how they were more limited in expressing their individuality (*Economic History of Women,* 49). Thus, Hawthorne's ghostlike Puritan women are probably jealous of Phoebe's freedom in the kitchen.

13. Hawthorne clearly attacks the descendants of Puritans in various guises. In "The Custom-House" introduction to *The Scarlet Letter,* we find a type very similar to the Pyncheons in the old Custom-House Inspector, who seems to be a relic of the past. As the "father of the Custom-House," he is the "patriarch, not only of the little squad of officials, but, . . . of the respectable body of tide-waiters all over the United States" (18). Hawthorne, working in the Custom-House, compares him to an animal, lacking all spirituality "Looking at him merely as an animal,—and there really very little else to look at,—he was a most satisfactory object" (18). Like Pyncheon, described in animalistic terms, the old Custom-House Inspector also seems to live for the pleasure of food: "One point, in which he had vastly the advantage over this four-footed brethren, was his ability to recollect the good dinners which it had made no small portion of the happiness of his life to eat. His gourmandism was a highly agreeable trait; and to hear him talk of roast-meat was as appetizing as a pickle or an oyster" (18). In his comic sketch, Hawthorne notes the Inspector's ability to evoke meals of the past and to allow his fellow workers to savor the "pig or turkey under one's very nostrils" (18-19). As a man who devoted "all his energies and ingenuities to subserve the delight and profit of his maw" (19), the Inspector almost becomes a historian of local dinners: "There were flavors on his palate, that had lingered there not less than sixty or seventy years, and were still apparently as fresh as that of the muttonchop which he had just devoured for his breakfast" (19). He is able to recollect in much more detail and with more relish the dinners of the past than the guests with whom he had eaten with, friends, who themselves "had long been food for worms" (19). Though seemingly humorous, the sketch shows the utter materialism of the "Custom-House" workers (and of the labor involved)—and clearly explains how Hawthorne's creative powers had diminished, and why he needed to leave to rediscover them.

14. In a novel which celebrates the matrilineal legacy and legitimacy (as with Phoebe and her mother) in contradistinction to patriarchal inheritance, it is not surprising that Clifford seems to be saved through the likeness to his mother. Hepzibah realizes that he does not have the criminal Pyncheon instinct, but that, rather, he has the gentleness of his mother: "they persecuted his mother in him! He never was a Pyncheon!" (60).

15. Hawthorne also attempted the utopian lifestyle at Brook Farm, but as we know from his Notebooks, he gave that dream up for wedded bliss to Sophia at the Old Manse, in Concord. He traded in his Fourierist ideas for domesticity,

much in the vein of Holgrave. It is noteworthy that Holgrave, like the Transcendentalist Thoreau (who preferred a vegetarian diet over meat), has a green thumb for growing beans; Clifford is delighted to see Holgrave's "scarlet-flowering beans" which have not grown in the Pyncheon garden for forty years (149).

16. Child, "How to Endure Poverty," *The American Frugal Housewife,* 111-113.

17. Robert K Martin sees the exchange between Hepzibah and Ned in a more ominous vein; he feels that Hepzibah is symbolically participating in the slave economy by basing her profits on the sale of the Jim Crow cookies ("Haunted Jim Crow: Gothic Fictions by Hawthorne and Faulkner," in *American Gothic: New Interventions in a National Narrative*, ed. Robert K. Martin and Eric Savoy. [Iowa City: University of Iowa Press, 1998], 129–142).

Little avaricious Ned Higgins, who demands charity of Hepzibah in the first shop encounter, can be likened to the organ-grinder's monkey, who incessantly sticks out his hand for more "lucre" so that even Phoebe is seduced into throwing him money. There is no way "of satisfying the covetous little devil," as the monkey takes little pleasure in the joyless and obsessive endeavor to accumulate: "Phoebe threw down a whole handfull [sic] of cents, which he picked up with joyless eagerness, handed them over to the Italian for safe-keeping, and immediately recommenced a series of pantomimic petitions for more" (164). Adam Smith's invisible hand of capitalism is insidious and not so invisible in Hawthorne's romance!

18. Hawthorne might have in mind an Andrew Jackson Downing rural and picturesque cottage with Phoebe's vision of the "gingerbread house" for Uncle Venner. Interestingly, what Child did for the culinary art of America, Downing might be credited for doing to American architecture—a simplifying but civilizing and also democratizing force in the wilderness of "New" England.

19. Although Tamar Heller and Patricia Moran make much of the apple imagery in their analysis of food by focusing on the association with women of transgressive activity ("Introduction." *Scenes of the Apple: Food and the Female Body in Nineteenth- and Twentieth-Century Women's Writing* [Albany: SUNY P, 2003], 1-44).

For Hawthorne, in this case, the apple simply represents solid and simple New England fare.

20. Lydia Maria Child obviously includes "dandelions" as important to the New England diet. She also comments on their hardiness: "If cut off, without injuring the root, they will spring up again, fresh and tender, till late in the season" (*The American Frugal Housewife,* 35). In some ways, dandelions represent Uncle Venner's stalwart and enduring ways, as he himself acknowledges.

21. Hawthorne's culinary imagination also corresponds with his notion of the "romance" as literary genre. In the prefaces to *The Scarlet Letter* and to *House,* he discusses the need for the romance to combine the supernatural or marvelous with the pedestrian and realistic using the right amount of light and shadow. In the preface to *House,* he even makes that distinction using food imagery. Describing the author as a host or cook, he speaks metaphorically of the

perfect ingredients: "He [the author] will be wise . . . to mingle the Marvellous rather as a slight, delicate, and evanescent flavor, than as any portion of the actual substance of the dish offered to the Public" (1). That the "Marvelous" can only be a seasoning shows Hawthorne's awareness of the audience's growing desire for substantial fare, or realism.

In his later journals and essays, after his Consular stay in England, Hawthorne evinces more ambivalence about the deteriorating state of both British and American cuisine, as it reflects upon deeper national characteristics. By the time Hawthorne writes the last sketch of *Our Old Home: A Series of English Sketches (1863)*, "Civic Banquets," he is not as apt to endorse the American character, even as he makes light of the English. It is a satirical sketch that exposes the weaknesses of both nations, through their appetites, cuisine, and table manners.

What Katy Ate:
Girls Eating and Reading in Classic Nineteenth-Century American Children's Fiction

Alice Jenkins

In their study of girls' fiction, Shirley Foster and Judy Simons recast the name of Susan Coolidge's classic novel, *What Katy Did*, as "What Katy Read." This essay is titled "What Katy Ate" because its concern is with the discourse of consumption and nutrition that surrounds images of girls reading in American children's literature in the middle and late nineteenth century. The analogy between tropes of food in children's literature and sex in adult literature has often been pointed out.[1] But the links between sexual and gustatory discourses can be more complex and ideologically various than this analogy suggests. During the nineteenth century, when children's literature and mass literature were developing legitimacy in the face of anxieties about the effects of widespread access to texts, the reading/eating metaphor was an important element in the rhetorical battery of writers from all points of the political compass. Reading, eating and sexuality were folded together in critical discourse about literature for girls as well as featuring, in appropriately coded ways, in the texts themselves. As Sarah Sceats puts it, "the use of food and eating as a deliberate sexual metonymy or metaphor is a long-established tradition".[2] In mid- and late-nineteenth-century America, the developing ideal of young womanhood was, as Joan Jacobs Brumberg notes, "an icon representing American exceptionalism and material progress."[3] Within this context, images linking girls' reading to consumption of foodstuffs assumed particular significance. Various kinds of food could stand for whole ideological positions; food became a coded expression of moral values.

As Donnalee Frega writes, "female hunger and eating habits have long been regarded as a form of discourse, a rich and complex metaphoric language of victimization, eroticism, and empowerment."[4] This discourse of hunger and food has been used as a way of thinking about female appetites of all kinds. The connections between the languages of hunger and sexual appetite are obvious, and have frequently been deployed to characterize the female as a state of lacking, emphasizing female physical emptiness and desire to be filled from outside. But almost as closely linked are discourses of eating and reading. Both are appetites for internalization of external matter; both exercise a kind of ownership over this external matter; both have the potential to change the individual as she consumes. Frega's trio of "victimization, eroticism, and empowerment" recur in the discourses surrounding female reading during the age of mass literacy and increasing juvenile access to texts. They figure both in representations of girls and women reading, and in the attempts to discipline and regulate such reading.

Steven Mailloux's work on the cultural uses of fiction in nineteenth-century America has emphasised the importance of what he calls 'the physicality of the tropes used to figure reading." Among these tropes, which include reading as discipline and reading as gymnastics, he lists the image of reading as eating, and comments: "these rhetorical interconnections enabled not only the development of a new kind of children's literature after the Civil War but also reforms in the cultural management of delinquency and perhaps even the institutionalization of literary study in the university."[5] David S. Downing elaborates on this suggestion about the role of the association of reading with nutrition in legitimising the academic study of vernacular literature: "If reading and learning were literally like eating and digesting, then it was an objectifiable process that could be measured, controlled, manipulated to fit certain criteria, and thus disciplinized into a coherent body of teachable knowledge."[6] The metaphor of text as sustenance lends itself to regulation, regularization and discourses of control, but a converse set of arguments were also being articulated during the later nineteenth century regarding the possible consequences of free, unregulated access to text. Mailloux's work concentrates on fears linking uncontrolled reading in boys to crime and delinquency; equivalent concerns over girls' reading habits in the same period tended to allude rather to the sexuality and physical health of the individual and her family.

Until the later nineteenth century, the dominant tradition in the use of images of girls reading in both American and British literature was disapprobatory or satirical. Girls were shown reading in order to indicate how misguided, foolish, and undiscriminating they were. Merging with the recurrent Christian confusion between fiction and lies, this tradition emphasized the wickedness of reading novels. At best such reading was a waste of time that could be used more profitably: Jane Hunter's study of nineteenth-century American girls' diaries shows how much guilt many girl readers felt over the time given to and pleasure derived from private reading.[7] At worst, reading for pleasure was believed to lead to the inculcation of vicious habits of mind and feebleness of body.

The imaginary girl in Lydia Signourney's 1838 essay on "Memory" prefers eating to reading. She confesses to her teacher:

> I forgot to get my lesson this morning," [. . .] "Did you forget to come to breakfast?" "No, Ma'am, I did not." "Then your body has a better appetite for food, than your mind for knowledge."
> [The teacher takes the opportunity to underline the moral.]
> "If you were sick you would not wish for breakfast. You would avoid the sight of food. Perhaps your parents would send for a physician. He would give you medicine. He would seek to remove the causes that had destroyed your appetite. What medicine will you take to restore the health of your mind?"[8]

The girl, we infer, has neglected her reading because the lesson-book – unlike her breakfast—is distasteful to her. Her story is compared to that of a boy who admits to his father that he cannot remember the sermon or the Sunday school lesson, although he can remember the story of Robinson Crusoe.[9] The boy's reading has been pleasurable; the girl's has not. Signourney splits the metaphor of eating as reading across the two children, so that the girl's taste for food is likened to the boy's for fiction, but both are condemned for putting appetite ahead of discipline.

A much better-known girl reader from the early part of the nineteenth century, Catherine Morland in *Northanger Abbey*, exemplifies the reverse of the fault Signourney reproves. Catherine is so avid a consumer of Gothic novels that she has no appetite for anything else, even for food: "Catherine was then left to the luxury of a raised, restless, and frightened imagination over the pages of *Udolpho*, lost from all worldly concerns of dressing and dinner."[10] Girls like Catherine Morland read to the exclusion of all other mental activities; rather than eating, indeed, they *become* food. They are consumed by the texts to which they devote themselves. They find the pleasure of the texts much greater than the pleasure of life, and this rejection, or rather postponement of engagement with life is figured as a postponement of mature relationships with men. Heroines of early nineteenth-century novels must renounce novel-reading before they can be assimilated into can be assimilated into the adult world—an assimilation signaled by participation in adult sexuality. Nor is their novel-reading replaced by any other kind of reading. Heroines do not forswear novels and turn to devotional or philosophical literature. Reading is a stage that must be grown out of along with adolescence.

The reading girls of the mid and late nineteenth-century novel maintain this tradition of reading as escape from, or postponement of, active participation in the outside world. With the development of a literature intended specifically for children, the texts read by girls in later nineteenth-century fiction are often not romances or Gothic productions, but stories about other children and young people. Where girls consumed adult fiction, though, the concern that reading is an immature taste which contributes to or at least reflects a delay in the onset of adult sexuality was complemented by a fear that some kinds of reading encourage premature sexual understanding. Just as some Victorian families tried to delay the onset of biological puberty by restricting their daughters' access to stimulating food, others sought to police girls' reading even into the late teens.[11]

Alberto Manguel argues that "the act of reading in time requires a corresponding act of reading in place, and the relationship between the two acts is inextricable."[12] There is interesting work to be done on the locations of reading in children's literature. Reading in private libraries, enjoyed by both Jo March and Katy Carr, clearly has different political implications from reading in sequestered spaces like Jo's attic and Katy's loft. What if the place of reading is not a library but a dinner table or a kitchen? C. S. Lewis felt that mealtime reading demands "a gossipy, formless book which can be opened anywhere".[13] His account of reading, though, is predicated on privileged circumstances involving almost no domestic tasks and a good deal of solitude. These circumstances were not available to most girl readers during the nineteenth century. Eating during meals would have been out of the question for most of the girls who read or featured in contemporary fiction. Instead, middle-class reading for pleasure was typically conducted in semi-formal setting of the family circle or privately during time taken from other duties, and any eating that accompanied it was likely to be supplementary or unofficial. But in critical writing the association between the discourses of reading and eating was far stronger than in material practice. In essays on girls' reading habits and in didactic passages in fiction for girls, the reading=eating equation was made again and again, and in ways that invoked numbers of related discourses and social anxieties about the health of the individual body and the nation.

Gunilla Theander Kester rightly notes that "The connection between the female subject and the act of eating as a criminal act [. . .] is deeply ingrained in Western culture."[14] During the early decades of mass female literacy, social anxieties about women's reading were encoded by analogies to women's eating in a tangle of metaphorical and discursive connections that expressed a range of attitudes from the guilty and punitive to the celebratory. In the remainder of this essay I shall argue that the linking of the discourses of eating, reading and sexual maturation provided nineteenth century writers for girls with a set of metaphors with which to explore and to encode social attitudes to female appetites. I shall begin by discussing the interactions of writing and eating in those classics of American girls'literature, *Little Women* and *What Katy Did*, and then shift my focus to the operation of these discourses in critical writing for girls in the same period.

Susan Coolidge's *What Katy Did*, the first of her hugely successful series largely for and about girls, plays a series of variations on the linked metaphors of reading and eating.[15] Coolidge often agrees with Jane Austen that reading and eating are in competition with one another; but the relationship between the two is more complex than that. During the first part of the novel Katy's delight in reading is encouraged by her father but feared by her friends: "the little girls to whose houses she went visiting [. . .] always hid away their story-books, when she was expected to tea".[16] In the second part of the book Katy takes over the housekeeping, and reads cookery books almost as obsessively as she previously read literature. Whether reading novels or cookery books, Katy, like Catherine Morland, finds that her hunger for text destroys her hunger for food. "Katy would send for every recipe-book in the house, and pore over them by the hour, till her appetite was as completely gone as if she had swallowed twenty dinners."[17]

Although her literary reading has been shown to be both eclectic and comparatively serious ("she read all sorts of things: travels, and sermons, and old magazines"), Katy's culinary reading becomes driven by a univocal ideology combining Puritanical distrust of pleasure with modern scientific doctrines on health.[18] By enforcing this ideology of plainness in her family's eating she destroys not only her own appetite but theirs as well. Her father, the book's symbol of benign male authority, is obliged to step in to break the link between reading and diet:

Katy got hold of a book upon "The Stomach", and was seized with a rage for wholesome food. She entreated Clover and the other children to give up sugar and butter and gravy and pudding-sauce and buckwheat cakes and pies, and almost everything else that they particularly liked. Boiled rice seemed to her the most sensible dessert, and she kept the

family on it until finally John and Dorry started a rebellion, and Dr Carr
was forced to interfere.

> "My dear, you are overdoing it sadly," he said, as Katy opened her
> book and prepared to explain her views; "I am glad to have the chil-
> dren eat simple food – but really, boiled rice five times a week is too
> much."[19]

Katy's appeal to the authority of text is trumped by the authority of
her father's status as a medical practitioner: once again, excessive reading is the enemy of healthy eating. It is interesting that Coolidge allows
her child characters a considerable degree of effective power, both to
enforce regulation and to rebel against it. John and Dorry's rejection of
Katy's plain food mirrors the younger Carrs' earlier rejection of her of-
fensively wholesome "religious paper" *The Sunday Visitor*, enforced
readings of which are stopped only when Clover and Elsie burn the
manuscript in the kitchen fire. Twice in two chapters, Katy's writings are
burnt in gestures that parody the act of cooking. As well as the destruction of her didactic writing, her fantastic narrative "The Blue Wizard, or
Edwitha of the Hebrides" is sent to the flames when discovered by Aunt
Izzie. These accounts of texts consumed by the flames of the kitchen fire
clearly owe something to the episode in *Little Women*, published by the
same Boston firm four years earlier, in which Amy March burns Jo's
book of fairy tales. But whereas Amy's is simply an act of calculated
vandalism, in both cases where Katy's writings are burnt, the destruction
is an act of literary criticism, readers condemning the texts as "trash."[20]
Coolidge empowers her child characters as readers, permitting them far
more scepticism, and ultimately more power, in their relationships with
both texts and food than Alcott permits in *Little Women*.

Alcott does, however, countenance the idea of solitary eating. In contrast, the Carrs' eating is almost always a familial activity. Even during
the literary fête involving reading and eating in the loft, the children's
eating away is outside the kitchen but within the family group. Where
girl characters are shown eating alone there is both greater danger and
greater potential for individual development. Jo March is found reading
and eating alone at the beginning of chapter 3 of *Little Women*.

> "Jo! Jo! Where are you?" cried Meg, at the foot of the garret stairs.
> "Here!" answered a husky voice from above, and, running up, Meg
> found her sister eating apples and crying over the *Heir of Redclyffe*,
> wrapped up in a comforter on an old three-legged sofa by the sunny
> window. This was Jo's favourite refuge; and here she loved to retire
> with half a dozen russets and a nice book, to enjoy the quiet and the so-
> ciety of a pet rat who lived near by and didn't mind her a particle.[21]

Already the book has made much of the motif of food. Nina Auerbach's striking comment that "the Christmas gift Marmee seems tenderly to offer her girls is hunger" refers to the opening chapter, in which the March girls give their Christmas breakfast away to a poor family, and are rewarded by the gift of a splendid festive supper by the wealthy old gentleman who lives next door.[22] This meal is shared not only by the family but by their Christmas guests, a collection of anonymous girls. Food links the familial and social contexts through the economy of charity. But in this scene in the garret, Jo's eating is not social but solitary, food taken from a private store and consumed privately, along with Charlotte M. Yonge's intensely moral, high-church novel of suffering and tragic redemption. There seems to be a creative conflict between Jo's passionate enjoyment of this story of renunciation, of the refusal of appetites, and her solitary and unnecessary consumption of food. This conflict can be read as expressive of Jo's difficulty in assuming the conventional gender identity offered to her; she is temporarily withdrawing from the world of socially-accepted desires.

Jo's choice of apples for her solitary eating reflects the straitened circumstances of the March household, in turn a reflection of the poverty of the Alcotts, who were reduced to living on apples and water during the final phase of Bronson Alcott's Fruitlands experiment in communal living.[23] These material considerations do not obscure the fact that Jo's choice is also a reminder of the apple that Anglophone Christianity has traditionally identified as the fruit eaten by Eve in Genesis 3:6. But Jo's apple-eating, unlike Eve's, is solitary and represents no threat to the ongoing life of her community (she is quite able to put the book away and resume her family responsibilities at Meg's call), although it does express a weaning from exclusive reliance on the familial context. Elaine Showalter argues that "eating apples also became identified in [Alcott's] mind with female creativity and sexuality, with writing, knowledge, and transgression."[24] The apples' suggestive allusion to Jo's growing sexual maturity contributes to the greater symbolism of the eating and reading in the garret, which is the desire for self-sufficiency. This desire is represented as essentially healthy: the apples are not only symbolic but also actually nutritious, and this in turn reflects well on Jo's choice of accompanying book. Alcott tends to make strong associations between wrong reading and wrong eating. Amy's teacher's attempts to police behaviour in his school climaxes in forcing Amy to discard her twenty-four pickled limes, and also includes making "a bonfire of confiscated novels and newspapers" and suppressing a "private post-office."[25] Similarly, in Alcott's 1870 novel *An Old-Fashioned Girl*, Polly's new city friends, evidently performing fashionable femininity, discuss sensation novels and are inclined to dismiss Polly's preference for novels with "history in them."[26] The reader is not at all surprised when a page later, Polly is subjected to peer pressure and foregoes the "honest brown cookies" that "Grandma had put in her pocket for luncheon" in order to eat unsustaining ice cream and macaroons with these fans of Ouida.[27] Unsustaining food goes with unsustaining literature; both ought to be rejected by wholesome girls.

In both Coolidge's and Alcott's novels, the ideological interactions of gendered eating and reading patterns are complicated by the introduction of important themes of writing. As Katy and Jo experiment with writing, seen in both narratives as a natural concommitant of reading, the discourse of consumption acquires fresh potency. When Jo moves from consumption into production, taking up writing as a serious pursuit, her ability to eat suffers as texts and food are dichotomised once again:

> She did not think herself a genius by any means; but when the fit came on, [...] sleep forsook her eyes, meals stood untasted, day and night were all too short to enjoy the happiness which blessed her only at such times, and made these hours worth living, even if they bore no other fruit.[28]

Hunger only returns after the urgent need to write has abated. Though consumption of texts may be compatible with eating, production of them in *Little Women* competes successfully with food preparation. David Waters notes that "Jo struggles to author texts kept in a "tin kitchen" which might be consumed in the parlor as an alternative to the expected women's kitchen production of meals."[29] Writing in this novel, is what reading is in *Northanger Abbey*: a bodily appetite so strong that it suppresses all others. The "fruit" that Jo's writing bears turns out, at first, to be unwholesome. Her forays into commercial literature make "her emaciated purse [grow] stout" but her conscience is awakened by Professor Bhaer's characterisation of sensation fiction in terms of bad food: "they haf no right to put poison in the sugarplum, and let the small ones eat it."[30] Jo's feeble appeal to market economics is met with the damning riposte: "there is a demand for whiskey, but I think you and I do not care to sell it."[31] Bhaer's extreme analogies activate what Patrick Brantlinger calls "the rhetoric of toxicity", the long-standing tradition of associating dangerous reading with poison, which was very powerful in the early decades of mass literacy.[32] As Brantlinger points out, metaphors comparing reading to eating "place novel-reading in the emergent category of mass consumption, rather than in that of high or elite culture", and it is very often in the context of fears for inexperienced readers (such as chil-

dren, women and the working class) that the rhetoric of toxicity is invoked.[33] Middle-class girls' reading was subject to these kinds of fears,
but was also considered to be valuable for its contribution to developing
individual, independent taste.[34]

Augusta Evans's *Macaria: Or, Altars of Sacrifice* is a sort of Confederate equivalent of *Little Women*, published in 1864; its most recent
editor describes it as "the quintessential war story for Confederate
women."[35] Like *Little Women*, *Macaria* makes connections between
girls reading and girls eating, but with a different construction of femininity from Alcott's. In an early scene, fourteen-year-old Irene is chided
by her Aunt Margaret (standing in for paternal authority) for carrying her
own books and lunchbasket to school:

> "You know very well your father can't bear to see you carrying your
> own satchel and basket to school. He ordered Martha to take them
> every morning and evening, but she says you will not let her carry them.
> It is just sheer obstinacy in you."
> "There it is again! because I don't choose to be petted like a baby or
> made a wax-doll of, it is set down to obstinacy, as if I had the temper of
> a heathen. See here, aunt Margaret, I am tired of having Martha tramp-
> ing eternally at my heels as though I were a two year old child. There is
> no reason in her walking after me when I am strong enough to carry my
> own books, and I don't intend she shall do it any longer."
> "But, Irene, your father is too proud to have you trudging along the
> road like any other beggar, with your books in one arm, and a basket
> swinging on the other. Just suppose the Carters or the Harrises should
> meet you? Dear me! they would hardly believe you belonged to a
> wealthy, aristocratic family like the Huntingdons. Child, I never carried
> my own dinner to school in my life."
> "And I expect that is exactly the reason why you are for ever complain-
> ing, and scarcely see one well day in the three hundred and sixty-five.
> [. . .]"[36]

Irene's solecism is to fail to display her family's wealth and prestige
by having a servant carry her lunch and schoolbooks. She seeks to demonstrate her growing independence and autonomy by taking control of
her materials for reading and eating, and the text endorses her association
of this control with physical health and mental wellbeing. The fact that
Irene's reading matter has materiality, having to be physically trans-
ported from one reading site to another, is part of its role in her development into a healthy adult.

As in this example, anxiety over reading as a factor in the formation
of the mind is often closely related to anxiety over the discipline of the
body. Regulating reading was in the nineteenth century part of the regu-

lation of health and sexuality. In the case of middle-class girls' reading, the urgency of the regulatory process derived from the double concern to delay the onset of adult sexuality and at the same time to educate the young female into the emotional constraints that support bourgeois heterosexual gender roles. That is, the girl should preserve her sexual innocence until far beyond puberty, avoiding sensation fiction, so-called "immodest" literature and any text which provokes a physical response in the reader. Equally, though, reading should prepare a girl for marriage by providing a series of examples which lead her to expect and endorse conventional sexual expression.

A combination of these ideological pressures and commercial opportunity meant that by the end of the nineteenth century in the United States the girl reader had come to occupy a particular niche within the reading public, with book marketing often directed explicitly at her supposed tastes and appetites, or at those of the adults who bought books for girls. In 1910 the editor of *Every Girl's Library*, Percy Kease Fitzhugh, wrote "I think we may dismiss, if we hold it, the view that there is any such thing as "girls' literature.""[37] Fitzhugh's enlightened critical views on gender and genre were, however, contradicted by the title (presumably chosen for commercial reasons) of his ten-volume collection. Judging by its size and its rather off-putting subtitle, "A Collection of Appropriate and Instructive Reading for Girls of All Ages from the Best Authors of All Time," this anthology was intended for purchase by adults to give to children or to be bought for libraries. The first volume opens with several essays on right reading practices for girls. These essays occupy an interesting generic position somewhere rather closer to advice literature than literary criticism; it is not at all surprising that they contain extensive material on the dangers of female reading. In order to enforce good reading habits they hyperbolise the discourses of nutrition and poison, partly to extol the harmlessness of the selection of texts appearing in the collection. Ella Wheeler Wilcox, for example, mobilises the discourse of health and discipline discussed earlier this essay, insisting that "However wisely we may regulate our reading after maturity, nothing eradicates wholly the influence left by the books we devoured in our adolescence."[38] She elaborates the indelibly-established metaphor of reading as devouring into just the type of admonitory narrative the Carr children in *What Katy Did* rebelled against:

> I have in mind a woman of ability and character who believes she has lost ten years of usefulness in the world by the unwise reading she was allowed to do in her childhood and early girlhood. [...] Sensation novels and "continued stories" running in weekly newspapers formed the main ingredients of her mental food.[39]

Kate Flint's study of the woman reader in the nineteenth century picks up the particular way in which metaphors of eating and reading were inflected in criticism of sensation fiction, which "deliberatedly catered to compulsive forms of consumption, and which [...] the reviewers prssented as being devoured by women".[40] Assuming "usefulness in the world" to be a goal of adult life rather than girlhood, Wilcox's argument is that a diet of cliffhanger narratives can retard the emotional and social maturation of girl readers. Margaret E. Sangster, similarly, condemns popular fiction as harmful to the reader, and improves on Wilcox's metaphor of bad food by referring to "sensational hot-house literature" as poison: "Whoever loves and appreciates [the girl reader] will be at pains to keep [such texts] from her, as the venom of the rattlesnake."[41]

In contrast with these two female commentators' attitudes to female literary appetites, Percy Fitzhugh's own essay explaining his rationale as editor of *Every Girl's Library* is remarkably optimistic about girls' ability to choose reading matter responsibly and not to be harmed by possible overindulgence. On the contrary, indeed, he writes strongly in favour of providing girl readers with substantial texts on which they can sate themselves, rather than presenting extracts and thereby implying that girls cannot make reading decisions for themselves. He mobilizes an extraordinary series of appetital metaphors to link female hunger, powerlessness and power, and sexuality, with the act of reading:

> From time immemorial, works partaking of the general character of this one have been published, and from time immemorial have their editors and compilers been charged with the grievous offence of whetting the literary appetite only to leave their disappointed readers hungry. Indeed, those responsible for the gathering and assortment of "gems" (as extracts from standard authors are usually called) may be likened to those ingenious prelates of the Spanish Inquisition who were wont, after binding their victims hand and foot, to place before them, but just beyond their reach, a steaming and savoury concoction, whose aroma, like some heedless coquette, would trifle with their palates, until they were well-nigh distracted.[42]

The image of the girl reader in bondage and in the power of an Inquisitor is quasi-pornographic: the female reader/victim yearningly desires the satisfaction that the male editor-Inquisitor deliberately withholds. But the stream of metaphors ends by gendering text as feminine, arousing but not satisfying the desires of the girl reader, herself now strangely re-coded as masculine or lesbian. This eminently respectable and indeed notably enlightened piece of writing nonetheless demonstrates that the confusion between the discourses of female appetite leads to a triple association between reading, eating and sexuality that offers constraint and subjection even as it promises liberation for the girl reader.

An extraordinary combination of cultural pressures and conflicting ideological intentions were present in contemporary thinking about the middle-class girl reader, who needed to be led towards adulthood but at the same time protected from too-early loss of innocence, and must be taught to aspire to heterosexual relationships but kept away from literature that provokes too much physical excitement. Fitzhugh's essay attempts to deal honestly with these conflicts, but the result is the breakdown of the gender identities he applies to his readers. Such clashing demands simply cannot be reconciled under assumptions of stable gender categorisation.

The eating/reading metaphor, then, focused a wide variety of social and political attitudes to the entrance of mid- and late-nineteenth-century American girls into literacy. While critical literature for and about girls often employed a semantic field based on health and nutrition (and conversely, addiction and poison), fictional images of girl readers were able to use describing eating as reading and reading as eating to indicate the pleasures of textuality, pleasures which gently and subtly suggest the pleasures of sexuality to come. As Flora Poste in Stella Gibbons's *Cold Comfort Farm* remarks, it is delightful to find a novel like *Macaria* in one's bedroom because it is the "kind of novel you could read while eating an apple."[43]

Notes

1. For instance, see Zohar Shavit, *Poetics of Children's Literature* (Athens: University of Georgia Press, 1986), 106.

2. Sarah Sceats, *Food, Consumption and the Body in Contemporary Women's Fiction* (Cambridge: Cambridge University Press, 2000), 23.

3. Joan Jacobs Brumberg, *The Body Project: An Intimate History of American Girls* (New York: Random House, 1997), 21.

4. Donnalee Frega, *Speaking in Hunger: Gender, Discourse, and Consumption in "Clarissa"* (Columbia: University of South Caroline Press, 1998), 1.

5. Stephen Mailloux, "Cultural Rhetoric Studies: Eating Bodies in Nineteenth-Century America," in *Reconceptualizing American Literary/Cultural Studies: Rhetoric, History, and Politics in the Humanities*, ed. William E. Cain (New York: Garland, 1996), 21-33 (22).

6. David S. Downing, "Feeding on American Fiction," in *Reconceptualizing American Literary/Cultural Studies*, 129-142 (133-34).

7. Jane H. Hunter, *How Young Ladies Became Girls: The Victorian Origins of American Girlhood* (New Haven: Yale University Press, 2002), 75-78.

8. L. H. Signourney, "Memory," in *The Girl's Reading-Book; in Prose and Poetry* (New York: Orville Taylor, 1838), 12-18 (12).

9. Signourney, "Memory", 12.

10. Jane Austen, *Northanger Abbey* (Oxford: Oxford University Press, 2nd edn, 1990), 34.

11. Brumberg, *The Body Project*, 10; Hunter, *How Young Ladies Became Girls*, 65.

12. Alberto Manguel, *A History of Reading* (London: HarperCollins, 1996; repr. Flamingo, 1997), 151.

13. C. S. Lewis, *Surprised by Joy: The Shape of My Early Life* (London: Bles, 1955; repr. Fontana, 1977), 116.

14. Gunilla Theander Kester, "The Forbidden Fruit and Female Disorderly Eating: Three Versions of Eve," in *Disorderly Eaters: Texts in Self-Empowerment*, ed. Lilian R. Furst and Peter W. Graham (University Park: Pennsylvania State University Press, 1992), 231-38 (232).

15. 'Susan Coolidge' was the pseudonym of Sarah Chauncy Woolsey. *What Katy Did*, her second novel for children, was published in 1872, and was followed the next year by *What Katy Did at School* and by *What Katy Did Next* in 1886. The sequence concluded with a novel focusing on Katy's younger sister *Clover* (1888).

16. Susan Coolidge, *What Katy Did: A Story.* (Boston: Roberts, 1872; Harmondsworth: Puffin, 1994), 46.

17. Coolidge, *What Katy Did*, 179.

18. Coolidge, *What Katy Did*, 46.

19. Coolidge, *What Katy Did*, 180.

20. Coolidge, *What Katy Did*, 60.

21. Louisa May Alcott, *Little Women, or, Meg, Jo, Beth, and Amy* (Boston: Roberts, 1868; Harmondsworth: Penguin, 1989), 23.

22. Nina Auerbach, "Little Women," in *Critical Essays on Louisa May Alcott*, ed. by Madeleine B. Stern (Boston: Hall, 1984), 129-40 (129).

23. Elaine Showalter, "*Little Women*: The American Female Myth," in *Sister's Choice: Tradition and Change in American Women's Writing* (Oxford: Clarendon Press, 1991), 42-64 (45).

24. Showalter, "*Little Women*: The American Female Myth", 45.

25. Alcott, *Little Women*, 67.

26. Louisa May Alcott, *An Old-Fashioned Girl* (Boston: Roberts, 1870; Harmondsworth, Puffin, 1996), 20.

27. Alcott, *An Old-Fashioned Girl*, 21.

28. Alcott, *Little Women*, 265-66.

29. David H. Waters, " 'A Power in the House': *Little Women* and the Architecture of Individual Expression," in *"Little Women" and the Feminist*

Imagination: Criticism, Controversy, Personal Essays, ed. Janice M. Alberghene and Beverly Lyon Clark (New York: Garland, 1999), 185-212 (202).

30. Alcott, *Little Women*, 355.

31. Alcott, *Little Women*, 355.

32. Patrick Brantlinger, *The Reading Lesson: The Threat of Mass Literacy in Nineteenth-Century British Fiction* (Bloomington: Indiana University Press, 1998), 5.

33. Brantlinger, *The Reading Lesson*, 11.

34. Hunter, *How Young Ladies Became Girls*, 86-90.

35. Drew Gilpin Faust, "Introduction," in Augusta Jane Evans, *Macaria; or, Altars of Sacrifice* (Baton Rouge: Louisiana State University Press, 1992) i-xxix (xv).

36. Evans, *Macaria*, 14.

37. Percy Kease Fitzhugh, ed., *Every Girl's Library: A Collection of Appropriate and Instructive Reading for Girls of All Ages from the Best Authors of All Time*, 10 vols (New York: Pearson, 1910), I, xvi.

38. Ella Wheeler Wilcox, "Impressions Upon the Youthful Mind," in *Every Girl's Library*, ed. Fitzhugh, I, xxv-xxxii (xxv).

39. Wilcox, "Impressions upon the Youthful Mind", xxv-xxvi.

40. Kate Flint, *The Woman Reader 1837-1914* (Oxford: Clarendon Press, 1993), 274.

41. Margaret E Sangster, "What a Girl Should Read, in" *Every Girl's Library*, I, xxxiii-xxxix (xxvi).

42. Fitzhugh, *Every Girl's Library*, I, ix.

43. Stella Gibbons, *Cold Comfort Farm* (London: Longmans, 1932; Harmondsworth: Penguin, 1938), 53.

Part III

Blood, Blockage, and Regurgitation: The Consumer's Modernity

The Queen's Coffee and Casanova's Chocolate: The Early Modern Breakfast in France

Jim Chevallier

Imagine a person having breakfast in eighteenth century France, around, say, 1760. Those familiar with France will probably envision such a person having a continental breakfast—that is, coffee, chocolate or tea with a croissant, a roll or some bread, joined perhaps by cheese and cold meats. But how accurate is such a picture? Coffee, after all, had only come to France in the previous century; had it already become part of breakfast, and before its introduction, what had people drunk or for that matter eaten for breakfast?

Though the question seems simple enough, familiar sources on food and private life offer little in the way of answers. The English version of the *Larousse Gastronomique*, with its convenient dual indexes—one in French, one in English—lists no entry in either language for "breakfast".[1] Though Alfred Franklin's numerous volumes on the history of French private life include at least three on the subject of food and meals, none devote a chapter to breakfast. Nor do Le Grand d'Aussy's three volumes on French food—a prime source for many later writers—list the subject anywhere in their very detailed indices.[2] The journals and travelers' diaries from the period, which so often itemize even simple meals, tend to pass unhelpfully over the first meal of the day with comments such as these: "We came back to breakfast at the hotel, and from there the porters took us to Saint Ouen";[3] "We breakfast every morning in a sort of kiosk";[4] "After breakfast we went to visit the Prince de Condé's château and gardens."[5] Often the meal is not mentioned at all. As we shall see, exceptions can be found, but typically the subject is more neglected than not.

This is the century in which France developed the culinary refinement for which it is known, the century when, as Alfred Franklin puts it, "the French, a gluttonous race too disposed to a blamable indifference to cuisine.. . .bit by bit became more knowledgeable and more difficult."[6] Supporting this, he quotes Duclos: "If those who died sixty years ago returned, they would not recognize Paris in matters of the table. . ."[7] and Mercier: "We have only known how to eat with refinement for half a century. The delicious cuisine of Louis XV was unknown even to Louis XIV."[8] Yet it is rarely made clear that as the later (and typically larger) meals of the day changed, so did breakfast, though not quite in the same way.

This paper seeks above all to answer a simple question: *when did breakfast in France start to become as it is today and what did it consist of before that*? But this in turn gives rise to others: was breakfast always a distinctly different sort of meal?; did breakfast—often referred to today as the most important meal of the day—play a special role in hygiene and/or nutrition?; how did breakfast differ between classes? These are some of the questions explored in this paper.

Breakfast – Just One More Meal?

It is a nutritional truism that breakfast is not only a distinct meal, but, because it begins the day, the most important meal we eat. But before asking what the French and their predecessors ate for breakfast in earlier times, it is useful not only to ask if they considered it a special meal, but did they think of it as a separate meal at all?

The concept of breakfast in fact dates back to long before there was a France, that is, all the way to classical times, when Xenophon mentions it among both the Greeks and their Persian adversaries. In *Anabasis*, he refers repeatedly to the Greek armies either having or missing breakfast, notably in this rather humorous passage:

> They had come to arrange a truce, and were persons competent to carry proposals from the king to the Hellenes and from the Hellenes to the king. He returned answer to them: "Take back word then to your master, that we need a battle first, for we have had no breakfast; and he will be a brave man who will dare mention the word 'truce' to Hellenes without providing them with breakfast."[9]

In *Cyropaedia*, Xenophon also frequently mentions the Persians' breakfasts, generally in conjunction with an evening meal, suggesting that the norm for this culture was two meals a day. But he also hints at more sober habits in former times:

Again, from the first it was their rule only to take a single meal in the day, which left them free to give their time to business and exercise. The single meal is still the rule, but it commences at the earliest hour ever chosen for breakfast, and the eating and drinking goes on till the last moment which the latest reveler would choose for bed.[10]

Note here the (apparently unique) idea of having a single meal at the start of day in order to, effectively, get the business of eating out of the way, and the contrast with a later more decadent lifestyle, giving undue attention to eating for its own sake— an image that brings to mind the excesses of Old Regime France.

The writers of the Bible also refer to the meal, if somewhat more obliquely. Writing in 1632, Guy Patin finds proof in Genesis 18 that the Biblical Israelites had breakfast:

The holy writings teach us that our first parents after being chased from the earthly Paradise, worked the earth and killed victims, whose flesh and viscera they could eat; but it is difficult to know how often they ate: nonetheless there is good reason to believe it was twice a day since we read that Abraham in *Genesis:18* begged three angels to stop and to take their refreshment at his house: *I will give you* (he said) *bread to fortify your hearts, after which you will go*; which he undoubtedly would not have done if it had not been the custom to eat something in the morning to maintain the body's strength. [11]

However, the original passage refers to "the hottest part of the day," which suggests a later hour. Exodus 16 might offer better evidence:

8 And Moses said, This shall be, when the LORD shall give you in the evening flesh to eat, and in the morning bread to the full; for that the LORD heareth your murmurings which ye murmur against him: and what are we? Your murmurings are not against us, but against the LORD.
12 I have heard the murmurings of the children of Israel: speak unto them, saying, At even ye shall eat flesh, and in the morning ye shall be filled with bread; and ye shall know that I am the LORD your God.

These verses clearly reflect a culture in which, to be properly fed, one had to have bread in the morning and meat at night.

Given such ancient antecedents, it is not surprising to find the concept of breakfast mentioned in medieval France. Already in the thirteenth century, breakfast was being formally cited as a separate meal:

At the end of the thirteenth century, the fullers went to work at break of day. They had their breakfast at their masters at six in the morning...

The statutes granted to the cloth workers in 1384 stipulate that workers would arrive at the workshop "at sun-up". They would take breakfast at nine.[12]

It was already being considered, too, in terms of health. At least one royal doctor—that of Henri IV, having instructed his monarch to relieve himself immediately upon waking, also suggested consuming prune juice or bouillons made of salads in case of obstruction.[13]

More often though, medical opinion seemed to favor skipping it, as when Jean Sulpice says (in *Civility*, published in 1483): "I do not approve of beginning to eat and drink as soon as you are out of bed. . . One should set an hour for taking meals, for example six or seven hours after getting up and taking sufficient exercise for the mind and body."[14] To which Rabelais (himself a physician) has Gargantua respond that "breakfast [makes] a good memory. . . I am very well after it and dine but the better."[15] Gargantua, it may be said, has just breakfasted on "good fried tripes, fair rashers on the coals, good gammons of bacon, store of good minced meat, and a great deal of sippet-brewis, made up of the fat of the beef–pot, laid upon bread, cheese, and chopped parsley strewed together."[16]

A doctor's regime for Henry III, noted in 1585, omits breakfast entirely, going (in summer) from waking at five to dining at nine, supping at five and retiring at nine. This varied by an hour or two between seasons, but always leaving four hours between waking and the first meal (of two).[17] Later, Louis XIII's doctor set similar hours for him while he was still a boy.[18]

The details given above for workers suggest that some, but not all, delayed eating for several hours after rising. If nothing else, though, the physical effort many exerted would have made it hard for all to limit themselves in the same way. Nor was the idea of leaving a large interval between rising and eating limited to royalty. Rabelais quotes an old proverb:

Rise at five, dine at nine,
Sup at five, to bed at nine,
Makes man live ten times nine.[19]

On the other hand, the lack of food at the start of day may have led to liquid replacements: "probably the habit of replacing the first meal of the day with spirits goes back to this period."[20]

Overall, there seems to have been a long period when skipping breakfast was actually considered healthy. While this may seem like one more erroneous idea from the past, it is worth noting that some new research does suggest that eating less may prolong life:

> A calorically restricted diet — including all necessary nutrients but 30 percent fewer calories than usual — has been found to extend the life span of rodents by 30 to 50 percent. Scientists hope, but do not yet know, that the same will be true in people.[21]

So the intuition that eating less was healthy may have been valid; it was the choice of the meal to skip that today would be considered questionable. If anything, if they did in fact limit themselves to one morning meal, it was the early Persians who came closest to these emerging concepts of nutrition.

It should be emphasized too that the fact that the first meal of the day was regarded as different in kind does not necessarily mean that it was different in substance (i.e., the same person who ate bread for breakfast might also have it for supper).

"Déjeuner" – A Special Case

Before looking further at breakfast in France, let us stop to note the evolution of the term itself.

In modern French, there is a word that means almost exactly to "break fast". That word is *déjeuner* (*dé* – a prefix suggesting, "to leave, quit or undo" – and *jeûner* –"to fast".) Inconveniently, as even speakers of phrasebook French will know, this word means "lunch". The modern word for breakfast is *petit déjeuner*, which would appear to mean, logically enough, "little lunch." But in fact the history of the term shows this not to be the case.

This is how Dr. Theodore Braun explains it:

> The aristocratic classes in the large cities tended to stay up gradually later, until many of them did not go to bed until 3 a.m. or later, after a night of playing cards and gambling. They would have their *déjeuner* later and later in the morning, until the time of it coincided with "*le dîner*" or the noontime meal. Their servants, however, continued to get up early, having a *déjeuner* in the morning, a *dîner* (which was a large meal) in midday, and a "*souper*" (more or less literally, a smaller meal usually consisting of bread and soup and some leftover meat and perhaps vegetables).[22]

While neither Franklin and Le Grand highlight this shift, they do discuss a similar shift in the hour for "dinner" time – that is, in modern

American terms, lunch. Le Grand, writing in the eighteenth century, says that dinner had always been between nine and ten, and supper at four, but that in the seventeenth century dinner moved to eleven (noon for the king) and supper to seven.[23] Then, as people wanting to see the king found themselves obliged to wait until one o'clock, many households adapted the later hour. At the start of the eighteenth century, he says,

> the custom of sitting down to eat at one o'clock was generally estab-
> lished among people of quality. Imperceptibly, for the convenience of
> business people, to favor the laziness and the dressing of the ladies,
> people waited until two. . . Presently. . . it is almost three o'clock and
> in many places near to four when one dines.

Clearly, breakfast would have followed these shifts, at least among "people of quality." Without tracing the steps before it, Franklin finally says that: "Since 1800. . . a meal much neglected until then has taken on a great 'importance'. . .that is breakfast, and it is served at noon."[24]

And so, by the end of the century, we have *déjeuner* firmly established as a noontime meal, even if it is still considered breakfast. But what about those whose days continued to begin at sun-up? Though neither author speaks much about them, Le Grand gives this note on workers' dinners: "still today. . . pavers, masons, stone cutters and others. . .according to the old customs . . . dine at nine in the morning."[25] And presumably breakfasted somewhat before, having what those more comfortable would have considered a "little breakfast" – *petit déjeuner*. While it is rare to see the noon meal described as the "big breakfast" – *grand déjeuner* –, Mercier uses exactly that term in referring to one of the two meals workers have in the late century, having replaced the morning meal with coffee.[26]

A French-English dictionary published in 1870 still translates *déjeuner* as "breakfast."[27] As a practical matter, in considering mentions and portrayals of *déjeuner* in the eighteenth century, it seems safe to interpret the word as meaning "breakfast." In upper class settings, however, the later the reference, the more likely that it refers to the kind of late-morning, expanded breakfast that Americans would now call "brunch."

Breakfast B.C. (Before Coffee)

Before coffee came to France, how did the French "break fast"? The answer is, much as the Romans had: with alcohol.

In ancient Rome, the working classes began the day with bread soaked in wine.[28] Centuries later, when a large portion of the Roman

Empire had become France, these items still formed the most common breakfast. For some, they may also have served for later meals. Several work contracts from Louis XI's time, for instance, mention bread and/or wine for the workers; though some got additional meat or fish, these two items would have formed the most basic allotment.[29] At the start of the eighteenth century, the prisoners in the Bastille—some of whom were surprisingly well fed—were still given bread and wine for their breakfast.[30]

Since wine, beer or brandy were more or less available in different areas, the specific form of alcohol would have varied by region. For some, an alcoholic drink was their whole breakfast; Le Grand is quoted above on the idea that the lower classes often replaced breakfast with spirits. When, writing around mid-century, Tobias Smollet has a Picard peasant girl serve Roderick Random chocolate and spirits for breakfast, the "modern" chocolate has been added to the meal, but spirits appear, even then, as a breakfast mainstay.[31]

The Hot Trio: Coffee, Tea and Chocolate

Alcohol, then, had been the basis for breakfast in the West for at least a millennium. The modern idea of a Western breakfast arose when coffee and its cousins, tea and chocolate, began to establish their ubiquitous roles in Western culture.[32] For the average person today, one vivid example of how much the modern era differs from those preceding it would be the absence in earlier times of these drinks. Neither Randle Cotgrave's very thorough English-French dictionary (1611), nor Nicot's French-Latin dictionary (1621) mentions any of these. In France, as late as 1666, the Abbé de Choisy served liqueurs after a meal, "because we were not familiar then with either coffee or chocolate, and tea was just appearing."[33] Once they were introduced, these drinks collectively played a significant role in transforming Western culture. Yet each arrived in Europe in very different ways.

Chocolate had first been brought to France either by Spanish nuns who introduced it to Cardinal Alphonse de Richelieu (died 1653) or later in 1661 by Maria-Theresa, Louis XIV's queen, who knew it from Madrid.[34] The Spaniards in turn had brought it from Mexico around 1510, despite their distaste for the Aztec version of the drink ("a rather disgusting gruel . . . called *chocollatl*" which included corn meal and red coloring, among other things).[35] Having modified its preparation to suit their tastes, they quickly adopted it as a favored drink. In France, it took some time to spread beyond Paris, and seems to have been regarded more as a (potentially dangerous) drug than as a normal drink.[36] By 1682, however, the king was already serving it at Versailles and in 1684 a Paris doctor said: "Chocolate, well made, is so noble an invention that it should be the food of the gods, rather than ambrosia or nectar."[37] By the time of the Regency (1715-1723), it was sufficiently established for favored courtiers to be "admitted to the chocolate" of the Regent—that is, to greet him as he took his morning cup of chocolate (since his libertine habits made it impolitic to have courtiers visit him—and whomever he was with— when he first awoke).[38]

The preparation of chocolate evolved differently in different countries: the Spaniards, having put vanilla and sugar in it, still took it with water, while one authority credits the English with adding milk to chocolate – as well as eggs, Madeira, etc.[39] In the late eighteenth century, says Le Grand, "we place the chocolate of Paris in the first rank, in which enters absolutely nothing but cocoa, vanilla, sugar and cinnamon."[40]

Soon after a Portuguese priest encountered tea in China in 1565, the Dutch—then linked with Portugal—became aware of it and the Dutch West Indies Company began to bring it from China.[41] It was mentioned in France from at least 1636.[42] Writing in 1680, Madame de Sevigné mentions another person's unusual habit of putting milk in tea (and suggests that her daughter use it in coffee as well).[43] But by the end of the eighteenth century, it was still favored most by the Dutch and the English. "It seems . . . that the thick air they breathe there, that the food and drink they consume make some such corrective necessary."[44] The *Encyclopedia's* entry on tea (1765) says that eight to ten million pounds of it are being sold in Europe.[45] In 1762, a commercial dictionary says that the Dutch bring most tea into Europe.[46] Le Grand however cites figures from 1766 naming England as the first importer of tea, followed by the Dutch, then the Swedes and Danes, and in last place the French. "One must be surprised. . . that the French consume the least; but we know that among us coffee has prevailed and that tea is far from being as general a fantasy."[47]

Tea was also the basis for a *bavaroise*, which in the eighteenth century referred to a mixture of tea and maidenhair syrup.[48]

Later, Le Grand says,

> It is a singularity worth noting, that of the four hot drinks used in France, the people have only adopted one. Tea they only consider a remedy in case of indigestion. They have never heard of a *bavaroise*; as far as chocolate goes, they have always viewed it with disgust; but almost everywhere, and down to the lowest classes, you see them seeking out, for their morning meal, coffee.[49]

Coffee was introduced by a Turkish ambassador in 1669, then un-successfully promoted by an Armenian peddler starting in 1672.[50] Though the first café was opened in Marseille in 1671, coffee had a very uneven history for a long while.[51] The medical establishment warned of its side effects—one degree candidate claimed: "The nerves relax, result-ing in paralysis and impotence."[52] Another doctor not only said that it caused impotence and frigidity, but that it "darkened the complexion; enflamed the liver and the spleen; led to disgust, vomiting, indigestion" and other drastic effects.[53]

When Louis XIV established the guild of *limonadiers* ("lemonade-vendors", though they sold a wide range of drinks) in 1676, they were authorized to sell coffee unground, ground and as a drink.[54] As time went on, coffee was sometimes viewed as a beverage, sometimes as a kind of tonic with various medicinal properties: "coffee, then, was regarded as a medicine rather than an agreeable drink."[55] But even as coffeehouses became ubiquitous in France, coffee's role shifted in importance. As a German living in France, the Princess Palatine may not be considered typical in her tastes when she complains in 1712 that, rather than tea, coffee or chocolate, she would rather have a good beer soup, but "the beer in France is worthless."[56] Still, when she says in 1716 "I rarely have breakfast and when I do, all I have is a *tartine au beurre*. . . I take neither chocolate, nor tea nor coffee",[57] it is clear that those around her do take such drinks with breakfast and that at the highest levels of French society, the modern "continental breakfast" was already widespread, if not neces-sarily the norm, at the beginning of the century. Others seem to have adapted it more slowly. Decades later, in 1744, a Swedish visitor to French Canada remarks that at breakfast, in addition to bread and brandy, only some were having chocolate and (especially the ladies) coffee.[58] But it was from 1750 on, says Le Grand, that coffee was established in its now familiar role in French private life:

Since 1750, . . . the consumption of coffee in France has tripled. There is not a bourgeois household where, at dinner, one does not offer you coffee. There is no shop girl, no cook, no chambermaid, who, in the morning, does not have a *cafe au lait* for breakfast. This taste. . . has reached even the lowest classes. In the public markets, in certain streets and passages of the Capital, women have established themselves who sell to the populace what they call *cafe au lait*; that is, bad milk, tinted with the dregs of coffee they bought from the officers of great houses, or from coffee dealers.[59]

While this date is necessarily approximate, given the universal influ-ence of French culture on Europe at this time, it is reasonable to assume that most people of any means across Europe regarded coffee or another hot liquid as part of breakfast by 1760.[60] The move from alcohol to caffeine was incremental and, as we have seen, not uniform across classes or regions. But it was, by the end of the century, definitive and far more significant than a simple change in taste. How many people, in an era when alcoholism is recognized as a disease and consumption of alcohol regulated, can imagine a society in which its use was ubiquitous? In describing a similar situation in England, the authors of *The World of Caffeine* say, "a nearly unmitigated state of alcoholic impairment was endemic."[61] The fact that these drinks took hold in Europe as it slowly moved towards a more mechanized, industrialized society may have been a coincidence, but if so, it was a happy one. Say the same authors:

> A new attitude towards alcohol, arising with and perhaps in part as a consequence of the beginnings of modern industrial society, began to predominate in Europe, an attitude that had less patience for drinking bouts or alcoholism as a way of life. Considered in the context of pandemic inebriation that plagued Europe before caffeine's arrival, some of the more effusive claims made on behalf of the health benefits of the temperance beverages seem more reasonable; after all, simply curtailing alcohol consumption would have made millions feel better and work better from morning to evening.[62]

The Latter Half of the Century

The change in what people drank for breakfast did not necessarily correspond to any change in what they ate—which, sometimes, as in the past, was nothing. When, writing in 1781, Mercier says, "At nine o'clock, the lemonade-vendors' boys. . . . carry coffee and *bavaroises* to furnished rooms,"[63] he mentions no foodstuffs with these drinks. Casanova had a distinct preference for chocolate, which he mentions more than once as his breakfast: "I took a cup of chocolate with her"[64]; "At eight o'clock one of the concierge's daughters brought me my chocolate."[65] Ironically, it is when he shares "an excellent chocolate I brought from Genoa" with some nuns in Chambèry that the meal becomes more sybaritic: "I breakfasted at the convent, and I recall that the chocolate, the biscuits and the jam were served with a care that bordered on flirtation."[66]

The *Encyclopedia* even offers an "instant" version of chocolate for those in a hurry:

> Chocolate made in this manner [with pepper, ginger and other spices] has this convenience, that when one is in a hurry to go out, or while voyaging does not have the time to make it as a drink, one can eat a

one-ounce bar of it and have a drink right after, letting the stomach act
to dissolve this impromptu breakfast.[67]

One innovation that may have made its way from the upper classes
into the general population is the use of butter on bread at breakfast
(think of the Princess Palatine with her buttered tartine). Le Grand says
that butter (as a food, rather than as a shortening) had been regarded by
many as limited to fast days.[68] It was not completely unknown as a food
otherwise; the Flemish love of butter was such that travelers were advised to take along a knife to taste it there and the common people elsewhere would have it with garlic in the morning, as a kind of home remedy.[69] But the earlier mentions above of bread for popular breakfasts do
not include butter, while, in 1763, Smollet says of a Parisian breakfast:
"one breakfasts deliciously upon their petit pains and their pales of butter,
which last is exquisite."[70] En route to Lyons, he later says, "About ten in
the morning we stopped to breakfast at some auberge, where we always
found bread, butter, and milk."[71] Already, Smollet is describing something very much like the continental breakfast a tourist might find today.

Brillat-Savarin, writing in the next century, recalls more substantial
breakfasts in the middle of the eighteenth century: "Ordinarily, we breakfasted before nine o'clock on bread, cheese, fruits, sometimes pâté and
cold meats."[72] When breakfast was a social event, it could resemble a
modern brunch, as when Duclos describes having a "breakfast" with a
friend and two women that lasted all day: "The breakfast, which was
brought from the local caterer, was of pigeons à la crapaudine, sausages
and other such things, with some very good wine."[73] He in fact uses a
term very much like brunch to describe subsequent meals of this sort:
déjeuners-dîners, or "breakfast-dinners."[74]

These variations—allowance made for financial means—did not depend on class alone; breakfast was as subject to individual variations in
taste as it is today. In his days as a lawyer in Arras, Robespierre had "a
meal of diary products" in the morning.[75] Even at mid-century, Louis XV
invariably had a bouillon made of one old capon, four pounds of beef,
four pounds of veal and four of mutton.[76] Since members of the court had
long been having coffee, tea and chocolate for breakfast, it is tempting to
think that this was for medical reasons. But not only did he have this
regularly, his dinner and supper were substantial enough to indicate a
healthy appetite. Marie Antoinette (a light eater overall) particularly sa-
vored her morning coffee, with which she had only "a sort of bread she
had grown used to, in her childhood, in Vienna" for breakfast.[77]

At the end of the century (1799), Madame de Genlis' phrasebook for émigrés offers an escalating variety of choices for breakfast before switching to items for supper and dinner:

> I would like for my breakfast, tea, chocolate, coffee. Fresh butter, wheat bread. Milk-bread. Black bread. Rye bread. Fresh eggs from to-day. Today's eggs, soft-boiled.
> Do not overcook the soft-boiled eggs.
> I would like hard-boiled eggs and fresh milk, good cream, very thick and sweet. I want the cream cold or warmed in a double boiler. Cooked or cold milk. Chocolate without vanilla or spices, or so-called health chocolate. Toasted slices of bread. Buttered bread. Bring us powdered sugar, lump sugar, sugar candy, coarse salt, fine salt, pepper, nutmeg, cinnamon, mustard, anchovies, capers, chopped herbs, radishes, soft cheese, cream cheese, Gruyère, Gloucester cheese, Sassenage cheese, Dutch cheese, parmesan, etc.
> Little raw artichokes, sausages, *cervelas*, dried sausages, ham, streaky bacon, cold veal, cold mutton, to make a *sandwich*.
> Punch, lemons, oranges, Seville oranges, biscuits, cakes, preserves, lemonade, orangeade, almond milk, orgeat, salad, compote, fresh oysters, green oysters, Muscat wine, white wine, beer, pastries, dry pastries, old bread, fresh bread.
> Do you have fruits? What fruits do you have?[78]

The breakfast section then ends with an exhaustive list of fruits.

Bearing in mind that a comprehensive phrasebook must offer every reasonable possibility, this selection suggests that the most common options (those listed first) were simple enough but also that some of her mainly upper-class readers would have had fairly luxurious breakfasts.

By the time of the Revolution, a more copious, later breakfast was becoming widespread, and it had a name. In 1806, the English traveler John Pinkerton wrote of Paris:

> *Le déjeuner à la fourchette*, or fork-breakfast, is so called, because in eating meat you have occasion for a fork. Since the lateness of the dinner hour, and the discontinuance of supper, this repast has become very common. It generally consists of cold meats, but broiled meats, kidneys, and sausages, are admitted with petits-patés. During the winter, oysters from the rock of Cancale, a public house so called, and much celebrated for this article, form the usual introduction.[79]

Earlier, in 1801, Blagdon unenthusiastically described another such meal, served around 11 o'clock:

> I there found eight or ten persons of very intelligent aspect, seated at a

round table, loaded with all sorts of good things, but, in my mind, better calculated for dinner than breakfast. Among a great variety of delicacies, were beef-steaks, or, as they are here termed, *bif-ticks á l'Anglaise*. Oysters too were not forgotten: indeed, they compose an essential part of a French breakfast; and the ladies seem particularly partial to them, I suppose, because they are esteemed strengthening to a delicate constitution. . .

I do not know that a man in good health, who takes regular exercise, is the worse for breakfasting on a beef-steak, in the long-exploded style of Queen Bess; but I am no advocate for all the accessories of a French *déjeuner a la fourchette*. The strong Mocha coffee which I swallowed, could not check the more powerful effect of the Madeira and *creme de rose*.[80]

Unlike the change in drinks and other elements of the morning meal which have endured until today, these accounts reflect a change in the meaning of "breakfast" itself: the hour had grown later, the meal was growing larger, and *déjeuner,* though the French did not yet realize it, was (however slowly) becoming lunch.

The Croissant Controversy

Some modern readers will be surprised not to see one item on Mme. Genlis' late century list: croissant. The *Larousse Gastronomique* tells a colorful (and much-repeated) tale of Austro-Hungarian bakers inventing this "crescent" roll in 1686, to celebrate their part in defending their city against a siege by the Turks.[81] Once one accepts that the croissant had been invented in Austria in the seventeenth century, it is a short step to the idea that Marie-Antoinette, an Austrian, brought the croissant to France, which, were it true, would represent an important milestone in the history of the French breakfast. Was this the bread, mentioned above, which "she had grown used to. . . in Vienna?" In an exchange in the French *Notes and Queries* – *L'Intermédiaire des Chercheurs et Curieux* – from 1933, one respondent cites Félix Dubois' account of the siege and his subsequent statement that: "It is queen Marie-Antoinette who made known in France the croissant, which, in Paris, was sold by a baker on the Rue Dauphine."[82] Raymond Calvel, in his *The Taste of Bread*, not only repeats the seventeenth century tale, but goes on to say, "A century later, following the marriage of the Austrian princess Marie-Antoinette to the future French King Louis XVI, the croissant began to be made at the Court of Versailles. It was successful there and little by little it was adopted by Paris and then by the rest of France."[83] He then says that it grew most popular after the Paris World's Fair of 1889, where it was made by Viennese workers and continues to say that, around 1920, French bakers began to make the "laminated, flaky croissant" we know today.

The idea that the most distinctive and graceful of French breakfast foods was invented in the elegant Austro-Hungarian empire and introduced at Versailles by a beautiful young queen has sufficient poetry to have endured, but it has not gone undisputed. *The Oxford Companion to Food* explicitly discounts the story of the siege, noting the first French use of the word in this sense in 1853 and the first recipe for it in 1905.[84] (The *pate feuillettée*, or puff pastry, often used to make croissants had been known in France since at least 1680.)[85] It seems unlikely too that if the croissant had already been adopted throughout France under the Old Regime, that (as is the case) no memoir, periodical, study or dictionary consulted for this paper would refer to it before 1853.[86] A book on Parisian workers from 1863 lists products commonly sold alongside croissants today—*brioches, chaussons aux pommes, pains aux lait*—but not croissants themselves.[87] By 1875, however, these were already known in the Anglophone world as a French product, as evidenced by an (undated) item from the *Pall Mall Gazette*, reproduced that year in *Littel's Living Age,* listing different items in a Prussian bakery, including (using the French word) *croissants.*[88] While neither the 1853 nor the 1875 reference disprove the croissant's Viennese origin, the first date is too far after Marie-Antoinette to support her role in introducing it into France and the second predates the supposed role of Viennese workers at the World's Fair.

Despite much legend and speculation, the true origins of the croissant appear at this point to be unknown. If in fact it was brought to (rather than invented in) France, no specific sources have yet been uncovered that document when and by whom. This paper concludes then with the observation that though the morning meal in France had fundamentally changed by the time of the French Revolution, becoming in most respects as it is today and, not incidentally, helping to wean the population from the ubiquitous use of alcohol, the available evidence—or the lack of it—suggests that one of its most cherished refinements would not be made until well into the following century.

Notes

1. Prosper Montagné, *Larousse Gastronomique,* Charlotte Turgeon and Nina Proud, eds. (New York: Crown Publishers, 1961), 1031-1098.

2. Le Grand d'Aussy, *Histoire de La Vie Privée des Français,* Vols. 1-3 (Paris: Ph.-D. Pierres, 1782).

3. Abbé P. Bernier, ed. *Voyage de Antoine-Nicolas Duchesne au Havre et Haute Normandie, 1762,* 38.

4. Maréchal Brune, *Voyages Pittoresque et Sentimental, dans plusieurs des Provinces Occidentales de la France* (London: 1788), 33.

5. Edward Rigby, *Dr. Rigby's Letters from France, &tc. In 1789* (London: Longman's, Green, and Co., 1880), 18.

6. Alfred Franklin, *La Cuisine.* La Vie Privée d'Autrefois (Paris: Plon, 1888), 207.

7. Charles Pinot Duclos, *Mémoires Sur la Vie de Duclos Ecrits Par Lui-Même,* Oeuvres Complètes de Duclos 10 (Paris: Fain et Compagnie, 1806): 6.

8. Mercier, *Tableau de Paris V-VII,* 383 (1783), 79. Gallica. *<http://visualiseur.bnf.fr/Visualiseur?Destination=Gallica&O=NUMM-89045>* (19 Jan. 2005.)

9. Xenophon. *Anabasis.* Trans. Henry Graham Dakyns. Project Gutenberg. *<ftp://ftp.ibiblio.org/pub/docs/books/gutenberg/etext00/cyrus10.txt>* (18 Jan. 2005.)

10. Xenophon. *Cyropaedia.* Trans. Henry Graham Dakyns, rev. F. M. Stawell. Project Gutenberg. *<ftp://ftp.ibiblio.org/pub/docs/books/gutenberg/etext00/cyrus10.txt>* (18 Jan. 2005.)

11. Guy Patin, *Traité de la Conservation de la Santé par un Bonne Regime* (Paris: Jean Lost, 1632), 70.

12. Except where noted, the discussion that follows is derived from Alfred Franklin's *Variétés Gastronomiques.* La Vie Privée d'Autrefois. (Paris: Plon, 1891), 98-110.

13. Alfred Franklin, *l'Hygiène.* La Vie Privée d'Autrefois. (Paris, Plon, 1890), Appendix: 12.

14. Jean Sulpice, *Libellus de moribus in mensa servandis* (Guillaume Durand, trans., 1545), cited in Franklin, *Variétés Gastronomiques,* 103.

15. François Rabelais, *Gargantua,* The Works of Rabelais. (London: Chatto and Windus), 44.

16. Rabelais, 43.

17. L. Joubert, *De la Santé du Prince,* in *Les erreurs populaires touchant la médecine,* 1579, cited in Franklin, *Variétés,* 105.

18. J. Hérouard, *De l'institution du prince,* following *Journal sur l'enfance et la jeunesse de Louis XIII,* II:342, cited in Franklin, *Variétés,* 108.

19. Rabelais, *Pantagruel,* Book IV, Chapter 64, cited in Franklin, *Variétés,* 102. Rabelais omits the third line, added by Franklin.

20. Franklin, *Variétés,* 108.

21. Nicholas Wade, "Study Spurs Hope of Finding Way to Increase Human Life", *New York Times,* 25 Aug. 2003.

22. Theodore Braun, "Re: continental breakfeast [sic] 1716". *18th Century Interdisciplinary Discussion* (5 May 2003). *<http://lists.psu.edu/cgi-bin/wa?A2=ind0305&L=c18-l&P=R5272>* (18 January 2005).

23. Le Grand, 264-265.

24. Franklin, *Variétés*, 120.

25. Le Grand d'Aussy, 264.

26. Mercier, *Tableau de Paris I-IV* 330 (1782): 155. Gallica. *<http://visualiseur.bnf.fr/Visualiseur?Destination=Gallica&O=NUMM-89044>* (19 Jan. 2005.) "Ainsi ils ne font plus que deux repas, le grand déjeûner et la *persillade* du soir".

27. A. Spiers, *Spiers and Surenne's French and English Pronouncing Dictionary* (New York: D. Appleton and Co., 1870), 177.

28. Duruy, Filon, Lacroix and Yanoski, *Italie Ancienne: Institutions, Moeurs et Coutumes* (Paris: Firmin Didot Frères, 1851), 582.

29. André Joubert, *Etude Sur La Vie Privée au XVe Siècle en Anjou* (Angers: Germain et G. Grassin, 1884), 40-41, 81-85, 93-97, 109.

30. Savine, Albert, *La Vie a la Bastille.* (Paris: Louis-Michaud, 1908), 114.

31. Tobias Smollet, *Adventures of Roderick Ransom.* Select Works of Tobias Smollet in Two Volumes II (Philadelphia, Lea and Blanchard, 1851), 122.

32. These might be more accurately called methylxanthine drinks, since chocolate's effect is due to theobromine as much as caffeine (see Bennet Alan Weinberg and Bonnie K. Bealer, *The World of Caffeine: The Science and Culture of the World's Most Popular Drug* (New York: Routledge, 2002), 227; Appendix B). However, since the two chemicals are closely related and chocolate does indeed contain caffeine, the collective term seems appropriate for our purposes.

33. François-Timoléon de Choisy, cited in Alfred Franklin, *Les Repas.* La Vie Privée d'Autrefois (Paris: Plon, 1889), 147.

34. Le Grand, 102-103. The information on chocolate is primarily derived from Le Grand, 102-108.

35. Le Grand, 102.

36. Le Grand, 104.

37. Le Grand, 106.

38. Alfred Franklin, *le Café, le Thé et le Chocolat,* 171.

39. Le Grand, 108.

40. Le Grand, 108.

41. Franklin, *le Café, le Thé et le Chocolat,* 116. Otherwise, the information on tea is primarily derived from Le Grand, 97-102.

42. Le Grand, 99.

43. Madame de Sevigné, letter of February 16, 1680, cited in Le Grand, 100, and in Franklin, *le Café, le Thé et le Chocolat,* 135.

44. Le Grand, 98.

45. Diderot, Denis, ed. *Encyclopédie ou Dictionnaire raisonné des sciences, des arts et des métiers, par une société de gens de letters* 16 (Paris, 1751-1780): 226.

46. *Manuel Historique, Géographique et Politique des Négocians.* III (Lyons: Jean-Marie Bruyset, 1762): 439.

47. Le Grand, 99.

48. Le Grand, 101-102.

49. Le Grand, 105.

50. Franklin, *le Café, le Thé et le Chocolat,* 36, 40.

51. Franklin, *le Café, le Thé et le Chocolat,* 26.

52. *Questions de médecine proposées part Messieurs Castillon et Fouque, docteurs de la Faculté d'Aix, à Monsieur Colomb, pour son agrégation au collège des médecins de Marseille, sur lesquelles on doit disputer le 27 février 1679 dans la salle de la Maison de Ville,* cited in Franklin, *le Café, le The et le Chocolate,* 27.

53. Daniel Duncan, *Avis salutaire à tout le monde contre l'abus des choses chaudes et particulièrement du café, du chocolat et du thé,* 1705, cited in Franklin, *le Café, le Thé et le Chocolat,* 77.

54. A. Chéreul, *Dictionnaire Historique des Institutions, Moeurs et Coutumes de la France* (Paris: Librairie Hachette et Cie., 1899), Seconde Partie:668.

55. Franklin, *le Café, le Thé et le Chocolat,* 40.

56. The Princess Palatine (Charlotte-Elizabeth of Bavaria, Duchess of Orleans), letter of December 12, 1712, cited in Franklin, *le Café, le Thé et le Chocolat,* 81.

57. The Princess Palatine, February 26, 1716, cited in Franklin, *le Café, le Thé et le Chocolat,* 82.

58. Kalm, Pehr, *Voyage de Kalm en Amerique.* Mémoires de la Société historique de Montréal (L. W. Marchand, trans.) (Montreal: T. Berthiaume, 1880), 138.

59. Le Grand, 125.

60. This was so much the case in Germany that: "Coffee . . . came under the scrutiny of mercantile economic policies. Measures by the state to restrict coffee consumption followed." Wolfgang Schivelbusch, *Tastes of Paradise: A Social History of Spices, Stimulants and Intoxicants* (David Jacobson, trans.) (New York: Vintage Books, 1993), 73.

61. Weinberg and Bealer, 98.

62. Weinberg and Bealer, 98.

63. Mercier, *Tableau de Paris I-IV,* 330:147.

64. Casanova, *Mémoires de J. Casanova de Seingalt,* VI (Paris: Editions de La Sirène, 1927): 252.

65. Casanova, VII (1928): 21.

66. Casanova, VII (1928): 273.

67. Diderot, *Encyclopédie,* 3:360.

68. Le Grand, II, 36.

69. Le Grand, II, 52-53.

70. Tobias Smollet, "LETTER VI PARIS, October 12, 1763", *Travels Through France and Italy*. Project Gutenberg. *<ftp://ftp.ibiblio.org/pub/docs/books/gutenberg/etext00/ttfail0.txt>* (20 Jan. 2005).

71. Smollet, "LETTER VIII To MR. M— LYONS, October 19, 1763", *Travels Through France and Italy*. *<ftp://ftp.ibiblio.org/pub/docs/books/gutenberg/etext00/ttfail0.txt>* (20 Jan. 2005).

72. Brillat-Savarin, *Physiologie du goût, ou Méditations de gastronomie transcendante* (Paris: Gabriel de Gonet, 1848) 245.

73. Duclos, *Memoires,* 41.

74. Duclos, *Memoires,* 44.

75. *Mémoires* of his sister Charlotte, from A. J. Paris, *La jeunesse de Robespierre et la convocation des Etats Généraux en Artois*, cited in Claude Manceron, *Their Gracious Pleasure 1782-1785* (Nancy Amphoux, trans.)(New York: Touchstone, 1980), 239.

76. Franklin, *La Cuisine*, 208.

77. Franklin, *La Cuisine*, 210-11.

78. Madame de Genlis, *Manuel de Voyage à l'Usage des François en Allemagne* (Berlin, P. T. de Lagarde,1799), 54-56.

79. John Pinkerton, *Recollections of Paris in the Years 1802-3-4-5* 2 (London: Longman, Hurst, Rees, and Orme, 1806): 201.

80. Francis W. Blagdon, *Paris As It Was and As It Is*, I (London: C. and R. Baldwin, 1803): 1972-74.

81. Prosper Montagné, *Larousse Gastronomique* (Paris: Librairie Larousse, 1938), 373.

82. Félix Dubois, *Histoire de la Boulangerie*, cited in "Croissant", *L'Intermédiaire des Chercheurs et Curieux*, XCVI, no. 1782 (15 January 1933): 611.

83. Raymond Calvet, *The Taste of Bread* (Ronald I. Wirtz, trans.) (United States: Aspen Publishers, Inc., 2001), 141.

84. Alan Davidson, *The Oxford Companion to Food* (Oxford: Oxford University Press, 1999), 232.

85. La Varenne, *Le Cuisinier François*, 11th edition (Lyon: Jacques Canier, 1680), 171-172.

86. The *Littré* dictionary from that year, cited in "Croissant2, subst. Masc.", *Trésor de la Langue Française informatisé* (TLF). *<atilf.atilf.fr/denden/scripts/tlfiv5/visuel.exe?12=133706700;r=1;nat=;sol=1;>* (8 November 2005).

87. Pierre Vincard, *Les Ouvriers de Paris: Alimentation* (Paris: Gosselin, 1863), 89.

88. "A Vandal Venice", *Littell's Living Age* (1844-1876): February 13, 1875; 124,1601; APS Online, 444.

Kantstipation

J.D. Mininger and Jason Michael Peck

What do Kant's dietary practices and digestive problems have to do with his intellectual production? To judge from Manfred Kuehn's recent biography of Kant, not much:

> Since we can no longer hope to discover the physiological cause (or causes) of these symptoms [of constipation] we should be careful in speculating about them. To claim that the affliction was psychosomatic, or that it was caused by his philosophy, is just as much a mistake as it is to claim that his philosophical achievement was in some sense caused by his hypochondria. Kant's critical philosophy may well be viewed as a 'dietetic' response to metaphysical excesses, but this is only one way of reading it—and not the most important one.[1]

While we fully understand and agree with Kuehn's reservations about a psychobiographical co-mingling of Kant's intellectual and excretory labors, the very fact of this resistance to the possibility of an inherent link between the two requires further investigation.

In order to fully understand this resistance, it will be important to dislodge this discussion of digestion and constipation from its physical manifestations, because Kant's actual gastrointestinal aggravations and his scatological obsession with them have long been well-documented. For instance, fellow eighteenth-century intellectual luminary Johann Georg Hamann wrote that "[Kant] is the most careful observer of his evacuations, and he ruminates often at the most inappropriate places, turning over this subject so indelicately that one is often tempted to laugh in his face. The same thing almost happened today, but I assured him that the smallest oral or written evacuation gave me just as much trouble as his evacuation a posteriori created for him."[2] Carefully noting the difference between his physical ailments and his intellectual figurations of digestion and constipation highlights the central place digestion and excretions (or their dysfunction) hold in Kant's philosophical thought. From the very beginning of his writing career, in its pre-critical phase, Kant showed a keen interest in both hypochondria in general (from which he claimed to suffer) and digestive problems in particular. Although his earliest investigations into these phenomena remained strictly physiological and anthropological in nature, these texts demonstrate that, in spite of their sources, these questions of digestion and excretion are primarily and for the most part philosophical. From the writing of the essay on mental illness (1764) to the better-known *Dreams of a Spirit-Seer* (1766), a transformation occurs from digestion and excretion as physical phenomena to their metaphorical use in philosophical elucidation. The philosophical underpinnings of this essentially physical problem dictate a study that, in essence, assumes that digestion, constipation, and excretion stimulate a philosophical investigation into the origins of reason and intellectual means of production, and inspire an examination of the ensuing blockage that philosophy erects for itself if it is to be grounded upon first principles.

In the wake of these earlier texts, Kant's critical philosophy found little success in extirpating these hindrances, as witnessed by his repeated emphasis on this lack of relief during the writing of the first critique. His *critical* position—to allow reason and understanding alone to set the limits of what can be known—still leads to a certain stoppage. Despite the shift in philosophical tone and purpose from Kant's early work to the critical period and beyond, he continued to associate an intellectual impediment with a physical obstruction. Though one may balk at the easy conflation supposed by this type of reading, what is indeed most remarkable is the way in which Kant himself foregrounded this reading. He frequently postponed discussion of his intellectual labor in favor of a closer investigation of the fickle workings of his bowels.

In the important correspondence Kant conducted with his former student, the medical practitioner and Berlin public intellectual Markus Herz, during the 1770s—the decade wherein Kant worked exclusively on his critical system—he more often than not substituted one form of discourse for the other. His confessions regarding lack of progress in his intellectual labors morphs into discussions of constipation and vice-versa. A letter from August 20, 1777 serves as an example of perhaps the most sustained instance of an outright amalgamation of these two discourses:

> Of the various indispositions that constantly plague me and often make me interrupt my intellectual endeavors. . .there is one complaint you may be able to help me with: I am not exactly constipated, but I have such a difficult and usually insufficient evacuation every morning that

the remaining feces that accumulate become the cause, as far as I can tell, not only of that gas I mentioned but also of my clouded brain.[3]

Here Kant quite explicitly yokes his gastrointestinal emissions to the opaque, unclear thoughts in his mind. In a letter to Herz from half a year prior, Kant confides that in spite of the urgency of his project of "a critique, a discipline, a canon, and an architectonic of pure reason,"[4] he can only work on filling his prescription for a purification of the techniques of reason "to the extent that [his] incessantly interrupted health will allow [him] to work."[5] Kant's constant constipation caused him such undue stress that the stakes of purgation extended to the roadblock it placed on his ability to produce writing. The need to 'flush out his system' resonated fully in both physical and philosophical valence. As becomes clear through the insights of these letters to Herz, the problem he has in loosing his clogged digestive system does not merely impede his ability to work, but becomes itself the paradigm of his intellectual difficulty. He must clear out the philosophical impurities and deformities that have accumulated in his philosophical system: "There is an obstacle to the completion of my 'Critique of Pure Reason,' and all my efforts are now devoted to removing it. . . The thing that detains me is the problem of presenting these ideas with total clarity."[6] From physical constipation to delays in work to the haze clouding and clogging his ideas, Kant clearly both saw and felt the knot that these elements constituted in his network of daily labors.

However, we do not wish to merely and naively read along with Kant, and argue blindly that his excretory adventures provide the single most important restraint to his work. That would be, in effect, to play the role of the analyst to his own overdetermined symptom (and oh my, what gifts and forces of transference might come to pass!). It remains our task to resist the facile psychological answers offered by these passages. Rather, in order to more productively read this relationship, and not merely find ourselves stuck in the biographer's hole, we will look at both the manifest and subsumed discourse of digestion and constipation in Kant's work. This requires an inversion of the order Kant suggests. We do not merely inquire after the essentially physically-delineated connection between psychosomatic symptoms and work hindrances. Instead, this essay probes how and why the philosophical problems Kant confronts manifest themselves in fundamental metaphors of digestion, constipation, and expurgation.

Additionally, any discussion of Kant's digestive problems (his physical discomforts, as well as the manner in which his philosophical problems stem from an inarticulate metaphor of digestion, generation, and expulsion) must map out the increasing marginalization of these problems in Kant's written work. The timing of the letters to Markus Herz—written during the genesis and production of the *Critique of Pure Reason*—rouses the temptation to hunt for clues or traces of these excretory problems in the dense and engorged prose of the *Critique of Pure Reason*. However, with the possible exception of the *Critique of Judgment*, the critical philosophy, moreover than not, excludes the necessary corporeal. To read for the constipatory paradigm in Kant's work is to constantly chase these fleeting passages on the margins of his work, and to understand that their very marginalization points to an unsolved problem within his thought. This would seem to lead back to the oft-cited mind/body problem that lingers unresolved—a crick in the back of Kant's philosophy. A marginalization of metaphors of digestion appears to privilege the intellectual foregrounding of the subject over its corporeal attribute. However, where Kant's work offers figures of digestion and expulsion, their use inevitably illustrates an epistemological problem of some sort. We suggest readings of three essays, which span the long tenure of Kant's writing career, and demonstrate how the metaphor of constipation always already mingles concomitantly with the larger philosophical problem of grounding and producing the subject in and of reason.

Dreams of a Spirit-Seer

Kant first addresses the connection between digestion and subjectivity in his short essay of 1764 "Essay on Mental Illness" [*Versuch über die Krankheiten des Kopfes*]. He appears here to favor an empirical approach to analyzing consciousness, and forgoes the critical investigations of his subsequent years. He ends his investigation on "die Gebrechen der Erkenntniskraft" [affliction of the powers of understanding] in the following manner:

> I have called the affliction of the powers of knowledge a sickness of the head in the same way one may call the loss of the will a sickness of the heart. I had also only to pay attention to the appearances of the same in the mind, without wanting to spy on the origin of the same, which appears to originate in the body and may very well have its place of origin in the digestive track [lit. digestion parts] rather than the mind.[7]

Kant explicitly links the digestive process to knowledge here, and further suggests that rather than philosophy's attempt to explain mental illness, it remains the purview of the physician to treat the unhealthy body in an effort to cure the mind. Approaching mental illness from a purely empirical perspective, the correlation between mind and body suggests that, through the effect of the digestive tract, the mind may be subservient to the body. This begs the question, what resides inside the intestines that would have so great a force over the mind?

Kant answers this question in his essay from 1766, *Dreams of a Spirit-Seer Elucidated by Dreams of Metaphysics*. Because the main thrust of the essay proffers an open critique of the mystic Swedenborg, who believed he could communicate with the spirit world, the figure of the spirit-seer appears simply a banal irritant. Kant spends the majority of the essay castigating both himself and philosophy for entering into dialogue with these charlatans through the back door of the otherwise venerable pursuit of metaphysics. He deems the ambiguous term "spirit" [Geist] an obstacle in the successful pursuit of metaphysical truth and thus, in a letter sent to Moses Mendelssohn after the publication of the *Spirit-Seer* book, Kant emphasizes his belief in the importance of metaphysics: "I am far from regarding metaphysics itself, objectively considered, to be trivial or dispensable; in fact I have been convinced for some time now that I understand its nature and its proper place in human knowledge and that the true and lasting welfare of the human race depends on it."[8] Seen in relation to the title of the first part of the *Spirit-Seer* book, "A Tangled Metaphysical Knot, Which Can be either Untied or Cut as one Pleases," Kant's investigation promises a necessary unwinding of this metaphysical knot, a release of the proper object of metaphysics from its entangled relationship with fanaticism. Again, Kant writes in his letter to Mendelssohn:

> My feeling is not the result of frivolous inconstancy but of an extensive investigation. Admittedly, my suggested treatment will serve a merely negative purpose, the avoidance of stupidity [*stultitia caruisse*], but it will prepare the way for a positive one. Although the innocence of a healthy but uninstructed understanding requires only an *organon* in order to arrive at insight, a *propaedeutic* [*catarcticon*] is needed to get rid of the pseudo insight of a spoiled head.[9]

Kant sees the *Spirit-Seer* essay as a force for extirpation. In order for metaphysics to realize its role in the welfare of the human race, it must purge its more fanatically stupid elements. Either wittingly or unwittingly, Kant begins to adopt the tone of philosophy's physician in prescribing a laxative for philosophy.

Nowhere is this more pronounced than in the third part of the *Spirit-Seer* essay, "Anti-Cabbala—A Fragment of Ordinary Philosophy, the Purpose of Which is to Cancel Community with the Spirit-World." By describing the maladies of the fantastical visionary through the methods of reason and physical science (i.e. understanding the corporeal origins of the spirit-seers delusion), Kant forestalls the conjoining of fanaticism and philosophy: "[T]o wish to offer, in a serious fashion, interpretations of the fragments of the imagination of fantastical visionaries instantly arouses grave doubts; and philosophy, which allows itself to be caught in such low company, falls under suspicion."[10] To accomplish this task would require a purification of metaphysics. All mysticism must be banned from the metaphysical speculation inherent in mapping out the limits of the understanding. Kant's *critical* philosophy truly begins here.

In reprimand of the spirit-seers who have debased and blocked the noble pursuit of philosophy, Kant advises: "whereas it was once found necessary in the past on occasion to *burn* some of them, it will now suffice simply to *purge* them."[11] This purging clearly relates to something corporeal—an excretion of the unfounded fanaticism that obstructs metaphysics with knots. In this vein, Kant wishes to offer a remedy, yet the remedy (by his own admission) remains incomplete. Kant sticks the following text (a paraphrase of a Samuel Butler rhyme) in the end of his discussion of eliminating the spirit-seer from philosophy: "if a hypochondriacal wind should rage in the guts, what matters is the direction it takes: if downwards, then the result is a f—; if upwards, an apparition or a heavenly inspiration."[12] He connects a metaphysical expurgation with a physical expulsion, manifested in a fart. Certainly the connection between the corporeal and the epistemological, which has been brewing since the earlier essay on mental illness, finds its logical conclusion in this particular passage. He equates routing out the spirit seer with the delusion of mistaking the hypochondriacal wind for a heavenly apparition. However, why does Kant choose to equate a metaphysical elimination with a corporeal effect that, when read in its full implication, only connotes the remnant of a purge? Indeed, the removal of the spirit seer in this case would not be a laxative at all, but merely point to signs of an irritation that cannot be dislodged. This discussion of purification, as evidenced from his autobiographical confession at the beginning of the *Spirit-Seer* essay as well as the letter to Mendelssohn, points to Kant's own desire to purge his investigations of his previous naïveté. Yet, the purgative ultimately fails, because the residue of the aborted purgative (i.e. the fart) lingers. It would take Kant another fifteen years to complete the critical philosophy first laid out in this essay, thus the metaphor of the incomplete purgative proves appropriate. If we are permitted to adopt Kant's tone—his irreverent masking of a true *metaphysical* problem through doggerel verse—then a truism found on many a bathroom stall seems apropos: "Here Kant sits all broken hearted / came to s— but only f—ed."

The Conflict of the Faculties

If our reading of *Dreams of a Spirit-Seer* outlines a certain procedure of diagnosing problems of the body that adversely affect the mind's use of reason, then this section inaugurates the related, but discrete task of reason's battle against physical and intellectual constipation: finding a remedy. Treatment of this arresting affliction assumes the same two formal categories that most ailments of stricture and obstruction do: on the one hand, curing the immediate symptoms, and, on the other, preventing the jam from amassing in the first place. The former will be treated in the following, final section on "What does it mean to orient oneself in thinking?" Kant addresses the latter, preventative option in a text from the final productive years of his life, published in 1798, *The Conflict of the Faculties* [*Der Streit der Fakultäten*].

In this work, Kant extols the virtues and importance of philosophy as the nerve-center that guides the body of various university faculties. Kant claims that philosophy serves as the vehicle and protector of critical reason, which provides the foundational lubricant necessary for each faculty to avoid frictional questions of unsound methodology and successfully traverse its own scientific trail. In the section of this work from which we will draw examples, "the Philosophy Faculty versus the Faculty of Medicine," Kant demonstrates that philosophy, in so far as it shepherds all uses of critical reason in an effort that none go astray, penetrates and guides the practice of medicine especially in the skill of prescribing what cures, for this is simultaneously the exercise of "the wisdom to prescribe what is also *duty* in itself."[13] What Kant means by "duty in itself" relates, on the one hand, to his moral philosophy, based on the categorical imperative. On the hand, however, and more specifically within this context, Kant refers to philosophizing as the condition of possibility for determining and following a regimen [*Diätetik*]; that is, the art of preventing disease.[14]

At this moment of preventative treatment, when critical reason is employed to insert a principle that determines a particular manner of (supposedly) healthy living, medical science envelops and embraces the practical force of philosophy. With his mention of philosophy dictating a physical and dietary regimen, Kant effectively slides the influence of the Stoics, and in particular the vegetarian commitment of Pythagoras, into his theory through the backdoor. He fails to mention their legacy as fundamental to such a theory, yet his schoolmarmish attachment to the necessity of conditioning the intellect by habituating the body recalls this tradition. However, true to his preoccupation with the inner-workings of his digestive system, Kant gives as an example of such philosophico-medical regimen-building the task of keeping, above all, the abdomen warm during the cold winter months.[15] Kant claims such warmth is crucial to maintaining the conditions necessary for proper digestive stimulation, and, ergo, to eventually and successfully emancipating the bodily waste that may otherwise hold one a constipatory hostage.

Above and beyond the manner in which the practice of medicine assumes a philosophical posture, Kant also suggests two ways in which philosophizing itself can positively 'treat' the body. In this first instance, for the maintenance of health, philosophy provides a stimulant to the mind that "keeps the vital forces from running down."[16] Kant also speaks of books as positive agitators of thought and reason. In the aforementioned 1777 letter to Markus Herz—the very same letter in which he implores Herz for advice on which purgatives will best incite a loosening and lessening of his burden—Kant compliments Herz on a recently published work, which Kant praises as "a stimulant to good taste and the knowledge of antiquity."[17] In the second instance, philosophizing can also compensate in times of poor health, acting as a form of temporary relief. This anesthetic quality derives from the manner in which philosophy, according to Kant, pursues the ends of reason (an absolute unity). The audacious, intrepid aspect of this pursuit produces a feeling of power that can soothe or compensate for physical weakness. Kant concedes, however, that opening up any new perspective on knowledge can stimulate such positive feelings as may compensate temporarily for (or simply distract one from) physical ailments.[18]

Kant's preventative medicine—his dutiful regimen—leans heavily on the concept of the proper diet for both physical and intellectual health and longevity. He insists that the aim of diets of both varieties is to prevent blockage and to encourage proper digestion and successful evacuation. In order to best regulate physical health, Kant recommends less liquids, and of those lesser liquids, greater proportions of more 'stimulating' drink, such as wine. He claims that these powerful potables, in combination with hearty food, stimulate circulation, which in turn promotes the vermicular movement of the intestines. Also in the interest of better digestion, Kant recommends sacrificing the evening meal as one gets older in years—apparently it disrupts first-stage digestion of the midday meal.

Diets pertain not only to food, however, but to intellectual sustenance as well. One must "go on a diet with regard to thinking," for "thinking is a scholar's food."[19] Kant strongly recommends the following course of action as intellectual diet: do not *think* when eating and walking. As with each of his regimen suggestions, the logical outcome of not following these habitually is, of course, an intestinal and intellectual jam. "Intellectual work diverts vital energy from the stomach and bothers it."[20] Instead of rigorous thinking during eating and walking, Kant advocates a banal movement: a "free play of imagination." The playfulness removes the tension of thoroughly focused and reasoned thought, and refreshes the intellectual spirits, not unlike a *digestif* for the mind. The "free play of imagination" helps to later avoid impediments to thinking, which disrupt the manner in which thinking holds "firmly onto a concept (of the unity of ideas connected in his consciousness)."[21] In other words, the mass that blocks thought's passageways arrives in the form of cloudiness and confusion, and an inability to string thoughts together consistently, which results in, for example, losing one's place in the progression of thought, or colloquially, intellectual flatulence: "now, where was I again?" For a philosopher, Kant contends, "healthy, unimpeded thought" proves vital, for a philosopher has to focus on an object not part by part, "but within the totality of a system (the system of pure reason)."[22] In order to best philosophize, care must be taken that one adheres to the preventative regimen, lest more muck clogs the spokes of thought.

What does it mean to orient oneself in thinking?[23]

What happens when the preventative regimen fails; when residues slip past the cleansing actions of habit and accumulate to the point of obstruction; when reason builds up pressure behind a dense wall of foggy thought? Relief must be sought—some radical stimulus unleashed which can provide the necessary remedy. For his strictly physical constipatory woes, Kant looked for catharsis in the form of purgatives:

> I have sought relief in the past three weeks (when nature did not help me out with an unusual evacuation) through gentle purgatives. They did sometimes help, by accelerating an unusual movement. Most of the time, though, they produced a merely fluid evacuation, without dislodging the bulk of the impure stuff, and caused not only a feeling of weakness (which diuretic purgatives always do) but also an ensuing constipation.[24]

Not only did blockage hinder his excretory and, consequently, his intellectual labors, but his initial attempts at unloading this burden through hydragogic purgatives proved unsuccessful and even counterproductive in that they exacerbated the constipation. Kant wanted a dosage recommendation from Herz, and also sought his advice on the benefits of

switching to an eccoprotic (laxative) purgative. In his search for an intellectual cure for the obstacles thrown in the way of the freedom to think
on the basis of pure reason, Kant embraces a strategy analogically similar
to the one he adopted for his bowels. The task of purifying the concept of
reason of the contradictions that impede its functioning must begin with
the correct prescription of a maxim that, accordingly, depurates the contradictions through reason's own self-limitation, and provides healthy
reason with relief from the one great pressure that strains against the limits of reason: reason's own "felt need [*gefühltes Bedürfnis*]." In his essay
from 1786 "What does it mean to orient oneself in thinking?" Kant provides an analysis of this therapy by explaining how a subject grounds
itself—the truth of its own thinking—in a process of orientation that allows reason alone to provide the remedy for its own need. In essence,
Kant delivers a laxative for reason.

Kant wrote the essay as a response to the so-called *pantheismusstreit*
(pantheism controversy), or *Spinozastreit* (Spinoza controversy), that
was brewing in German-speaking intellectual circles in the 1780s, and
that consisted primarily of the opposed efforts of F.H. Jacobi and Moses
Mendelssohn. Generally speaking, the immediate stakes of the debate
surrounded the tension between two philosophical stances, rational nihil-
ism and irrational fideism. The *Spinozastreit* was, prima facie, the opportunity for Jacobi to deliver his critique of the Enlightenment, which consisted essentially of the thesis that rationalistic inquiry—represented by
the proper name Lessing (*mutatis mutandis* for Spinoza)—led ultimately
to atheism (or a kind of fatalism). This sparked a wider debate that included a major contribution from Kant: "What does it mean to orient
oneself in thinking? [*Was heißt, sich im Denken orientieren?*]." By insisting that reason provide the remedy for its own needs, hindrances, and
limitations, Kant, in this essay, strives to save the autonomy of reason
from self-destruction at the hands of both obscurantism and dogma-
tism—that is, in both cases, the limitation of reason from outside itself.

Kant ostensibly defends Moses Mendelssohn from Jacobi's criticisms by picking up Mendelssohn's concept of "healthy reason" and its
corresponding maxim, "that it is necessary to orient oneself in the speculative use of reason."[25] However, Kant clearly inserts his argument in the
cracks of Mendelssohn's: "it is not *cognition* but a felt *need* of reason
through which Mendelssohn (without knowing it) oriented himself in
speculative thinking."[26] Kant allegedly does it for Mendelssohn because
he is a friend, but parenthetical comments like this one suggest that, at
bottom, Kant seeks a solution for what sits behind his own theoretical
troubles: a purifying self-remedy for reason—that is, how a subject can
ground truth claims using and appealing only to pure reason.

Kant begins his description of how orientation in thinking corresponds to the use of "healthy reason" with the example of geographical orientation, in particular, how the *feeling* of differentiating left from right anchors the basic act of locating oneself in a room, or under the stars, etc. He calls this a feeling, and not knowledge through cognition, "because these two sides outwardly display no designatable difference in intuition."[27] His emphasis on the procedure of geographical (and also mathematical) orientation as grounded in a feeling leads him to insist that, regardless of how much objective data presents itself, the subject orients itself "only through a *subjective* ground of differentiation."[28] He then applies greater explanatory pressure to the concept of orientation, embedding it into the faculty of orienting oneself not merely geographically or mathematically, but in thinking in general (i.e. logically). He calls on reason to establish its purview through the subject's act of orienting itself in the realm of supersensible thought, where familiar objects of experience must be left behind. Here the subject (of pure reason) passes through a crucial stage, where

> it is no longer in a position to bring its judgments under a determinate maxim according to objective grounds of cognition, but solely to bring its judgments under a determine maxim according to a subjective ground of differentiation in the determination of its own faculty of judgment. This subjective means still remaining is nothing other than reason's feeling of its own need.[29]

This *need* of reason derives from the dynamic that arises when reason, in the realm of the supersensible, must presuppose or assume something which it otherwise may not presume to know through objective grounds.[30] This need reflects the growing tension reason confronts at the moment it assumes a subjective ground of thought—a ground reached when objective principles of reason prove insufficient for orientation in thinking.

The 'felt need' through which the subject orients itself draws extra force from its poetics and rhetorical use. The use of the word *Bedürfnis* here is quite curious, since it, in connotation if not in literal meaning, more often than not signals a corporeal need. With respect to the current essay, there are any number of phrases that use the word *Bedürfnis* that evoke the act of relieving oneself: *Bedürfnis verrichten* (to defecate) and *Bedürfnisanstalt* (public toilet) are just two examples. Reason's *Bedürfnis* amounts to a presupposition or assumption of the concept of something unlimited or unconditioned that provides the ground of the concepts of all limited or conditioned beings. Thus, the body, at least through poetic force, informs and helps ground reason's most supersensible and abstract thoughts, and it is the body's digestive scheme (consumption, digestion, excretion) that serves as the vital metaphorical landscape for reason's own reflection on the process of its self-purification; or, as Kant writes, "only a critique of this same faculty of reasons can fundamentally remedy this ill."[31]

Kant sharply admonishes that this 'felt need,' which amounts to reason's own subjective self-grounding in an act of assuming an intelligent cause that it cannot objectively prove, does not constitute an insight. This conflation that makes the act of assuming a ground for certainty into an insight—a 'fact' of knowledge that has been proven—turned out to be Descartes' great mistake upon importing God into his method.[32] Of this status of the 'need' in relation to its presupposition of an intelligible ground, Kant writes:

> Although we cannot prove the impossibility of such a purposiveness apart from an intelligent cause (for then we would have sufficient objective grounds for asserting it and would not need to appeal to subjective ones), given our lack of insight there yet remains a sufficient ground for assuming such a cause in reason's need to presuppose something intelligible in order to explain this given appearance, since nothing else with which reason can combine any concept provides a remedy for this need.[33]

Proof cannot be offered, yet reason's need constitutes grounds for assuming an intelligible cause. The need to find subjective orientation compels a presupposition of something independent, unlimited, and unconditioned, but only on the basis of an admission of the insufficiency of an objective principle of reason. Hence, the subject manages "the only use of reason allowed by its limits—a corollary of its need—and . . . *by itself alone*."[34] In order to pronounce reason "healthy," however, and to have appropriately relieved its "felt need," Kant points out the following fallout from the subjective ground necessitated by reason's self-limitation: healthy reason can potentially be mistaken for a rational insight or a rational inspiration. Thus, as essentially the only possible laxative for reason that provides the correctly measured dosage, Kant summons the concept of *rational belief or faith*. "Every belief, even the historical, must of course be *rational* (for the final touchstone of truth is always reason); only a rational belief or faith is one grounded on no data other than those contained in *pure* reason."[35]

This conceptual laxative purges more than reason's 'felt need,' for it also recalls some of his earliest constipational-intellectual concerns, such as ridding philosophy of fanaticism and bald stupidity, which he treats in the *Spirit-Seer* essay. In relation to that early project, prescribing the use of rational belief in this essay works to root out and abolish *Schwärmerei* [enthusiasm; zealotry], *Aberglaube* [superstition], and *Unglaube* [unbelief], all of which block the pathways of free thinking, and thus enlightenment. Kant defines freedom in thinking as the subjection of reason to no law that it does not give itself, thus his laxative for reason's felt need, rational belief, works to immediately dislodge the accumulated difficulty of grounding the subject in reason alone. Though rational belief operates from a subjective ground, and hence cannot offer proof for its anchor in principles of objective reason, the real proof of Kant's laxative for reason lies, as it were, in the relief. We hope he felt it; we surely do.

Notes

1. Manfred Kuehn, *Kant: A Biography* (Cambridge: Cambridge University Press, 2001), 239.

2. From Hamann's *Briefwechsel* vol. 5, p. 36, quoted in: Kuehn, *Kant*, 239.

3. Immanuel Kant, *Philosophical Correspondence, 1759-99*, trans. and ed. Arnulf Zweig (Chicago: University of Chicago Press, 1967), 88.

4. Kant, *Correspondence*, 86.

5. Kant, *Correspondence*, 86.

6. Kant, *Correspondence*, 89.

7. Immanuel Kant, *Versuch über die Krankheiten des Kopfes*. In: *Vorkritische Schriften bis 1768*. Werkausgabe II, ed. Wilhelm Weischedel (Frankfurt am Main: Suhrkamp, 1977), 900. Our translation.

8. Kant, *Correspondence*, 55.

9. Kant, *Correspondence*, 55.

10. Immanuel Kant, *Dreams of a Spirit-Seer Elucidated By Dreams of Metaphysics*. In: *Theoretical Philosophy, 1755-1770*. trans. and ed. David Walford (Cambridge: Cambridge University Press, 2003), 335.

11. Kant, *Spirit-Seer*, 335-6.

12. Kant, *Spirit-Seer*, 336.

13. Immanuel Kant, *The Conflict of the Faculties*, trans. Mary J. Gregor (Lincoln: University of Nebraska Press, 1992), 175.

14. Kant, *Conflict*, 177.

15. Kant, *Conflict*, 185.

16. Kant, *Conflict*, 185.

17. Kant, *Correspondence*, 89.

18. Kant, *Conflict*, 185.

19. Kant, *Conflict*, 199.

20. Kant, *Conflict*, 199.

21. Kant, *Conflict*, 207.

22. Kant, *Conflict*, 207.

23. This section was inspired, in part, by conversations with Dr. Andreas Gailus at the University of Minnesota.

24. Kant, *Correspondence*, 88.

25. Immanuel Kant, *What Does It Mean to Orient Oneself in Thinking*? In: *Religion and Rational Theology*. trans. and eds. Allen W. Wood and George Di Giovanni (Cambridge: Cambridge University Press, 1996), 7.

26. Kant, *What does it mean*, 12.

27. Kant, *What does it mean*, 8.

28. Kant, *What does it mean*, 9.

29. Kant, *What does it mean*, 9-10.

30. Kant, *What does it mean*, 10.

31. Kant, *What does it mean*, 11.

32. Kant, *What does it mean*, 11.

33. Kant, *What does it mean*, 12.

34. Kant, *What does it mean*, 12-3.

35. Kant, *What does it mean*, 13.

A Chubby Orpheus: Handel's Corpulence as a Prerogative of Genius

Ilias Chrissochoidis

Handel's Reputation

No composer in eighteenth-century Britain enjoyed the lofty reputation of George Frideric Handel (1685-1759).[1] A German by birth, he came of artistic age in Italy and quickly moved to England in search of financial reward. Handel dominated London's opera scene during the 1720s and 1730s before establishing a new type of musical entertainment, English oratorio. A favorite of the Hanoverian dynasty,[2] he eventually commanded respect across the political gamut for his uplifting oratorios and their deployment for charitable aims.[3] At the time of his death, Britons considered him a cultural institution and placed his remains at Westminster Abbey.

Handel's Orphean Image

The virtuosity of Handel as a keyboard player and the affective power of his music called for the highest praise. From an early age, he saw his name linked to Orpheus.[4] His London debut in 1711, earned him the title "Orfeo del nostro seccolo."[5] In the years to follow, he received eulogies as a master of harmony and even pleas for restoring civil order in the kingdom.[6] By the 1730s, his admirers could readily portray him as "a man of the vastest genius and skill in music that perhaps has lived since Orpheus."[7] The culmination of Handel's Orphean image came in the mid-1730s with a popular setting of Dryden's *Alexander's Feast* (1736)[8] and the erection of a life-size statue of the composer in the Vauxhall Gardens (1738): "FAM'D *Orpheus* drew the *Thracians* with his lyre; / The *Britons Handel*'s sweeter power admire."[9]

A Chubby Orpheus

The legendary control of Handel over sound corresponded poorly, however, with his carnal appetites. Handel's fondness for rich meals and good wine was common knowledge among his contemporaries. And so was his corpulence, through regular appearances in public as a performer of oratorios. The mental conflict between an Orpheus who charmed modern ears and a man whose unyielding body challenged the eye caught the attention of his admirers. None of his public images, including two statues by Roubiliac, offers a hint to his actual body size. And no biography acknowledges his corpulence without excuses. The paradox of a chubby Orpheus and contemporary exegetical efforts to sublimate it in public narratives make the subject of this essay.

Handel's Physique

There is historical consensus on Handel's appearance. Early biographers, who personally knew the composer or his friends, describe him as a "large made and very portly man"[10] who was "somewhat corpulent, and unwieldy in his motions."[11] A contemporary satirist marveled: "How amply your Corpulence fills up the Chair? / . . . / Three Yards, at the least, round about in the Waist, / In Dimensions your Face like the Sun in the West; / . . . / Needs must that your Gains and your Income be large, / To support such a vast *unsupportable* Charge!"[12] The unflattering description of Handel's hand as foot and his fingers as toes is confirmed by Charles Burney, who explains that "his hand was . . . so fat, that the knuckles, which usually appear convex, were like those of a child, dinted or dimpled in, so as to be rendered concave."[13] Handel and corpulence would form a strong link in the historian's mind; in 1770, Burney wrote that the Italian composer Jomelli, who "was then corpulent, . . . reminded me of the figure of Handel."[14] A large body, of course, may be genetically determined. However, biographers of Handel readily acknowledge his strong eating habits: "he had a great appetite"[15]; "His chief foible was a culpable indulgence in the sensual gratifications of the table"[16]; and he was "a person always habituated . . . to an uncommon portion of food and nourishment."[17]

Contemporary Reactions to Handel's Gluttony

Handel's corpulence became a topic of anxiety for friends and admirers. In the spring of 1737, the composer had a major health crisis, variously mentioned as rheumatism, palsy, and stroke, which caused the temporary paralysis of his right arm.[18] Modern studies have explained his condition as lead poisoning caused by drinking fortified wines from Portugal.[19] In the following years, which saw relapses of his condition, close friends would vent their concern for his table habits: "Mr. Handel instead of goeing to Scarborough to drink the waters, drinks wine with Mr Furnes at Gunsbury[,] and I fear eats too mutch [sic] of those things he ought to avoid. I would fain methinks preserve him for a few years longer."[20] Protracting the life of a celebrated artist is a noble concern. But there may have been other, cultural and moral, reasons for this anxiety about Handel's gluttony.

Gluttony as Vice

Like any sensual excess, overeating and heavy drinking were viewed as morally degrading habits at the time.[21] An instruction manual for "The Young Gentleman and Lady" from 1747 summarizes contemporary views on the subject:

> it is our duty to regulate ourselves in the indulgence of the loose pleasures of sensuality, the brutishness of gluttony, and the mad sallies of excessive drinking, and of other sensual appetites... each vice directly tends to blast our private character, and to render us unfit to be trusted in public; they cloud the understanding, and stupefy the judgment; they dissipate our fortunes, and dispose us to a general neglect of the duties, which we owe to our friends, our families, and our country; they are attended with miserable intervals of remorse and self-dislike, and at last bring on an untimely old age, with a long train of infirmities and diseases, which are seldom felt by the chaste, temperate, and virtuous liver.[22]

For a society that put increased emphasis on civic duties, gluttony eroded one's ability to properly function in the public sphere. Aside from being a superb artist, Handel was also a recognizable public figure. Each theatrical season, he would appear before audiences twice-a-week for a minimum of three months. And beginning in the late 1730s, he would accumulate social capital as a composer of morally uplifting music and a benefactor to charities.[23] His evident corpulence provided a contrast with

a long-earned reputation as modern Orpheus and a recently acquired one
as a philanthropist.

The Conflict Visualized: Goupy's Caricature

The brewing conflict between a master of music and a slave of the palate
found expression in a caricature by Joseph Goupy, an intimate friend of
the composer.[24] This satirical depiction of Handel survives in a number
of versions.[25] In the last and popular one, Handel "is delineated sitting on
a hogshead, with the profile of a boar, a bill of fare, and other emblems
of voluptuousness scattered round him,"[26] or "symbols of gluttony."[27] A
scroll by his left foot reads "I AM MYSELF ALONE." Nothing makes
the image more explicit than the stanzas at the bottom of the print:

THE Charming *BRUTE*

The Figure's odd—yet who wou'd think?
(Within this Tunn of Meat & Drink)
There dwells the Soul of soft Desires,
And all that HARMONY inspires:

Can Contrast such as this be found?
Upon the Globe's extensive Round;
There can—yo[n] Hogshead is his Seat,
His sole Devotion is—to Eat.[28]

Existing accounts relate that Goupy was reacting to a dinner party, in
which Handel catered his friends with plain port while himself stealthily
enjoying good wine in the adjacent room.[29] Published in March 1754, at
the peak of Handel's oratorio season, this print must have affected the
pubic image of the composer. Handel had been blind for at least a year,[30]
and the inevitable reduction in his physical activity must have rendered
his corpulence even more visible to others.[31] In 1760, his first biographer
would admit that Handel's eating habits "have been so much the subject
of conversation and pleasantry."[32]

The contrast mentioned in the Goupy print surely complicated Handel's reputation. Conscious of his posthumous fame, the composer himself had requested a burial in Westminster Abbey, and he allocated £600
of his fortune for a commemorative monument.[33] His friends and admirers, who had supported him for decades in a variety of ways,[34] were even
more eager to preserve his legacy. With Britain engaged in the most
widespread conflict of the century (Seven Years War), the country

needed heroes and cultural models.[35] The growing use of Handel's oratorios for charitable purposes had cemented his moral reputation. Personal
flaws like his gluttony had at least to be addressed, if not to be excused.
A major shift in British aesthetics at this period would facilitate such an
operation.

A New Concept of Genius: Exceptionalism

The amount of critical attention paid to the arts in Georgian England
brought about a paradigm shift in aesthetics. For a country that had
achieved liberation from Roman Catholicism and absolute monarchy, the
concept of imitation was losing its appeal. Adhering to ancient models
indicated a slavish attitude to the past and certainly clashed with England's spearheading progress and becoming a global empire. Innovation
was imperative; and originality comprised the engine of progress:
"Something new may be expected from *Britons* particularly; who seem
not to be more sever'd from the rest of mankind by the surrounding sea,
than by the current in their veins; and of whom little more appears to be
required, in order to give us *Originals*, than a consistency of character,
and making their compositions of a piece with their lives."[36] In the
course of half-a-century, English critics demoted imitation as plagiarism
and championed originality as the highest force in artistic creation.[37] A
dictionary from this period is quite explicit: "*If a Man has a bright Genius, he will excel, if he follows his Genius; but where the Genius is either
poor or constrain'd, the best Instructions will never bring it to bear good
Fruit; one might as well suppose it possible to make a* RAPHAEL, *a*
POPE, *or a* HANDEL, *in Painting, Poetry, and Musick, by Education
only.*"[38] Learning to follow models was not enough; one had to embrace
what is unique in one's own self.

The vehicle for originality was genius, which loosely referred to
one's mental faculties.[39] Around the middle of the century, this term acquired a very specific content.[40] The work that helped establish the new
understanding of genius was Edward Young's *Conjectures on Original
Genius* (1759). An open letter rather than a structured treatise, Young's
publication is an ecstatic celebration of originality. "*Originals* are, and
ought to be, great Favourites, for they are great Benefactors; they extend
the Republic of Letters, and add a new province to its dominion: *Imita-
tors* only give us a sort of Duplicates of what we had, possibly much better, before."[41] Writing at the height of the Seven Years War, Young often
frames his discussion in political and moral terms. "Hope we, from Plagiarism, any Dominion in Literature; as that of *Rome* arose from a nest of

Thieves? / Rome was a powerful Ally to many States; antient [*sic*] Authors are our powerful Allies; but we must take heed, that they do not succour, till they enslave, after the manner of *Rome*."[42] He associates the glory of the original writer with "*Caesar*, who declared he had rather be the First in a Village, than the Second at *Rome*."[43] And he finds that "Modern Writers have a *Choice* to make. . .They may soar in the Regions of *Liberty*, or move in the soft Fetters of easy *Imitation*; and *Imitation* has as many plausible Reasons to urge, as *Pleasure* had to offer to *Hercules*. *Hercules* made the Choice of an Hero, and *so* became immortal."[44]

The new understanding of genius was hinged on its stark contrast with learning: "Learning we thank, Genius we revere;. . . Genius is from Heaven, Learning from man. . . Learning is borrowed knowledge; Genius is knowledge innate, and quite our own."[45] Not only is genius superior to learning, but it also can stand on its own. Young writes "I would compare Genius to Virtue, and Learning to Riches. . . As Virtue without much Riches can give Happiness, so Genius without much Learning can give Renown. . . so to neglect of Learning, Genius sometimes owes its greater glory. Genius, therefore, leaves but the second place, among men of letters, to the Learned."[46] It follows that genius radiates in conditions of absolute independence, "For Rules, like Crutches, are a needful Aid to the Lame, tho' an Impediment to the Strong."[47] Learning, on the other hand, presupposes dependence on the past: "Too great Awe for them [=the ancients] lay Genius under restraint, and denies it that free scope, that full elbow-room, which is requisite for striking its most masterly strokes."[48] The new concept of genius demanded freedom from rules and maximum independence from earlier models: "Genius can set us right in Composition, without the Rules of the Learned; as Conscience sets us right in Life, without the Laws of the Land."[49] Genius shines only as an exception to the rule.

Handel's Exceptionalism as Artistic and Social Independence

Handel matched this new aesthetic paradigm more than any other composer, if not artist, in Georgian Britain. His fierce independence was both a cause for celebration and a reason for his frequent troubles.[50] "[Y]ou. . . scorn to be subservient to, or ty'd up by Rules, or have your Genius cramp'd," a satirical pamphlet from 1733 charged him.[51] This tendency applied both to his life and to his art. Unlike most musicians of his caliber, Handel began his musical education against the wishes of his father.[52] During a celebrated sojourn in Italy in the late 1700s, he firmly resisted overtures to join the Catholic dogma.[53] His decision to stay in England in violation of his contract with the Hanoverian court, led to his dismissal from the Elector's service.[54] During the 1720s, when he was composing operas for the Royal Academy of Music, his refusal to submit to the demands of spoiled singers brewed tensions that expedited the company's downfall.[55] Much more consequential was his rift with opera star Senesino in 1733. For the next four years, he was officially competing with a company supported by some of the most powerful members of British nobility.[56] And in 1745, he would be brought on his knees after refusing to collaborate with the same forces and even ignoring the wishes of the Prince of Wales.[57]

In his art, too, Handel was more often than not uncompromising. According to John Hawkins, "Mr. Handel declared that, after he became master of the rudiments of his art, he forbore to study the works of others, and ever made it a rule to follow the suggestions of his own fancy."[58] He also developed a dislike for older music: "he seems to have disdained all imitation, and to have looked with contempt on those pure and elegant models for the church style."[59] In 1719, actually, he wrote that, "as we have been liberated from the narrow limits of ancient music, I cannot see of what use the Greek modes can be to modern music."[60] This is not to say that Handel avoided borrowing material from other composers,[61] a widely used technique at the time for generating a music piece. But unlike most contemporary artists, he retained full control over the production and dissemination of his works. Their frequent and successful performances in Britain and elsewhere confirm their originality and explain why in 1759 Handel was "allowed by all Europe to be the greatest Musical Genius that ever lived."[62]

Handel's Gluttony as Prerogative of his Genius

The exceptionalism that characterized Handel's life and art, and its centrality in the new concept of genius provided the exegetical framework to deal with the composer's gluttony. The first instance appears in the *Memoirs of the Life of the Late George Frideric Handel*. Published anonymously in the spring of 1760, this was the first extensive biography of a composer. Evidently a celebration of Handel's life and achievements, the book features on its title page an excerpt from Longinus: "I readily allow, that Writers of a lofty and tow'ring Genius are by no means pure and correct, since whatever is neat and accurate throughout must be exceedingly liable to Flatness."[63] Printed in the original Greek, the excerpt signals that the following narrative is more than a factual account; it is also an effort to understand a great artist. Indeed, the biography ends with a reference to Handel's character:

> Those who have blamed him for an excessive indulgence in this lowest of gratifications, ought to have considered, that the peculiarities of his constitution were as great as those of his character. Luxury and intemperance are relative ideas, and depend on other circumstances besides those of quantity and quality. It would be as unreasonable to confine HANDEL to the fare and allowance of common men, as to expect that a London merchant should live like a Swiss mechanic. Not that I would absolve him from *all* blame on this article. He certainly paid more attention to it, than is becoming in any man: but it is some excuse, that Nature had given him so vigorous a constitution, so exquisite a palate, and so craving an appetite; and that fortune enabled him to obey these calls, to satisfy these demands of Nature. They were really such.[64]

As a genius, Handel stands beyond common humanity. Whatever his excesses may have been, we may not apply to him general standards. If a genius is by definition closer to Nature, then his uncommon appetite also relates to that Nature. By turning a violation of normal behavior into an emanation from the supreme nature of a genius, the author seeks to integrate both virtues and flaws under a common roof. This is the basis for the idea of a flawed genius: free from rules and human constraints, the genius can both reach the highest peaks of the mind and sink into the deepest recesses of depravity.

The second part of the argument is strictly utilitarian:

> besides the several circumstances just alledged [*sic*], there is yet another in his favour; I mean his incessant and intense application to the studies of his profession. This rendered constant and large supplies of nourishment the more necessary to recruit his exhausted spirits. Had he hurt his health or his fortune by indulgences of this kind, they would have been vicious: as he did not, they were at most indecorous.[65]

The fact that Handel remained creative was proof of his ultimate control over his carnal desires. Constant work and prodigious mental effort made it inevitable that he would require large quantities of food and drink. The argument is actually problematic, especially if one recalls that Handel is supposed to have written *Messiah* in only three weeks, while taking a minimum of food. More significant, here, too, there is a reversal of the evaluative polarity: what is by definition irrational (excessive food intake) turns into a rational reaction (the mental effort of a genius is prodigious, therefore it requires a prodigious amount of food).

The author of the *Memoirs* was not the first to make such arguments. About the same time, David Hume proposed that

These indulgences are only vices, when they are pursued at the expence. [*sic*] of some virtue, as liberality or charity; in like manner as they are follies, when for them a man ruins his fortune, and reduces himself to want and beggary. . . . To be intirely [*sic*] occupied with the luxury of the table, for instance, without any relish for the pleasures of ambition, study, or conversation, is a mark of gross stupidity, and is incompatible with any vigour of temper or genius.[66]

Since Handel died a very rich and widely celebrated man, it follows that his gluttony was not as vicious as one might initially have thought. The aims and achievements of a genius are of paramount significance and can justify whatever excessive behavior.

Placing Handel's gluttony within the new discourse of boundary-free genius provided a compelling solution for this shadowy aspect of the composer's life. It would be duly followed by subsequent Handel biographers:

His chief foible was a culpable indulgence in the sensual gratifications of the table; but this foible was amply compensated by a sedulous attention to every religious duty, and moral obligations.[67]

The figure of HANDEL was large, and he was somewhat corpulent . . . but his countenance . . . was full of fire and dignity; and such as impressed ideas of superiority and genius.[68]

HANDEL, with many virtues, was addicted to no vice that was injurious to society. Nature, indeed, required a great supply of sustenance to support so huge a mass, and he was rather epicurean in the choice of it; but this seems to have been the only appetite he allowed himself to gratify.[69]

It is impossible to defend, or even to excuse, Handel [for his gluttony];— but we may extract from the fact some comfort for mediocrity of talent, by calling attention to the almost invariable truth, that, as if in mercy to the weakness of human nature, which cannot endure any pretension to entire superiority, the balance is generally pretty accurately adjusted between great excellence and great deficiency.[70]

Concluding Reflections

There is little doubt that Handel's corpulence was a biographical detail in need of cultural editing. Although his posthumous fame was secure, his position as a national symbol had yet to be fixed.[71] Anecdotes of his difficult character were still in circulation and native composers like Thomas Arne were eager to unseat him from the throne of British music.[72] Moreover, the victorious ending of the Seven Years War called for institutions and cultural heroes to solidify Britain's global superiority.[73] It is not difficult to understand the concern of Handelians for aspects of his biography that might complicate his canonization.

The existence of an editorial attitude towards Handel's life should not, however, be taken as biographical distortion. Interpretation is a natural form of cultural editing and is part of how we constantly update aspects of the past for the needs of the present. Handel himself probably did not consider his gluttony a vice to be either suppressed or bemoaned. But given that most of his contemporaries could not reach the mental heights and creative aspirations of a genius, they were unable to properly evaluate his addiction to excessive food and drink. Far from excusing his gluttony, early biographers sought to apply a perspective that would render such indulgence understandable. They were translators of their own time as much as we aspire to be translators of their actions.

Notes

1. See Ellen T. Harris, "Handel's Ghost: The Composer's Posthumous Reputation in the Eighteenth Century," in *Companion to Contemporary Musical Thought*, edited by John Paynter, Tim Howell, Richard Orton, and Peter Seymour, 2 vols. (London and New York: Routledge, 1992), 1:208-25. Also, Ilias Chrissochoidis, "Early Reception of Handel's Oratorios, 1732-1784: Narrative-Studies-Documents" (Ph.D. dissertation, Stanford University, 2004), 602-06.

2. For Handel's Hanoverianism, see Chrissochoidis, "Reception," 620-24.

3. See Chrissochoidis, "Reception," 585-88; Donald Burrows, "Handel and the Foundling Hospital," *Music and Letters* 58 (1977): 269-84.

4. For a general discussion of the topic, see Robert James Merrett, "England's Orpheus: Praise of Handel in Eighteenth-Century Poetry," *Mosaic* 20/2 (Spring 1987): 97-110. See also, Chrissochoidis, "Reception," 603-06.

5. Giacomo Rossi, "Il Poeta al Lettore," in [Aaron Hill], *Rinaldo, An Opera* (London: Tho. Howlatt, 1711), no pagination.

6. "What Pow'r on Earth, but Harmony like Thine, / Cou'd *Britain*'s jarring Sons e'er hope to join?": *An Epistle to Mr. Handel, upon his Operas of Flavius and Julius Caesar* (London: J. Roberts, 1724), 1; see also Daniel Prat, *An Ode to*

Mr Handel, On his Playing on the Organ (1722): Otto Erich Deutsch, *Handel: A Documentary Biography* (London: Adam and Charles Black, 1955), 143; Aaron Hill, "An Ode, on Occasion of Mr. Handel's Great Te Deum, at the Feast of the Sons of the Clergy": *The Gentleman's Magazine* 3 (1733): 94. For a comprehensive discussion of the topic, see Ruth Smith, *Handel's Oratorios and Eighteenth-Century Thought* (Cambridge: Cambridge University Press, 1995), 202-10.

7. Diary of Viscount Percival, 31 August 1731: *Manuscripts of the Earl of Egmont: Diary of Viscount Percival afterwards First Earl of Egmont. Vol. I. 1730-1733* (London: His Majesty's Stationery Office, 1920), 201.

8. See Newbrugh Hamilton's dedicatory poem in [John Dryden], *Alexander's Feast; Or, The Power of Musick. An Ode. Wrote in Honour of St. Cecilia, by Mr. Dryden. Set to Musick by Mr. Handel* (London: J. and R. Tonson, 1739), 6.

9. *The London Magazine: And Monthly Chronologer* [7] (1738): 251; see also David Bindman, "Roubiliac's Statue of Handel and the Keeping of Order in Vauxhall Gardens in the Early Eighteenth Century," *The Sculpture Journal* 1 (1997): 22-31.

10. John Hawkins, *A General History of the Science and Practice of Music*, 5 vols. (London: T. Payne, 1776), 5:412.

11. Charles Burney, *An Account of the Musical Performances in Westminster-Abbey, and the Pantheon...in Commemoration of Handel* (London: printed for the Benefit of the Musical Fund, 1785; reprint, New York: Da Capo Press, 1979), 31.

12. "The Scandalizade," in *Remarkable Satires* (London: Mrs. Newcomb, 1760), 121.

13. Burney, *Account*, 35.

14. Charles Burney, *A General History of Music, from the Earliest Ages to the Present Period...Volume the Fourth* (London: the author, 1789), 566.

15. Hawkins, *History*, 5:409.

16. [William Coxe], *Anecdotes of George Frederick Handel, And John Christopher Smith* (London: W. Bulmer and Co., 1799), 27.

17. [John Mainwaring], *Memoirs of the Life of the Late George Frederic Handel* (London: R. and J. Dodsley, 1760; reprint, New York: Da Capo Press, 1980), 140.

18. See Milo Keynes, "Handel and his Illnesses," *The Musical Times* 123 (1982): 613-14. Keynes' diagnosis is "recurrent muscular rheumatism" (613).

19. See William A. Frosch, "Moods, Madness, and Music. II. Was Handel Insane?" *The Musical Quarterly* 74 (1990): 31-56 (45).

20. The 4th Earl of Radnor to James Harris, 8 August 1741: Donald Burrows and Rosemary Dunhill (editors), *Music and Theatre in Handel's World: The Family Papers of James Harris, 1732-1780* (Oxford and New York: Oxford University Press, 2002), 119.

21. For a general discussion of gluttony and its moral standing in Western culture, see William Ian Miller, "Gluttony," *Representations* 60 (Autumn 1997): 92-112.

22. *The Young Gentleman and Lady instructed in such Principles of Politeness, Prudence, and Virtue, as will lay a sure Foundation for gaining Respect, Esteem, and Satisfaction in this Life, and eternal Happiness in a future State*, 2 vols. (London: Edward Wicksteed, 1747), 1:104-05.

23. See, for instance, reports and public letters in *The London Daily Post, and General Advertiser*, Tuesday 1 April 1740, [1-2], and in *George Faulkner. The Dublin Journal*, Tuesday 13 – Saturday 17 April 1742, [2].

24. Hawkins, *History*, 5:412; on Goupy, see Horace Walpole, *Anecdotes of Painting in England . . . Volume the Fourth* (Strawberry-Hill: Thomas Kirgate, 1771), 93-94; and Sheila O'Connell, "Goupy, Joseph," *Oxford Dictionary of National Biography* (Oxford University Press, 2004), <*http://www.oxforddnb.com/view/article/11159*>, accessed 1 September 2005.

25. For discussions and readings of these depictions, see Edward F. Rimbault, "Goupy's Caricature of Handel," *Notes and Queries*, Series V, Vol. 5 (1876): 263-65; Richard W. Wallace, "Joseph Goupy's Satire of George Frideric Handel," *Apollo* 117 (1983): 104-05; *Handel: A Celebration of his Life and Times, 1685-1759*, edited by Jacob Simon (London: National Portrait Gallery, 1985), 40-42; and Ellen T. Harris, *Handel as Orpheus: Voice and Desire in the Chamber Cantatas* (Cambridge, MA, and London: Harvard University Press, 2001), 247-65.

26. John Ireland, *Hogarth Illustrated from his Manuscripts*, 3 vols., 2nd edition (London: the author, 1804), 3:179n.

27. Horace Walpole, *Anecdotes of Painting in England*, 2nd edition, 4 vols. (London: J. Dodsley, 1782), 4:203.

28. Deutsch, *Handel*, 768/69.

29. Ireland, *Hogarth*, 3:180n; see also Deutsch, *Handel*, 748. The version of the story, as told by historian John Hawkins, appears in Laetitia-Matilda Hawkins, *Anecdotes, Biographical Sketches and Memoirs. Vol. I* (London: F. C. and J. Rivington, 1822), 196-97.

30. Unidentified London newspaper, 27 January 1753, in Deutsch, *Handel*, 731.

31. An anecdote recorded by Boswell in 1783 confirms that "Handel had always a good dinner" even after the loss of his sight: Ruth Smith, "Thomas Morell and his Letter about Handel," *Journal of the Royal Musical Association* 127 (2002): 191-225 (222).

32. [Mainwaring], *Handel*, 141.

33. Deutsch, *Handel*, 814.

34. See Chrissochoidis, "Reception," 613-20.

35. See, for instance, *A New History of England, from the Time of its First Invasion by the Romans. . .to the Present Time*, 4 vols. (London: J. Newbery, and W. Owen, 1757), 4:494-95.

36. [Edward Young], *Conjectures on Original Composition* (London: A. Millar and R. and J. Dodsley, 1759), 75-76.

37. For a succinct account of the conflict between originality and imitation and the role of genius in mid-to-late eighteenth-century Britain, see George J. Buelow, "Originality, Genius, Plagiarism in English Criticism of the Eighteenth Century," *International Review of the Aesthetics and Sociology of Music* 21/2 (December 1990): 117-128 (119-25).

38. Noel Chomel, *Dictionaire Oeconomique: Or, The Family Dictionary*, edited by R. Bradley, 2 vols. (Dublin: J. Watts, 1727), 1:Preface.

39. See Samuel Johnson, *A Dictionary of the English Language*, 2 vols. (London: J. Knapton et al., 1756), 1:GEN-GEN.

40. For a general discussion of the topic, see Peter Kivy, "Mainwaring's *Handel*: its Relation to English Aesthetics," *Journal of the American Musicological Society* 17 (1964): 170-78.

41. [Young], *Conjectures*, 10.

42. [Young], *Conjectures*, 25.

43. [Young], *Conjectures*, 11.

44. [Young], *Conjectures*, 19.

45. [Young], *Conjectures*, 36.

46. [Young], *Conjectures*, 29.

47. [Young], *Conjectures*, 28.

48. [Young], *Conjectures*, 25.

49. [Young], *Conjectures*, 31.

50. For a general discussion of Handel's independence, see Chrissochoidis, "Reception," 589-602.

51. *Harmony in an Uproar* (London: R. Smith, 1733), 13.

52. [Mainwaring], *Handel*, 4-5.

53. [Mainwaring], *Handel*, 64-65.

54. See Donald Burrows, "Handel and Hanover," in *Bach, Handel, Scarlatti Tercentenary Essays*, edited by Peter Williams (Cambridge: Cambridge University Press, 1985), 35-59.

55. See Burney, *Account*, *24, n; the letter by Paolo Rolli to Giuseppe Riva, 18 October 1720, in Deutsch, *Handel*, 114; *The Devil to pay at St. James's* (London: A[.] Moore, 1727), 7.

56. Carole Taylor, "Handel's Disengagement from the Italian Opera," in *Handel: Tercentenary Collection*, edited by Stanley Sadie and Anthony Hicks (London: Macmillan, 1987), 43-60; Donald Burrows, "Handel and the London Opera Companies in the 1730s: Venues, Programmes, Patronage and Performers," *Göttinger Händel-Beiträge* 10 (2004): 149-65.

57. See letters by Christopher Smith to James Harris, 4 and 11 October 1743, in Burrows/Dunhill, *Handel's World*, 167, 171.

58. Hawkins, *History*, 5:412.

59. Hawkins, *History*, 5:271.

60. Handel to Johann Mattheson, 24 February 1719: Deutsch, *Handel*, 87-88.

61. See, for instance, John H. Roberts, "Handel's Borrowings from Telemann: An Inventory," *Göttinger Händel-Beiträge* 1 (1984): 147-71; John H. Roberts, "Handel's Borrowings from Keiser," *Göttinger Händel-Beiträge* 2 (1986): 51-76.

62. Mr. Wilkes [=Samuel Derrick], *A General View of the Stage* (London: J. Coote, and W. Whetstone, 1759), 76.

63. *Dionysius Longinus on the Sublime*, translated by William Smith (London: J. Watts, 1739), 78-79.

64. [Mainwaring], *Handel*, 140-41.

65. [Mainwaring], *Handel*, 141.

66. David Hume, *Essays and Treatises on Several Subjects*, new edition, 4 vols. (London: A. Millar; Edinburgh: A. Kincaid and A. Donaldson, 1760), 2:25-26.

67. Coxe, *Anecdotes*, 27.

68. Burney, *Account*, 31.

69. Burney, *Account*, 32.

70. Hawkins, *Anecdotes*, 197.

71. See, for instance, the debate on Handel's qualifications as the head of the English School in music: *The British Magazine* 1 (1760): 74-76, 181-84.

72. Arne attempted to establish his own oratorio season at Drury Lane Theatre in 1761 and 1762: Chrissochoidis, "Reception," 326-27, 329-31.

73. See, for instance, John Brown's proposal for an Academy of Poetry and Music: John Brown, *A Dissertation on the Rise, Union, and Power, The Progressions, Separations, and Corruptions, of Poetry and Music* (London: L. Davis and C. Reymers, 1763), 238-42.

The Insatiable I:
Intoxication and Desire in the
Baudelairian Aesthetic

Guilan Siassi

Post-Disenchantment and the Turn to Artificial Paradises

It would quickly become clear to even the most casual reader of Charles Baudelaire that his is not your ordinary *mal du siècle*. His poetry bemoans no receding waters of the Sea of Faith, dramatizes no simple romantic melancholy or disillusionment with the world. In fact, it is hard to identify the source of disillusionment in many of his poems,[1] as his "illusions" are of an entirely different order than those of his Romantic predecessors: they relate not to an idealized vision of the real world, but to his aesthetic idealism of artificial worlds. Indeed, Baudelaire's poetical and theoretical elaboration of artificial paradises suggest a sort of inverted phenomenology of the Romantic artistic "spirit." Having exceeded classical forms of disillusionment (discovery of the falsehood of the real), modern poetic consciousness must instead come to terms with a more elusive sense of emptiness and loss: with a numbing perceptual overstimulation and "shock experience" of modern life,[2] which is punctuated only by the violent intrusion of reality into the realms of deliberate self-mystification.

Jacques Derrida characterizes such an existential state of what one might call post-disenchantment and its concomitant urge for the illusory world of drugs in the following way:

> When the sky of transcendence comes to be emptied, and not just of Gods, but of any Other, a fatal rhetoric fills the void, and this is the fetishism of drug addiction. Not religion as the opiate of the people but

drugs as the religion of the atheist poets—and of some other, more or less atheists, more or less poets.[3]

Much of Baudelaire's poetry, and his prose poems in particular, reflect the evacuation of that sky and the consequent tension within a bipolar world of Spleen and Ideal that folds out beneath it. But they also bespeak a poetic experience so pervasive that it merits allegorization as such; in doing so, they also raise two fundamental questions: Firstly, what aspects of modernity empty the sky of romantic transcendence and give the poet recourse only to a simulated "beyond" of nostalgic longing or opiate dreaming? Secondly, what is the nature of the violent, intrusive "Truth" that causes such artificial worlds to collapse? To the extent that we can read in Baudelaire's poetry a diagnosis of the social "traumas" of nineteenth-century France as well as an almost frantic urge to fill the sky with aestheticized substitutes for its lost metaphysical and romantic ideals, his oeuvre constitutes an excellent springboard for an inquiry into these questions. More importantly, however, we look to Baudelaire because his poetics of excess and intoxication enact a broader crisis of representation; one which concerns the intrusion of the "real" into a seemingly "pure" world of art.

Post-romantic Escapism and the Consumption of Poetry

We see Baudelaire's inversion of such romantic tropes when we compare two allegories of disenchantment among his prose poems in the *Spleen de Paris*: "La Chambre Double" (1862) and "Laquelle est la vraie?" (1863, 1867). The first describes a dreamlike room, where the soul, languishing in its torpid inactivity, is aromatized by a wistful desire [*le regret et le désir*]. Every object, every form, every color in the room has assumed the aspect of a "pure dream," and the sylph-like queen of this fantasy kingdom [*l'Idole, la souveraine des rêves*] lies asleep on the bed. The complete disappearance of time further underscores the unreality of this space to whose "eternity of delights" [*éternité de délices*] the speaker abandons himself:

> O beatitude ! That which we generally call life, even in its happiest expansion, has nothing in common with this supreme life that I now know.
>
> [*Ô béatitude! ce que nous nommons généralement la vie, même dans son expansion la plus heureuse, n'a rien de commun avec cette vie suprême dont j'ai maintenant connaissance.*][4]

And yet, in a characteristically Baudelairian reversal, the dream comes to a crashing halt: an intruder—the sinister specter of time—trespasses upon this paradisiacal refuge, bringing with it a violent reminder of the life the speaker naïvely thought he had escaped:

> Horror! I remember! I remember! Yes, this dump, this place of eternal boredom is indeed mine. . . .
> In this narrow world, but so full of disgust, a single recognizable object smiles at me—the flask of laudanum, an old and terrifying friend; like all girl-friends, alas! teeming with caresses and betrayals.
> Oh! Yes! Time has reappeared ; Time reigns as a sovereign here ; and with the old man has returned all his demonic convoy of Memories, Regrets, Spasms, Fears, Anguishes, Nightmares, Angers, and Neuroses.
>
> [*Horreur! je me souviens! je me souviens! Oui! ce taudis, ce séjour de l'éternel ennui, est bien le mien. . . .*
> *Dans ce monde étroit, mais si plein de dégoût, un seul objet connu me sourit: la fiole de laudanum; une vieille et terrible amie; comme toutes les amies, hélas! féconde en caresses et en traîtrises.*
> *Oh! oui! Le Temps a reparu; Le Temps règne en souverain maintenant; et avec le hideux vieillard est revenu tout son démoniaque cortège de Souvenirs, de Regrets, de Spasmes, de Peurs, d'Angoisses, de Cauchemars, de Colères et de Névroses.*]

There is a similar undercurrent of feeling in "Laquelle est la vraie." Here, the speaker remembers a "miraculous girl" who, too beautiful to live long in this imperfect world, died shortly after he made her acquaintance. This Bénédicta, he tells us, radiated an aura of ideality [*remplissait l'atmosphère d'idéal*]; her eyes "emanated the desire for grandeur, beauty, glory, and all that would make one believe in immortality." When she died, he tells us, he himself buried her in a well-sealed and perfumed coffin, such that she would remain uncorrupted in death. As he stares nostalgically at the site where he has buried his beloved, his melancholy daydream is interrupted by the sight of a small person who bears a striking resemblance to the girl. Laughing caustically and trampling the fresh grass, she announces that she is the true Bénédicta, a whore whom the speaker, as a punishment for his foolish blindness, must love as she is:

> And as my eyes remained fixed upon the site where my treasure was buried, I suddenly saw a small person who oddly resembled the deceased and who, stomping on the fresh earth with a hysterical and bizarre violence and bursting into laughter, said, "It's me, the true Benedicta. It's me—an infamous slut! And in order to punish your madness and your blindness, you will love me just as I am!"

[*Et comme mes yeux restaient fichés sur le lieu où était enfoui mon trésor, je vis subitement une petite personne qui ressemblait singulière-
ment à la défunte, et qui, piétinant sur la terre fraîche avec une violence hystérique et bizarre, disait en éclatant de rire: "C'est moi, la
vraie Bénédicta! C'est moi, une fameuse canaille! Et pour la punition
de ta folie et de ton aveuglement, tu m'aimeras telle que je suis!"*][5]

Again, the violence of this appearance and the speaker's ensuing expulsion from his imaginary Eden cannot be overemphasized. Furious, the
speaker cries out his objection to such a fate, and to accentuate his refusal to accept this "truth," stomps his foot into the grave, where it remains stuck until now, entrapping him perhaps forever in the pit of the
ideal [*comme un loup pris au piège, je reste attaché, pour toujours peut-
être, à la fosse de l'idéal*].

These two poems are emblematic of Baudelaire's ambivalent relationship to the two major forms of escapism he stages in much of his literary work: namely, retreat into a timeless present on one hand, and into
an idealized past on the other. One "artificial paradise" is produced
through the torpid consciousness of opium dreams, and the other through
the melancholy reminiscences of nostalgic contemplation. Both entail a
major distortion of temporal experience and an act of self-alienation
(through retreat into a purely subjective world of the mind).

Baudelaire's opiate dreams of eternal bliss, as well as his simulated
souvenirs of lost utopia constitute a symptomatic response to the increasingly commodified forms of art that were being produced for and consumed by the bourgeois reading public of the poet's time. Indeed, it is
hard to dissociate Baudelaire's textual output and his obsession with artificial paradises from the increasingly pervasive ideologies of bourgeois
consumerism precipitating from the expanding market economy of nineteenth-century France. His work bears witness to effects of this expansion—particularly the deterioration of social relations and the reification
of temporal experience—while experimenting with the new forms of
subjectivity that these processes engender.

Thus, the disjunctures of subjective experience which Baudelaire's
poetry both embraces and resists are rooted in the new forms of sociality
which become prevalent in the era of high capitalism. Pasi Falk traces
the emergence and constitution of the modern subject along these lines,
identifying it with the severing of individualized selves from the larger
social body—a severance which engenders new patterns of consumption
as well. It is this shift in the praxis of consumption from rituals of social
communion to acts of individual communication and self-expression that
is intricately tied to various forms of Romantic consumerism. Baudelaire's engagement with themes of intoxication and addiction thus consti-

tute a partial response to the idea that consumption is implicated in a project of self-building and self-completion—and by extension, to the notion that the force of desire driving excessive consumption and commodity fetishism, regardless of its material object, aims ultimately as such (self) fulfillment.

Modern subjectivity likewise issues from new temporalities of the capitalist economy, reflecting a shift from the dominance of what Walter Benjamin calls *Erfahrung*—authentic temporal experience in its fullest sense—to *Erlebnis*—moments lived through but not assimilated into consciousness and memory.[6] In her study, *Dead Time*, Elissa Marder investigates the "temporal disorders" of modernity from this perspective, distinguishing between trauma and "addicted time." In the case of trauma, Marder explains, the subject is haunted, and even possessed by time, whereas in addiction the subject is exiled from it.[7] The addict, she argues, is driven by a need to forget, to numb him or herself to the passage of time and to instead simulate experience through various forms of consumption. And yet, a closer look at Baudelaire's *poésie de l'idéal* reveals that in many ways, the addict's transfiguration of time originates from the same kind of unassimilated and inassimilable "knowledge" that haunts the trauma victim. That is, addictive desire stems from the psychic residue of an ineffable lack whose only trace is the forgetting it sets in motion.

Baudelaire's literary representations of intoxication and other excessive or "decadent" forms of consumption respond precisely to this lack in the modern condition: a lack, we could say, of ontological fullness, epistemological security, social cohesion and historical continuity among other things. As Ross Chambers has put it, "It is the sense of an absence, of a lack of ground, that marks the sorrow in Baudelaire, the presence of a vaporizing Devil implying the disappearance of the God who presided over the traditional *theatrum mundi*."[8] Indeed, Baudelaire's own reorganization of time in his poetry serves as an anesthetic (and less convincingly, as a corrective) for such disturbances in modern temporal experience. We can say, then, that intoxication not only stimulates new, ostensibly transgressive desires but also simulates experiences that the modern subject is otherwise unable to assimilate "naturally" in their organic or authentic temporal form.

Perhaps the poem of *Les Fleurs du Mal* that most effectively expresses this anxiety of the modern subject before the "sinister god" of Time is "L'Horloge." Neatly composed of twenty-four lines of verse in six stanzas (corresponding to the number of hours in a day), the poem presents the ominous admonition of the clock to "remember":

Three thousand six hundred times per hour, the Second
Whispers, "Remember! Quickly, with his insect-like voice.
The Time of Now says, 'I am Time Past,
And I've sucked up your life with my abominable trumpet peal.'

Trois mille six cent fois par heure, la Seconde
Chuchote: Souviens-toi! Rapide, avec sa voix
D'insecte, Maintenant dit: Je suis Autrefois,
Et j'ai pompé ta vie avec ma trompe immonde![9]

The poem depicts a sense of time as an unrelenting flood of instants that leave no room for the subject to digest his or her experience. As Marder has pointed out, the six-times-repeated imperative of the clock to remember also "leaves no time for memory."[10] Presence (*Maintenant*) has lost the kind of fluidity and elasticity of an Augustinian notion of time, where temporal experience stretches beyond the immediacy of "Now," in both the direction of things past (as memory) and the direction of things future (as anticipation).[11] Modernity can no longer fully incorporate these three aspects of time in the consciousness or *animus* of the subject. Indeed, it has made obsolete such existential time as well as the sense of authentic being that would accompany it.

If the shocks of modernity are conveyed through this degradation of existential time, then Baudelaire's prose poem, "Enivrez-vous" (1864) proposes perpetual intoxication not only as a numbing agent for the jarring perceptual overload, but also as a kind of remedy for it: "In order not to feel the horrible weight of Time who crushes your shoulders and bends you towards the earth, you must get drunk without pause." [*Pour ne pas sentir l'horrible fardeau du Temps qui brise vos épaules et vous penche vers la terre, il faut vous enivrer sans trêve*].[12] That is, the counter-force in the battle against Time would be the "other" temporality of intoxication—an unremitting [*sans trêve*] power that would yield to no "truce" [*trêve*]. In contrast to "L'horloge," where the clock rants without pause while the diminutive subject ("toi") remains mute, it is the respected reader of this poem ("vous") who shall ask the time of "all that flees." And in response, all that speaks to human life—including the clock—will tell him that it is the time to become inebriated: "And the wind, the wave, the star, the bird, the clock will respond to you: 'It is the time to get drunk!'" [*Et le vent, la vague, l'étoile, l'oiseau, l'horloge, vous répondront: 'Il est l'heure de s'enivrer!'*]. Thus, these two poems suggests that as long as the ticking of the terrible Clock inundates our mind and senses with excessive demands, desires, and other stimuli, intoxication allows for the possibility of synchronizing perception with those jolts: of responding to the "overdose" of life itself.

Temporalities of Desire and Baudelaire's Consuming Nostalgia

If we consider the fundamental lack at the heart of social experience with respect to a basic theory of desire, we note a certain irreducibility of the two terms, on the order of the proverbial chicken and egg. On one hand, we see lack as the precondition or source of desire, desire being understood as a force generated by that deficiency. On the other hand, from a deconstructive perspective, such a deficiency comes to be only when an additional element—akin to the Derridean *supplément*—creates and articulates it as such. In this sense, it is *excess* which implies deficiency—the outside supplement which, to some degree *creates* an inside lack.[13] Thus, it would appear that insofar as modern desire functions within the logic of surplus value in a capitalist economy, it is *necessarily* excessive—and occasionally, in the case of Baudelaire, transgressive. From this perspective, Baudelaire's consumption of the (sub)cultural commodities of art and drugs and his embrace of intoxication as the praxis of poetic excess *par excellence*, can be understood as a symptomatic response to a culturally and historically specific mode of desiring enabled by the collapse of this binary relation.[14]

Baudelairian desire—the sign of simultaneous excess and lack—responds to the emptiness of the present by expressing that lack in terms of an ineffable loss suffered in the distant past; but it is a past that constitutes the idealized dimension of futurity. Indeed, Baudelaire's poems often conflate projective longing with retrospective wistfulness. This temporal oscillation is perhaps most visible in the poet's opiate dreams of a primordial paradise and his simulated souvenirs of a lost utopia—both of which are pervaded by an ersatz or imagined nostalgia. As Arjun Appadurai has aptly demonstrated, such nostalgia "inverts the temporal logic of fantasy" and "creates the simulacra of periods that constitute the flow of time, conceived as lost, absent, or distant."[15] And yet, the utopian future-past that the nostalgic seeks has never existed except as an ideological fiction; the aim of such desire being precisely the absence which generates it.[16]

We find the clearest link between such escapism and nostalgia in "La Chevelure."[17] The speaker imagines the hair he addresses not only to hold a reserve of "*souvenirs*," but also to house the exotic and languorous lands of "an entire distant, absent world" that is nearly extinct [*"Tout un monde lointain, absent, presque défunt"*]. This "ebony sea" into which the speaker can plunge his "love-drunk head" contains a "dazzling dream" which envelops his longed-for "other" [*Tu contiens, mer d'ébène, un éblouissant rêve.... Je plongerai ma tête amoureuse d'ivresse/ Dans ce noir océan où l'autre est enfermé*]. The speaker's yearning for the ideal in this poem conforms on many levels to Susan Stewart's general characterization of antiquarian longing: "His search. . . is primarily an aesthetic one, an attempt to erase the actual past in order to create an imagined past which is available for consumption. In order to awaken the dead, the antiquarian must first manage to kill them."[18]

Thus, we can understand the poet's aesthetic self-distancing from the woman behind the hair and his enterprise of "immobilizing desire"[19] to transform her into a symbolic vehicle of transport as expressive of a murderous impulse towards the feminine other. Indeed the female figure of this poem, like the many other mute and/or dead women in Baudelaire's lyric poetry, is significant not so much for *who* she is inherently, but for what she *represents* symbolically. If feminine beauty is to serve as an aesthetic filter through which the poetic consciousness can perceive the world in the eternal light of his own fantasy, then Woman must be kept at the level of abstraction, she must remain de-humanized as an empty, unchanging vessel for the poet's fantasies. Thus, the "real" woman behind the hair must be killed in order to be resurrected in poetry as a "pure" symbol of the speaker's desire. Only when woman is thus represented as a non-conductive *receptacle* for the speaker's desire can she become a symbol designating the hidden *source* and ultimate *aim* of that desire. In other words, as the symbol of that-which-is-desired, "woman" can acquire absolute meaning and point to an inviolable, eternal "truth" only when she becomes one of many interchangeable objects, when she ceases to be recognized as a subject in her own right. The mythic past in which Baudelaire locates this ideal and to which he, like an addict, repeatedly returns serves to help him both "remember" the sign of this truth and to "forget" the absence to which that sign ultimately refers.

Furthermore, the image of woman as a source/vehicle of intoxication—as the "gourd" from which the poet can drink the wine of memory—becomes what Marder describes as a primary "shock absorber" in Baudelaire's oeuvre. Feminine presence, in various "controllable" forms, is required not just to mediate but to correct the poet's temporal relationship to the world.[20] As we see in this poem, however, although the woman connected to this inanimate *chevelure* is disembodied, the speaker's pure synecdochic address lapses in the last stanza as he finally distinguishes between the "you" and the "mane" that essentially constitutes her:

For a long time! Forever! My hand in your heavy mane
Will sow ruby, pearl, and sapphire
So that you should never be deaf to my desire!
Are you not the oasis where I dream, and the gourd
Where I gulp down the wine of memory?

[*Longtemps! toujours! ma main dans ta crinière lourde*
Sèmera le rubis, la perle et le saphir
Afin qu'à mon désir tu ne sois jamais sourde !
N'es-tu pas l'oasis où je rêve, et la gourde
Où je hume à longs traits le vin du souvenir?][21]

The steady alternation between present and future tense in the seven stanzas is interrupted in these last lines with a subjunctive clause and an interrogative phrase, indicating both anxiety and doubt on the poet's part that the "longtemps" of his reverie could become the "toujours" of his ideal. This skepticism, as we have seen, is fully exploited in later ironic and allegorical poems like "Laquelle est la vraie" and "La Chambre Double."

We can thus view the nostalgic escapism of Baudelaire's *poésie de l'idéal* as an intoxicated mode of representation which simulates "memories" that render the passage of time meaningful within a poetic space of mobile *correspondances*. Like any aesthetic contemplation, nostalgia is not only a mode of experience and representation but also a form of consumption whose temporality is not dissimilar to that of an opium dream. Indeed, the nostalgic turn to a primordial *vie antérieure* effects the same temporal reconfigurations of desire as the addict's turn to an artificial paradise, creating the intoxicating illusion of the simultaneity of past and present: a sense that one is moving through the present out of time. Such addicted temporalities reveal how desire in the context of modern consumerism becomes both mnemonic and fantastic, both nostalgic and eschatological. Indeed, taken to their extremes, nostalgic reminiscence and intoxicated forgetting in Baudelaire's poetry become the same thing: forms of consumption and modes of exchange that only further drive the circulation of sign-values within the market and libidinal economies.[22] Engendered and promoted by the capitalist ethos, nostalgia and intoxication manufacture desires which drive consumption and sustain the means of their own reproduction. From this perspective, both are deeply embedded within the temporal logic of modernity's most addictive *paradis artificiels*.

Towards a Definition of the Baudelairian Aesthetic: Intoxication vs. Inspiration

Baudelaire's poetics of intoxication not only problematizes the temporal dynamics of desire within the cultural logic of his age, but also reflects his ambivalent relationship to the aesthetic ideals embraced and promoted by his Romantic predecessors. However much Baudelaire sees the modern condition to be marked by an irremediable loss—by the disappearance of any transcendental signifier—he remains suspicious of theological paradigms locating the moment of recovery in the afterlife (as a sort of redemption in the kingdom of God) and, as we see from poems like "La Chevelure" and "Laquelle est la vraie," skeptical about ideals of a similar kind of redemption through love on earth. Indeed, his poetry rarely if ever conveys a simple, hopeful vision of a future "return" to oneness through union with the Other, be it woman, nature, or God. Recognizing that such ideals of love, communion with nature, or Christian redemption no longer make sense within the cultural imaginary of his time, Baudelaire stands at the threshold of a romantic tradition and a precociously modern sensibility. At a time when literature had become a prime commodity, the consumption of which was hoped to gratify readers' spiritual hunger, offering consolation or self-knowledge, Baudelaire rejected the role of poet holding up the refining mirror of his text, and thereby reflecting a harmonious image of the natural world, his social milieu, and himself.

But even if Baudelaire did not write his poems to recuperate some sort of psychic or spiritual unity of Being, it does seem, as Jean Paul Sartre has noted, that he often did so "in order to rediscover his own image in them."[23] And yet, the poet often constructs this image in order to shatter it, dramatizing his own impossible pursuit of these ideals of self-creation and self-possession and frustrating his own desire for subjective coherence and meaning within the context of his larger poetic project. As much as Baudelaire depicts the modern subject in his fragmentation and contingency and attempts to conceive and construct a new, distinctly *modern* artistic identity, his poetry remains haunted by what Alina Clej describes as the pseudospiritual and rhetorical forms through which Romantic subjectivity had long been construed and put into circulation for the bourgeois reading public.[24] However much the poet resists the popular rhetoric of revelation, synthesis, and a self-contained unity of being, his work is still "possessed" by similar metaphysical, existential, and aesthetic aspirations.

In his *Paradis Artificiels* (1860), Baudelaire explains that it is the persistent, ghost-like presence of such ideals which drives the artist to seek them out through artificial means: "It is a kind of haunting, but an intermittent haunting, from which we should pull, if we were wise, the certitude of a better existence and the hope to attain it by the daily exercise of our will" [*C'est une espèce de hantise, mais de hantise intermittente, dont nous devrions tirer, si nous étions sages, la certitude d'une existence meilleure et l'espérance d'y atteindre par l'exercice journalier de notre volonté*].[25] This abnormal state is the trace and the promise of a longed-for spiritual condition which would allow man to transcend the "heavy shadows" [*lourdes ténèbres*] of his daily life and make it possible for him to attain a state of poetic beatitude through his natural fervor and free will: it is "a true blessing, a magic mirror in which man is invited to see himself in his beauty, that is, as he should and could be" [. . . *une véritable grâce, un miroir magique où l'homme est invité à se voir en beau, c'est-à-dire tel qu'il devrait et pourrait être*].[26] However, we are not "wise" enough to settle for, and aspire to this promise of a "better existence" in the future. Indeed, instead of comforting us with hope, this haunting arouses within us an irritating desire for which we seek immediate gratification. Consequently, we are tempted to pursue the means of escape through false ideals and artificial sources of intoxication. It is thus that our "taste for the infinite," as Baudelaire says, "often gets lost on its way" [*le goût de l'infini. . . se trompe souvent de route*].[27]

Thus, we see that on one hand, Baudelaire respects the ideal of wholeness—of unity of self and world—attainable through patient and faithful poetic endeavors. But on the other hand, he rebels against it, seeking instead in his artificial paradises further fragmentation as he pursues a means of "multiplying individuality."[28] This preoccupation becomes evident in the poet's appetite for self-possession on one hand and self-evasion on the other. More importantly, however, it finds expression in his insatiable urge to incorporate otherness, or, as he puts it, in the desire of *le moi insatiable du non-moi*[29]: a voracity of desire which can be understood in terms of the poet's simultaneous recognition and disavowal of the romantic illusions he both consumes and reproduces in his art.

Baudelaire elaborates this notion of artistic insatiability in his essay on Constantin Guys, "Le Peintre de la vie moderne" (1863). Here, he depicts the artist as one whose exceptional creativity and heightened perception stem from his power to recapture a state of childlike intoxication. According to this ideal of the *homme de genie*, what Bersani has called "psychic scattering" and "self-disseminations" become both the primary modality and the end of modern art. That is, the Baudelairian aesthetic is not one of *transcendent inspiration* leading to a total unity of being but of *transgressive intoxication* whose purpose is, to use the words of Alina

Clej, the "multiplication and decentering of the self through verbal dissemination."[30]

Thus, the artist's openness to the crowd and his insatiable desire for the "intoxicating spectacle of otherness" in the urban center[31] shows him seeking a confirmation of difference: not a self-dissolution in unity, but a self-dispersion in multiplicity. As Baudelaire explains in *Paradis Artificiels*, the drug experience, like the experience of the man of the crowds, also facilitates an escape from the self to the extent that it induces oblivion: "The contemplation of external objects makes you forget your own existence, such that you soon become mixed up with them." [*La contemplation des objets extérieurs vous fait oublier votre propre existence, et que vous vous confondez bientôt avec eux*].[32] But this artificial paradise is different from the sublime experience of nature (or love, or God) insofar as the disintegration of the ego it effects in this case comes about not through metaphorical union but through the multiplication and objectification of the self.

In the same vein, we can see the aesthetic of intoxication, as a sort of "antidote" to Baudelaire's notion of art as prostitution.[33] In the latter, art is not in the service of reflecting an image of the world (mimetically or otherwise), but of reflecting an image of the Self onto the world. Self and Other, subject and object thus dissolve into one another and difference is effaced through an artistic act of "avid narcissistic appropriation."[34] The kind of art Baudelaire characterizes as prostitution disseminates such signs of ontological unity, ipseity, and harmonious intersubjectivity, thus serving as a sort of ideological commodity that seems to have been manufactured precisely with the wishes of nineteenth-century consumers in mind.

Baudelaire, however, recognizes that with the rise of urban industry and the increasing alienation of the individual in society, the ideals of romantic union, social communion, and the sublime experience of nature persist as nothing but empty forms and commodified souvenirs of utopian days of "yore." The illusions to which nature (like beauty or romantic love) give rise instead induce a merely *temporary* loss of self, lulling the poet into a dream-like state from which he must awaken with an even greater sense of contingency and with a more desperate awareness of the lack he had tried to fill with those ersatz illusions.

The temptation to buy into this derivative model of transcendence and the rude awakening which the failure of this attempt induces is precisely the experience that is depicted in Baudelaire's prose poem, "Le Confiteor de l'Artiste" (1862).[35] The poem describes a scene of sunset in autumn, where the speaker delights in immersing himself in the vastness of the surrounding natural world. Describing his sensations at first in universals, the speaker feels pierced by the "infinity" surrounding him: "Oh how penetrating are the end of autumn days. . . A great pleasure it is indeed to drown one's vision in the immensity of the sky and the sea!" [*Que les fins de journées d'automne sont pénétrantes!* . . . *Grand délice que celui de noyer son regard dans l'immensité du ciel et de la mer!*]. This experience seems, at first glance, to be one that attempts to fill the sky of modernity with sublime meanings through communion with nature. However, the transcendent Other is lost along with the contingent Self: the poet's connection to the world causes his ego to disintegrate as everything coincides and becomes one with everything else. He can no longer even distinguish between his subjective perceptions and objective, external reality. Watching a sail flapping in the horizon, a miniscule and isolated boat that seems to imitate his "irremediable existence," and day-dreaming to the monotonous melody of the waves, the speaker marvels, "All these things think through me, or I think through them (since, in the grandeur of reverie, the *I* is quickly lost!)" [*Toutes ces choses pensent par moi, ou je pense par elles (car dans la grandeur de la rêverie, le moi se perd vite!)*]. But he no longer knows whether these too-intense thoughts originate within himself or whether they "shoot off from things" [*s'élancent des choses*], and is overwhelmed by the excessive "energy in voluptuousness" [*energie dans la volupté*] that he feels. He is confounded and exasperated—indeed revolted—by the "insensitivity of the sea" and the "immutability of the scene."

When, at the end, he pleads with his "rival," the pitiless enchantress of Nature, to stop tempting his "desire" and his "pride," we have a clue as to the source of his anxiety. This impassive and omnipotent Other, like the "Beauté" that Baudelaire envisions as a "dream of stone,"[36] is impenetrable and yet deceives him into forgetting himself in a moment of artistically-simulated, and largely contrived communion. This false death of the ego, this dramatization of an inspiring but manufactured moment of harmony with the universe (or, the universal Other), threatens to annihilate his self-conscious sense of difference and to thus render him poetically impotent. Needless to say, such self-effacement in a moment of symbolic coincidence—this displacement of the boundaries between perceiving subject and object of perception—is very similar to the experiences of intoxication that Baudelaire describes in his essays on wine, hashish, and opium. And yet, ironically, we see here what we do not see there: a bad trip. This romantic moment has tempted him to seek his ideal in life itself—through natural, as opposed to artificial means.

Conclusion

All the foregoing notwithstanding, Baudelaire's attempts "to dismiss defined structures of self and society"[37] and to construct new forms of modern subjectivity are not unproblematic. While Baudelaire's oeuvre—his later works in particular—present a radical re-evaluation of identity and undermine many assumptions of Romanticism, he continues to display a conflicted attitude towards the ideal of inebriation that he places in their place at the heart of his poetic vision. As Leo Bersani writes, "Baudelaire's work gives us images of this psychic fragmentation at the same time that it documents a determined resistance to all such ontological floating."[38] Considered in this light, Baudelaire's necrophilic obsessions, his anti-naturalism, and his cultivation of the "artificial sublime"[39] suggest a similar "process of partly willed, partly rejected self-recognition or self-identification" with the Other.[40] This process is essential to Baudelaire's aesthetic as it gives rise to an "impersonality" and "objectivism" which become the distinguishing mark of what he himself calls "the excessive development of the poetic spirit"[41] in modern art and life.

The rhetoric of intoxication and addiction which pervades Baudelaire's prose and verse thus speaks to a general condition of epistemological insecurity and existential anxiety that shapes and distorts subjectivity in the modern world. As we have seen, the so-called shock experience of modernity and the addictive response it sets in motion is directly tied to a collective spiritual or existential dilemma reflected in the degradation—if not deliberate perversion—of the old Romantic aesthetic and sensibility. Baudelaire's awareness of the insufficiency of religious beliefs, of the limitations of artistic expression, and of the absurdity of any sense-making projects or fabricated ideals consequently gives rise to another prominent feature of his poetics: irony.

Baudelairian irony derives not only from the poet's radical re-evaluation of Romantic tropes, but also from a questioning of his own poetic identity and his assumptions about the redemptive value of art. It is for this reason that he often appears to undermine his own aesthetic and metaphysical ideals and to lampoon the very notion of symbolic synthesis or transcendence through art. Indeed, the aesthetic logic of Baudelaire's mature, or "demystified" poetry suggests a sort of "self-deconstruction." As Barbara Johnson has pointed out, metaphorical harmony is dislodged and displaced to expose the illusory character of the *correspondances* that constitute it.[42]

We note in these poems a sense of loss, a certain lack in the object of poetry itself corresponding to the lost hope for a sublime epiphany accompanying artistic creation. Baudelaire's prose poems in particular stage these aesthetic losses, enacting the tension between the poet's own desire for meaning and his sense that meaning always inevitably collapses. As he exploits this tension between lyricism and irony, *correspondances* and *différences*, spleen and idéal, Baudelaire offers a critique of the very notion that consumption of such ideological and aesthetic forms could lead to self-realization and fulfillment or, indeed, constitute any ontological wholeness in the modern world. It is thus that Baudelaire's poetical, critical, and theoretical elaborations of modernity's *paradis artificiels* become a major underpinning of his personal aesthetic and his general theory of post-romantic art.

Keeping in mind the ironic undercurrent of Baudelaire's poetry and the way it constitutes an indirect critique of culture consumption, we can now take another look at the two prose poems with which we opened up this inquiry into Baudelaire's aesthetics of intoxication. In "Laquelle est la vraie" the poet demystifies a feminine ideal assumed to be immortalized in death through nostalgic memory. By turning the speaker's fantasy or "repaired" memory of the illustrious Bénédicta into a nightmarish vision of "Malédicta," the "true" woman of his dreams, Baudelaire satirizes his pretensions, his attempt to construct some kind of transcendent truth by retaining an idealized and doubtless artificial memory of a woman whom he barely knew. With this image of a nostalgic lover who is neither able to "remember" illusory perfection in death nor to "forget" the horrid reality of life—Baudelaire questions the ability of poetic language to construct any true or lasting meaning. In this sense, it would seem that he also portrays his own tragic fate as a lover, and more importantly, as a poet.

Similarly, the Idol or *sylphide* of "La Chambre Double" is overshadowed and replaced by her nightmarish double, the Specter. Here, once again, ideality degrades into reality. If it is the ghost of reality that haunts the poet's artificial Ideal, it is his splenetic conscience—his melancholy awareness of this haunting—that either speaks to, or is silenced by the tension between life and art. Ross Chambers has pointed out the relationship of this splenetic consciousness to the activity of memory, arguing that memory is a source of melancholy, just as melancholy is a mechanism of memory.[43] But in its extreme form—as Ennui—melancholy no longer seems to stem from representations that refigure past lost as present lack. Instead, it appears to be a symptom of the *general* impossibility of such representation at all.

If desire corresponds, as I have argued, to the locus of a lack always already present, it is the mind's distension of time into the past that transforms this melancholy awareness into a "remembrance" of loss. But it is only when desire can be *articulated* as such—as a past to be recalled and perhaps mourned, rather than as an empty present to be brooded silently—that an authentic human time of the symbolic order becomes possible. We can understand the interference of an ironic reality (or is it truth?) in Baudelaire's allegorical representations of artificial paradise along these lines. That is, while we may identity the phantom haunting Baudelaire's "addicted time" with a more "authentic" metaphysical truth or historical reality, we must also understand this ghost of reality as a sign whose meaning is above all rhetorical and symbolic. When an artificial paradise is interrupted by such a sign of reality, artistic creation inaugurates its own deconstruction and, at the same time, destabilizes the very binaries—consumption and production, addiction and free will, intoxication and sobriety, artifice and truth—upon which that sign is built. The perpetual self-deconstruction into which the Baudelairean text falls as it simultaneously affirms and denies ideals of artistic redemption or self-fulfillment, reflects the haunting of his own aesthetic by the falsehood of the so-called truth itself—which is, perhaps, the only "truth" of art.

Notes

1. Of course, in "Au Lecteur," the opening poem of the *Fleurs du Mal*, the poet's dread of Ennui is quite explicit, suggesting, if not a cause, then a major effect of Baudelaire's disillusionment. At issue here, however, is not the poet's elaboration of *ennui* as such (a problematic that has already received a good deal of critical attention), but rather the underlying socio-psychological dynamics that give rise to this state of splenetic torpor and the paralysis of creativity that accompanies it. Specifically, I propose to address how the turn to artificial paradises and patterns of excessive consumption in Baudelaire's *oeuvre* feeds the vicious cycle of poetic inspiration and disillusion in which Ennui comes to occupy so central a role.

2. I am, of course, alluding to Walter Benjamin's characterization of Baudelaire's experience as a "lyric poet in the era of high capitalism." See "On Some Motifs in Baudelaire," in *Illuminations*, ed. Hannah Arendt (New York: Schocken Books, 1968), 155-200. See also "Paris, the Capital of the Nineteenth Century," in *Charles Baudelaire: A Lyric Poet in the Era of High Capitalism*, trans. Harry Zohn (London: NLB, 1973).

3. Jacques Derrida, "The Rhetoric of Drugs," *differences: A Journal of Feminist Cultural Studies* 5, no. 1 (1993): 11.

4. Charles Baudelaire, *Oeuvres Complètes* (Paris: Robert Laffont,1980), 163. All translations from this text are my own.

5. Baudelaire, *Oeuvres Complètes*, 200.

6. Elissa Marder, *Dead Time: Temporal Disorders in the Wake of Modernity* (Stanford: Stanford University Press, 2001), 93.

7. Marder, *Dead Time,* 132-133.

8. Ross Chambers, "Poetry in the Asiatic Mode," in *The Writing of Melancholy: Modes of Opposition in Early French Modernism* (Chicago: University of Chicago Press, 1993), 143.

9. Baudelaire, *Oeuvres Complètes*, 59.

10. Marder, *Dead Time,* 64.

11. See Saint Augustine, "Book XI: Time and Eternity," in *Confessions,* trans. Henry Chadwick. (Oxford: Oxford University Press, 1991), esp. 242-243.

12. Baudelaire, *Oeuvres Complètes*, 197.

13. As Pasi Falk puts it, "The additional (forbidden) element both creates and articulates the lack, the latter being an expression of desire as much as the desire is. an expression of lack." See *The Consuming Body: Theory, Culture & Society* (London: Sage Publications, 1994), 98. On the *supplement*, see Jacques Derrida, *Of Grammatology*, trans. Gayatri Spivak. (Baltimore: John Hopkins University Press, 1998), esp. 143-45.

14. Falk elaborates this point more specifically, arguing that the logics of modern consumption by which commodities and other objects are transformed into "a chain of substitutes or representations," are rooted "in the existential conditions of individual self-construction involving an historically specific mode of the reproduction of lack—and desire." See *The Consuming Body*, 143-144.

15. Arjun Appadurai, "Consumption, Duration, and History," in *Modernity at Large: Cultural Dimensions of Globalization* (Minn.: UMP, 1996), 77.

16. On this point, see Susan Stewart, *On Longing: Narratives of the Miniature, the Gigantic, the Souvenir, the Collection* (Durham: Duke Univ Press, 1993), 23.

17. Baudelaire, *Oeuvres Complètes*, 19.

18. Stewart, *On Longing*, 143.

19. For an elaboration of this concept, see Leo Bersani, *Baudelaire and Freud* (Berkeley: University of California Press), 1977.

20. Marder, *Dead Time*, 34-35.

21. Baudelaire, *Oeuvres Complètes*, 19.

22. I borrow the term "libidinal economy" from Jean-François Lyotard. For a further elaboration of this concept, see his *Libidinal Economy*, trans. Iain Hamiltaon Grant. (Bloomington: IUP, 1993). See also Jean Baudrillard's analysis of sign form and sign value in *For a Critique of the Political Economy of the Sign*, trans. Charles Levin. (Telos Press, 1981), esp. 143-163.

23. See Jean-Paul Sartre, *Baudelaire*, trans. Martin Turnell. (New York: New Directions, 1950), 51 & 157.

24. Alina Clej, *A Genealogy of the Modern Self* (Stanford: SUP, 1995), 135 & 255.

25. Baudelaire, *Oeuvres Complètes*, 111.

26. Baudelaire, *Oeuvres Complètes*, 110.

27. Baudelaire, *Oeuvres Complètes*, 111.

28. Bersani, *Baudelaire and Freud*, 3.

29. Baudelaire, *Oeuvres Complètes*, 795.

30. Clej, *Genealogy*, 14.

31. Bersani, *Baudelaire and Freud*, 19.

32. Baudelaire, *Oeuvres Complètes*, 133.

33. I recall here Baudelaire's famous phrase from his *Journaux Intimes* : "Qu'est-ce que l'art? Prostitution." See *Oeuvres Complètes,* 389.

34. Bersani, *Baudelaire and Freud*, 19.

35. Baudelaire, *Oeuvres Complètes*, 162.

36. See "La Beauté" in *Oeuvres Complètes*, 15.

37. Bersani, *Baudelaire and Freud*, 3.

38. *Baudelaire and Freud*, 4.

39. I borrow this term from Fredric Jameson. See his "Baudelaire as Modernist and Postmodernist: The Dissolution of the Referent and the Artificial 'Sublime'," in *Lyric Poetry: Beyond New Criticism,* eds. C. Hosek & Patricia Parker. (Ithaca: Cornell University Press, 1985), 247-263.

40. Bersani, *Baudelaire and Freud*, 19.

41. See Baudelaire's "Paradis Artificiels" in *Oeuvres Complètes*, 101.

42. Barbara Johnson, *Défigurations Du Langage Poétique* (Paris: Flammarion, 1979), 46.

43. See "Memory and Melancholy," in *The Writing of Melancholy*, 167-169.

No "Mere Modernity": Biopolitics, Media, and the Breeding of the Modern Consumer in Bram Stoker's *Dracula*

Jared F. Green

Anthropology and Biopolitics: The Gothic Origins of the Modern Subject

The London imagined by Bram Stoker's 1897 novel, *Dracula*, as is true of the metropolis as figured in much of late-Victorian Gothic fiction and urban exploration alike, is a cardiac structure, the heart of an imperial corpus imperiled by destructive forces exerting pressure from both within and without. The logic of vampirism, perforce, binds the city homologically to the bodies of its citizenry, and both are systemically altered as the Count circulates doubly: within the metropolitan grid and the biological bloodstream. In this respect, Stoker's novel, for all its overtly Gothic conventions, might best be understood as a symptom (in the Lacanian sense) of a massive epistemic shift in the conceptualization and regulation of the metropolis and its constituent bodies. Regarded in light of *Dracula*'s intersecting and competing discursive fields—that is, its ideological conflict between a decayed social order and an emerging modern subjectivity that Stoker renders as Gothic narrative—the novel may be read as a dramatization of what Giorgio Agamben has termed the biopolitical turn of modernity.[1] Much of the extensive body of *Dracula* criticism has focused on the vampire's violation of Victorian codes of sexuality and thus the Count's embodiment of sexual danger his subversion of culture-stabilizing gender roles. While it would seem a critical blindness to ignore the obvious importance of sexual discourse in

Stoker's text, it is my intention to move beyond the limiting psychosexual reading in order to understand *Dracula* as an exemplar of late-Victorian ipsography in order to explore how biopolitics links late-Victorian Gothic literature, anthropology and social science in the production and normalization of modern subjectivity.[2] These biopolitical *dispositifs* I insist, work in tandem to situate readers as consuming subjects, that is, as nodal points in the matrix of forces that binds the individual body to the state and its political economy and confirms and reiterates that relationship by way of the practice of commodity consumption as a form of imperial citizenship.[3]

Significant steps have already been taken in the interest of offering historical rather than psychoanalytic readings of Stoker's novel. Carol Senf, Patrick Brantlinger and Stephen D. Arata, for example, have all contributed to a growing field of *Dracula* criticism which suggests reading the text in terms of a generalized cultural anxiety that an overextended imperial Britain could fall prey to a reversal of its own colonial practices. This reversible logic is certainly inherent in the Hegelian master-slave dialectic that defines the practices of imperialism and which always problematizes the master position with the fear of the slave's seizure of the very power that enslaves. Yet what I wish to interrogate is the sufficiency of the ahistorical, ineluctably psychoanalytic condition of "cultural anxiety" to fully account for the cultural work of the Gothic text as a medium for the socialization of relations of state power to the body it seeks to discipline and render knowable.[4]

By contrast, Nicholas Daly eschews the psychologization of culture by reading *Dracula* in the context of emerging modern British class positions. In *Modernism, Romance and the Fin-de-Siècle,* Daly posits that *Dracula* "uses anxiety to produce as both necessary and natural a modern form of professional, male, homosocial combination—the team of experts."[5] Daly insists that Stoker's novel limns the parameters of a new professional class—the "class of experts" —that was crucial to the expansion of British home power. What he does not explore, however, is how the figures of the vampire-hunters *advertise* modes of class-affiliated desire that may be attained through the consumption of transportation, medical and information technologies. Given that *Dracula* emerges from a period of imperial expansion abroad, sharp industrial competition with the Continental European powers (Germany in particular) and resultant economic decline, the case can be made for situating the novel within a British mass culture that both markets to and promulgates the consumer class that was instrumental to the health of capitalism's circulatory system. It is in this sense, then, that I will presume, along with Daly, that *Dracula* is a novel that "ideologically [. . .] belongs to a specifically modernist culture,"[6] especially insofar as Stoker's text employs the long-standing discourse of racial difference to articulate modern consumerist practices that collapse clear distinctions between the body and its commodified, technological prostheses.

If it is at all possible to speak of literature as a reflection of "cultural anxieties," then, the most significant such fear articulated by Stoker's text is at the nexus of modern biopolitics and the (pseudo)science of race: the polygenist fear about the consequences of contact between the colonizer and colonized, particularly when the technologies that ensure the hegemony of empire wind up in the hands of those under imperial dominion. Such ambivalent logic, belonging as it does to the pre-Mendelian account of the heritability of acquired characteristics, is already evident in blood theories such as that of Dr. James Hunt, the president of the Anthropological Society of London whose 1863 essay, "On the Negro's Place in Nature," negates the pretense of the "civilizing mission" of empire while advancing a vexed account of racial admixture: "It is assumed that great improvement had taken place in the intellect of the Negro by education, which we much doubt. It is simply the European blood in their veins which renders them fit for the places of power, and they often use this power far more cruelly than either of the pure-blooded races."[7] An adherent to the polygenist account of evolution, Hunt maintains that the "negro race," being a separately evolved species from the white European could only advance through the literal incorporation of European blood. The inherent Gothicism of the concept is clear in Hunt's implied warning against the hybrid creature that results: a mutant whose racial stock is improved by the blood he consumes, thereby making him a more cunning and voracious threat to the imperial power that has itself already been proportionately compromised by such "miscegenation."

If some late-Gothic texts, most notably Robert Louis Stevenson's *The Strange Case of Dr. Jekyll and Mr. Hyde,* represent the monogenetic view of decadence as a slide into a primitive evolutionary state, *Dracula* coalesces around an account of degeneration that echoes Hunt's. In resonance with Hunt's account of race, Stoker's novel imagines the Count as a multifarious pathogen, for not only does his vampirism drain away the life blood of the English subjects he consumes, it also allows the Count to replicate indefinitely, thereby threatening to alter British culture quite literally from the inside by turning its productive citizens into consumers of other citizens rather than "proper" consumers of modern commodities. Through the central conceit of vampiric consumption, however, Stoker's novel departs from the specificities of anthropological theory (and thus proffers a thematization—rather than mere reflection—of cultural anxiety) for an idiosyncratic conflation of monogenism and polygenism. Here, the threat of atavism is reimagined as a universal potential situated within the individual psyche and externalized as an exogenous and pathogenic force that can replicate itself within *both* the biological and cultural body. This version of degeneration as a communicable, contaminating force is most clearly manifested in the criminology of Cesare Lombroso, who is specifically named in the text,[8] and the eugenic theories of Sir Francis Galton, with which Stoker's novel is most closely aligned. According to Galton, as well as other followers of Jean-Baptiste Lamarck and Herbert Spencer, degeneration was understood as a complex outcome of heritability, that is, as the passing on of undesirable characteristics acquired from the equally anathematic sexual miscegenation and cultural assimilation. For race scientists like anatomist Sir William Lawrence (an early nineteenth-century monogenist, although his account of race shares much with polygenist beliefs), race divided humans as starkly as species did animals and "un-natural unions" or crossings which introduced the "stain" of black blood could lead only to the "deterioration" of the white race.[9] It was this pessimistic version of heredity that would give rise to the "one drop of blood" theory of race pollution as well as the idea of cultivated racial improvement, codified as Galton's eugenics at the beginning of the twentieth century.[10]

After 1900, Galton fused nascent genetic science and the Liberal notion of ameliorism to produce his highly influential concept of eugenics.[11] It is clear from his full elaboration on the subject, *Eugenics, Its Scope and Aims* (originally published in 1904) that Galton's eugenics is a socio-economic program mapped onto the Darwinian schema. Here, Galton adopts Charles Booth's class categories to discern between the genetic types that comprise the "natural" hierarchy of urban dwellers. Quoting Booth directly, Galton proffers the same unsparing view of "Class A," or the poorest of London's poor: "Their life is the life of savages, with vicissitudes of extreme hardships and occasional excess. From them come the battered figures who slouch through the streets and play the beggar or the bully. *They render no useful service, they create no wealth; more often they destroy it.* They degrade whatever they touch, and as individuals are perhaps incapable of improvement."[12] At a time when the propagation of a solid consumer base was instrumental to the perpetuation of the imperial economy, Galton could hardly have raised a more abhorrent spectre than that of the urban savage who not only cannot create wealth but can actually actively "destroy it." Galton goes on to state that the goal of eugenic science is to "represent each class or sect by its best specimens; that done, to leave them to work out their common civilisation in their own way."[13] Eugenics, in other words, is not to be conceived of as a wholly repressive praxis, but rather as a *productive* biopolitics, the aim of which is to encourage a human breeding stock "better suited to fulfill our vast imperial opportunities."[14] While Galton does stress that "it would be an economy and a great benefit to the country if all habitual criminals were resolutely segregated under merciful surveillance and peremptorily denied opportunities for producing offspring," he is actually far more interested in "augmentation of the favoured stock" than in the forcible elimination of undesirable populations.[15] The ultimate outcome, as Galton's logic would have it, would be an English culture purified of both the criminal, indolent poor and the decadent aristocracy, in the wake of which would rise a vigorously healthy, more productive middle class. Evoking the same images of parasitism and vampirism that animate Stoker's articulation of eugenic concepts, Galton notes that in the social body as in the animal kingdom, there is a "contrariety of ideals between the beasts of prey and those they prey upon, between those of the animals that have to work hard for their food and the sedentary parasites that cling to their bodies and suck their blood."[16]

That the blood theories that link mid-Victorian anthropologists and Galtonian eugenics bear no small resemblance to the tropes of infection and contamination that suffuse *Dracula* is unsurprising, given that much of the horror in Stoker's novel consists in the reappropriation of the already-Gothic imagination that subtends the discourse of racial "science" in both its ethnographic and ipsographic applications. Indeed, such theories as Hunt's would not sound out of place coming from *Dracula*'s Van Helsing, who proves himself conversant in the pseudoscientific physiology of Eugene Talbot[17] when quizzing his colleague, Dr. Seward: "Do you know the altogether of comparative anatomy, and can say wherefore the qualities of brutes are in some men and not others?"[18] Yet while the eugenic strain of *Dracula*'s vampire-hunting narrative is most obviously borne out in the text's biological concepts, it has a material cultural component as well that is consonant with the economic imperatives that I have emphasized in Galton's work: If the Count and the atavistic aristocratic order he represents are to be permanently removed from the site of cultural reproduction, his literal death must also be hastened—and outlasted—by the propagation of the ideal type of the modern consumer as epitomized by the vampire hunters.

II. The Circulatory System: Information and/as Capital

In *Signs Taken for Wonders* (1983), Franco Moretti posed the possibility of interpreting *Dracula* as a text which allows two parallel readings, the psychoanalytic and the material historic, yet he himself ultimately admits to being at a loss to demonstrate where these critical trajectories meet. The problem, in part, is that Moretti reads *Dracula* as though Stoker's text were a deliberately Marxist allegory, with Count Dracula operating as the symbolic representative of capital itself. Moretti's rationale for imposing a schematic Marxism on the novel appears to be derived from a rather literal uptake of Marx's assertion that "Capital is dead labour which, vampire-like, lives only by sucking living labour, and lives the more, the more labour it sucks."[19] Yet the text of *Dracula* cannot support such a conclusion, as the very mechanics of Stoker's plot deliberately privilege those characters who are conversant with and capable of working within the emergent communications-transportation matrix of late-nineteenth century capitalism.

Representative of this interpretive gap is Moretti's insistence on associating the Count with monopolistic capitalism. As a counterpoint, he cites Mina Harker's comment regarding the "wonderful power of money" as an entreaty for the use of capital for the ultimate goal of social justice. For Moretti, then, *Dracula* winds up providing an allegory of the proper moral application of money: "Money must not have its end *in itself*, in its continuous accumulation. It must have, rather, a *moral*, anti-economic end to the point where colossal expenditures and losses can be calmly accepted."[20] While Moretti is correct in noting that the pure accumulation of capital is problematic in *Dracula*, he refuses to associate this sort of non-productive orientation toward capital with the old-order aristocracy that Count Dracula himself represents. Yet the text repeatedly demonstrates that the reason Mina and company are exemplars of "money properly applied" is that they allow capital to circulate freely between each another and out into the general British economy by way of the distinctly modern products, services and technologies that they consume. As Friedrich Kittler puts it in *Gramophone, Film, Typewriter* (1999), *Dracula* is ultimately about "the final victory of technological media over the blood-sucking despots of old Europe."[21]

A more apt precedent for the homology between the circulatory system and capital in *Dracula* might be that offered by Herbert Spencer's "The Social Organism" (1860), with its "analogy between the blood of a living body, and the circulating mass of commodities in the body politic."[22] This is the triumphalist view of consumerism's systolic and diastolic flow and exchange. Spencer pursues his analogy still further, however, uniting it with a vision of cultural evolution that posits the body of the capitalist society as that which possesses the more advanced vascular system, and in turn, the greater fitness for survival and domination than the more "primitive" feudal order. Similarly, in lieu of Marxism, the procapitalist economic theories of Friedrich A. von Hayek, who saw the health of capitalism as being based upon its ability to organize disparate bits of information into a comprehensive system, seems a more useful model for interpreting *Dracula*'s metanarrative of information-gathering.[23]

A slight adjustment of Moretti's use of the term "monopoly," then, points us toward what I believe is a more productive reading of the text's multiple economies. Thomas Richards also uses the term "monopoly" but in a sense much closer to the spirit of Hayek's information systems, to describe the "British monopoly over knowledge" that is threatened by Dracula's challenge to the "ordinal scheme of historical morphological development."[24] It is in this respect that the vast information network of the vampire-hunters animates Weber's notion that bureaucracy can be a brutally efficient armature of power for those who know how to control it. *Dracula*, after all, is a novel in which God is imagined as a sort of transcendental bureaucrat, as when Dr. Seward, resigning himself to the scientist's life of perpetual record-making, declares: "So it will be until the Great Recorder sums me up and closes my ledger account with a balance to profit or loss."[25]

Stripped of the generic tropes of Gothic romance, *Dracula*, reveals itself to be what mark Seltzer has termed a "romance of the market in machine culture,"[26] that is, a narrative about conflicting information systems and their attendant modes of class affiliation: the outmoded and technologically primitive one that defines Dracula's feudal order and the accelerated, technologically enhanced one that defines British capitalism. As Geoffrey Wall has so aptly put it: "The 'scientific, sceptical, matter-of-fact nineteenth century' equips its world-historical representatives, three Englishmen, a Texan and a Dutchman, its present, its future and its past, equips them with a phonograph, typewriter and railway timetable in the struggle to defend woman, family and empire against the archaic remnant of a feudal aristocracy."[27] For Stoker's vampire-hunters, just as for Hayek, information *is* capital and the mutually entailing relationship between the two is carefully elaborated through the text's networked sites of discourse: the medical-ethnographic account of biology, the archive, and finally, communications technologies as apotheosized by the typewriter, which yields the final typescript as an archivable redoubt against the degenerate forces of the primitive. Jonathan Harker says as much himself, proudly identifying his own shorthand method as "nineteenth century up-to-date with a vengeance."[28] Although Harker will also voice the novel's underlying note of fear that "the old centuries had, and have, powers of their own which mere 'modernity' cannot kill,"[29] the phrasing here is telling, for while "mere 'modernity'"—that is, simple linear temporality—may not be able to kill off the powers of the old centuries, a *specific*, technological modernity most certainly can.

Of all of *Dracula*'s information-hunters, it is perhaps Harker who is most representative of the modern, imperial gaze that translates human beings into the disciplinary subjects that Seltzer calls "statistical persons,"[30] units of data that can quite literally be accounted for and organized in the master technology of the "imperial archive."[31] Harker, who first appears in the novel as archived information himself—his diary and letters are part of the overall tissue of textuality sutured together by Mina's typescript—has prepared for his journey to Dracula's castle (to finalize the details of the Count's newly-acquired London estate) by consulting the British Museum's books and maps. The term Harker uses for the goal of his preparatory activities, "foreknowledge," is significant in that it sums up the relationship between *Dracula*'s personae and their natural, social and cultural environments, even as it underscores how benighted Harker remains upon this first encounter. In the narrative's many instances of information-processing, archival classification tends to precede empirical experience, as when Harker enumerates the precise ethnic categories of the various peoples he spies through his carriage window during his trip to Transylvania, assessing each as "picturesque," or to put it another way, as human figures who have been reduced to little more than a living simulation of the photographic images that have preceded them. Armed with his shorthand-coded notebooks, his Kodak and his travel guides—firmly situate him as the novel's representative of the practices of ethnography and travel, as well as its representative of consumerism as a fundamental attribute of imperial subjectivity.[32] Harker penetrates the Count's sphere of influence much as Burton, Stanley and others forayed into Africa, reaffirming the advancements of English civilization by noting their absence with every step further into the heart of darkness. The arc of technological devolution is readily apparent from the outset of the text, as when Harker notes that "the further East you go the more unpunctual are the trains. What ought they to be in China?"[33] Yet Harker's journey is not, in fact, the simple "first contact" narrative it resembles. Rather, the Gothic elements of the text arise not from difference but from uncanny similarity and Harker is repeatedly surprised by the extent to which the Count—in spite of the "strange intonation" and mannerisms which satisfy the need of both Harker and the text to mark him as other—has absorbed English language and literature.

This oscillation between similitude and alterity finds an apt correlative on the body of the Count himself, as when Harker comments: "Hitherto I had noticed the backs of his hands as they lay on his knees in the firelight, and they had seemed rather white and fine; but seeing them now close to me, I could not but notice that they were rather coarse—broad, with squat fingers. Strange to say, there were hairs in the centre of the palm."[34] The trope of the body as a bearer of sameness that both conceals and reveals the mark of difference brings Freud's language of the uncanny as the homely-unhomely/native-stranger before us here. Everything about this first encounter is an inversion of surface and depth; although Harker remarks upon his pleasure at seeing the familiar elements of Englishness in the Count's home, he cannot recognize in the Count's library the signs of an acquisitive activity that mirrors his own research in the British Museum.

> In the library I found, to my great delight, a vast number of English books, whole shelves full of them, and bound volumes of magazines and newspapers. A table in the centre was littered with English magazines and newspapers, though none of them were of very recent date. The books were of the most varied kind—history, geography, politics, political economy, botany, geology, law—all relating to England and English life and customs and manners. There were even such books of reference as the London Directory, the 'Red' and 'Blue' books, Whitaker's Almanack, the Army and Navy lists, and—it somehow gladdened my heart to see it—the Law List.[35]

Unbeknownst to Harker, it is against the Count's shadow archive that the text will play out its most pitched battle. In fact, it will take almost the entirety of the narrative before D. Van Helsing, the Dutch physician and Dr. Seward's mentor, fully appreciates the enormity of the Count's knowledge acquisition:

> With the child-brain that was to him he have long since conceive the idea of coming to a great city. What does he do? He find out the place of all the world most of promise for him. Then he deliberately set himself down to prepare for the task. . . He study new tongues. He learn new social life; new environment of old ways, the politic, the law, the finance, the science, the habit of a new land and a new people who have come to be since he was.. . . It help him to grow as to his brain. . . He have done this alone; all alone! from a ruin tomb in a forgotten land. What more may he not do when the greater world of thought is open to him.[36]

Although entirely unacknowledged by Harker at the outset of the text, such early intimations are already clear in what at first he misinterprets as the Count's self-effacing appraisal of his own learning:

> Well I know that, did I move and speak in your London, none there are who would not know me for a stranger. That is not enough for me.

> Here I am noble; I am *boyar*; the common people know me, and I am
> master. But a stranger in a strange land, he is no one; men know him
> not—and to know not is to care not for. I am content if I am like the
> rest, so that no man stops if he see me, or pause in his speaking if he
> hear my words, to say 'Ha, ha! a stranger!'.[37]

In his drive to efface the marks of difference, the Count, like one of
Homi Bhabha's "mimic men," has absorbed the logic of the archive to
such an extent that he has learned to speak of himself as situated within
ethnographic discourse. In this sense, he has already begun to practice a
rudimentary sort of consumerism—that is, by internalizing the system of
knowledge-production in which he is configured—but not one that is yet
mapped onto the world of commodities (although one assumes that his
acquisition of the London estate will mark his entryway into the marketplace of English goods as well as English bodies). The effect of the
Count's mimicry is not simply uncanny in its mirroring of Harker's classificatory system, it borders on the carnivalesque in the sense that the
Count threatens to exhaust the categories of ethnographic representation.
Although he identifies himself as a scion of the Szekely family, Dracula
appears to have thoroughly internalized the ethnographic mode of representing through type, for he claims that "in our veins flows the blood of
many brave races." His own account of his racial lineage (delivered, in
the manner of the true archival composite, in the first person plural),
charts a world-historical genesis in the "whirlpool of European races, the
Ugric tribe," to their proliferation throughout "Europe . . . Asia and Africa too,"[38] an all-consuming racial profile which well exceeds any classificatory system that would attempt to contain it.[39]

Whereas the Count is himself an embodied composite, the vampire-
hunters, according to Van Helsing "have the power of combination—a
power denied to the vampire kind; we have resources of science; we are
free to act and think."[40] While the Count's mirror archive of out-of-date
texts and periodicals on British subjects testifies to little more than the
fruitlessness of attempting to keep pace with the rapidly-evolving culture
of England without its attendant information technologies, the British
Museum as a comprehensive repository of things past allows for more
than adequate knowledge of the Count. Even Van Helsing's ominous
question, "what more may he do when the greater world of thought is
open to him" is mitigated by his insistence that the Count's "child-brain"
is still in the process of learning how to decode the full genome of modern urban life.

Troy Boone has persuasively argued that in the text's privileged
model of combination is an insistence on developing a more flexible sort
of scientism, one which can absorb rather than simply write over super-

stition and magic. Herein lies the secondary meaning of Harker's comment on the insufficiency of "mere 'modernity',," or the fear that positivism might err by unwittingly effacing the knowledge of the past. Indeed, Dr. Seward begins to accept just such a possibility late in the text, as when he comments that "Van Helsing is off to the British Museum looking up some authorities on ancient medicine. The old physicians took account of things which their followers do not accept, and the Professor is searching for witch and demon cures which may be useful to us later."[41] The Dutch physician's role is therefore especially significant as a mediator of cultural positions. With "various armaments—the spiritual in the left hand, the mortal in the right," Van Helsing's ultimately successful synthetic approach poses the possibility of a science that is not defined strictly by its opposition to older forms of belief. While the threat remains that the archive which subjugates is the same as that which can empower, the significant difference that still separates the Count's efforts from those of the vampire-hunters is that Dracula must process his information alone, while their "power of combination" is both enabled by and enabling of the technologies of communication that the Count has yet to master.

III. Consuming Machine Culture: From Writing Type to Type-Writing

While ethnographic discourse—the writing of types—dominates the novel's epistemophilia, another sort of type-writing, the mechanical sort, emerges as the mechanical process most suited for the ethnographic enterprise. In response to Moretti's inability to bridge the Marxist and Freudian interpretations he finds in *Dracula*, Jennifer Wicke's "Vampiric Typewriting: *Dracula* and its Media" (1992) remains one of the most persuasive attempts to ground Stoker's text in the specific material culture that circulates throughout the narrative. Her provocative reading of the novel's competing communication systems stems from the central assumption that "The social force most analogous to Count Dracula's as depicted in the novel is none other than mass culture, the developing technologies of media in its many forms, as mass transport, tourism, photography and lithography in image production, and mass-produced narrative."[42]

Wicke's focus on the "technologies that underpin vampirism," rather than any allegorical interpretation of the Gothic melodrama, allows her to historicize Stoker's peculiar version of the degeneracy debates and to tease out of the novel's various scare tactics a sustained engagement with the specific forms of consumerist modernity which lead her to proclaim

Dracula as the "first great *modern* novel in British literature."[43] In Wicke's reading, the material culture that circulates in *Dracula* effectively complicates the otherwise too-easily drawn series of binaries that critics tend to use to reduce the text to a compendium of resolvable oppositions (Oriental/Occidental, heterosexual/homosexual, civilized/primitive and so on). I wish to pursue Wicke's emphasis on *Dracula*'s media to show the extent to which the text's ethnographic structure discursively positions its characters as representatives of two competing social orders, broadly characterized here by "improper" and "proper consumption." Although *Dracula* works to reposition the source of degenerative influence from inside the self (where it resides in *Dr. Jekyll and Mr. Hyde*) to outside the self, it does so in a doubly uncanny way, since vampirism always threatens to "come inside," as it were, and reverse these categories. As a result, the self/other and primitive/civilized binaries become untenable and the text must rely on the only distinction that can be concretely demonstrated: the difference between proper and improper consumption. While it might seem an altogether too obvious pun to suggest that the Count's feeding on English bodies is "improper consumption"—one which leads to an equally improper reproduction—the negative example of vampirism as that which stands outside of and "other" to middle-class culture allows for a clearly delineated set of proper consumer practices to be represented as ontologically stable.

This is certainly the case, but Wicke's critical framework for interpreting how "the social force most analogous to Count Dracula's as depicted in the novel is none other than mass culture. . . " can be resituated to shift the focus from mass culture's resemblance to vampirism and place it instead on how such apparent homologies in fact attest to the divide *between* the modern and the pre-modern. Consider, for example, Dr. Seward's deduction of a link between his patient, Renfield, and the Count that points toward the discursive roles of these characters as ciphers for information; Renfield not only resembles the Count in his "zoophageous" habits, but is "mixed up with the Count in an *indexy* kind of way."[44] When Dr. Van Helsing first arrives in London to aid Seward in diagnosing the vamped Lucy Westenra's as-yet unclassifiable ailment, he re-emphasizes the parallel between organic systems and information systems when he cautions Seward to exercise discretion and not yet reveal anything of the mysterious case: "So you shall keep knowledge in its place, where it may rest—where it may gather its kind around it and breed."[45] As with Van Helsing's numerous other "composite" concepts— and here the reference to the Count's coffin and his harem of female vampires is unmistakable—an uncomfortable and uncanny parallel appears to confer the same ontological status on vampirism and knowledge-gathering.

Wicke's treatment of phonography offers another useful example of how apparent homologies are deployed by Stoker's text so as to re-establish the terms of absolute difference as policed by the possession of the technologies of the modern. Noting the diary entry in which Van Helsing's voice is recording Dr. Seward's diary onto phonograph cylinders, Wicke interprets the "immaterialization of the voice" effected by phonographic reproduction as constituting a restructuring of the relationship between speech and voice; a "vampiric exchange," in which one man's voice is effectively usurped and reproduced by another. Rather than seeing this as a directly homologous form of vampirism mapped onto the technology of phonography, however, I would suggest that such parallelism can only emphasize *Dracula*'s precisely patrolled boundary between proper (technological) and improper (vampiric, telepathic) methods of information reproduction. While Wicke reads the "immaterialization of. . . voice" as an example of "speech already colonized, or vampirized, by mass mediation," a reversal of this formula reveals an instance in which the vampire hunters assert the power of mass mediation to triumph over an older order that links language directly to the body—an association that has deadly consequences in *Dracula*. In fact, technologies of "immaterialization" are valorized in the novel and insistently privileged over the embodied authenticity of Dracula's voice, handwriting, telepathic commands and so on, because they render the gathering corpus of information non-localizable and therefore immune to destruction at Dracula's hands. Indeed, if there is any explicit link to vampirism to be found in *Dracula*'s representation of phonography, it seems to be more closely linked to the declaration made in an 1877 *Scientific American* that with the phonograph, "speech has become, as it were, immortal."[46]

Van Helsing's speaking for Seward, then, is not the property of the text's Gothic narrative but is rather one of the privileged methods by which Gothic elements are resolved and normative order re-established. The process of extricating speech from the body and typewritten language from speech is nothing short of an evolutionary process in action. When Mina first offers to transcribe Seward's diary, she remarks on the strangely *un*mediated contact it maintains with the doctor's private interiority: "That is a wonderful machine, but it is cruelly true. It told me in its very tones, the anguish of your heart. It was like a soul crying out to almighty God. No one must hear them spoken ever again! See, I have tried to be useful. I have copied out the words on my typewriter, and none other need now hear your heart beat, as I did."[47] As valuable as the phonograph is to the vampire-hunters' process, however, its ability to capture the voice maintains an indexical yoke to the physical body and requires a further remove through the reproductive technology of type-writing, which bears the mark of neither hand nor voice. After all, in vampirism's somatic economy, nothing could be more vulnerable than information that is still linked to the heart.[48]

Type gains control over speech in more ways than one: if the phono-graph has the possibility to make speech "immortal," the physical fragil-ity of its medium (the wax cylinder) nonetheless requires further media-tion. The vulnerability of human voice and body as well as fragile phonographic media are all attested to in the sequence of events which begins with Mina's vamping and which leads to the Count's destruction of the manuscript and phonograph cylinders. This would appear to be an event of consummate disaster, with all of the central nodes of the infor-mation network—both the records and their recorder alike—threatened with obliteration. Yet this would only be the case if Stoker's text privi-leged the notion of the authentic document and maintained writing's in-dexical links between the body and the word. On the contrary, and thanks to the intervention of the typewriter, neither Mina's body nor the printed words she produces bears the status of the original. The same cannot be said for the Count himself, whose vampiric communication network will necessarily disappear once his embodied, centralized control has been destroyed. Far from signaling the sort of lamentable unlinking of the body from the word that both Wicke and Heidegger insist upon, the technologically-mediated   process   of   becoming   *in*authentic— disseminatable—through the consumption of technologies of reproduc-tion is absolutely essential to the novel's drive to formal closure. Mere modernity, or that which is bound to unicity, authenticity and the econ-omy of the body, is that which the Count most challenges. And it is only technological reproducibility—that is, the final manuscript's multiple copies—that ensures that the vampire-hunters will still be able to exact their violence on the all-too-original body of the Count, thus eliminating the primitivized practices of "improper" consumption and linking proper consumption to an equally proper idea of cultural and biological repro-duction.

Notes

1. Giorgio Agamben, *Homo Sacer: Sovereign Power and Bare Life*, tr. Dan-iel Heller-Roazen (Stanford: Stanford University Press, 1988).

2. Along with Agamben's understanding of the term "biopolitics," I also have in mind Foucaults's more well-known elaboration of biopolitics as the emergence of the modern subject as the subject of disciplinary power (see Foucault's now-classic texts, *Discipline and Punish* [New York: Vintage Books, 1979] and *The History of Sexuality*, vols. I-III, [New York: Pantheon, 1978]).

3. Of the relatively few critical attempts to differentiate the late nineteenth-century Gothic from its earlier counterparts, Kathleen L. Spencer's notion of what she terms the "urban Gothic" is especially suggestive. In "Purity and Danger: *Dracula,* the Urban Gothic, and the Late Victorian Degeneracy Crisis" Spencer claims that the fantastic that develops at the end of the nineteenth century…is identifiably different from the Gothic of one hundred years before. First and most important, the new authors insist on the modernity of the setting…. A modern setting means, most profoundly, an urban setting, as by the end of the nineteenth century, well over half the population of the British Isles lived in cities. To be modern also means that science is the metaphor that rules human interactions with the universe, so the new fantastic adopts the discourse of empiricism even to describe and manipulate supernatural phenomena. (Kathleen L. Spencer, "Purity and Danger: *Dracula*, the Urban Gothic, and the Late Victorian Degeneracy Crisis," *ELH* 59:1 [1992], 200). Spencer also suggests that, in counterpoint to French and American naturalism (linked to Zola, James and Howells), "urban Gothic" fiction participated in a more general revival of romance genres that signified a "patriotic" attempt to establish a "healthy *English* fiction" (Spencer, 202). Spencer's idea of a Gothic inflected by urbanization, scientific empiricism and technological change is compatible with Patrick Brantlinger's concept of an "imperial Gothic," which "combines the seemingly scientific, progressive, often Darwinian ideology of imperialism with an antithetical interest in the occult" (Patrick Brantlinger. *Rule of Darkness: British Literature and Imperialism 1830-1914* [Ithaca: Cornell University Press, 1988], 227). In a somewhat different account of Gothicism's articulation of modernity, Brantlinger goes on to say that the imperial Gothic "expresses anxieties about the waning of religious orthodoxy, but even more clearly it expresses anxieties about the ease with which civilization can revert to barbarism or savagery and thus about the weakening of Britain's imperial hegemony. The atavistic descents into the primitive experienced by fictional characters seem often to be allegories of the larger regressive movement of civilization."(Brantlinger, 229).

4. For example, Arata argues that "In *Dracula* vampirism designates a kind of colonization of the body. Horror arises not because Dracula destroys bodies, but because he appropriates and transforms them. Having yielded to his assault, one literally "goes native" by becoming a vampire oneself…. In turn [his victims] receive a new racial identity, one that marks them as literally 'Other.' Miscegenation leads, not to the mixing of races, but to the biological and political annihilation of the weaker race by the stronger" (Stephen D. Arata, "The Occidental Tourist: *Dracula* and the Anxiety of Reverse Colonization," *Victorian Studies* 33:4 [1990], 630). Much as I agree with Arata's reading of the racial

component of vampirism, I believe that the overly schematic claim that "*Dracula* enacts the period's most important and pervasive narrative of decline, a narrative of reverse colonization" (Arata, "The Occidental Tourist," 623) still leaves the text's representation of material culture unaccounted for.

5. Nicholas Daly, *Modernism, Romance and the Fin-de-Siècle: Popular Fiction and British Culture, 1880-1914* (Cambridge; Cambridge UP, 1999), 30.

6. Daly, *Modernism, Romance,* 30.

7. James Hunt, "On the Negro's Place in Nature," *Memoirs Read Before the Anthropological Socoiety of London,* 1 (1863), 98.

8. The theory of atavism in the concatenated fields of physical anthropology, psychology and criminology come fully into the foreground with Dr. Seward's observation that "The Count is a criminal and of a criminal type. Nordau and Lombroso would so classify him, and *qua* criminal he is of imperfectly formed mind." Against the backdrop of the increasing anti-immigrant sentiments that marked the century's final decade, *Dracula*'s equation between the Count's criminality and his ethnic—and therefore racialized—primitivism anticipates the trend toward eugenics as it plays out a number of simultaneous fantasies of degeneration, atavism, sexual corruption, social parasitism, and finally, cultural purification and domestic resolution. "By the late nineteenth century," notes Nancy Stepan, "the urban poor, prostitutes, criminals, and the insane were being construed as "degenerate" types whose deformed skulls, protruding jaws, and low brain weights marked them as 'races apart,' interacting with and creating degenerate spaces near at home" (Stepan, 98). In the semiotic system of degeneration, race already marked a degenerate condition and racial characteristics (prognathism, "simian" cranial angles and noses, and so on) offered a code of visibility and legibility which could be used to pick out the primitive, criminal individual in the crowd. "The meanings attached to racial 'degeneracy,' and the technologies they encapsulated became constituent elements, therefore, of the doctrine of social decay" (Stepan, 98).

9. William Lawrence, cited in Stepan, 107.

10. For the blood theorists, cultural degradation was literalized as a symptom of simultaneously endogenous and exogenous pathogenic invasion, and as such, established a direct parallel between the individual body and the cultural body that made culture legible as a physiological phenomenon. Although the idea of the individual operating within culture as an organ operates within the body is not new to the nineteenth century, then-recent discoveries such as germ theory and heredity, along with such historical factors as immigration and the transformations of urban populations made such homologies appear to be more than merely metaphorical. For the blood theorists, cultural degradation was literalized as a symptom of simultaneously endogenous and exogenous pathogenic invasion, and as such, established a direct parallel between the individual body and the cultural body that made culture legible as a physiological phenomenon. Although the idea of the individual operating within culture as an organ operates within the body is not new to the nineteenth century, then-recent discoveries

such as germ theory and heredity, along with such historical factors as immigration and the transformations of urban populations made such homologies appear to be more than merely metaphorical. The analogy between the individual body and the state has a key precursor in Rudolf Virchow's *Cellular Pathology* (1858), which stressed an equivalence between the cells in the human body and individuals in the social body. Of Virchow's account of degeneration, Sander L. Gilman notes: "Disease arose from only two sources: an active external source ("irritation") and a passive internal source. The latter he labeled 'degeneration'" (Sander Gilman, "Sexology, Psychoanalysis and Degeneration: From a Theory of Race to a Race to Theory" in Chamberlin and Gilman, ed. *Degeneration: The Dark Side of Progress* (New York: Columbia University Press, 1985). Throughout the nineteenth century, explanations of pathogenic causality bound ideas of race to class to form what was fostered as a scientific method of interpreting and improving culture, especially in the work of Herbert Spencer. Although it would require the rediscovery of Gregor Mendel's genetic theory in 1900 to give heredity a truly scientific (and non-Spencerian) foundation, the idea of being able to select out the degenerate in favor of the fit is already present as the primary aim of Galton's composite photography.

11. It is particularly important here to note that there is a difference between what is traditionally called "positive" eugenics and the more infamous "negative" version put into practice in the fascist European regimes of the 1930s and 40s. The former, which is closer to Galton's intent than the programs of extermination associated with the latter, is "positive" in the sense that it is intended to encourage those qualities which contribute to fitness and thereby hasten the disappearance of those that lead to degenerescence. Although Galton's eugenics grew out of the liberal ideal of improvability—and while liberals were the majority of the program's proponents in Britain between 1900 and 1914—its implicit intent to eliminate the populations who bore the mark of degeneration (i.e. racial and class others) cannot be overlooked. The conservative grain of Galton's theories is particularly evident when seen as a direct reaction of the welfare-state interventionism that characterized the Liberal party in the 1890s. According to Galton and his partner in the Eugenics Laboratory, Karl Pearson, welfare was counteracting the natural competition that would lead to the survival of the fittest. Since the popularly held notion was that the poorest and most feeble were also breeding at an unchecked rate, eugenics was considered one way to restore balance and to eliminate what Pearson called the "survival of the most fertile." (see Robert Nye, "Sociology and Degeneration," in Chamberlin and Gilman, *Degeneration*, 63-65).

12. Charles Booth, quoted in Francis Galton, "Eugenics: Its Definition, Scope and Aims," *Essays in Eugenics* (London: The Eugenics Education Society, 1909) 19-20; my italics.

13. Galton, *Eugenics*, 37.

14. Galton, *Eugenics*, 38.

15. Galton, *Eugenics*, 20.

16. Galton, *Eugenics*, 36.

17. Talbot, an American dental surgeon, claimed in *Degeneracy: Its Causes, Signs and Results* (1898), criminals (along with prostitutes, sexual perverts and "persistent paupers") shared with the "lower races" the easily identifiable physiognomy of the unnaturally shaped skull, thus uniting the criminal, the poor, the "Negro" and the ape as exact evolutionary counterparts. Talbot goes so far as to entertain a bizarre theory of racial development from anthropoid apes:

> The orang descendant would have long arms and red hair. The chimpanzee descendant would be of small size, dark colour with slender bones and jaws. The gorilla race would have massive chest, big bones, massive jaws and teeth. These three types appear in Great Britain and Ireland and traces of their blood are still detectable in living men. (Talbot 94)

18. Bram Stoker, *Dracula* (New York: Penguin Books, 1993), 247.

19. Karl Marx, quoted in Franco Moretti *Signs Taken for Wonders*, tr. Susan Fischer, David Forgacs and David Miller (London: Verso, 1988).

20. Moretti, *Signs*, 94.

21. Friedrich Kittler, *Gramophone, Film, Typewriter* (Stanford: Stanford University Press, 1999), 86.

22. Herbert Spencer, "The Social Organism," *Herbert Spencer on Social Evolution*, Ed. J.D.Y. Peel, (Chicago, University of Chicago Press, 1972); 53-70; 65.

23. For an elaboration of Hayek's notion of economic equilibrium and its necessary relation to the equilibrium of knowledge and data, see Hayek, "Economics and Knowledge": "...economics has come nearer than any other social science to an answer to that central question of all social sciences: How can the combination of fragments of knowledge existing in different minds bring about results, if they were to be brought about deliberately, would require a knowledge on the part of the directing mind which no single person can possess?" In "The Use of Knowledge in Society," Hayek defines the price system in equally suggestive terms: "Fundamentally, in a system in which the knowledge of the relevant facts is dispersed among many people, prices can act to co-ordinate the separate actions of different people in the same way as subjective values help the individual to co-ordinate the parts of his plan.... It is more than a metaphor to describe the price system as a kind of machinery for registering change, or a system of telecommunications."

24. Thomas Richards, *The Imperial Archive*, (New York: W.W. Norton & Co., 1993), 49.

25. Stoker, *Dracula*, 96.

26. Mark Seltzer, *Bodies and Machines,* (New York: Routledge, 1992), 48.

27. Geoffrey Wall."Different from Writing: *Dracula* in 1897,"*Literature and History* 10:1.Spring 1984, 19.

28. Stoker, *Dracula*, 51. *Dracula*'s insistence upon its own modernity was certainly not lost on its contemporary readers; in an echo of Harker's comment,

an early review in *The Spectator* praised the novel's "up-to-dateness" (*The Spectator* 79. 31 July 1897, 151).

29. Stoker, *Dracula*,51.

30. Seltzer, *Bodies and Machines*, passim.

31. The term here is borrowed from Thomas Richards, *The Imperial Archive*, passim.

32. Jennifer Wicke, "Vampiric Typewriting: *Dracula* and its Media," *ELH* 59:2 (1992), 467-493.

33. Stoker, *Dracula*, 9.

34. Stoker, *Dracula*, 28.

35. Stoker, *Dracula*,30-31.

36. Stoker, *Dracula*, 412-13.

37. Stoker, *Dracula*, 31-32.

38. Stoker, *Dracula*, 42.

39. Much later on in the text, Van Helsing repeats this formulation, speaking of the vampire's ethnic lineage in terms so diffuse that the classificatory value of ethnography appears to lose all potency, as the Count is represented as coextensive with all forms of Orientalism and archaism: "he is known everywhere that men have been. In old Greece, in old Rome; he flourished in Germany all over, in France, in India, even in the Chersonese; and in China, so far away from us in all ways, there even is he, and the people fear him at this day. He have follow the wake of the berserker Icelander, the devil-begotten Hun, the Slav, the Saxon, the Magyar" (Stoker, *Dracula*, 307).

40. Stoker, *Dracula*, 306.

41. Stoker, *Dracula*, 352.

42. Wicke, *Vampiric Typewriting*, 469.

43. Wicke, *Vampiric Typewriting*, 467.

44. Stoker, *Dracula*, 320, emphasis added.

45. Stoker, *Dracula*, 156.

46. *Scientific American*, 1877, cited in Kittler 1999, 21.

47. Stoker, *Dracula*, 285-6.

48. In *Parmenides*, Martin Heidegger makes the especially resonant observation that

> It is not accidental that modern man writes 'with' the typewriter and 'dictates' [*diktiert*] (the same word as 'poeticize' [*dichten*]) 'into' a machine. This 'history' of the kinds of writing is one of the main reasons for the destruction of the word. The latter no longer comes and goes by means of the writing hand, the properly acting hand, but means of the mechanical forces it releases. The typewriter tears writing from the essential realm of the hand, i.e. the realm of the word. The word itself turns into something 'typed.' Where typewriting, on the contrary, is only a transcription and serves to preserve the writing, or turns into print something already written, there it

has a proper, though limited, significance.... Mechanical writing deprives the hand of its rank in the realm of the written
word and degrades the word to a means of communication. In
addition, mechanical writing provides this 'advantage,' that it
conceals the handwriting and thereby the character. The typewriter makes everyone look the same. (Martin Heidegger,
Parmenides, tr. André Schuwert and Richard Rojcewicz
[Bloomington: Indiana University Press, 1992], 80-81, 85-86).

Aside from "proper, though limited significance" which he begrudgingly confers
upon the typewriter as a mode of preservation, Heidegger finds little to celebrate
in a machine whose ability to "[tear] writing from the essential realm of the
hand" signals the degenerate aspect of modern culture. Nonetheless, each of his
negativized terms (e.g. the intimation that typewriting cannot be said to have any
proper "history," that it "conceals the hand and thereby the character" and that it
reduces the word to a symptom of mechanical force and a unit of communication) defines the exact reasons for which this modern innovation proves so une-
quivocally triumphant in Stoker's text.

Helen Pike Bauer is a Professor of English at Iona College. Her research and teaching concentrate on nineteenth-century fiction, recently on the work of British novelists who treat India. She has published a full-length study, *Rudyard Kipling: A Study of the Short Fiction*, and has published essays and presented papers on Anglo-Indian culture, and on the work of Flora Annie Steel and Sara Jeannette Duncan.

Sumangala Bhattacharya is Assistant Professor of English and World Literature at Pitzer College in Claremont, California. She is currently working on a book entitled "Victorian Hunger" and has forthcoming essays on nineteenth-century representations of hunger.

Ron Broglio teaches British Romanticism, Animal Studies, and literary theory at Georgia Institute of Technology. His research focuses on how philosophy and aesthetics can help us rethink the relationship between humans and the environment. His book "Technologies of the Picturesque: Art, Poetry, and Instruments 1760-1830" will be published by Bucknell University Press in 2007. Broglio is associate editor of *Romantic Circles* and book review editor of *Configurations*. His essays appear or are forthcoming in *The Wordsworth Circle, Praxis, New Formations, TEXT Technology, Visible Language* and *Visual Culture*, among others.

Jim Chevallier is an unaffiliated researcher whose interest in the 18th century derives from his efforts at historical fiction, but now includes research into and translations of a variety of material.

Ilias Chrissochoidis holds a Ph.D. in Musicology from Stanford University. He specializes on the life, career, and image of Handel in Georgian England and, especially, the reception of his English Oratorios during1732-1784. A former residential fellow at Stanford Humanities Center, he has received fellowships and grants from Harvard, Yale, UCLA, UT-Austin, the Huntington and Folger libraries, ASECS, and the American Handel Society. He is completing a volume of studies on Handel's early reception in Britain and a collection of documents on the composer.

Dr Helen Day is currently a Research fellow for the Centre for Employability through Humanities at the University of Central Lancashire. Her research interests include Mrs Beeton, Victorian Dining at Home and in London Clubs and the Pedagogy of English Language and Literature. She is currently teaching modules on Food Writing and Television and Live Food Project and bakes exceedingly good cakes!

Monika Elbert, Professor of English at Montclair State University and Asssociate Editor of *The Nathaniel Hawthorne Review*, has published extensively on Hawthorne and on other nineteenth-century American authors. Recently, her co-edited collection, *Reinventing the Peabody Sisters*, was published. Her edited collection on acculturation and social values in nineteenth-century American children's literature is forthcoming.

Jared Green is Associate Professor of Modern Literature and Culture at Stonehill College in Easton, MA, USA. His research areas include British and Continental Modernism, theories of urban modernity, technology and commodity culture, nineteenth- and twentieth-century visuality, early cinema, and anthropology. He is currently at work on a book-length study, "White Primitives: Anthropology and Cinema in the Empire of the Image, 1895-1926."

James Gregory is lecturer in modern British history at the department of Languages and European Studies in the University of Bradford, England. Educated at the Universities of Oxford, Cambridge and Southampton, he has previously taught at Southampton and the University of Durham. His publications include *Of Victorians and Vegetarians. The Vegetarian Movement in Nineteenth Century Britain* (I.B. Tauris, May 2007), biographical essays on food reformers and vegetarians in the *Oxford Dictionary of National Biography* and *Dictionary of Labour Biography*, and essays on the uses and meanings of 'eccentricity' in British culture.

Narin Hassan is Assistant Professor in the School of Literature, Communication and Culture at The Georgia Institute of Technology. Her research and teaching areas include Victorian literature and culture, postcolonial theory, gender studies and the history of medicine. Her book manuscript, "Foreign Bodies: Medicine, Gender and Colonialism in Nineteenth Century British Culture" is currently under review for publication. She has published articles in *Mosaic, South Asian Review* and *Public*.

Alice Jenkins is a Senior Lecturer in English Literature at the University of Glasgow. Her research is mainly in the field of nineteenth-century literature and science. She is the author of *Space and the 'March of*

Mind': Literature and the Physical Sciences in Britain, 1815-1850 (Oxford University Press, 2007) and the editor of *Gerard Manley Hopkins: A Routledge Literary Sourcebook* (Routledge, 2006). With Juliet John she co-edited the essay collections *Rereading Victorian Fiction* (Macmillan: 2000) and *Rethinking Victorian Culture* (Macmillan, 2000). She has published articles on Michael Faraday, Mary Somerville, John Tyndall, Humphry Davy and others. She is the Chair of the British Society for Literature and Science.

Tamara Ketabgian is Assistant Professor of English at Beloit College, where she teaches courses in nineteenth-century British literature, critical theory, science fiction, and the history of technology. She is currently completing a book entitled "The Lives of Machines: The Industrial Imaginary in Victorian Literature and Culture." Her essays have appeared in *Victorian Studies, Women's Writing*, and other journals.

Tara Moore's dissertation combines her love of the Victorian with her historical interest in the English Christmas. She teaches writing and literature at Penn State York.

Beyond digesting Kant together, Peck and Mininger maintain an on-going collaboration on the poetry of Paul Celan, which has yielded several presentations and publications thus far. Dr. Peck teaches in the Modern Languages and Literatures department at the University of Rochester and Dr. Mininger teaches Literature and Philosophy at LCC International University (Klaipeda, Lithuania). Both are recent Ph.D's from the University of Minnesota in German and Comparative Literature, respectively.

Christine Rinne is currently a Postdoctoral Scholar in German at the University of Nevada, Reno. This essay is a revised version of a chapter in her dissertation, which is entitled "Mastering the Maidservant: Dienstmädchen Fantasies in Germany and Austria, 1794-1918" (Indiana Univ., 2005). Her research interests include German colonial literature, popular literature, and depictions of material consumption.

Guilan Siassi is a Ph.D. candidate in the Department of Comparative Literature at the University of California, Los Angeles, where she works in modern French, Persian, and English literatures with an emphasis in psychoanalytic and social theory. Her dissertation is entitled "Un(der)writing Home: Nostalgia, Nomadism and the Transnational Poetics of Desire in Modern Literatures of Iran and the Maghreb."

Tamara S. Wagner obtained her PhD from the University of Cambridge in 2002 and is currently assistant professor of English Literature at the School of Humanities & Social Sciences, Nanyang Technological University, in Singapore. Her books include *Longing: Narratives of Nostalgia in the British Novel, 1740-1890* (Bucknell University Press, 2004) and *Financial Speculation in Victorian Fiction: Plotting Money and the Novel Genre, 1815-1901* (Ohio State University Press, forthcoming). Wagner's current projects are a study of Victorian cultural fictions of the "shabby genteel" and representations of the Regency period. She is also editing a special issue on silver-fork fiction.

Adele Wessell teaches history at Southern Cross University in Australia. She has published in the field of colonial history and food and is currently working on a book introducing food history in terms of historical themes such as colonialism, industrialisation and identity. Her most recent publication is "Reading Religion and Consuming the Past in the Feast of Guadalupe" in *Anthropology of Food: Food, Religious Groups and Conflicts of Norms* Spring 2006.

Andy Williams recently finished his PhD on advertising and the serial works of Charles Dickens at Cardiff University's Centre for Critical and Cultural Theory. He has written a number of academic articles and book chapters on Victorian consumer culture and poststructuralist textual theory. He has taught in the fields of English and Cultural Criticism, and is currently a Research Fellow in the Department of Journalism, Media, and Cultural Studies at Cardiff University.